Developing Minority Language Resources

BILINGUAL EDUCATION AND BILINGUALISM
Series Editors: Professor Colin Baker, *University of Wales, Bangor, Wales, Great Britain* and Professor Nancy H. Hornberger, *University of Pennsylvania, Philadelphia, USA*

For more details of these or any other of our publications, please contact:
Multilingual Matters, Frankfurt Lodge, Clevedon Hall,
Victoria Road, Clevedon, BS21 7HH, England
http://www.multilingual-matters.com

BILINGUAL EDUCATION AND BILINGUALISM 58
Series Editors: Colin Baker and Nancy H. Hornberger

Developing Minority Language Resources
The Case of Spanish in California

Guadalupe Valdés, Joshua A. Fishman,
Rebecca Chávez and William Pérez

MULTILINGUAL MATTERS LTD
Clevedon • Buffalo • Toronto

The research reported in this book was made possible (in part) by a grant from the Spencer Foundation. The data presented, the statements made, and the views expressed are solely the responsibility of the authors.

Library of Congress Cataloging in Publication Data
Developing Minority Language Resources: The Case of Spanish in California/
Guadalupe Valdés ... [et al.]. 1st ed.
Bilingual Education and Bilingualism: 58
Includes bibliographical references and index.
1. Spanish language–Study and teaching (Higher)–California.
2. Bilingualism–California. 3. Languages in contact–California.
I. Valdés, Guadalupe. II. Series.
PC4068.U5D48 2006
468.0071' 1794–dc22   2006003665

British Library Cataloguing in Publication Data
A catalogue entry for this book is available from the British Library.

ISBN 1-85359-898-4 / EAN 978-1-85359-898-2 (hbk)
ISBN 1-85359-897-6 / EAN 978-1-85359-897-5 (pbk)

Multilingual Matters Ltd
UK: Frankfurt Lodge, Clevedon Hall, Victoria Road, Clevedon BS21 7HH.
USA: UTP, 2250 Military Road, Tonawanda, NY 14150, USA.
Canada: UTP, 5201 Dufferin Street, North York, Ontario M3H 5T8, Canada.

Typeset by TechBooks Ltd.
Printed and bound in Great Britain by MPG Books Ltd.

Contents

Acknowledgments

As is the case with most books, the work and the thinking that led to the writing of this book began many years before it was written. There are, therefore, many people to whom we owe a debt of thanks for the role they have played in its writing. We are first of all indebted to Kenji Hakuta for his encouragement and support as we sought funding for this project. We drew energy from his work on bilingualism in California and from his deep interest in the teaching of heritage languages. We are grateful for his wise counsel and his friendship.

We are also grateful for the generous support of the Spencer Foundation for our project and to the anonymous scholars at Spencer who reviewed our proposal and who raised key questions about our proposed work. We profited much from their suggestions and know that our work was greatly strengthened by the changes we made in response to their feedback.

At Stanford University we had the good fortune of working with an outstanding group of graduate and undergraduate students who assisted us in both data gathering and analysis. We owe a special thanks to undergraduates Jose Reséndiz, Yolanda Ochoa, Nati Rodríguez, Gabriel Domínguez, Robert Martínez, Alvaro Soria, and Esteban Galván, who helped us by contacting and interviewing our California professionals, scheduled multiple appointments, patiently made indices of each tape, transcribed interviews, coded interviews, and entered codes into the databases for analysis. They also assisted us during the school survey compiling the envelopes, coding responses and entering the codes into their respective databases. We also wish to thank graduate students Mari Negrón, Ali Miano, Raquel Sánchez, and Martha Castellon, who were part of the team that visited classrooms at the 12 institutions surveyed, and Ben Thomas who transcribed the interviews conducted during these visits. Their deep commitment to Spanish language maintenance and their knowledge of heritage language teaching as well as their careful attention to detail was essential to the work we carried out. We are particularly grateful to Raquel Sánchez for being willing to play multiple roles in both data gathering and data analysis. We deeply appreciate her good cheer in the face of mountains of data as well as her analytical insights and exceptional organizational skills. We also want to acknowledge Ona Andre for coordinating facilities for our project and Christopher Wesselman for his excellent technical support during all phases of the project.

We are very grateful as well for the generous support we received from many individuals in putting together the various lists that we used in drawing our samples of California Latino professionals and secondary and postsecondary institutions with established Spanish heritage language programs. Duarte Silva, the director of the California Foreign Language Project made available to us the list of secondary institutions that offered Spanish heritage language programs and was immensely helpful in providing us information about heritage language instruction in California. David Goldberg of the Modern Language Association generously shared with us data on California institutions of higher education that reported offering heritage programs in Spanish. We deeply appreciate his interest in our project as well as his deep understanding of the challenges surrounding the maintenance of heritage languages in the United States. We are also thankful to the California La Raza Lawyers, Hispanic Business Journal, and the American Medical Association for discounting their lists of professionals so that we could purchase lists for the purpose of our research.

We owe a special debt of gratitude to the California professionals who agreed to participate in the telephone interviews as well as to the faculty members at secondary and postsecondary institutions for responding to our mail survey on the teaching of heritage languages. We are especially grateful to faculty at the six secondary and six postsecondary institutions that allowed us to visit their classes and to the individuals who graciously and generously were willing to talk about their heritage students, the successes they have enjoyed, and the challenges they still face.

Finally, we wish to thank Tommi Grover and Marjukka Grover of Multilingual Matters for their wise counsel, for their interest in bilinguals and bilingualism, and for their enthusiasm for our project. We are grateful as well to Colin Baker and Nancy Hornberger for their comments and suggestions and for their willingness to move forward with this project in spite of their very busy schedules.

Introduction

The Development of Non–English-Language Resources in the United States

The United States is a profoundly English-speaking country. Even before the much publicized activities of organizations such as US English, citizens of this country have imagined themselves (Anderson, 1991) as part of a Christian monolingual nation where individuals from many lands abandon old loyalties and become simply American. As Ricento (1998), has argued, "deep values" within the society have, from the beginning, rejected the idea that the maintenance of either immigrant or indigenous languages is intrinsically, socially, or economically valuable. In spite of the presence of persons who continue to speak non-English languages in this country, our position has been to ignore available non–English-language resources and to assume that the loss of ethnic languages is part of the price to be paid for becoming American. Bilingualism, as Haugen (1972a, 1972b) argued, has been seen not as a characteristic of an educated citizenry, but as a characteristic of the poor and disadvantaged.

Not surprisingly, given national ideologies about the importance of English, Americans have felt strongly ambivalent about the study and teaching of foreign languages in this country, and, as Lambert (1986) and Tucker (1990, 1991) have pointed out, the foreign language competency of most Americans is abysmally low. Few students acquire functional proficiencies in the languages they study. Many reasons have been given for this state of affairs. Some individuals (e.g. Lambert, 1986) have blamed the small amount of time devoted to foreign language study, the relatively low competencies of foreign language teachers, and the lack of agreement about effective pedagogies.

Others have argued that the United States does not produce large numbers of individuals who are fluent and competent in foreign languages because negative attitudes toward bilingualism are deeply embedded in what Schiffman (1996) has termed "American linguistic culture." According to Schiffman, English has been established as the dominant language in the United States by a "masked language policy" in place from the beginning of the colonial period. Schiffman argues (1996: 234) that covert policies toward language have maintained that English is the language of liberty, freedom, justice, and American ideals; that non-English languages are the languages of tyranny, oppression, injustice, and un-Americanness; that children cannot learn American ideals through non-English languages, and that bilingualism is bad for children and should be discouraged in schools.

Following language-related controversies in the early part of the century (e.g. *Meyer v. Nebraska*, 1923),[1] educational involvement in language issues has been limited to the teaching of "foreign" (i.e. non-English and not personally linked) languages as academic subjects to students who are monolingual speakers of English. Typically, foreign languages have been studied in high school by college-bound students. They are also studied in colleges and universities as one of several general education requirements. In spite of efforts by some individuals (e.g. Lambert, 1986) who have proposed the development of a coherent strategy designed to augment the capacity of American businesses to be competitive in global markets and increase the effectiveness of our foreign affairs specialists, there have been few fundamental changes in the study and teaching of foreign languages during the past century.

The events of September 11, however, have made evident what Brecht and Rivers (2002) have referred to as a "language crisis" surrounding national security. In the last several years, therefore, there has been an increasing interest by the intelligence and military communities (Muller, 2002) in expanding the nation's linguistic resources by both teaching non-English languages and by maintaining the heritage or home languages of the 47 million individuals who reported speaking both English and a non-English language in the latest census (US Census Bureau, 2000). For many individuals concerned about language resources, the development of strategic languages can only be brought about by expanding the mission of departments of foreign languages to include the maintenance and expansion of the varieties of non-English languages currently spoken by immigrants, refugees, and their children.

For non-English languages in the United States, these are times of possibility. There has been an increasing interest in the teaching of indigenous and immigrant ancestral or heritage languages not only from language-teaching professionals but also from other educators committed to the maintenance of non-English languages in this country. For the first time, individuals who teach both commonly and less commonly taught languages at both the secondary and postsecondary levels have come into contact with individuals who through immersion programs, dual immersion programs, and community-based language schools are working to develop the next generation's proficiencies in both indigenous and immigrant languages. For the first time also, professionals engaged in the teaching of such languages as Spanish and French have found themselves in conversations with teachers of what Gambhir (2001) referred to as the "truly less commonly taught languages" such as Bengali, Zulu, and Khmer.

Some individuals dare to be optimistic about the development of a coherent language-in-education policy that can support efforts to revitalize and maintain non-English languages (whether or not these languages are presently strategic) using the resources of existing educational institutions. In spite of Fishman's (1991) cautionary statements concerning the limitations of educational institutions in reversing language shift, many individuals – including newly funded national defense grantees – continue to see educational institutions as a very large part of the solution.

The Study of Heritage Languages in California

In this book we report on a project that has many implications for the development and maintenance of heritage languages in the United States and for the establishment of language policies that can support not only the revitalization and maintenance of indigenous and immigrant languages, but also the dissemination of theoretical insights and pedagogical approaches across very different languages that nevertheless share a common societal context. The study focused on two fundamental questions:

- How can the United States meet the challenge of maintaining non-English language resources?
- How can direct instruction in heritage/immigrant languages be used to reverse or retard the process of language shift?

To answer these two questions, we examined the challenges of developing existing language resources on Spanish, a world language that is currently spoken in California by 8.1 million of California's residents 5 years and over out of a total population in this age group of 33.8 million (US Bureau of Census, 2003). We selected California as the site for our study because California is by any measure the most linguistically diverse state in the United States. Approximately 40% of the population 5 years and over speaks languages other than English. Moreover, as noted in Table 1, California is also home to a disproportionate share of the US population who are speakers of strategic languages, such as Arabic, Chinese, Hindi, Japanese, Korean, Persian, and Russian.

For example, 40% of the speakers of Chinese in the US, 49% of the speakers of Persian, and 18% of the speakers of Arabic reside in California. California, therefore, is an ideal setting for investigating the issues and problems likely to be encountered in the implementation of educational initiatives intended to maintain and develop language resources for use in economic, diplomatic, and geopolitical arenas. We elected to focus on Spanish because it is both an immigrant language that is seen as a threat to English as well as a "foreign" language taught as an academic subject in high schools and universities. It is our position that important lessons about the dilemmas and difficulties surrounding the development of a coherent

Table 1 Non-English languages spoken at home – United States and State of California

Language	Number of speakers in the United States	Number of speakers in California	Percentage of US speakers residing in California
Population 5 years and over	262,375,152	31,416,629	0.12
Speak only English	215,423,557	19,014,873	0.09
Speak a language other than English	46,951,595	12,401,756	0.26
Speak a language other than English	46,951,595	12,401,756	0.26
Spanish or Spanish Creole	28,101,052	8,105,505	0.29
French (incl. Patois, Cajun)	1,643,838	135,067	0.08
French Creole	453,368	4,107	0.01
Italian	1,008,370	84,190	0.08
Portuguese or Portuguese Creole	564,630	78,403	0.14
German	1,383,442	141,671	0.10
Yiddish	178,945	8,952	0.05
Other West Germanic languages	251,135	30,796	0.12
Scandinavian languages	162,252	28,653	0.18
Greek	365,436	28,847	0.08
Russian	706,242	118,382	0.17
Polish	667,414	23,435	0.04
Serbo-Croatian	233,865	23,872	0.10
Other Slavic languages	301,079	28,696	0.10
Armenian	202,708	155,237	0.77
Persian	312,085	154,321	0.49
Gujarathi	235,988	33,112	0.14
Hindi	317,057	76,134	0.24
Urdu	262,900	31,588	0.12
Other Indic languages	439,289	112,119	0.26
Other Indo-European languages	327,946	37,750	0.12
Chinese	2,022,143	815,386	0.40
Japanese	477,997	154,633	0.32
Korean	894,063	298,076	0.33
Mon-Khmer, Cambodian	181,889	71,305	0.39

(*Continued*)

Table 1 (*Continued*)

Language	Number of speakers in the United States	Number of speakers in California	Percentage of US speakers residing in California
Miao, Hmong	168,063	65,529	0.39
Thai	120,464	39,970	0.33
Laotian	149,303	41,317	0.28
Vietnamese	1,009,627	407,119	0.40
Other Asian languages	398,434	76,013	0.19
Tagalog	1,224,241	626,399	0.51
Other Pacific Island languages	313,841	113,432	0.36
Navajo	178,014	1,774	0.01
Other Native North American languages	203,466	6,729	0.03
Hungarian	117,973	19,231	0.16
Arabic	614,582	108,340	0.18
Hebrew	195,374	34,647	0.18
African languages	418,505	45,471	0.11
Other and unspecified languages	144,575	35,548	0.25

Source: US Census Bureau, Census 2000 Summary File 3, Matrix PCT10.
Source: US Census Bureau, 109th Congressional District Summary File (Sample), Matrix PCT10.

language-education policy can be learned in a context in which there are (1) strong anti-immigrant sentiments, (2) established Spanish high-school and university programs for foreign language learners, and (3) an increasing number of new programs designed to accommodate students who have been raised in Spanish-speaking homes and communities.

While particularly important within the United States, the study of Spanish heritage language teaching Spanish in California may also be of value in other contexts in which there is an interest in the reacquisition or development of regional, minority, and immigrant languages and an effort to maintain such languages through established educational programs. Our examination of the role of such programs in promoting the use and development of one widely spoken minority language in the United States has many implications for other areas of the world in which the reversal of language shift is a desired goal. Our study lends direct support to the claim made by Edwards and Newcombe (2005) that in some communities school is not enough. As was the case in Ireland, for example, the study of Spanish in California suggests that formal education programs do not see their role as providing support for language maintenance.

To answer the research questions posed above, we first conducted a survey of Latino professionals to determine the degree to which Spanish is being maintained by first-, second-, and third-generation Latinos in California. We then carried out a survey of current practices used in the teaching of Spanish as a foreign language at the high-school and university levels to students who, although educated entirely in English, acquired Spanish at home as their first language. Finally, we carried out visitations and observations of 12 institutions that have implemented special programs for these Spanish-speaking students who are known in the foreign language teaching profession as *heritage* speakers.

As part of our work in answering the study's central questions, we focused on the following subquestions:

- Are current goals guiding existing direct instruction for heritage speakers of Spanish coherent with those of successful Latinos working in a variety of professions in which they have experienced a need for Spanish?
- Are current practices used in the teaching of Spanish as a heritage language coherent with existing theories of individual and societal bilingualism?
- To what degree are present programs successful in achieving their own institutional goals as well as contributing to the maintenance of Spanish?
- What features do heritage programs have to include to support heritage language maintenance?
- What kinds of policy recommendations might result in the implementation of educational programs designed to support the development and maintenance of heritage language?

Synopsis of Chapters

To provide a broad context for the study, we begin this book with a chapter written by Joshua Fishman entitled "Acquisition, Maintenance, and Recovery of Heritage Languages: An 'American Tragedy' or 'New Opportunity'?" This chapter problematizes the new interest in *heritage languages* as strategic resources and examines the challenges involved in the cultivation of such resources throughout the lifespan and the role of educational institutions in this effort.

Chapter 2, also written by Joshua Fishman, will focus specifically on the United States and on existing challenges for the United States in maintaining language resources, including enduring ideological challenges (one nation–one language sentiments), pressures to assimilate, etc. It includes information from Fishman's extensive work on existing language loyalty in the United States.

Chapter 3, written by Guadalupe Valdés, traces the presence of Spanish in California from the time of the conquest to the present. It provides an overview of the segregation and exclusion of Spanish-speaking individuals after the imposition of English in California and a discussion of major state policies directed at Spanish-speaking persons in recent years. In this chapter, Valdés argues that Spanish language maintenance efforts in California are faced with deep ambivalence within the Latino population of the state and with extreme hostility by the anglophone majority.

Chapter 4, written by all four authors, presents the findings of the telephone survey of Latino professionals. In this chapter, we provide information about the personal and professional characteristics of the individuals surveyed, the need and use of Spanish by these individuals in their current professions, their preference for particular varieties of Spanish, and their recommendations for the teaching of Spanish as a heritage language in California. We present evidence that a clear pattern of ongoing language shift among Latino professionals is emerging in California.

Chapter 5, also written by Valdés, provides an introduction to the work of the foreign language profession in the United States and to its traditional work in teaching commonly taught languages to monolingual speakers of English. It describes the profession's more recent efforts to engage in the teaching of commonly and uncommonly taught languages to heritage students. The chapter includes a definition and description of various types of heritage learners, an overview of the bilingualism of proficient heritage language speakers, and a discussion of the questions raised by these particular learners about the acquisition/development of a nondominant, first language.

Chapters 6 and 7, written by all four authors, report on the survey of professional practices in secondary and postsecondary Spanish heritage programs in California and on the observations of heritage language teaching carried out at six secondary and six postsecondary heritage programs. These two chapters provide detailed information about current practices in high schools and colleges/universities that have implemented special programs for heritage speakers. These chapters also describe the challenges and difficulties of maintaining/developing non-English languages through formal instruction in traditional educational settings.

Chapter 8 examines the challenges in the teaching of Spanish as a heritage language in California. Written by Valdés, this chapter argues that in order for post-9/11 efforts aimed at developing existing language resources in this country to be successful, sustained attention must be given to the development of theories of heritage language development/reacquisition and to the examination of the impact of language ideologies on the teaching and learning enterprise.

Finally, chapter 9, written by Fishman, imagines linguistic pluralism and argues that the lack of protected ethnolinguistic pluralism in the United States is a byproduct of its peculiar settlement history and its intellectual parentage. Our Founding Fathers did not oppose Languages Other Than English (LOTEs) nor their cultivation for posterity; they merely operated in a universe of ideas and values that were sociolinguistically uninformed and alinguistic. The massive presence of Spanish in current American life represents a last opportunity to rectify a gap that has needlessly impoverished our internal and our external modus vivendi. It represents a last chance for cultural democracy to also become a part (a long-overlooked part) of the American dream and for publicly supported linguistic repair, conservation, and growth to be added to our efforts to save from erosion and firmly establish a proactive policy in behalf of the community languages that still dot our landscapes.

Note

1. In *Meyer v. Nebraska*, 262 US 390 (1923), the Supreme Court overturned the conviction of Robert Meyer, a parochial school teacher who violated a 1919 Nebraska statute mandating English-only instruction by teaching a Bible story in German to a child. The Court concluded that the state law prohibiting the teaching of foreign languages until the pupil had passed eighth grade was unreasonable because it interfered with the power of parents to control the education of their children and with the calling of foreign language teachers.

References

Anderson, B. (1991) *Imagined Communities*. New York: Verso.
Brecht, R., and Rivers, W. P. (2002) The language crisis in the United States: Language, national security and the federal role. In S. Baker (ed) *Language Policy: Lessons from Global Models* (pp. 76–90). Monterey, CA: Monterey Institute for International Studies.
Edwards, V., and Newcombe, L. P. (2005) When school is not enough: New initiatives in intergenerational transmission in Wales. *International Journal of Bilingual Education and Bilingualism* 8 (4), 298–315.
Fishman, J. A. (1991) *Reversing Language Shift*. Clevedon: Multilingual Matters.
Haugen, E. (1972a) Active methods and modern aids in the teaching of foreign languages. In R. Filipovic (ed) *Papers from the Tenth Congress of the Federation Internationale des Professeurs de Langues Vivants* (pp. 1–14). London: Oxford University Press.
Haugen, E. (1972b) Language and immigration. In A. Dil (ed) *The Ecology of Language* (pp. 1–36). Stanford, CA: Stanford University Press.
Lambert, R. D. (1986) *Points of Leverage: An Agenda for a National Foundation for International Studies*. New York: Social Science Research Council.
Meyer v. Nebraska (1923), 262, US 390.
Muller, K. E. (2002) Addressing counterterrorism: US literacy in languages and international affairs. *Language Problems and Language Planning* 26 (1), 1–21.

Ricento, T. (1998) National language policy in the United States. In T. Ricento and B. Burnaby (eds) *Language and Politics in the United States and Canada* (pp. 85–115). Mahwah, NJ: Lawrence Erlbaum.

Schiffman, H. F. (1996) *Linguistic Culture and Language Policy*. London: Routledge.

Tucker, G. R. (1990) Second-language education: Issues and perspectives. In A. M. Padilla, H. H. Fairchild, and C. M. Valadez (eds) *Foreign Language Education: Issues and Strategies* (pp. 13–21). Newbury Park, CA.: Sage.

Tucker, G. R. (1991) Developing a language-competent American society: The role of language planning. In A. G. Reynolds (ed) *Bilingualism, Multiculturalism, and Second Language Learning* (pp. 65–79). Hillsdale, NJ: Lawrence Erlbaum.

US Census Bureau (2003, October) *Census 2000 Brief: Language Use and English-language Ability* (No. C2KBR-19). Washington, DC: US Census Bureau.

Chapter 1

Acquisition, Maintenance, and Recovery of Heritage Languages

An "American Tragedy" or "New Opportunity"?

JOSHUA A. FISHMAN

Introduction

When it comes to heritage languages (HLs), modern America is as divided today as it was throughout the 20th century. The American mainstream is as convinced as ever that foreign languages are not really necessary in this modern age, when "the whole world speaks English." If this is true relative to the great languages of the Western and Eastern civilizations and the great religious traditions, all of which have shaped human intellect, spirituality, and morality since the dawn of history, then it is doubly true of the colonial, indigenous, and immigrant languages other than English (LOTEs; in Michael Clyne's usage, 1991: 3) of the United States.

Those scholars, teachers, and educated laymen who have been laboring in the American "language vineyards" for the past generation must feel a certain déjà vu. They haven't thrown in the towel but they, nevertheless, are not consoled when their friends reassure them that owing to the current war and "war prospects" in South Asia, "languages are going to pick up now." The life and death of cultures, communities, and collective memories cannot be demeaned to the tactics of war. How are the languages of America supposed to function in the daily lives, dreams, and hopes of millions of Americans if they have to constantly worry that they may not be useful to the military or the espionage services? Well, mainstream America isn't really sure that there are any such LOTEs that should function in the daily lives, dreams, and hopes of its citizenry, or that there should be. Usually most Americans most of the time are convinced that "those folks will work their ways up" – or their children will – and "they will forget all that foreign language stuff" that is regrettably occupying space in their minds.

The view that America need not concern itself with LOTEs is supported by a small cluster of accompanying views: (i) that schools don't really succeed in teaching languages anyway ("I had four years of French and I couldn't say a blessed thing then and I certainly can't do so now!"); (ii) that

1

raising monolingual English speaking, reading, and writing children is the only decent and patriotic way to socialize children into "the American way of life"; (iii) that a multitude of languages will confuse the American mind as well as American society as a whole and result in lowered GNP, as well as a higher frequency and intensity of Civil Strife; or, even worse, (iv) that fostering multilingualism is tantamount to fostering political unrest, sedition, and other dangers to American stability; and finally, (v) that English is and of right ought to be the national or only official language of the United States (minor exceptions being made for Amerindians, most of which/whom are dying out anyway).

Into this rather inhospitable cauldron of negative views, beliefs, and attitudes we now come to introduce the topic of HLs, a slim read, indeed, in the backwater where FLES (foreign language in the elementary school), bilingual education, foreign language instruction in schools and colleges, language-related day schools, and supplementary afternoon foreign language education are all contending for a smidgeon of social acceptance and dignified stable support. In this chapter we will discuss HLs both in general terms and with special attention to its possible role for Spanish and Hispanics and in the constant context of common biases such as those enumerated here. Can HLs reverse or improve the rather bleak picture of the present and future of LOTEs in the United States, or is it merely "more of the same but in a different disguise"? What goes through the minds of Hispanic parents when they ponder whether and when to permit their children to register for "Spanish for Native Speakers"? Do their concerns increase or decrease with the successive developmental stages at which their children can access HL programs and experiences? In general, can HLs possibly enable America to more properly appreciate and use its rich LOTE resource, a resource that is second to none in the world?

Heritage Languages: Meeting the New White Hope

"Heritage languages" is a designation that has fairly recently "arrived" in the United States to indicate languages other than the nationally dominant one that are historically associated with the ethnicity (the ethnocultural heritage) of particular minority populations. Such languages, by whatever name, are currently, and have for a good long time been, devalued in many settings. It is even crucial to determine not just why they are underacquired, undermaintained, and underrecovered but why it has taken so long to undertake such a basic inquiry. At the beginning of the 21st century it is no exaggeration to say that as America goes, so goes, for better or for worse, the world. Therefore, it behooves us to ask how we can assist America overcome its self-denial of the many benefits that would accrue to it by means of a more positive and fitting regard for HLs, both as public and as particular-group resources.

The sometimes implied contradiction between languages as distinctly human and humanistic *indices of culture* and, simultaneously, as *part and parcel* of the cultures that they express is more imagined than real. All nonmaterial culture serves simultaneously as a carrier, and an essential part, of what it carries. Literature, religion, law and folklore, oratory and negotiation, politics, and celebrations are all examples of linguistic culture that both express the traditional association of the various cultures and help constitute these cultures and the identities they foster. Accordingly, it will be the explicit position of this volume that heritage languages (e.g. Spanish, first and foremost in terms of numbers of speakers) constitute noteworthy resources, material and nonmaterial, for the United States as a whole and for its constituent populations (as groups and as individuals).

Languages (and Heritage Languages) as Resources

The problems of viewing languages as resources (by now, not a new or original metaphor at all) must be brought to the fore at the very outset. Are languages really resources? Do they have tangible, monetary, or "public benefit" value and, furthermore, will the use of the term *resources* in conjunction with *languages* orient our discussion in an overly materialistic direction? Even the humane and humanistic terra lingua view that relates linguistic diversity to the diversity in animal and plant life (Mafi, 2003) also tends to deal primarily with material resources. However, "diversity" need not necessarily be valued and evaluated in material terms alone. Environmental impact studies, required throughout the United States before beginning to build a new edifice, highway, or dam are indicative of a modern sensibility for the preciousness of co-territorial life.[1] That preciousness is not necessarily expressible either in monetary terms or in terms of any possible hard-and-fast parallelism with human life. Furthermore, even the widespread positive expectation that languages are resources (and, therefore, are directly translatable into monetary or other power-related terms) not only runs counter to some of our own experiences, but it strikes many threatened cultures as a characteristic Western non sequitur. In much of modern Western culture, "resources" are primarily material and quantitatively expressible (Hinton, 2003) and the overuse of this metaphor in conjunction with matters ethnolinguistic may well tell others more about ourselves than about languages in culture. As it is with other resources, those who control contextually crucial languages have a potential for greater power in relevant human affairs than those who do not; uncommon languages are not, therefore, necessarily more valuable (as Whorf, 1942 once believed). On the other hand, many reasonably widely used languages continue to be powerless and unvalued to this very day (viz. Woloff, Oromo, Quechua).

Languages (and Heritage Languages) as Conflicted Resources

Nevertheless – or perhaps precisely because – language in general and heritage languages in particular are so complexly associated with all other aspects of culture that their propagation and cultivation frequently turn out to be problematic. But, this problematic aspect or attribution is often overdone. Furthermore, there is no aspect of society or culture – ethnicity, religion, education, class, age gender – that cannot become a cause for intergroup conflict. The coauthors of this volume believe that the conflicted aspects of language resources are so often overdone (Fishman 1985), and even given disproportional attention, that in exploring the positive potential aspects of heritage languages we must take caution not to reply in kind and to overlook the negative contexts or co-occurrences entirely. Keeping both in mind is not just an expression of intellectual honesty – something always morally desirable – but it enables us to better understand why the potentially positive contributions of heritage languages in the United States are so often overlooked, unrecognized, and even found to be suspect.

Furthermore, recognition of the problematic nature of heritage languages is necessary in order to understand how to overcome these problems at the societal level and, absolutely so, how to better appreciate their variability from place to place and from time to time. To begin with, therefore, we will look at the language enculturation process throughout the lifespan as a means of appreciating whatever constraints the American scene imposes on the process of HL acquisition, use, and loss.

The First Intergenerational Ethnolinguistic Continuity Stage: Early-Childhood Heritage Language Acquisition

Early childhood is generally any individual's most crucial period of language acquisition. This is the fascinating and brief period of unconscious transition from primarily nonverbal to verbal interaction. No matter how often we have observed language acquisition, even in our own children and grandchildren, it still unfolds miraculously before our very eyes. First language acquisition is also frequently accompanied by national or official language acquisition, although sometimes the opposite sequence obtains. This is so primarily because in multicultural societies with a single national or official language it is the national or official language that is commonly the lingua franca and, therefore, the main language of real power in the community. Minority inhabitants, accordingly, become bilingual during early childhood, frequently in their own homes or family environs.

An HL cannot remain the only language for that proportion of a heritage community that wants or needs to interact (or parents who want their children to be able to interact) with mainstream society. Nevertheless, even early-childhood bilingualism, in which both languages (HL and national or official language)[2] are of about equal vintage for a sizable minority population, does not automatically ensure a positive role for the HL in the lives of such individuals. There are, of course, a goodly number of minority individuals for whom there is a clear absence of an HL. Cases of absence of any HL are encountered among African children raised entirely in English or French, Amerindian or Aborigines children raised entirely in English, ethnically Tibetan children raised in Potinguah, or the children of Israeli immigrants who gave up their mother tongues for Israeli Hebrew or the children of Latin American immigrants to the US who gave up their mother tongues "for the children's sake." Similarly far from rare, on the other side, are those children who grow up in ethnically mixed households in which each "side" continues to speak its own HL, doing so precisely in order to enable their children to interact comfortably with both sets of grandparents (not to mention aunts, uncles, cousins, etc.). At this time, in the still brief history of inquiry into HLs in the United States it is not yet known whether each of the etic distinctions vis-à-vis the possible types of HL combinations that exist corresponds to the emic differences either in language facility or attitudes, or whether any differences between them in these respects that may still obtain by adulthood are more related to initial degree and age of mastery.

Turning to factors that may impinge on parental readiness to pass on an HL to their children, we once again find ourselves more in the realm of logical supposition than in the realm of empirical research. We can all, however, surmise that many parents who *could* pass along an HL during the early childhood of their offspring, do not, in fact, do so. The proportion doing so will vary with the local status of the HL involved and, therefore, its public recognition, public valuation, and the sense of security on the part of the parents of newborns. Parents who are insecure about their own ethnic identity are likely to associate that language more with disadvantages than with advantages and, therefore, identify with it less and discontinue using it more often. Languages associated primarily with indenture, or with poverty, or with lack of literacy or schooling; languages that threaten to foreclose their speakers' access to upward social mobility and social acceptance; languages lacking any widely recognized literary or historical role; and languages of small speech communities lacking in potential political prowess will all suffer a relative loss of intergenerational use and transmission in comparison to others that are known or believed to posses these desiderata. Parents often mistakenly believe that they make a far greater contribution to the happiness of their children by denying their children any exposure to their HLs than by exposing these children to the predictable difficulties and satisfactions of a group-identity–related childhood, adolescence, and adulthood like the ones they themselves (the parents) have experienced.

Wherever some ethnoculturally, and therefore ethnolinguistically, identifiable groups are disadvantaged while ethnic group membership generally remains open to voluntary (i.e. self-initiated and self-maintained) membership and to the absence of racially interpreted stigmata, all socially penalized groups will "underperform" (i.e. they will practice socially patterned membership avoidance) insofar as ethnolinguistic continuity is concerned. Early childhood is the earliest point at which parents who have maintained ethnolinguistic continuity with *their* own parents frequently decide whether or not to opt for early disengagement from such continuity for their own offspring. Even such disengagement is not irrevocable, however, because parents can still change their minds during their children's early childhood, parents are not the only influences on their children's early language development (grandparents, neighbors, child-contemporaries, churches, and other neighborhood voluntary organizations that aim their efforts at toddlers are also effective in this connection, as the Maori Katango Reo have so amply demonstrated), and because early childhood itself is not the be-all and end-all of intergenerational ethnolinguistic continuity opportunities vis-à-vis minoritized speech communities in the United States (see later). Nevertheless, infancy is the primary age of HL acquisition (or nonacquisition), and that it is marked in the United States by a high degree of "opting out" is a major problem for HL acquisition. The fact that California Hispanics may well opt out (of Mexicanness identity and of HL continuity) less frequently than do others is one of the major forces favoring Spanish as an HL in the United States at this time.

The Second Opportunity for Intergenerational Language Acquisition: The Nursery School and Early Grades

A common feature of HLs is that neither the homes and neighborhoods nor the voluntary neighborhood institutions associated with them are really culturally intact and primarily under their own guiding control. Another problem that "bedevils" the earliest intergenerational language transmission processes is its informality and lack of formal times and places set aside for language in particular. Perhaps *bedevils* is not the right word to use in this connection, since it deals with the unvarnished daily life (and language life) of many HLs. Indeed, it is the very informality, spontaneity, and motivational self-direction of HLs at this point that makes them real mother tongues to begin with and imbeds them in cultural reality and in interpersonal intimacy from the very outset. These are desiderata that courses and other postchildhood formal efforts can never duplicate or replicate. Indeed, the more the time that elapses between the age of informal language acquisition until organized measures are undertaken on behalf of HL acquisition, the less likely it is that full spontaneity, emotional attachment, and native-like fluency will ever be attained at all (Fishman, 2001).

The downside to the above is the ubiquitous nature of two interrelated mainstream views of Southwestern Spanish and its speakers that its speakers have absorbed, at least in part. The first view is the negative stereotype that minority tongues are not "real" languages, such as those of Europe, but rather a variety of dialects, patois, and gibberish ("Tex-Mex"). The second is that these minority languages cannot be written ("because they are unstandardized") and have no true literary traditions of their own. Youngsters at the high school level are more exposed to charges such as the above, because it is in high school that serious literacy instruction begins. This is not so much because of interest in literacy per se or in the development of standard (literary) English, as because of the assumption that control of the latter is an asset in the work sphere. The fact that non-Anglos also necessarily speak some dialect or other, and that the latter is not written, any more than is the spoken informal Spanish of local Hispanics, and is often quite unlike the written standard for their region (English, unlike French or German, has no supra-regional standard, nor any institutions for deriving and elaborating any such thing) is lost upon most Anglo-Americans, whether pupils or teachers. Furthermore, the fact that their American counterparts are still learning how to read and write "school English" (because the latter is nowhere fully interchangeable with the English of home, street, and community) and, indeed, will continue doing so for many postschool years to come and that this task is, probably, a much harder task than is learning standard school Spanish (for Hispanics) is never used as a critique of the standard itself or of the learners thereof. These are common facts of language reality wherever two languages of groups of vastly different status meet in the same schools. The classroom per se cannot equalize them, and the status gaps between the languages and their speakers will reappear every occasion in which children of the conquered and children of the conquerors are in close quarters with one another. A little sociolinguistic perspective might be highly desirable, particularly for HL students (of both types).

That being said, there is also no denying that the structured language teaching so common for second-stage entry into an HL effort can and does commonly result in language learning. In many cases, throughout the world, where the informal initial stage is most commonly missed (e.g. for Maori in New Zealand, for Basque in the Autonomous Basque Community, for Andamanese in India, and for Breton in France), the early school-related stage is an invaluable entry stage in the total HL-acquisition process. This stage also encompasses school-sponsored outings, clubs, camps, choruses, teams, and other activities or projects that involve students under "qualified supervision" in after-school and out-of-school life. Indeed, not only can schools *produce* second-entry HL learners but they can do so more successfully than minority society as a whole can provide for the *absorption, maintenance,* and *activation* of such speakers in non–school-related affairs more generally. This *production–maintenance disparity* is a crucial dilemma to ponder because it repeats itself from one entry point in the intergenerational transmission process to another. At each such stage, minority society is often too weak to absorb, activate, and maintain its own partial successes. As a result, parents who initially delayed exposing their children to their HL (for the very reasons that have been suggested at length above), may very well believe that by and during ages 5–10 their children are strong enough to "take it" in terms of a somewhat more formalized exposure, teaching, and learning process within a supervised framework. Nevertheless, the school requires a great deal of help from the surrounding HL society if the HL acquired there is to be maintained.

Unfortunately, leave-it-to-the-school (church, youth group, etc.) approaches often have a higher attrition rate and a lower language maintenance rate than do most of the earlier-mentioned informal processes. I repeat: this is not because schools either do or must fail to teach HLs successfully but because schools cannot reproduce anything like the total sociocultural and interpersonal reality that languages themselves require for postadolescent language maintenance, not to mention linguistically fluid, native-like maintenance. Obviously, middle entry into HL acquisition requires for its success access to the same kinds of privileges and rewards (or their equivalents) that are available to students who are not "burdened" with an HL and its more intensive and crowded total curricular concomitants. Nevertheless, because the school is an omnipotent societal agency, with a staff and budget of its own, it is often (and increasingly) expected to enter these thickets and must have or prepare an approach to acquiring and maintaining HLs that are congruent both with reality and with it own obligations to serve society with professional competence.

The Third Entry Point for Heritage Languages: In the Early High School or the Early College Years

The difficulties faced by adults and children alike vis-à-vis the earliest entry level are primarily ideological and political. The difficulties faced at the intermediate entry level are primarily pedagogical and operational. The next major opportunity to interest a large number of parent and pupils in HL involvement is when the high school to college transition occurs. The problems encountered at this level may include most of those we have encountered before, plus a few others. Chief among the latter are the jurisdictional and pedagogical claims of FL instruction, on the one hand, and of HL instruction, on the other. Assuming that these can be peacefully resolved within a single unified department,[3] the major remaining concerns are more attitudinal/ideological in nature and revolve around issues of identity. Although these transition points arouse anxieties for all students when they enter high school and college, the HL students are somewhat unique in that their choice brings them into interaction with HL peers embarking on a part of their identity that they could have, but elected not to, activate and acknowledge.

Choosing to become or not to become an FL student or teacher is much different for Hispanics than choosing to participate in a long-term involvement with HL events, activities, groups, and community life as a whole. When some of those doing so have twice before passed up (or been forced or persuaded to pass up) opportunities of this same kind and with the same implications, a certain amount of tension related to insecure self-discovery should be expected. Unless this choice is buttressed by a goodly portion of moral support, recognition, and acceptance, it is likely to be terminated before it comes to fruition via political, communal, and ideological identity formation at the adult level. This is a lot to expect as outcomes of educational exposure from the very outset, but it is particularly unlikely in conjunction with HL students in HL courses.

Frankly, the entire educational involvement with HLs in educational institutions, processes, and goals is contraindicated. As long as HL involvement is tied to Spanish courses, we have lost all those who take no such course or who do not perform well or successfully in such courses, and these may well be the majority of youngsters in the Hispanic HL fold. An HL is not a course and not a job program, and we must be careful of proceeding as if it were. Not only that far from all Hispanic youngsters attend institutions offering them an HL link, but most of those that do are pursuing programs that make no demands for HL-language-in-community commitments. Clearly, HL courses offered at the secondary and tertiary entry points must be viewed as merely possible staging grounds, rather than as the basic building blocks of a national program for maximizing the acquisition and maintenance of Spanish as an HL and of Spanish even more holistically viewed. For such a national program to be launched and then optimized, it must provide for students both within and outside the school settings.

The Heritage Language Movement: A Focus Both for Students and Adults

If Spanish as an HL is to become what it should be, both for the country as a whole and for the Hispanic community in particular, it needs to become a youth movement rather than just a school course-sequence, and it must seriously pursue, attain, and maintain home, school, and community outreach. The "movement" must not be defined by age, gender, or occupational goal. It must be explicitly for focusing a home, school, and community partnership with respect to the intergenerational promise of Spanish as a permanent feature of the American scene.

There are many features of American society that militate against the attainment of goals such as those outlined in this chapter (brief reference has also been made to them in discussing earliest and intermediate entry into HL-friendly efforts). Fears of political and social fractionalization of American life along language lines must be exposed as the remnants of flat-earth thinking that they are, as the recent Indian (South Asia Indian) decision to virtually double the number of indigenous languages that are "scheduled" (i.e. that will receive governmental recognition, support, and functions), with 35 further additions in the offing). Such increased recognition of diversity actually cements national unity and clears the boards for more rapid progress toward English mastery too. If HL efforts ultimately get to be understood as contributing to America's sense of safety, rationality, and goodwill – as well as to internal HL community feelings of community intergenerational continuity and acceptance – that will be akin to an "ugly-duckling" rebirth of America's idealistic promise to "crown [its] good with brotherhood, from sea to shining sea."

The Burden of Heritage Languages in America

Thus far we have seen that at every level of entry into HL linkages, there are many members of the HL community who see their HL as something whose cost-benefit analysis must be carefully pondered. It is not an open-and-shut case with benefits clearly seen as outweighing debits. Many of the quandaries introduced to the reader in this chapter will be empirically investigated at a more data-anchored level in Chapter 4. In Chapter 2, we begin by presenting a historical overview of the place of HLs in this country.

Notes

1. New Bird Species Threatened. *Stanford Daily*. January 13, 2004, p. 3. "Scientists have discovered a new bird species in southeastern Venezuela.... Males are light grey with blue feathers whereas females are different shades of brown. Currently only three individuals have been sighted.... The discoverers had little time to celebrate though since a hydroelectric dam is being built on the Caura River and can destroy the birds' only known habitat. Conservation International has called on the Venezuelan government to designate the area as a wildlife reserve."
2. Although the difference between them is often disregarded in practice, "national languages" are those that are native to a people or nationality, whereas "official languages" are those that are employed by state offices or their representatives.
3. There will only be three kinds of programs, teachers, and pupils: (i) those *not* from any appropriate HL background and primarily pursuing FL credits and/or certificates; (ii) those from HL backgrounds who are interested in pursuing FL

credits and/or certificates; and (iii) those from HL backgrounds who are interested in HL credits and/or certificates. Types (i) and (ii) are reasonably combinable into largely similar and traditional treatments, but Type (iii) requires different and more innovative planning, either together with or separate from Types (i) and (ii). There is also a fourth type of HL student, namely, the type that will not show up at all in a Spanish-language course either in high school or in college. The latter type is discussed later.

References

Clyne, M. (1991) *Community Language*. Cambridge, UK: Cambridge University Press.

Fishman, J.A. (1985) Positive pluralism: some overlooked rationales and forefathers. In J.A. Fishman, M.H. Gertner, E.G. Lowy, and W.G. Milan (eds) *The Rise and Fall of the Ethnic Revivial: Perspectives on Language and Ethnicity* (pp. 445–495). Berlin: Mouton Publishers.

Fishman, J.A. (ed) (2001) *Can Threatened Languages Be Saved?* Clevedon: Multilingual Matters.

Hinton, L. (1994) *Flutes of Fire: Essays on California Indian Languages*. Berkeley, CA: Heyday Press.

Mafi, Louisa (2004, January 13) New bird species threatened. *The Stanford Daily*, p. 3.

Whorf, B. (1942) Language, mind and reality. *Theosofist (The Theosophical Society-Madras, India)*, 63 (January), 281–291 and No. 2 (April) 25–37.

Chapter 2

Three Hundred–Plus Years of Heritage Language Education in the United States[1]

JOSHUA A. FISHMAN

All of us – individuals, societies, cultures, and nations alike – live by our fondest myths, beliefs whose importance transcends their value as truth. One of the myths held in the United States is that our Pilgrim fathers first left England and resettled in the Netherlands, then left the Netherlands for Plymouth Rock because their children were becoming monolingual Dutch speakers and losing their command of English. Whether this is pure myth or has some confirmed truth, it is beyond doubt that since the time of the Pilgrims, millions upon millions of refugees and immigrants have arrived on America's shores with strong hopes of maintaining the ethnolinguistic traditions that defined them to themselves, to their neighbors, and to their God.

If we define HLs as those that (a) are LOTEs (languages other than English), in Michael Clyne's usage (1991: 3), and that (b) have a particular family relevance to the learners, then we will find schools devoted to teaching these languages and to developing literacy and promoting further education through these languages among the indigenous, the colonial, and the immigrant groups that have come to this country by choice and good fortune or by force and the winds of cruel history.

Indigenous Heritage Languages

We have no record of HLs in the United States before the arrival, on foot and by boat, of the Amerindians. Amerindian schools were initially the schools of life, the noninstitutional means by which the young were socialized into the daily rounds, beliefs, and practices that constituted the culture of their parents. Such enculturation still goes on, of course, but increased contact with others (conquerors, settlers, and governmental officials) has led Amerindian educators to create their own brick-and-mortar institutions – formal schools associated with literacy or, as is increasingly common, biliteracy in an Indian language and in English. Given the sad state

12

of intergenerational cultural transmission – particularly, mother tongue transmission – in most Amerindian groups today, it is instructive that never before in this century has such a high proportion of Amerindian children been engaged in HL schooling, from prenursery to college institutions, under tribal control or with tribal input (McCarty *et al.*, 1999; McCarty & Zepeda, 1998).

Despite a discouraging history of intermittent governmental intrusion (in blatant disregard of treaty obligations), many Amerindians have managed to liberate their lives and their educational institutions from outside influences that deprecate their values, beliefs, and community ties. The conference series "Stabilizing Indian Languages" (Cantoni, 1996; Reyhner, 1997, 1998), the annual summer American Indian Language Development Institute, housed at the University of Arizona (see McCarty *et al.*, 1997), the Mentor-Apprentice Program in California (see Hinton, 1994), and the slowly but steadily growing number of Amerindian junior colleges offering indigenous languages are all evidence that HL concerns are alive among Amerindians, whether or not they will be supported by local, state, or federal funds. The fact that an Indian teacher, researcher, and poet, Ofelia Zepeda, was a recipient in 1999 of a MacArthur ("Genius") Award is a sign that at least in some mainstream quarters Amerindian interests and welfare are finally considered to be in the public interest.

The combination of Indian primum mobile (they were here first) and mainstream guilt feelings over past injustices to Indians have finally resulted in much greater language consciousness among Amerindians themselves and more sympathy among mainstream authorities and foundations for Amerindian heritage education. It is unfortunate that we often wait until matters become extreme before paying attention to them and taking ameliorative steps that are in everyone's best interest. The improved state of affairs with regard to Amerindian heritage education does not derive from a mainstream conviction that Amerindian societies that preserve their own languages are better off – richer, healthier, less dislocated, less alienated and hopeless, and, therefore, less problem-prone. Rather, it is a result of what Amerindians themselves have accomplished in terms of HL revitalization, acquisition, and maintenance.

Colonial Heritage Languages

Heritage language education for speakers of colonial languages – nonindigenous languages that were already established here before the United States of America came into being – usually have neither the justification of primum mobile nor mainstream guilt to support them. Indeed, some have already lost contact with their colonial roots, and their current existence in the United States is an outgrowth of immigrant reinforcement rather than colonial origins. In this category are found such small language groups as Dutch (introduced in the 17th century into Manhattan and for miles along the Hudson River in New York State), Swedish and Finnish (Sweden and Finland were at times under single rule, and many immigrants from these countries were bilingual Swedish–Finnish speakers even before coming to our shores), and Welsh. All of these languages have long since faded away as intergenerationally transmitted vernaculars in the United States, leaving only place names to remind us of their erstwhile presence. We also find such worldwide giants as French, Spanish, and German. It speaks volumes about our lack of appreciation for HLs that there has been almost no intergenerational mother-tongue language transmission among the speakers of this trio of languages, who can trace their roots back to colonial times. Certainly the Franco-Americans in New England and Louisiana have only rarely been able to transmit their language across generations, and the success of Spanish speakers in the rural, small-town Southwest is only insignificantly greater. It is recent immigration that largely explains the present prevalence of Spanish, not only in the country as a whole but even in the same small towns in the agricultural Southwest to which the forebears of today's residents came hundreds of years ago.

Only German in its Pennsylvania German incarnation can claim significant intergenerational mother tongue transmission. It holds the distinction of being the only colonial language with an uninterrupted, though not completely unaltered, tradition of HL community life and, therefore, of heritage schooling in the United States. Once again, it is to internal forces that we must turn to fathom the ability of Pennsylvania German groups to maintain their language across generations. That ability (not unlike the ability among some Amerindian groups and ultraorthodox Jews) is primarily attributable to their jealously guarded physical and cultural distance from the American mainstream. Without some kind of self-imposed cultural boundaries, there would be virtually no colonial HL education in the United States today, notwithstanding the huge numbers (relative to total population size) that were once involved in HL education and the obvious governmental, commercial, and cultural value of these languages for America's own well-being. This fact is well worth keeping in mind as we turn next to the immigrant languages and their associated HL efforts.

Immigrant Heritage Languages

How can we hope for a national agenda on immigrant HL education – one that supports the acquisition, retention, and active use of immigrant languages in private and public life – when we consider the sad experiences of indigenous and colonial HL maintenance? The colonial languages lacked the assets of the indigenous languages (primum mobile and mainstream guilt), but at least three of them enjoyed the advantages of huge numbers and worldwide utility. In contrast, most immigrant languages have lacked even these advantages, although the major ones: French, German, Spanish, Italian, Polish, and Yiddish claimed around one million or more speakers in the United States during almost all of the 20th century. Whether widely spoken or not, immigrant languages have rarely been regarded as a national resource, and for the most part have suffered the same sad fate here that immigrant languages typically suffer around the world. Even so, as a testament to the human spirit, the immigrant languages, large and small, have refused to fade quietly away. The determination of immigrants to develop and maintain HL schools for their children should have been documented by the US Department of Education or by the separate state departments of education. However, as far as these official agencies were concerned, no such schools have existed, unless they have been cited for lack of bathrooms, windows, or fire escapes.

Already in the late 19th and early 20th centuries, when immigration to the United States was still in full swing, HL schools made important contributions to American education and the development of education-related laws. Among the most instructive benchmark languages to follow in those early days is German, not only because it was for so long the largest immigrant language in the United States, and of major importance in the world at large (particularly in the areas of science, commerce, and diplomacy), but also because it was one of the most controversial. In 1886, the German-American writer K. W. Wolfradt published a study showing that in the United States 280,000 children were studying German in 2066 German ethnic heritage elementary schools (cited in Kloss, 1966: 234). That these figures are not out of line is clear from the Commissioner of Education's 1902 Report of the year 1900–1901 (Viereck, 1902, cited in Kloss, 1966: 234), which notes that there were 3984 such schools with 318,000 students. In addition to the above, the number of public elementary schools that taught German also grew during this period because a large proportion of their students were of German immigrant extraction. By the end of the 19th century, as public schools rapidly multiplied and spread, particularly throughout the Midwest, the number of schools that taught German and that were officially German–English bilingual public elementary schools began to equal the number of nonpublic ethnic heritage schools. The legal basis for such public elementary schools was explicitly incorporated into state education law in many states. An example is the Nebraska education law of 1913, just before the outbreak of World War I, which permitted such bilingual schools to be established (in English plus any other language) when requests to do so were received from the parents of 50 pupils in urban areas.

German is also a good example of how US foreign policy and other national interests can affect HL education. World War I led to such severe antiforeigner (and particularly anti-German) propaganda that many ethnic heritage schools were closed, both voluntarily and by state directives. Legislation against foreign language instruction, aimed particularly at the elementary education level, both public and private, was passed. *Meyer v. Nebraska* (1923, 262 US 390) is the US Supreme Court decision that overthrew such legislation, on the grounds that it constituted unjustified state intrusion into the educational preferences of parents and the professional freedom of teachers to practice a legally certified occupation. The Nebraska state government's argument that early exposure to a living foreign language was injurious to the national loyalty and to the intellectual development of children was explicitly rejected by the Supreme Court as contrary to reason and unsupported by evidence. Thus, Nebraska lawmakers and German educators were involved in both the high and low points of ethnic heritage education in the United States. Although the Supreme Court came to the rescue of parents and teachers in connection with the constitutionality of ethnic HL education, the atmosphere was already poisoned. We did not fully recover for another quarter century, when minority civil rights were more positively located on the national agenda.

Before the Ethnic Revival

It was my good luck to come of age as a sociolinguistic researcher in the late 1950s and early 1960s, just when the Sputnik scare moved various federal agencies to recognize that HLs might make an important contribution to the national interest, even important enough, it turned out, for some funding to be directed toward trying to understand just how much of a resource these languages constituted, at individual and institutional levels. As a result, I was able to undertake a national study to determine by myself what the government had studiously ignored. This 1960–1963 study (Fishman, 1966) was the first modern call to conserve and foster our nation's HL resources by developing capacity in the various HLs before they were assimilated out of existence. I located 1885 ethnic community schools operating in dozens of different languages, most of them Southern and Eastern European. Undoubtedly, there were several hundred more that I had failed to uncover or that had hidden from me, in fear of government-related probing during what were still the McCarthyite Cold War years. I cannot say that any public agency was really interested in my research – other than the FBI, which paid me a visit to see if any of these schools were communist-dominated. When I replied that I hadn't the slightest idea, nor would I ever have, I lost the FBI's interest as well.

After the Ethnic Revival

From 1980 through 1983, the National Science Foundation, the National Institute of Education (now the Office of Educational Research and Improvement), and the National Endowment for the Humanities all demonstrated that the argument of my 1966 book – that HLs were a national resource that should be preserved and encouraged – had finally gotten through, at least to those organizations. They enabled me to repeat and extend my study of nearly 20 years earlier (Fishman, 1985a, 1985b). By then, I was both a more experienced and a better-known researcher. I knew where to look for HL schools, and, perhaps, some of them understood by then that I was a trustworthy researcher as well. Perhaps even more important, this took place after the ethnic revival of the mid- to late 1960s, and by then HL schools were a more self-confident breed. They were being maintained by a younger generation of advocates who were more secure in their own ethno-American identities. Although I identified 6553 schools at that time (Fishman, 1985a, 1985b, pp. 243–44), I still had the impression that there were 1000 or more that I had not located. Once more I felt the need for a stable government interest that would realize the value of up-to-date files, and I happily deposited mine at the National Clearinghouse for Bilingual Education in the hope that such interest would materialize. Alas, that was not to be. Like all files, the longer my school data just sat there, the less useful they became, as schools moved, closed, and changed addresses, programs, and affiliations. To my knowledge, that was the last nationwide study of HL schools in the United States. Just as the second study came 20 years after the first, so another 20 years is about to elapse since the second. A new benchmark study would now be extremely welcome. With what other national resource would we wait 20 years to find out its status? It is my hope that a call for such an updated benchmark study will go out from our ranks and reach the ears of those who are concerned that we maximize, rather than trivialize, our country's HL resources.

The Early 1980s

The more than 6500 HL schools that I located in the early 1980s, all of them outside of the public sector, involved 145 languages, 91 of which were Amerindian, with Chinese, French, German (including Pennsylvania German), Greek, Hebrew, Italian, Japanese, Korean, Polish, Portuguese, Spanish, Ukrainian, and Yiddish accounting for approximately 90% of the total number of schools. Note that Asian languages had become nationally important for the first time, as a result of the rise of legal immigration from China and South Asia after World War II. The century's "big six" languages (French, German, Italian, Polish, Spanish, and Yiddish) were all present and prominent in the ranks of HL school sponsors. Every state in the Union was represented. Another noteworthy finding was the high correlation between the number of schools associated with any particular language and the number of local religious units (churches, mosques, synagogues, and temples) associated with that language, giving us a clear insight into what has thus far been the major and most durable support for HL schooling in the United States.

One other point about our HL schools in the early 1980s deserves mention: They varied greatly as to the amount of time spent on language instruction per se. Day schools (about a quarter of the total) both devoted most time to language study and most frequently used their HLs as media for other areas of substantive instruction. Those schools with the longest curriculum (again, the day schools) also tended to claim a higher proportion of graduating students who spoke the language moderately well or better (which only a third or so of the responding schools claimed). The 1960–1980 growth rate for HL schools was 228%, compared to a growth rate of 63% for public schools and 24% for Catholic schools as a whole. Clearly, the HL schools constituted an educational sector whose social significance goes beyond HL instruction. Has their rate of growth continued? Has their image as successful transmitters of HLs improved? What would be the roughly equivalent number of years of study needed in public high schools in these languages to reach the level of moderate spoken facility or better? These would be important questions to answer, if we have in mind the recent Australian model of providing public high school credit for HL study (Fishman, 1991: 262–69).

Can the Two Worlds Be Bridged?

Thus far, we have perused HL study, particularly since the end of World War II, as if it were totally unrelated to the world of public school language study. The last large-scale link between public schools and HL education that we have examined pertained to the study of German before World War I. In recent years, however, there have been two other links between HL education and the public schools. The first pertains to Spanish. The second pertains to a longish list of smaller HL groups that have succeeded in establishing programs with local public school authorities, often doing so with more success than the Spanish groups did. Let us look at both of these attempts to bridge what would otherwise be two isolated worlds, HL schools and public schools, making first the case of Spanish in American elementary and secondary school education.

Spanish in the 1990s

It took decades before it was recognized that Spanish was the most popular foreign language in American high schools and colleges, effectively replacing French and all but obliterating German in most departmental offerings (Huber, 1996). A good proportion of Spanish language students (estimates as high as 25% beyond the first year of study seem reasonable) already speak Spanish, and certainly understand it, when they show up in our mainstream classrooms. Efforts are being made to develop special teacher training programs to cope more adequately with these students (many of whom speak Spanish more fluently but less "correctly" than their teachers); to prepare appropriate curricula, lesson plans, and course materials for them; and, above all, to keep our attention focused on the important community roles and responsibilities that these students and their parents play in relation to the future of Spanish in their own lives and in the commercial, diplomatic, intellectual, and cultural life of the country as a whole.

Although various parallels exist with German in the late 19th and early 20th centuries, there are many differences as well. There is no huge religious sector backing Spanish now, as there once was for German, the Catholic Church having become a more mainstream American (and less immigrant) church. Indeed, there may be fewer community-maintained Spanish HL schools today than there were in 1980, when there were around 250, and incomparably fewer than existed for German a century ago. Latinos have been incorporated into the American public school system so fully that they may have neglected cultural institutions of their own. Dependent on the American school system for Spanish language education, Latino parents have not organized to push for more suitable Spanish courses for their native (or near-native, quasi-native, or submerged-native) Spanish-speaking children. Furthermore, unlike most German-speaking parents in the last century, Spanish-speaking parents frequently have low literacy skills. This affects their comfort level in negotiating with school authorities for more appropriate courses for their children; questions regarding their legal status serve to further complicate the situation. Finally, low literacy within the Latino speech community reflects negatively on the entire image of Spanish in American society. Rather than being viewed as the literary and standardized language that it has been for centuries, Spanish is widely viewed as the dialectally splintered and socially stigmatized language of lower-class illiterates. As a result, it is severely undervalued as a language resource. For the sake of the entire country's enrichment, its New World dialects need to be recognized as legitimate, thereby fostering its grassroots and intergenerational maintenance. This type of attention (involving appropriate instructional programs, placement, and evaluation) is only just beginning to be seriously pondered.

Other Heritage Languages and the American Public School

The picture is somewhat different on the middle-class side of the HL street, whether the languages involved pertain to more visible or less visible minorities. I first became aware that something new was afoot in 1956, when I became a research associate (and later vice president for research) at the College Entrance Examination Board. The first test development project to which I was assigned was an English language listening test, and the second was an achievement test for Hebrew. The latter was requested by community groups fostering Hebrew as an HL, both in the public high schools and in private HL schools, most of which were attached to local synagogues or other religious organizations. Students studying in all-day schools (Yeshivas) were exposed to the language (or to its closely related cousin Judeo-Aramaic) through the intensive study of religious classical texts every day, for many hours, for a period of 8–12 years. For some of the students, Hebrew was also the medium of instruction in other Judaic studies. Public high school (and, more rarely, elementary school) students were exposed to the language only through secular texts and topics, for far fewer hours per day, and for far fewer years of study. Since both groups of students had to be tested for their Hebrew language achievement in connection with college entrance, a variety of different language testing instruments, as well as different sets of norms, had to be prepared to accommodate students of widely different educational and community backgrounds. That was the first experience in dealing with differing community programs in connection with heritage vernacular and heritage classical languages.

Since then, other middle-class groups have succeeded in providing public school and college authorities to recognize their respective HLs in one way or another. In Palo Alto, California, next door to Stanford University, HL schools teach Arabic, Chinese, Japanese, and Korean, as well as French, German, Hebrew, Persian, and Spanish. Some of these schools meet (rent-free or at nominal cost) in public school or university quarters. The students who attend these language courses for a specified number of years can receive high school foreign language credit for doing so. In many cases, they can also be examined on College Entrance Examination Board tests for college admission, and then they can complete or go beyond their college's foreign language requirement by taking further courses in their HL. In many cases (particularly where Japanese and Korean are concerned), the parents of these students are literate in the HLs involved. The standardized varieties of these languages are, therefore, part of the home heritage that students bring to their language study. Dialect versus standard and classical versus vernacular problems may be more common for Arabic and Chinese, but in those cases, too, community HL schools are commonly available to students before their graduation from high school. Although none of these cases has been researched (let alone researched well), the contrasts between these languages and Spanish as an HL – with respect to both school–community cooperation and community profiles (parental income, education, and exposure to literacy in their own standard varieties) – need to be fully appreciated.

Conclusion

If we want to foster the language resources of our country, we cannot do so by dealing only with the smaller and relatively problem-free cases. Other languages will come and go as catastrophes continue to plague different parts of the globe. (Witness the influx of speakers of Albanian, Arabic, Bosnian, Croatian, Kurdish, Persian, Russian, Ukrainian, and Vietnamese, just to mention several recently arriving languages.) However, our geographic location is the best guarantee that while other languages may come and go (most Kosovar Albanians, for example, are now returning to their homeland), Spanish will keep on arriving on our shores forever. We must face up to this opportunity quickly, constructively, and inventively. We in the United States are now more multilingual than we have been for quite a while. We are perhaps even more so than we were in the latter part of the 19th century, when European immigration was at its height and 10% of the white population was German speaking, even though further mass immigration from Germany had already ended.

The goal of promoting HL proficiency will revitalize our entire approach to non–English-language instruction. It will not only give us more individuals proficient in these languages, it will also dignify our country's HL communities and the cultural and religious values that their languages represent. It will help language instruction to connect with cultural and intellectual creativity, which it has often been speciously distant from. It will help connect instruction with business and governmental needs for expertise in the languages involved. Finally, it will help us break out of the penumbras of fear and contention that English-only and antibilingual education policies have cast on HLs, as Valdés (1995) has pointed out. These languages will be brought into the scholarly and professional orbits of our schools and colleges, away from the battlefield that public elementary and secondary bilingual education has become, in large part because of the ties to poverty and politics that HLs are perceived to have. We all embrace English and accept its crucial importance in this country. But our country and our educational systems also have other needs – in science and in math, in history and in literature, in world consciousness and in world sensitivity. We desperately need competence in languages – to become "a language-competent society," in Tucker's phrase (1991) – and our huge and varied HL resources have a definite role to play in achieving such competence.

Along with the contributions that industry, government, and language teaching are already making in this connection, we must find and refine the ways and means of bringing these HLs into the educational "main tent," where our national well-being is given its most serious attention and most ample support. This will not be easy to do because we have shamelessly neglected our HLs for far too long. However, we are beginning the intellectual, tactical, pedagogical, and organizational struggle to give these languages the support they deserve, and we may well be remembered by posterity for having done so.

Note

1. From Peyton, J. K., Ranard, D. A., and McGinnis, S. (eds) (2001) *Heritage Languages in America: Preserving a National Resource.* McHenry, IL: Delta Systems and Center for Applied Linguistics. Copyright Center for Applied Linguistics and Delta Systems Co., Inc. Used with permission. See http://calstore.cal.org/store/detail.aspx?ID=166.

References

Cantoni, G. (ed) (1996) *Stabilizing Indigenous Languages.* Flagstaff, AZ: Northern Arizona University, Center for Excellence in Education.

Clyne, M. (1991) *Community Language.* Cambridge, UK: Cambridge University Press.

Fishman, J. A. (1966) *Language Loyalty in the United States.* The Hague: Mouton.

Fishman, J. A. (1985a) *The Rise and Fall of the Ethnic Revival.* Berlin: Mouton de Gruyter.

Fishman, J. A. (1985b) Mother-tongue claiming in the United States since 1960: Trends and correlates. In J. A. Fishman, M. H. Gertner, E. G. Lowy, and W. G. Milan (eds) *The Rise and Fall of the Ethnic Revival: Perspectives on Language and Ethnicity* (pp. 107–94). Berlin: Mouton.

Fishman, J. A. (1991) *Reversing Language Shift.* Clevedon: Multilingual Matters.

Huber, B. J. (1996) Variation in foreign language enrollments through time (1970–1990). *ADFL Bulletin* 27 (2), 57–84.

Kloss, H. (1966) German-American language maintenance efforts. In J. A. Fishman (ed) *Language Loyalty in the United States.* The Hague: Mouton.

Meyer v. Nebraska (1923), 262, US 390.

McCarty, T. L., Yamamoto, A., and Watahomigie, L. J. (eds) (1999) Reversing language shift in indigenous America. *Practicing Anthropology* 20 (special issue, 2), 39–43.

McCarty, T. L., Yamamoto, A., Watahomigie, L. J., and Zepeda, O. (1997) School-community-university collaborations: The American Indian language development institutes. In J. Reyner (ed) *Teaching Indigenous Languages: Proceedings of the 1997 Stabilizing Indigenous Languages Conference* (pp. 85–104). Flagstaff, AZ: Northern Arizona University, Center for Excellence in Education.

McCarty, T. L., and Zepeda, O. (eds) (1998) Indigenous language use and change in the Americas. *International Journal of the Sociology of Language*, 132 (special issue).

Reyhner, J. (ed) (1997) *Teaching Indigenous Languages: Proceedings of the 1997 Stabilizing Indigenous Languages Conference.* Flagstaff, AZ: Northern Arizona University, Center for Excellence in Education.

Reyhner, J. (ed) (1998) *Revitalizing Indigenous Languages: Proceedings of the 1998 Indigenous Languages Conference.* Flagstaff, AZ: Northern Arizona University, Center for Excellence in Education.

Tucker, G. R. (1991) Developing a language-competent American society: The role of language planning. In A. G. Reynolds (ed) *Bilingualism, Multiculturalism, and Second Language Learning* (pp. 65–79). Hillsdale, NJ: Lawrence Erlbaum.

Valdés, G. (1995) The teaching of minority languages as 'foreign' languages: Pedagogical and theoretical challenges. *Modern Language Journal* 79 (3), 299–328.

Viereck, L. (1902) *German Instruction in American Schools: Report of the Commission of Education for 1900–01.* Washington, DC: US Govt. Printing Office.

Chapter 3
The Spanish Language in California

GUADALUPE VALDÉS

The Current Presence of Spanish in California

In this chapter, we trace the presence of Spanish in California from the time of the conquest to the present. We discuss the segregation and exclusion of Spanish-speaking individuals after the imposition of English in California as well as major state policies directed at Spanish-speaking persons in recent years. We argue that, because of the status of Spanish in California, Spanish language maintenance efforts are faced with extreme hostility by the non-Latino population.

Spanish is currently spoken in California by 8.1 million of California's residents aged 5 years and over, out of a total population of 33.8 million (US Census, 2003). Spanish is both a colonial language that pre-dates the establishment of English in California as well as an immigrant language that is spoken by recent arriving immigrants from Mexico and other Spanish-speaking countries. Because recent immigrants often struggle with the English language (Hill & Hayes, 2002), many English-speaking, monolingual Calfornians view Spanish not as a major world language spoken by more than 400 million individuals, but as persistent threat to English, a language of the undocumented and the uneducated that has little value for ordinary Americans who do not plan to work in immigrant communities.

The Early Presence of Spanish in California

The Spanish language entered California in 1542 with Juan Rodríguez Cabrillo's arrival at the port of San Diego. There has been some debate about the exact origin of the name *California*, but according to Chapman (1939) it is generally assumed that the name was taken from *Las Sergas de Esplandián*, one of the popular chivalric novels of the period. Chivalric novels involved an endless series of adventures and struggles against monsters and giants and were read widely in Spain at the time of the "discovery" of California. Chapman (1939) believes that Fortún Jiménez first used the name California when he reached Baja California in 1533–1534 to refer to a number of islands called collectively the Californias.

California's existence was further established for the Spanish crown by Sebastián Vizcaíno, who arrived in Monterrey Bay in 1602. However, it was not until 1769 that Gaspar de Portolá – at the urging of José de Gálvez, the *visitador general* of New Spain – established a Spanish presence in *Alta California*. Unfortunately, the struggles of the final years of the Spanish conquest and the challenges of the northwestward advance were not yet over. Chapman (1939) speaks of the period of 1773 to 1776 as a precarious period in which a limited Spanish military presence in a vast expanse of territory faced hostilities from the native populations. Because of an inadequate supply route from New Spain, settlements lacked adequate provisions and domestic animals. Missions failed to attract neophytes, and the conduct of soldiers toward native women provoked deep antagonisms. It was only the threat of Russian and other European aggression that led to the establishment of a stable supply route and a more extensive presence of the Spanish in California.

The Imposition of the Spanish Language

In spite of the challenges present in the early years, segments of the period 1769–1848 are referred to by historians as the pastoral period (Bancroft, 1888), the romantic period (Chapman, 1939), and the halcyon days (Pitt, 1998/1966). It was an epoch in which Spanish-speaking *Californios* dominated – first, a Spanish California and, after 1823, a California that had become a part of Mexico. It was a time of *fandangos*, *rodeos*, songs, dances, beautiful horses, and gracious and generous hospitality. It was also a period of linguistic domination, of forced conversion of the native population (Haas, 1995), and of the establishment of rigid boundaries reflecting race and class that divided the world into *gente de razón* (people of reason) and *gentiles*, the native population.

As was the case in other parts of New Spain (Mar-Molinero, 2000), Spanish was established in California as the language of interaction and imposed on the native peoples. According to Mar-Molinero (2000), there were three types of pressures that led to the imposition of Castillian during the colonial period: the pressure toward centralization, the belief that the native peoples would not adopt Christian values as long as they spoke their original languages, and the belief that other tongues could not convey Christian beliefs. Blanco's research (1971) supports that view in that he found numerous documents that discuss the teaching of both Christian doctrine *and* the Spanish language to native populations. Blanco contends that in a number of the texts he reviewed, missionaries questioned the wisdom of teaching catechism in Spanish, a language that the natives did not comprehend. However, Blanco also states that few of these individuals took on the task of mastering the native languages. Schiffman (1996) emphasizes that, within the Spanish colonial society of California, indigenous peoples had no language rights. The acquisition of Spanish was empha-sized, and special privileges were given to natives who spoke Spanish to some degree. Pablo Tac, for example, a young man from the Mission San Juan Capistrano who apparently learned Spanish very well, was taken to Rome at the age of 12 so that he could engage in further study. Tac's writ-ten description of the conquest and of mission life is cited by Haas (1995) as presenting a complex account of the lives of both converted and un-converted native peoples of the San Juan Capistrano area (in which the Spanish language played an important role): "Tac's approach to this story of conversion and his use of language denote a quiet resistance to the hu-miliations of conquest, particularly the renaming practices that threatened group history and identity" (Haas, 1995: 19).

For example, renaming was prominent after being baptized, when young natives were subsequently given Spanish names (e.g. Juan Bautista). This practice was also in evidence in the renaming of places. Blanco (1971) – because of his interest in the use of the Spanish language in California – speaks of renaming as an important contribution by the Spaniards to the New World:

> La eufonía maravillosa que en la geografía tiene la palabra California concuerda con el encanto de los nombres que los españoles supieron aplicar aquí en su paso. Hemos comparado con otros países del cen-tro de América y con México e incluso con las otras antiguas regiones españolas de Estados Unidos y es California la que tiene menos nom-bres geográficos procedentes de las antiguas lenguas indígenas: Tu-lares, Pechanga, Coachella, Jamul Pacoima, Islay, etc., son algunos de los pocos que se conservan. Nada nos extraña después de haber leído los diarios de Crespí, Portolá, Costansó, Font, etc., en los que además de admirar lo natural de lo extraordinario entre los españoles mientras descubren California, vemos como siempre es un franciscano el que marcha delante bautizando lugares. (Blanco, 1971: 90)

From today's perspective on the study of colonialism, however, the change in linguistic geography is a clear manifestation of the power relationship between the European conquerors and the vanquished native peoples. The newly "baptized" rivers, streams, mountains, canyons, and valleys were very likely less "enchanting" than they appear to Blanco, a Spaniard writing in the twentieth century about the place of Spanish in the history of California.

What Haas's and Blanco's perspectives do highlight, however, is that Spanish in California was a colonial language that was imposed by con-quest on the indigenous populations. As is the case in all such encounters, the Spanish established their language as the only legitimate means of communication. The history of Spanish in California, moreover, is closely linked to racial ideologies that assumed the superiority and nobility of pure-blooded *españoles* (Spaniards) in comparison to *castas* (individuals of mixed blood) and *indios*. As Mapes (1992: 26) points out, the racial ideology present among *Californios* divided the population into three different groups:

> Racial identity was an indicator of one's total social personality which included race, legitimacy of birth, ancestry, occupation, citizenship and religion and social status as much as one's skin color or blood count. Based on these categories, Californians divided themselves into Castillians and Spaniards, the supposedly racially pure and certainly economically powerful; Mexicans who were considered mixed bloods; and neophytes or Indians who were at the very bottom of the hierarchy.

Haas (1995: 30) concurs with Mapes (1992) and further contends that these categories "undergirded the legal system that evolved to define people throughout the Spanish Americas in the late sixteenth century." However, Haas emphasizes (1995: 31) that within the Spanish system, race categories were relatively flexible. "Whiteness was thus not a singular or static category but included a range of color. 'White' lineage could be purchased from the crown with gold or other goods". Like Haas, Blanco (1971) also determined that the term *gente de razón* was not synonymous with Spaniard and that this classification included artisans, soldiers, colonists, and missionaries who were *mestizos*, *criollos*, or Spaniards. Only *indios* were not included in the designation *gente de razón*, reflecting "the theological debates of the sixteenth century that addressed such questions as whether Indians had souls" (Haas, 1995: 31).

Ironically, as we will point out below, the ultimate decline of the *Californios* and the continuing implementation of restrictive language policies aimed at the Spanish language after the Anglo-Americans established themselves in California was also undergirded by a racial ideology – an ideology that viewed – and continues to view – all Spanish-speaking people as inferior to Anglo-Americans.

The Imposition of the English Language

In 1823, after a bitter war of independence with the mother country, the provinces of New Spain – including California – became provinces of the new Republic of Mexico. For *Californios*, who had not been involved in the war of independence, the change was a difficult one. They did not see themselves as Mexicans, and they deeply resented the administrative modifications made by Mexican government officials, especially the secularization of the missions. *Californios* subsequently resented the Mexican government even more strongly when they learned that California had ceded to the United States as an outcome of the Mexican War.

The English language arrived officially in California in 1846, when Sloat raised the American Flag in Monterrey, thé capital of California. In 1848, Mexico and the United States signed the Treaty of Guadalupe Hidalgo.

According to Schiffman (1996), the treaty included guarantees of rights of the citizens within the ceded territories, including customs, religion, and language. Unfortunately, according to Adams and Brinks (1990: 317), Article VIII, the "only article in the treaty which might be relevant to language rights," has been rejected by state courts when appeals for such rights have been attempted.

The first California Constitution, ratified in 1849, still interpreted the language of the treaty as ensuring that Mexican citizens would receive the same freedom and privileges granted to other citizens of the United States. Thus, the convention delegates accepted the proposal of delegate Noriega from San Luis Obispo, which established that

> All laws, regulations, and provisions emanating from any of the three supreme powers of this State, which from their nature require publication, shall be published in English and Spanish. (Constitution of the State of California 1849, Article VI, Section 21)

The debate about this matter, as cited in Blanco (1971), is an interesting one. Mr. Noriega argued that the present inhabitants of California would not learn English in 3–4 years and that people could not obey laws they did not understand. Opponents were concerned about the future expenses incurred in the translation of all laws. They argued that the provision was unnecessary because in the course of 20 years, everyone in California would speak English. Noriega maintained that his proposal was necessary in order to protect the older inhabitants of California. At that time the older inhabitants were greatly outnumbered due to a recent arrival of more than 68,000 Anglo-Americans during the course of 1 year. Not convinced of the need to protect *Californios* by using their language, another delegate countered that the act of appointing original citizens as constitutional convention delegates would not only ensure their participation in the debates but also ensure that, by giving them a voice, no wrong would ever be done to them:

> It has been the custom of other nations, who were the conquerors, to trample to the dust the rights of the conquered; but what do you see here? You see these gentlemen admitted to exactly the same platform that you occupy yourselves taken to your hearts as friends and brothers; and here when they sit upon this floor, treated with a degree of deference and respect that no other members in this convention can command, is not that a guaranty – a sufficient guaranty – that they who have done this will never do them wrong? (Debates of the Convention of California on the Formation of the State Constitution, as cited in Blanco, 1971: 333)

Unfortunately, by 1878, as Crawford (1992) points out, not a single Spanish-speaking delegate was present at the constitutional convention that revised the constitution. Perhaps, as a result of the limited participation by *Californios*, the California Constitution of 1879 revoked its earlier policy on publishing laws in English and in Spanish and established (by 46 ayes to 39 nays) that the publication of all official proceedings in the state of California would be limited to English. In the debates carried out during the convention, arguments made by opponents of the English-only stance met with counter arguments that claimed the original residents had had 30 years to learn English and that the Treaty of Guadalupe Hidalgo was not an implied contract to protect language rights.

Historical accounts of the period after 1846 suggest that, as had been the case with the first group of conquerors of California (the Spanish), the second group also viewed themselves as racially and culturally supe-rior to the vanquished population. Examinations of the Anglo-American views toward the Spanish and Mexicans during the period (Almaguer, 1994; Haas, 1995; Mapes, 1992) make evident that Anglos who arrived in California felt great disdain for the wealthy and aristocratic *Californios*. The second group saw the wealthy *Californios* as indolent, unproductive, and lazy. Accounts of the lifestyles of wealthy ranchers written by easterners traveling in California and cited by historians (e.g. Mapes, 1992; Pitt, 1998) emphasize the differences between Anglo protestant values stressing fru-gality and hard work and the disdain felt toward the wealthy ranchers who represented exploitative paternalism. Anglos viewed the ranchers as fail-ing to really work the land, exploiting the native peoples, and constantly displaying their wealth in a conspicuous manner. Commonly, ambitious young Anglo males married into *Californio* families and spoke of the great beauty of the females. However, there was widespread doubt about the racial purity of even the *gente de razón*, who appeared to be the offspring of *Californios* and the universally despised Indians. Almaguer (1994: 55) argues that

> Those whose class position and ostensible European ancestry placed them at the top of the hierarchy during the Mexican period, the "gente de razón," were reluctantly viewed as "white" by Anglo Americans. The dark complexioned, mestizo population (the "greasers" or gente sin razon – literally, "people without reason"), on the other hand, were viewed as "nonwhite" and not significantly different from pure-blood, Indian "savages" in the state.

Feagin (1997: 16), in tracing the deep roots of modern nativism in the United States, contends that the fierce commitment to "English norms, values, and ways of operating" was established in the early settler societies of the Puritans. The Puritans had the "arrogant notion that these English settlers would make better use of what they saw as undeveloped "wilder-ness" than "wild savages" who were the present occupants." The belief in Anglo-Saxon superiority was clearly present in the 1840s and 1850s, and used against certain categories of white immigrants and as a justification for Manifest Destiny (the westward expansion of the United States to extend across the continent) (Almaguer, 1994; Feagin, 1997).

The English-only and anti-Mexican stance that influenced the new constitution became present in the daily lives of the Spanish-speaking population of California. According to Macías (2001), by 1852, state funds were made unavailable to private schools and by 1855 the State Bureau of Public Instruction decreed that all schooling, both public and private, should take place exclusively in English. Up until that time, Spanish was used in 18% of all schooling in both private and Catholic schools. In 1870, a state law further supported the 1855 regulation requiring that only the English language be used in education in both public and private schools. Macías (2001: 347) concludes that by the beginning of the 20th century,

> California had subjugated non-English languages, especially Spanish. ...English was the official language of instruction in the schools, English literacy was required for voting, and English was the language for administration of government.

Present-Day California Policies toward the Spanish Language and toward Spanish-Speaking Persons

The legacy of racial tensions and conflicts present in the early days of the American period are still present today in the beginning years of the 21st century. Racial intolerance and exclusion – both related and unrelated directly to language – have remained a part of present day California. The exclusionary policies directed at Spanish-speaking residents and the English-only policies that have received extensive publicity in the last decade are, unfortunately, not a recent phenomenon. Moreover, overt policies directed at Spanish-speaking residents of California have often masked covert policies designed to limit the use of Spanish. While overt policies directed at language have often masked policies directed against the rapidly increasing Mexican-origin population.

The segregation of Spanish-speaking students

The early segregation of Mexican-origin students in California schools is an example of a policy directed, in theory, at providing language services for English learners. However, an examination of school segregation in California as it has impacted African American, Asian, and Mexican children reveals that "throughout the state's history there has been a conflict between those who have seen the schools as universal and unifying institutions and those who have seen the schools as particularist and separated institutions" (Wollenberg, 1976: 6).

In the case of Mexican students in California, Wollenberg presents evidence of the routine segregation of children of Mexican workers, which began in 1910. By the 1920s 10% of the state's total school population consisted of Mexican-origin students. According to Wollenberg, this increased enrollment of Mexican children led to the opening of separate Mexican schools in many areas of the state and of segregated swimming pools, theatres, and restaurants. Schools segregated children largely in response to the demands of white parents who feared educational retardation for their own children. Segregation was justified on linguistic grounds because Mexican children were said to need special instruction and special programs in order to learn English.

It was not until 1945 that Mexican parents took legal action against the schools, which prohibited their children from attending schools attended by Anglo-American youngsters. Wollenberg reports that the favorable decision in the1946 case of *Mendez v. Westminster* held that the State Education Code did not provide for the segregation of children of Mexican origin and that no clear valid educational reason justified the segregation of the children. Unfortunately, even though the plaintiffs prevailed in the appeal, the decision had an impact only on *de jure* and not on *de facto* segregation. What this reveals about the early history of California language policies is that, while manifested in linguistic and racial prejudice, the policies have not been exclusively or even primarily about language.

Segregation of Mexican children continues in California today. Because of residential segregation, majority minority-populated schools, with nearly 100% Latino enrollment are common in many parts of the state. According to Frankenberg *et al.* (2003) Latino students are currently segregated in schools around the country by race, poverty, *and* language. Spanish-speaking English language learners "attend schools with many more low-income minority, and non-English-speaking students than do other groups, including non-LEP Hispanic and non-Spanish-speaking LEP students" (Van Hook & Balistreri, 2002: 650).[1] Moreover, as the papers filed in support of *Williams v. The State of California*[2] make evident, in 30 of the 46 schools listed in the complaint, over 30% of the students are English language learners. Even in those schools where native English speakers are present, language-based tracking ensures that Mexican-origin students are kept separate from Anglophone white youngsters. Valdés (2001) contends that overt policies on language assessment and student language reclassification create ESL ghettos – that is, hermetically sealed tracks from which English-language learners are seldom exited. State guidelines for assessing the language proficiency of students whose primary language is not English are elaborate and take the position – when convenient – that students need extensive support until they acquire enough English to succeed in mainstream courses, thus justifying their continued segregation.

Bilingual education policy

As pointed out above, an 1870 state statute established English as the sole language of instruction in both private and public schools in California. This statute, directly prohibiting the teaching of subject matter in languages other than English was repealed in 1967. In 1976, the California legislature approved the passage of the Chacon-Moscone Bilingual-Bicultural Education Act (1976), which made it legal to give non–English-speaking students access to the curriculum through their primary language. Macías (2001) argues that federal policies (e.g. the Civil Rights Act of 1964, the Bilingual Education Act of 1968, and the 1974 *Lau v. Nichols* US Supreme Court decision requiring schools to take "affirmative steps" to provide equal educational opportunities to non–English-speaking youngsters) created a context in which states, for example California, were encouraged to repeal existing laws limiting or prohibiting the use of non-English languages in education. The Chacon-Moscone Bilingual-Bicultural Act (1976) required schools to provide pupils who were limited – or non–English-speaking – with equal educational opportunities. In 1980, the Bilingual Education Improvement and Reform Act mandated schools to provide bilingual education of limited English-speaking students.

These two statutes, however, expired (or sunsetted) in 1987 and were not renewed. By that time, controversies surrounding the vagueness of the language of the *Lau* decision had provoked a debate around the country about the types of remedies considered legitimate in providing equal educational opportunities to English language learners.[3]

As a language policy, the California Chacon-Moscone Bilingual-Bicultural Act (1976) overtly dealt with the implementation of instruction in non-English languages. Moreover, as a civil rights policy it obligated the state of California to provide a meaningful and equitable education for all students. However, to some degree the Bilingual Education and Reform Act (1980) could be seen as a covert exclusionary policy. It allowed Spanish-speaking students to be educated separately from other students, and it justified this separation – as was done in the case of *Mendez v. Westminster* – by arguing that the special language needs of certain groups of students required the development of educational programs designed to meet their special needs. For those concerned about segregation, bilingual education appeared to be a language policy that masked exclusion. For those concerned about the futility of educating students in a language they did not understand, bilingual education was a compensatory education policy that focused on language, the condition that prevented students from accessing the curriculum. Finally, for those concerned about providing too many benefits to an undeserving population, bilingual education was an employment policy for Spanish-speaking teachers, an expensive drain on state resources, a Spanish-language program designed to prevent students from learning English, and a manifestation of new immigrants' refusal to become American. Over time, negative views about bilingual education culminated in the passage of Proposition 227, an initiative directed at prohibiting instruction in non-English languages.

The anti-immigrant propositions

From 1976 to 1995, immigration to California increased dramatically. According to the Population Resource Center (2004), by 1994, one-third of the foreign-born population in the United States resided in California. Between 1960 and 1990, the total population of California almost doubled, increasing from 15.7 million to 29.7 million. The influx of both documented and undocumented immigrants, combined with the increase of immigrants from Mexico, provoked strong anti-immigrant sentiments in California. The negative sentiments reflected the state's emergent economic distress as well as the growing unease present around the country about the costs of immigration, the federal government's role in providing states relief for the burdens imposed on them by "out-of-control immigration," and an only slightly disguised distress about the "browning" of America.

The effects of immigration were hard to estimate, and a number of reports using different methodologies disagreed strongly about the actual costs of immigration for residents of the state of California. A Rand report (McCarthy & Vernez, 1997) concluded that immigration reduced job opportunities for natives and stated that immigrants as a group did not pay enough taxes to cover the costs of public services. Organizations such as the Federation for American Immigration Reform (FAIR) argued that immigration seriously affected the quality of life and environment in California. Immigration increased population, caused increased traffic, led to reduced open space and farmland, resulted in crowded housing and lack of affordable housing, affected directly the state's health care budget, water supply, and air quality, caused school overcrowding, and led to massive expenditures in the incarceration of illegal aliens.

Beginning in 1983 with Proposition O (a citizens' initiative directed at urging the federal government to amend the Voting Rights Act) and ending in 1998 with Proposition 227 (an initiative designed to prohibit bilingual education) a series of anti-immigrant, anti–Spanish-speaking and anti-Mexican legislative initiatives were proposed and approved. In 1986, 73% of California voters passed Proposition 63, declaring English to be the official language of California. In 1994, 58.9% of the citizens of the state of California voted to pass Proposition 187, an initiative designed to bar illegal immigrants from receiving public health, education, and welfare benefits and calling upon schools and health and welfare agencies to ask students and clients to prove their legal status before receiving services.

It also made it a felony to manufacture, sell, or use false citizenship or residence documents. In 1996, 54% of voters in California passed Proposition 209 and agreed to end affirmative action by amending the California Constitution. Finally, in 1998, 61% of California voters agreed to dismantle bilingual education.[4]

Services in multiple languages

Because federal policies have precedence over state policies, services in languages other than Englishs are still available in California. Federal court decisions (e.g. *Lau v Nichols*), federal legislation (e.g. the Civil Rights Act of 1964, the Voting Rights Act of 1975, the Court Interpreters Act of 1978), and guidelines and regulations set up by the administrative bodies created by such legislation (e.g. EEOC Guidelines, Lau Remedies) have been extremely important in providing a basis for state actions. In spite of antiimmigrant and anti-Spanish views, the state must still follow federal laws. It must also ensure the health and safety of its residents, and it must respond to newly passed legislation, to new lawsuits, and to new court decisions directly affecting language use. Moreover, as Schiffman (1996) points out, the state must enforce the California State statutes already part of the California code that require the use of non-English languages. An excellent summary of these codes is provided by an article on bilingual public services authored by the American Civil Liberties Union of Northern California (ACLU, 1992) including a description of

- *The Dymally-Alatorre Bilingual Services Act (1973)*
  The Dymally-Alatorre Bilingual Services Act (1973) requires state and local agencies to ensure that their services are accessible to substantial populations of limited-English-speaking individuals. The Dymally-Alatorre Bilingual Services Act specifically requires that when state and local agencies serve a "substantial number of non-English speaking people," they must employ a "sufficient number of qualified bilingual staff in public contact positions."
- *The California Codes governing social, health and emergency services*
  These codes set forth the responsibilities of state agencies to publish informational materials about disability insurance, workers compensation, unemployment benefits in English, Spanish, and other non-English languages as required. These codes also cover the obligation of state agencies to provide information in English and Spanish about public assistance, the Medi-Cal Program, rights of the mentally retarded, patients' rights, and emergency and disaster relief. All applications for disaster relief, food stamps and the like need to be provided in languages accessible to the population.

- *The California Codes guiding fair employment and housing*
  These codes prohibit discrimination based on language, which is considered to be a form of national-origin discrimination. The Department of Fair Employment and Housing is required to publish Spanish language posters and pamphlets on existing laws. Farm labor contractors must provide information about compensation in English and Spanish. The Departments of Industrial Relations, Employment Development, the Housing and Community Development Office, and the Office of economic Opportunity must provide for bilingual services.

In addition, the Master Plan for Special Education requires that students with special needs be identified in the appropriate language. The Department of Motor Vehicles must provide examinations in 23 different languages, and the Departments of Real Estate, Consumer Affairs, and Water Resources, and the Franchise Tax Board must make available materials in languages needed by the population served and/or provide interpreters. Finally, all non-English persons charged with a crime have a constitutional right to an interpreter (Cal. Const. Art. I §14 [adopted, Nov. 5, 1974]).

It is important to emphasize that in California efforts to advance the state of the law on language rights reflect deliberate and systematic attempts by civil rights attorneys to expand legal protection against language discrimination. For example, the Language Rights Project of the American Civil Liberties Union Foundation of Northern California is an advocacy project established in 1994. It has as its purpose providing "legal assistance to those who have been unfairly targeted in the workplace, in the marketplace, or in other important arenas because (a) they choose to communicate in their native, non-English language, or (b) they are unable to speak standard English" (ACLU, 1996: 2). The project currently runs a Language Rights Hotline providing legal advice and referrals to individuals who have been victims of language discrimination, as well as identifying cases that can potentially expand legal protections against language bias. Attorneys working with ACLU, the Equal Employment Opportunity Commission (EEOC), the Asian Law Center, Mexican American Legal Defense Fund (MALDEF), Puerto Rican Legal Defense Fund (PRLDF), and Multicultural Education Training and Advocacy Project (META) are currently engaged in litigating a wide variety of language-related cases. The organizations were also directly involved in challenging all four anti-immigrant propositions. These challenges were successful in the case of Proposition 63 (which became largely symbolic) and Proposition 187 (which was declared unconstitutional and not appealed by Governor Grey Davis).

Activities supporting language rights have also continued in the California legislature. In January 2000, a new California law (originally Assembly Bill 800) sponsored by Assemblyman Herb Wesson and supported by ACLU added a section to the government code that outlawed all workplace English-only rules. It implemented the constitutional protections provided by Section 8, Article 1, of the California Constitution, while claiming to recognize the statement policy found in Section 6, Article III, of the California Constitution that English is the official language of California.

SEC. 2. §12951 is added to the Government Code, to read: 12951.

(a) It is an unlawful employment practice for an employer, as defined in subdivision (d) of Section 12926, to adopt or enforce a policy that limits or prohibits the use of any language in any workplace, unless both of the following conditions exist:
    (1) The language restriction is justified by a business necessity.
    (2) The employer has notified its employees of the circumstances and the time when the language restriction is required to be observed and of the consequences for violating the language restriction.
(b) For the purposes of this section, "business necessity" means an overriding legitimate business purpose such that the language restriction is necessary to the safe and efficient operation of the business, that the language restriction effectively fulfills the business purpose it is supposed to serve, and there is no alternative practice to the language restriction that would accomplish the business purpose equally well with a lesser discriminatory impact. (Cal. Gov Code §12951)

In 2001, Latino Senator Escutia introduced Senate Bill 987 to amend the 29-year-old Dymally-Alatorre Bilingual Services Act. The bill intended to hold state agencies accountable for the degree to which they provide bilingual services and to add services in additional languages. Although Governor Gray Davis vetoed the bill resulting from SB 987, Assembly Bill 2408 covering the same issues passed in July 2004. The struggle, however, continues.

The Challenge of Developing Spanish Language Resources in California

Language maintenance and heritage language development

Language maintenance refers to the continued use of an indigenous or immigrant minority language in a majority language context. To be considered language maintenance, it is not sufficient for a language to be present in a particular community and for it to be spoken, for example, by newly arrived immigrants. The process of language maintenance refers to the retention of language and its transmission over several generations. The scholarship on language shift and language maintenance (e.g.

Fishman, 1991, 2000) has examined a variety of language contexts around the world in which speakers of indigenous languages (e.g. Welsh, Irish, Basque, Navajo) have struggled to preserve their languages. The task of maintaining or developing minority or heritage languages in the various settings described involves different challenges. In the case of indigenous languages that are not spoken outside of one particular setting, the task of reversing language shift – once the abandonment of the language is underway – is enormously challenging. Especially, if there are no other communities of speakers that can be brought in to revitalize the language. As Fishman (2000) has argued, language maintenance efforts in those cases may need to begin with the reconstruction of the language from elderly and vestigial users. Those committed to reversing language shift must understand the functional disruption of their particular language in social space and must focus and prioritize their efforts in clear stages in order to be successful. They may need to move from reconstructing the language, to using the language once again in the community, to language use and transmission within the family, and to the use of schools for literacy acquisition for both young and old. In some communities, the advantage may be that all its members as well as outside majority language members can be made conscious of the costs involved in the total shift by the community to the majority language: language endangerment and eventually language death.

In the case of languages that are widely spoken, such as Spanish or Arabic, language maintenance appears to be much less pressing in settings such as the United States. Language endangerment and language death are not an issue since these languages are widely spoken elsewhere in the world. Moreover, new groups of immigrants appear to be constantly revitalizing and maintaining the language with their very presence. The presence of new immigrants and the language's constant use in receiving communities does not mean that the language will be maintained over generations by the children and the grandchildren of newcomers. For those youngsters who are born here and who are educated only or primarily in English, there are few advantages to retaining or developing high-level proficiencies in languages other than English.

Maintaining and developing Spanish in California

In California, as is evidenced by the passage of Proposition 63, there are strong views against the development and maintenance of Spanish by Latinos. It was most unusual, therefore, that on February 17, 1999, the *San Jose Mercury News* (San Jose, California) published a front-page article entitled "Latino Lawmakers Study Their Spanish: Some Were

Fluent as Kids but Stumble Today" (Jordan, 1999). The article pointed out that newly elected Latino lawmakers, as products of a public-school system that emphasized English, and immigrant parents who wanted their children to assimilate, were wrestling to recover the Spanish that they had spoken fluently as children. Many found themselves struggling to discuss complicated issues of policy such as health care as they accompanied Governor Gray Davis to Mexico. The politicians were faced with the need to campaign in Spanish and to court the Latino population, the article stated, many Latino lawmakers reported taking intensive courses in Spanish and immersing themselves in the language among family members and Spanish-speaking aides in order to improve their skills.

Although Spanish is widely spoken in the United States, the impact of national language ideologies stressing the rapid acquisition of English and the exclusive use of English is clearly apparent in the patterns of language shift in Latino communities in this country. Recent research on language use in Latino communities has made clear that in spite of the influx of monolinguals into Latino communities the shift toward English among Latinos is unmistakable. Several scholars (e.g. Fishman 1985, 1987; Veltman, 1983, 1988) have demonstrated that present-day immigrants to the United States, including Latinos, are regularly acquiring English and shifting away from the use of their ethnic languages. Moreover, research conducted from a variety of perspectives directly supports these findings. For example, a survey of Latinos carried out by de la Garza *et al.* (1992)[5] revealed that no more than 10% of each of three groups of 1546 Mexican, 589 Puerto Rican, and 682 Cuban respondents considered themselves to be monolingual in Spanish or English. This is especially noteworthy given that 13% of Mexican respondents, 66% of the Puerto Rican respondents, and 71% of Cuban respondents were born outside the US mainland. In the case of young Latinos, Solé (1990) recently demonstrated that ongoing language shift toward English is absolute. One third of the youngest Latinos, for example, have no skills in the ethnic language, and monolingualism in Spanish among Hispanics is weak, encompassing only 16% of Puerto Ricans, 12% of Mexican Americans, and 1.6% of Cuban Americans. Support for Solé's conclusions have been provided more recently by the study carried out by Portes and Hao (1998), who found that less than half of the Latino students they surveyed were fluent bilinguals.

Other work on language maintenance and language shift carried out in Cuban and Puerto Rican communities (e.g. Solé, 1980, 1982; Zentella, 1997) reveals a similar pattern of increased use of English among young Latinos. Similarly, research conducted on Mexican-American communities (e.g. Bills, 1989; Bills *et al.*, 1995; Hart-Gonzalez & Feingold, 1990) coupled with sociolinguistic work carried out among first-, second-, and third-generation speakers of Spanish (e.g. Gutierrez, 1996; Lope Blanch, 1990; Silva-Corvalán, 1994) provides strong support for the position that Latino communities are shifting to English. Furthermore, Hart-Gonzalez and Feingold (1990: 28) conclude that there is "a clear overall tendency toward home language shift."

Other research carried out in Mexican-American communities on the Spanish language itself also supports the position that Spanish is the non-dominant language of most third-generation speakers. Research by Silva-Corvalán (1994) led to the conclusion that while Spanish is being maintained at the societal level because of the influx of new immigrants, at the individual and family level, there is a clear shift to English. In Los Angeles, where Silva-Corvalán did her research, speakers of Spanish could be located at very different ends of a continuum of proficiency ranging from fully fluent speakers of Mexican Spanish to users of emblematic Spanish. Silva-Corvalán (1994) found clear differences between Group 1 (Los Angeles speakers who were born in Mexico who immigrated to the United States after the age of 11), Group 2 (Los Angeles speakers who were born in the United States or came to the United States before the age of 6) and Group 3 (Los Angeles speakers born in the United States who had one parent fitting the definition of group 2). Members of Groups 1 and 2 could converse in Spanish with ease. However, speakers in Group 3 spoke Spanish with difficulty. More importantly, in the Spanish of Group 3, Silva-Corvalán found clear evidence of simplification of grammatical categories, overgeneralization of forms, and the direct and indirect transfer from English. Other similar work (e.g. Gutierrez, 1996; Lope Blanch, 1990) supports the position that the Spanish spoken in Mexican-American communities is characterized by lexical limitations and morphological insecurities. Still further research on language maintenance and loss in Mexican-background high school students (Hakuta & D'Andrea, 1992; Hakuta & Pease-Alvarez, 1994; Pease-Alvarez, 1993) very strongly supports the above conclusions.

While it is encouraging that a recent newspaper article spoke positively of the advantages of retaining and developing Spanish for Latino legislators, efforts to maintain Spanish in California and/or to develop Spanish language resources are faced with a number of specific challenges. First, there is a challenge of motivating individuals to take on the task of maintaining Spanish in a context in which there has been and continues to be open hostility to Spanish and Spanish-speaking individuals. Second, there is the challenge of utilizing existing educational institutions to bring about the development of advanced literacy-related proficiencies in Spanish in light of current policies toward bilingual education and confronted with the ideologies of correctness present in Spanish language departments. In the sections that follow, we present an overview of these two challenges.

The context of hostility toward Spanish

The political climate toward Spanish-speaking persons is a hostile one in California. In the current anti-immigrant climate, the image of Latinos has been deeply tainted by the debates surrounding the passage of the four initiatives discussed above. Labeled by numerous scholars as nativist and reactionary (e.g. Feagin, 1997; Gibbs & Bankhead, 2001; Schockman, 1998), these four propositions (63, 187, 209, and 227) have created a context in which racial and ethnic prejudices that had previously been alluded to indirectly have now become part of the public discourse (Cain, 1998). This openly racist public discourse surrounding the passage of the four initiatives has resulted in what Gibbs and Bankhead (2001: 174) refer to as a "sociodemographic schism" within which it is now safe to propose a constitutional amendment that would determine whose children will be allowed to be America's future citizens (Roberts, 1997). As Roberts argues, fears about the browning of America and the "loss of cultural as well as and numerical preeminence" have led to the thinking that "assumes that American culture is synonymous with the culture of white people and that the cultures of the new immigrants are inconsistent with a national identity" (p. 211). The solution for those who object to "racially undesirable immigrants" and who support the limitation of the production of "home-grown foreigners" (p. 212) is an amendment to the Constitution that denies American citizenship to the children of undocumented immigrants. It also provides for an immigration quota that increases the numbers of southern- and eastern-European immigrants.

Santa Ana (2002) in his study of public discourse in California points out (as have other scholars; e.g. Cain, 1998; Gibbs & Bankhead, 2001) that nativist ideologies became part of the public discourse in 1993 with Governor Pete Wilson's Open Letter to the President of the United States on Behalf of the People of California. In this letter, Wilson spoke of "massive illegal immigration," "perverse incentives," and "stemming the flow." Santa Ana points out that California voters experiencing an economic downturn approvingly received this nativist rhetoric:

> Immigration became an emotionally charged political issue, as it has been in other recessionary times, and the mood of the dominant constituencies of California political life became perceptively negative toward Latinos. . . . Once the governor expressed anti-Latino sentiment, xenophobia was no longer confined to private discussions. It became the stuff of public discourse. (Santa Ana, 2002: 6)

Santa Ana argues that the conventional views of the American nation within which Mexicans had a certain limited place were reaffirmed by way of metaphors such as: "awash in a brown tide, the relentless flow of immigrants, like waves on a beach, these human flows are remaking the face of America" (p. 7). These common and unquestioned metaphors created an even more negative image of Latinos in the public imagination. Analyzing articles published in the *Los Angeles Times* from 1992 to 1998, during the period of three of the four statewide referenda – Proposition 187, Proposition 209 and Proposition 227 – Santa Ana found that Latinos were metaphorized in particular patterns (e.g. immigration as dangerous waters, immigration as invasion, politics as war, success as race, language as barrier). Furthermore, Santa Ana concluded that these terms reproduced and reaffirmed existing ideological assumptions about race, ethnicity, and citizenship.

Strictly speaking, only propositions 63 and 227 can be considered language policies. As Macías (2001) points out, however, within the state's political context, these initiatives were "wedge issues" used to polarize the electorate by race and class. Moreover, these language policies directly reflect racist and exclusionary ideologies such as those historically present among Anglo-Americans in California. As Wiley (2000: 73) argues,

> In U.S. history, and in its prior English colonial history, race has always been a more salient maker of group boundaries than language. Nevertheless, in Nativist and Neo-Nativist ideologies, cultural and linguistic differences have been used as quasi-racial markers to define inter-group boundaries even among European-origin peoples.

A study of the vote on Proposition 187 (the anti-immigrant initiative) conducted by Mac Donald and Cain (1998) revealed that "there was a substantial overlap between the vote for the English only and Prop. 187 initiatives." There was "almost a one-to-one correspondence between county support levels for Props 63 and 187" (pp. 296–97). Those who voted for the English-only Proposition (63) also tended to vote for the anti-immigrant Proposition (187).

What kind of Spanish? Perspectives on the Spanish of California

Spanish is currently spoken in Latin America, Spain, the United States, Equatorial Guinea, Guam, North Africa, Andorra, and the Philippines. It is spoken by 400 million people around the world, 40 million of whom are in Spain and 22 million of whom are in the United States (Stewart, 1999). Varieties of Spanish spoken in different parts of the world reflect the same kinds of differences observed in varieties of English spoken in Great Britain, Canada, the United States, Belize, and India. Like English, Spanish varieties or dialects vary primarily in pronunciation and vocabulary. As is the case with English, speakers of Spanish have strong attitudes toward what they consider to be both "good" and "bad" Spanish. Speakers of Latin American Spanish often have negative and stereotypical views of speakers of Peninsular Spanish, and speakers of Peninsular Spanish have equally negative perceptions of the varieties of Spanish spoken by Latin Americans. There have been proposals to classify the various regional varieties of Spanish spoken in Latin America according to the patterns and routes of Spanish colonization, regional origins of original settlers, social and occupation origins of original settlers, and contact with particular indigenous languages. None of these descriptions are considered entirely adequate (Lipsky, 1994). As Penny (2000: 1) argues, "it is a universal characteristic of human language that speakers of the 'same' language who live in different parts of a continuous territory do not speak in the same way." There is as much social and geographical variation within the Spanish spoken in Spain as there is in the Spanish spoken in Latin America.

The relationship between Latin American Spanish and Peninsular Spanish has been a focus of debate among intellectuals beginning in the 19th century after the Latin American nations had won their struggle for independence from Spain. According to del Valle and Gabriel-Stheeman (2002), Spain sought to retain a strong influence in Latin America through language. Acrimonious debates took place during the 19th century about "what Spanish is, what it represents, and who has the authority to settle linguistic disputes and dilemmas" (p. xii). Some Latin American intellectuals (e.g. Sarmiento) disagreed strongly about the need for the Spanish spoken in Latin American countries to be limited to the prescriptions of the *Real Academic Española.*[6] While others (e.g. Bello) felt strongly that linguistic unity must be created and expanded. During the last half of the 19th century, intellectuals of the stature of Juan Valera, Miguel de Unamuno, and José Ortega y Gasset were deeply engaged in polemical discussions focusing on nationhood, Hispanic unity, and language.

During the early 20th century, acrimonious discussions about *la unidad de la lengua* (the unity of the language) still continued. A number of respected philologists and writers engaged in these discussions. For example Cuervo (1900a, 1900b, 1901, 1903) expressed extensive concern about the possible fragmentation of Spanish (parallel to that of Latin) and of the development of mutually unintelligible languages originally based on Spanish but directly influenced by indigenous languages. Menéndez Pidal (1918, 1944, 1951, 1956), on the other hand, argued strongly that the circumstances leading to fragmentation were not present in Latin America. Many other Spanish scholars disagreed and continue to disagree. In 1956, for example, in a meeting of the Academies of Language[7] Dámaso Alonso, disagreed with Menéndez Pidal and expressed strong concern about the fragmentation of Spanish because of lexical differences in the various zones of Latin America. More recently, in the Congreso del Internacional del Español held in Valladolid, Spain, in 2001, the same disquiet about language unity and diversity of language was once again expressed. (The conference program and papers presented can be seen at: http://cvc.cervantes.es/obref/congresos/valladolid/ponencias/unidad_

diversidad_del_espanol.) The paper presented by Lope Blanch (2001) once again argues for an "ideal norm" that ensures the unity of the Spanish language. The papers on Spanish in the United States include examinations of the "problems" faced by Spanish in the United States (Palacios, 2001) as well as more serious linguistic studies of US Spanish (Otheguy, 2001; Silva-Corvalán, 2001). Every paper, however, in the section reveals a strong preoccupation with the characteristics of contact varieties of Spanish and ultimately with language change.

Historical accounts of Spanish in California

There have been few historical studies of the Spanish language in California. One such work is *La lengua española en la historia de California* (1971) written by Antonio Blanco and presented as a doctoral dissertation under the direction of Dámaso Alonso at the University of Madrid. The work is based on Blanco's fieldwork at the Bancroft Library at the University of California Berkeley, in the Archivo de Indias de Sevilla, and the Archivo General de la Nación de México. For Blanco (1971), who set out to describe the evolution of the Spanish of California, the background of the early population and their pride in the language was particularly important. In carrying out his work, Blanco attempted to follow the methodology used by Boyd-Boman (1956, 1964), who investigated the geographical and social-class origins of 40,000 Spaniards who came to America in the 16th century in order to identify the social and regional features of the language brought to the New World. Using a variety of written documents, Blanco describes the Spanish brought to the New World by the missionaries, the chronicle writers, and the military. He also includes some discussion of indigenous languages.

As a student of Dámaso Alonso, a member of the Real Academic Española who was concerned about lexical fragmentation, Blanco looked for evidence of *indigenismos* in the Spanish of California. Finding very little evidence of such "contamination," he argues that, as opposed to other areas of the New World, in California, the *gente de razón* remained very separate from the indigenous masses. According to Blanco, the Spanish spoken by the Jesuits and Franciscans, as seen through their early writings about California reveals "la belleza de un estilo 'franciscano' de una exquisita sencillez, elegancia y diáfana sinceridad." Citing passages taken from the works of Father Jaume and Father Crespí, Blanco points out "expresiones llanas y castizas" (p. 79) as well as "lenguaje sencillamente coloquial." He attributes the quality of Spanish spoken and written by missionaries as due to intellectual traditions in the Jesuit and Franciscan orders and to their rigorous preparation.

Blanco is much less effusive about the Spanish brought to the New World by the soldiers, but he is certain that there were important linguistic differences between the language of the officers and the common soldiers. Vulgar and careless pronunciation were present in New Spain as well as:

> mexicanismos necesarios o innecesarios, vulgarismos plebeyos y lenguaje de arrabal o de ranchería, aztequismos, mezcla de palabras indígenas junto con el castellano propio del refinamiento de la más culta y sensorial cuidad de América ... (p. 101)

Proud Spaniards and *criollos* (Spaniards born in the New World) had great pride in maintaining their language. Moreover, in California, mestizo soldiers and families arrived from Sonora and Sinaloa and mixed with the *criollo* population already there.

> El mestizo en California emparentó fácilmente con el criollo y de esta forma se hizo un culto de la sangre Española. Se diría que en este rincón de la nueva España se había formado una raza diferente que se distinguía por su superior inteligencia, su educación y su capacidad para ocupar los puestos preeminentes. Casi todos eran o habían sido o precedían de militares distinguidos y formaban un aristocracia sencilla. (p. 120)

Blanco states that the population of California up to 1840 consisted of old soldiers and their descendants. In contrast with what occurred in Mexico, *Californios* did not mix with the natives and:

> en California no hubo división de castas y la sociedad se mantuvo más pura y más unida, sin que existieran tampoco (al menos no hemos encontrado mención de ello) las rivalidades propias de las innumerables divisiones de la sociedad colonial. (p. 128, our emphasis)

Both racial and linguistic purity seem to be important to Blanco. He concludes (p. 128) that the language used by *Californios* incorporated few mexicanisms or other terms that signaled differences between classes and castes. He also concludes that indigenous languages did not influence the Spanish of the *Californios*.

The portrait of the Spanish of California presented by Blanco begins with the arrival of the Spanish in California and ends in the 1960s, the period when he conducted his fieldwork. The work includes a list of *Californianismos* (California vocabulary), a linguistic description of changes in vowels and consonants, and a discussion of irregular uses during the Spanish period. It also includes an examination of what he terms "la anglización del español" at the beginning of the American period and concludes that the language was by then in danger. He criticizes the Spanish of the documents translated from English during that period and lists a number of anglicisms, to which he objects strongly. He refers to this era as one in which mexicanization took place (p. 342) and concludes that linguistic fragmentation, if it occurs, will first take place in Mexico. For Blanco, changes in the language are "un cancer profundo de la esencia, del tuétano de la lengua castellana" (p. 343).

From the early days of California and the Gold Rush, Blanco's work jumps forward to the period beyond the 1940s and includes a discussion of *pachuco* argot, a bibliography on *pachucos*, and a listing of *pachuco* vocabulary. In speaking of the contact between two cultures, Blanco refers to the war of languages that he witnessed and laments that Spanish has not been able to liberate itself from the influence of the dominant language. Furthermore, Blanco characterizes the Spanish spoken by Spanish-speaking youngsters in California, as follows:

> Los jóvenes que formaron la primera y segunda generación de descendientes de aquellos emigrantes aprendieron el español en casa directamente de sus padres y heredaron las mismas deficiencias... Aparece así el problema sociológico y sicológico del bilingüe en el que el lenguaje al reflejar una cultura de la cual es símbolo, es insustituible por otro. (p. 344, our emphasis)

This particular quote suggests that Blanco was influenced by views about the sociological and psychological problems of bilingualism that were part of the literature on bilingualism at the time the book was written.

For Blanco, the solution is for the state of California to provide instruction in Spanish, to provide courses in Latin American culture, and to motivate students to carry out university studies on the indigenous and Spanish past. The state has, in Blanco's view, a historical obligation to conserve and extol its Spanish and Mexican past.

Nevertheless, Blanco is cautious about the actual possibilities of teaching Spanish in this country to the children of immigrants. Having been a faculty member at various California universities, he warns (pp. 593–94) that people who can really teach Spanish must be found, that great care must be taken to prevent demagogues from taking over departments of Spanish, and that extremist students should not be allowed to control the curriculum. Instruction should have as its goal solving existing sociological, psychological, economic, and educational problems.

As compared to the work of Espinosa (1911) on the Spanish of New Mexico , which is cited frequently by students of Spanish in the Americas and which simply documents but does not condemn the numerous contact features identified in the Spanish of that state, Blanco's history of Spanish in California is not a work that is well known by students of US Spanish. The work, however, received the *Premio Conde de Cartagena* awarded by the Real Academia Española in 1968. It is important to note that, although it is a product of the period during which it was written, it is an important work for those concerned about the maintenance of Spanish in California because it emphasizes the pervasiveness of the long-standing and ongoing preoccupation with both linguistic and racial purity.

Present-day contact varieties of Spanish in California

The Spanish varieties that are spoken in the United States by individuals who have lived here for an extensive period of time are contact varieties of the language[8] that are used among Latinos to interact with both monolingual and bilingual speakers of Spanish. Residents of long-standing Latino communities include both newly arrived Latinos who are monolingual in Spanish, bilingual Latinos who have acquired English and retain Spanish, young bilingual Latinos who have acquired both languages in their communities, and monolingual English-speaking Latinos. In these communities, individuals interact with one another using Spanish, English, or both. A choice of language is often made depending on the language proficiencies of the individuals engaged in interaction, on the topic of interaction, on the setting, and on the relationship between the interlocutors. Children who are born and raised in such communities acquire the ability to use both languages to some degree to communicate with newly arrived individuals, as well as with monolingual members of the majority Anglophone community (Zentella, 1997).

The Spanish spoken in California by bilingual individuals of many different types is not identical to that spoken in the monolingual areas of the Spanish-speaking world. As is the case with other contact varieties of language, in the United States and in California, Spanish has borrowed numerous elements from the language with which it is in contact, particularly nouns and verbs, to talk about new or unfamiliar experiences, objects, concepts, and activities.

As is well known to students of bilingualism, the process of borrowing has been studied extensively in many other languages in bilingual contexts. Einar Haugen (1953), for example, in his classic study *The Norwegian Language in America* developed a complex classification for different types of loan words found in American Norwegian. These borrowings or loans were integrated into American Norwegian as speakers of Norwegian became aware that their language did not have a term for a particular concept or object or when they wanted to make particular distinctions made in English that were not made in Norwegian.

Similarly, in the case of Spanish, when newly arrived individuals are momentarily at a loss for an exact equivalent of an English term (e.g. *hang out*, *spell*, *truck*), they may use the term in Spanish conversation, adapting its phonology and morphology to that of Spanish (*jenguiar*, *espeletiar*, *troca*). Over time, other bilingual individuals in the community may begin to use the same terms because they also find them useful. If these terms come to be used by Spanish-speaking monolinguals in the entire community, the terms are classified as established loans or integrated borrowings and as part of that variety of the language. As is the case with borrowings in general (e.g. *menu* and *garage* in English), many bilingual and monolingual individuals who use them may not be aware that these terms were originally adapted from English.

What is often not obvious to monolinguals unfamiliar with contact varieties of a language are the kinds of distinctions that are being made when speakers use such borrowings. In numerous cases, bilingual individuals borrow terms from the dominant language because their first language does not make distinctions that have become important in their new context. For example, while English makes a distinction between *lock* and *close*, Spanish does not. The verb *cerrar* is used for both. Over time, the verb *cerrar* begins to be perceived as unnecessarily ambiguous by bilinguals who are used to making the English distinction. They therefore "borrow" the term *lock* and integrate it both phonologically and morphologically into Spanish, creating the verb *laquear*. The verb can then be conjugated in all tenses of both the indicative and the subjunctive.

Logical and useful as the process of borrowing might be to communicate more effectively in bilingual settings, for many individuals who are concerned about correctness, erosion, and the contamination of the Spanish language, such uses are examples of *Spanglish*, a type of speech that in the popular mind is neither English nor Spanish. Such individuals are even more intolerant of the process of code-switching, the alternating use of the two languages at the word, phrase, clause, and sentence levels.

For students of language, code-switching is a well-known and familiar phenomenon found in bilingual communities all over the world. It has been studied extensively in many pairs of languages (e.g. Auer, 1998; Dabene & Moore, 1995; Gibbons, 1987; Jacobson, 1998; Milroy & Muysken, 1995; Myers-Scotton, 1993a, 1993b; Poplack, 1980), and it is considered the unmarked code for informal communication between bilinguals in many settings. Scholars agree that code-switching is a rule-governed process that requires extensive knowledge of two grammatical systems, as well as knowledge of where in an utterance a switch can take place.

It has also been established that code-switching carries social meaning and is indexical of personal rights and obligations (Scotton, 1988). Even though in many cases bilinguals may switch languages because of lexical need, more frequently by switching, they signal changes in role relations, suggest changes in attitude toward the topic being discussed, and foreground particular aspects of the message. Rather than limiting themselves to a six-string guitar (one or the other of the languages), bilinguals use the entire range of a 12-string guitar (two languages) to create complex nuanced utterances.

Unfortunately, current examinations of bilingual communication in the popular press (e.g. Stavans, 2003) while attempting to speak positively of the contact variety of Spanish known as *Spanglish*, describe it as a creative hodgepodge and a broken mix of English and Spanish, rather than a legitimate variety of Spanish that continues to make essential morphological and syntactic distinctions. Interestingly, Stavan's rewriting of *Don Quijote* in *Spanglish* directly violates the syntactic constraints of code-switching that have been carefully researched by scholars since the early 80s (e.g. Poplack, 1980). The negative reaction to Stavan's work has not come from linguists who have studied English/Spanish bilingualism in this country, but rather from Latino intellectuals and writers. Some of them are members of Spanish department faculties, who find *Spanglish* offensive and who view it as evidence of the fact that US Latinos have mastered neither language.

Research on US Spanish in California (e.g. Silva-Corvalán, 1994) has established that the contact variety spoken by US Latinos is indeed Spanish. What is also clear is that the contexts of acquisition for Spanish in this country are very different from those found in Spanish-speaking countries. As a result, the language experiences of US Latinos who grow up in bilingual communities in the United States are very different from those of persons raised in Latin America or Spain. Because many Latino speakers have not had access to the range of situations and contexts in which formal varieties of Spanish are used, their language is characterized by a somewhat narrower range of lexical and syntactic alternatives than is found in the language of monolingual upper-middle-class speakers from Spain or Latin America. Perhaps more telling, in bilingual communities, the use of Spanish is restricted to largely low-level functions and private sphere interactions, over time – as Huffines (1991) points out – "the immigrant language falls into disuse" (p. 125). As a result, many young people in bilingual communities may not acquire a full mastery of the registers and styles characteristic of Latino monolinguals.

The complexity of issues involving language and status and opportunities for acquisition of particular varieties or registers is intensified within California. Speakers of Spanish inhabit worlds in which English surrounds them and in which the maintenance of their HL often represents a rejection of mainstream values to mainstream Americans. As Santa Ana (2002) argues, in California the Spanish language is the language spoken by the "brown tide" of new immigrants that is rapidly "rising." It is, therefore, viewed as a threat to English and to the American common culture. It is also viewed as a direct barrier to the successful assimilation of Latino immigrants. Not surprisingly, in such a climate, there is likely to be little enthusiasm for language maintenance among Latinos.

In the chapter that follows, we present the results of the survey of Latino professionals that we conducted in California which sought to determine the frequency of use of Spanish by educated professionals as well as their attitudes toward particular varieties of Spanish and toward the role of formal language instruction in the maintenance and development of Spanish among Latinos in California.

Notes

1. The term *limited English proficient* (LEP) was used until recently by official government agencies in the United States to refer to children who arrived in school with no English, little English, or flawed English. More recently, the terms *English Language learner* (ELL) or *English language developing student* (ELD) have been used. We use the term here as it was originally used by others in the material we cite.
2. The *Williams v. State of California* class action suit filed in 2000 sought to require the State of California to provide educational essentials in all schools in California. The amended complaint argued that many California students do not have access to legible or current textbooks, permanent teachers, fully credentialed teachers, classrooms with sufficient seats, libraries, functioning toilets, and facilities in good repair. The plaintiffs claimed that substandard conditions are present in schools attended by low income and nonwhite students.
3. For a discussion of the debates surrounding the Lau remedies, see Crawford (1989).
4. A number of scholars have given attention to the analysis of the debate surrounding the passage of these propositions as well as to their effects. For an analysis of the debates surrounding the passage of these initiatives, the reader is referred to Adams and Brink (1990) and Crawford (1992a, 1992b) for Proposition 63, to Herrera (1995) and McLaughlin *et al.* (1995) for Proposition 187, to Gibbs and Bankhead (2002) for Proposition 209, and to Butler *et al.* (2000) and García and Curry-Rodríguez (2000) for Proposition 227.
5. The Latino National Political Survey (LNPS) was designed to collect basic data describing Latino political values, attitudes, and behavior. Supported by the Ford, Spencer, Rockefeller, and Tinker Foundations. The research was conducted between 1989 and 1990 in 40 Standard Metropolitan Statistical Areas and involved a sample representative of 91% of the Mexican, Puerto Rican, and Cuban populations of the United States.
6. The Real Academic Española was founded in 1713 and had as its motto *limpia, fija y da esplendor* ("it cleans, fixes and brings splendor"). Modeled on the *Academie Française*, its purpose was to standardize the language, a process Mar-Molinero (2000: 23) points out is "an essential part of linguistic nationalism." The Academy has published a series of dictionaries and grammars setting forth what was almost universally accepted as "good" Spanish. Currently, according to Stewart (1999), the academy currently seeks to reflect and not to prescribe use.
7. During the 19th century, national *academias* were established in Latin America. Twenty-one *academias corresponsales* continue to exist today (including an Academia Norteamericana de la lengua). A description of each academy, its history, and membership is included on Real Academia's Web site: http://www.rae.es/.
8. Languages are said to be *in contact* when they are used alternately by the same speakers (Weinrich, 1974).

References

Adams, K. L., and Brink, D. T. (Eds.) (1990) *Perspectives on Official English: The Campaign for English as the Official Language of the USA.* Berlin: Mouton de Gruyter.

Almaguer, T. (1994) *Racial Fault Lines: The Historical Origins of White Supremacy in California.* Berkeley, CA: University of California Press.

Alonso, D. (1956) Unidad y defensa de la lengua. _Memorias del Primer Congreso de Academias de la Lengua Española_, 33–48.

American Civil Liberties Union of Northern California. (1992) Bilingual public services in California. In J. Crawford (ed) _Language Loyalties_ (pp. 303–11) Chicago: University of Chicago Press.

Auer, P. (1998) _Code-switching in Conversation: Language, Interaction and Identity_. London: Routledge.

Bancroft, H. H. (1888) _California Pastoral 1769-1848_. San Francisco: A. L. Bancroft.

Bills, G. D. (1989) The US Census of 1980 and Spanish in the Southwest. _International Journal of the Sociology of Language_ 79, 11–28.

Bills, G. D., Hernandez-Chavez, E., and Hudson, A. (1995) The geography of language shift: Distance from the Mexican border and Spanish language claiming in the U.S. _International Journal of the Sociology of Language_ 114, 9–27.

Blanco, A. (1971) _La lengua española en la historia de California: Contribución a su estudio_. Madrid: Ediciones Cultura Hispánica.

Boyd-Bowman, P. (1956) The regional origins of the earlist Spanish colonists of America. _Publications of the Modern Language Association_ 71, 1152–72.

Boyd-Bowman, P. (1964) _Indice giobiográfico de 40,000 pobladores españolas de América en el siglo XVI_. Bogotá: Instituto Caro y Cuervo.

Butler, Y. G., Orr, J. E., Bousquet Gutierrez, M., and Hakuta, K. (2000) Inadequate conclusions from an inadequate assessment: What can SAT-9 scores tell us about the impact of Proposition 227 in California? _Bilingual Research Journal_ 24 (1–2), 141–54.

Cain, B. E. (1998) The politization of race and ethnicity in the nineties. In M. B. Preston, B. E. Cain, and S. Bass (eds) _Racial and Ethnic Politics in California_ (Vol. 2, pp. 457–68). Berkeley, CA: Institute of Governmental Studies Press.

Chapman, C. E. (1939) _A History of California: The Spanish Period_. New York: Macmillan.

Crawford, J. (1989) _Bilingual Education: History, Politics, Theory and Practice_. Trenton, NJ: Crane.

Crawford, J. (ed) (1992a) _Language Loyalties: A Source Book on the Official English Controversy_. Chicago: University of Chicago Press.

Crawford, J. (1992b) _Hold Your Tongue: Bilingualism and the Politics of English Only_. Reading, MA: Addison Wesley.

Cuervo, R. J. (1900a, September 24) Sobre la duración del habla castellana. _El Imparcial_.

Cuervo, R. J. (1900b, December 2) Carta. _La Nación_.

Cuervo, R. J. (1901) El castellano de America. _Bulletin Hispanique_ 3, 35–62.

Cuervo, R. J. (1903) El castellano de América. _Bulletin Hispanique_ V, 58–77.

Dabene, L., and Moore, D. (1995) Bilingual speech of migrant people. In L. Milroy and P. Muysken (eds) _One Speaker, Two Languages_ (pp. 17–44). Cambridge: Cambridge University Press.

de la Garza, R. O., DeSipio, L., Garcia, F. C., Garcia, J., and Falcon, A. (1992) _Latino Voices: Mexican, Puerto Rican, and Cuban Perspectives on American Politics_. Boulder, CO: Westview.

del Valle, J., and Gabriel-Stheeman, L. (2002) _The Battle over Spanish between 1800 and 2000_. London: Routledge.

Espinosa, A. (1911) _The Spanish Language in New Mexico and Southern Colorado_ (Vol. 16). Santa Fe, NM: New Mexican.

Feagin, J. R. (1997) Old poison in new bottles: The deep roots of modern nativism. In J. F. Perea (ed) _Immigrants Out: The New Nativism and the Anti-immigrant Impulse in the United States_ (pp. 13–43). New York: New York University Press.

Fishman, J. A. (1966) _Language Loyalty in the United States_. The Hague: Mouton.

Fishman, J. A. (1985a) *The Rise and Fall of the Ethnic Revival*. Berlin: Mouton de Gruyter.

Fishman, J. A. (1985b) Mother-tongue claiming in the United States since 1960: Trends and correlates. In J. A. Fishman, M. H. Gertner, E. G. Lowy, and W. G. Milan (eds) *The Rise and Fall of the Ethnic Revival: Perspectives on Language and Ethnicity* (pp. 107–94). Berlin: Mouton.

Fishman, J. A. (1987) What is happening in Spanish on the US mainland. *Ethnic Affairs* 1, 12–33.

Fishman, J. A. (1991) *Reversing Language Shift*. Clevedon: Multilingual Matters.

Fishman, J. A. (2000) From theory to practice (and vice versa): Review, reconsideration and reiteration. In J. A. Fishman (ed) *Can Threatened Languages Be Saved?* (pp. 451–83). Clevedon: Multilingual Matters.

Frankenberg, E., Lee, C., and Orfield, G. (2003) *A Multiracial Society with Segregated Schools: Are We Losing the Dream?* Cambridge, MA: The Civil Rights Project, Harvard University.

Garcia, E. E., and Curry-Rodriguez, J. E. (2000) The education of limited English proficient students in California schools: An assessment of the influence of Proposition 227 in selected districts and schools. *Bilingual Research Journal* 24 (1/2), 15–35.

Gibbons, J. (1987) *Code-mixing and Code Choice: A Hong Kong Case Study*. Clevedon: Multilingual Matters.

Gibbs, J. T., and Bankhead, T. (2001) *Preserving Privilege: California Politics, Propositions, and People of Color*. Wesport, CT: Praeger.

Gutierrez, M. (1996) Tendencias y alternancias en la expresión de condicionalidad en el español hablado en Houston. *Hispania* 79 (September), 567–77.

Haas, L. (1995) *Conquests and Historical Identities in California, 1769-1936*. Berkeley: University of California Press.

Hakuta, K., and D'Andrea, D. (1992) Some properties of bilingual maintenance and loss in Mexican background high-school students. *Applied Linguistics* 13 (2), 72–99.

Hakuta, K., and Pease-Alvarez, L. (1994) Proficiency, choice and attitudes in bilingual Mexican-American children. In G. Extra and L. Verhoeven (eds) *The Cross-linguistic Study of Bilingual Development* (pp. 145–64). Amsterdam: North Holland.

Hart-Gonzalez, L., and Feingold, M. (1990) Retention of Spanish in the home. *International Journal of the Sociology of Language* 84, 5–34.

Haugen, E. (1953) *The Norwegian Language in America: A Study in Bilingual Behavior*. Philadelphia: University of Pennsylvania Press.

Herrera, L. Q. (1995) Majority will v. minority rights: Proposition 187 and the Latino Community. Unpublished honors thesis in political science, Stanford University.

Hill, L. E., and Hayes, J. M. (2003) California's newest immigrants. In H. P. Johnson (ed) *California Counts: Population Trends and Profiles* (Vol. 5, No. 2, p. 20). San Francisco, CA: Public Policy Institute of California.

Huffines, M. L. (1991) Pennsylvania German: Convergence and change as strategies of discourse. In H. W. Seliger and R. M. Vago (eds) *First Language Attrition* (pp. 127–37). New York: Cambridge University Press.

Jacobson, R. (1998) *Codeswitching Worldwide*. New York: Mouton de Gruyter.

Jordan, H. (1999, February 17) Latino lawmakers study their Spanish. Some were fluent as kids but stumble today. *San Jose Mercury News*, p. 1.

Lau v. Nichols, 1974 414 U.S. 563.

Lipsky, J. (1994) *Latin-American Spanish*. London: Longman.

Lope Blanch, J. M. (1990) *El español hablado en el suroeste de los Estados Unidos: Materiales para su estudio*. México, DF: Universidad Nacional Autonoma de Mexico.

Mac Donald, K., and Cain, B. E. (1998) Nativism, partisanship, and immigration: An analysis of Prop. 87. In M. B. Preston, B. E. Cain, and S. Bass (eds) *Racial and Ethnic Politics in California* (Vol. 2, pp. 277–304). Berkeley, CA: Institute of Governmental Studies Press.

Macías, R. (2001) Minority languages in the United States with a focus on California. In G. Extra and D. Gorter (eds) *The Other Languages of Europe: Demographic, Sociolinguistic and Educational Perspectives* (pp. 332–354). Clevedon: Multilingual Matters.

Mapes, K. A. (1992) Race and class in nineteenth century California. Unpublished master's thesis, Michigan State University, Lansing, MI.

Mar-Molinero, C. (2000) *The Politics of Language in the Spanish-speaking World: From Colonisation to Globalisation*. London: Routledge.

McCarthy, K., and Vernez, G. (1997) *Immigration in a Changing Economy: California's Experience*. Santa Monica: Rand.

McLaughlin, B. (1978) *Second-language Acquisition in Childhood*. Hillsdale, NJ: Erlbaum.

McLaughlin, K., Kramer, P., and Legon, J. (1995, November 21) Judge guts core of Prop. 187. *San Jose Mercury News* p. 1A.

Mendez v. Westminister School Dist. of Orange County, 64 F.Supp. 544 (D.C.CAL. 1946).

Menendez Pidel, R. (1918) La lengua española, su unidal. *Hispania* 1, 1–14.

Menendez Pidal, R. (1944) *La unidad del idioma*. Madrid.

Menendez Pidal, R. (1955) El castellano en América. *Cuadernos Hispanoamericanos* 20, 490–92.

Menendez Pidal, R. (1956) Nuevo valor de la palabra hablada y la unidad del idioma. *Memorias del Primer Congreso de Academias del a Lengua Española*, 33–34.

Milroy, L., and Muysken, P. (1995) *One Speaker, Two Languages: Cross Disciplinary Perspectives on Code-switching*. Cambridge, England: Cambridge University Press.

Myers-Scotton, C. (1993a) *Duelling Languages: Grammatical Structure in Codeswitching*. Oxford, England, and New York: Clarendon Press and Oxford University Press.

Myers-Scotton, C. (1993b) *Social Motivations for Codeswitching: Evidence from Africa*. Oxford: Clarendon Press.

Otheguy, R. (2001) Simplificación y adaptación en el español de Nueva York. Paper presented at the Congreso Internacional del Español, Valladolid, Spain. Retrieved March 21, 2006, from http://cvc.cervantes.es/obref/congresos/valladolid/ponencias/unidad_diversidad_del_espanol/1_la_norma_hispanica/lope_j.htm

Palacios, O. B. (2001) El español en los Estados Unidos: Problemas y logros. Paper presented at the Congreso Internacional del Español, Valladolid, Spain. Retrieved March 21, 2006, from http://cvc.cervantes.es/obref/congresos/valladolid/ponencias/unidad_diversidad_del_espanol/1_la_norma_hispanica/lope_j.htm

Pease-Alvarez, L. (1993) *Moving In and Out of Bilingualism: Investigating Native Language Maintenance and Shift in Mexican-descent Children* (No. 6). Santa Cruz, CA: University of California, Santa Cruz.

Penny, R. (2000) *Variation and Change in Spanish*. Cambridge: Cambridge University Press.

Poplack, S. (1980) Sometimes I'll start a sentence in Spanish *y termino en español*: Toward a typology of code-switching. *Linguistics* 18, 581–618.

Population Resource Center (2004) Immigration to California. On www at http://www.prcdc.org/summaries/immigrationca/unmigratienca.html. Accessed 26.8.2004.

Pitt, L. (1998) *The Decline of the Californios: A Social History of the Spanish-speaking Californians, 1846-1890* (Updated with a New Forward by Ramon Gutierrez, ed). Berkeley, CA: University of California Press.

Portes, A., and Hao, L. (1998) *E Pluribus Unum*: Bilingualism and loss of language in the second generation. *Sociology of Education* 71, 269–94.

Roberts, D. E. (1997) Who may give birth to citizens? In J. F. Perea (ed) *Immigrants Out: The New Nativism and the Anti-immigrant Impulse in the United States* (pp. 205–19). New York: New York University Press.

Santa Ana, O. (2002) *Brown Tide Rising: Metaphors of Latinos in Contemporary American Public Discourse.* Austin: University of Texas Press.

Schiffman, H. F. (1996) *Linguistic Culture and Language Policy.* London: Routledge.

Schockman, H. E. (1998) California's ethnic experiment and the unsolvable immigration issue. In M. B. Preston, B. E. Cain, and S. Bass (eds) *Racial and Ethnic Politics in California* (Vol. 2, pp. 233–76). Berkeley, CA: Institute of Governmental Studies Press.

Scotton, C. M. (1988) Code-switching as indexical of social negotiations. In M. Heller (ed) *Codeswitching* (pp. 151–86). Berlin: Mouton.

Silva-Corvalan, C. (1994) *Language Contact and Change: Spanish in Los Angeles.* New York: Oxford University Press.

Silva-Corvalán, C. (2001) Aspectos lingüísticos en el español de Los Angeles. Paper presented at the Congreso Internacional del Español, Valladolid, Spain. Retrieved March 21, 2006, from http://cvc.cervantes.es/obref/congresos/valladolid/ponencias/unidad_diversidad_del_espanol/1_la_norma_hispanica/lope_j.htm

Solé, C. (1980) Language usage patterns among a young generation of Cuban–Americans. In E. L. J. Blansitt and R. V. Teschner (eds) *A Festschrift for Jacob Ornstein: Studies in General Linguistics and Sociolinguistics* (Vol. 274–81). Rowley, MA: New Bury.

Solé, C. (1982) Language loyalty and language attitudes among Cuban-Americans. In J. Fishman and G. D. Keller (eds) *Bilingual Education for Hispanic Students in the United States* (pp. 254–268). New York: Teachers College Press.

Solé, Y. R. (1990) Bilingualism: Stable or transitional? The case of Spanish in the United States. *International Journal of the Sociology of Language* 84, 35–80.

Stavans, I. (2003) *Spanglish: The Making of a New American Language.* New York: Harper-Collins.

Stewart, M. (1999) *The Spanish Language Today.* London: Routledge.

US Census Bureau. (2003 October) *Census 2000 Brief: Language Use and English-language Ability* (No. C2KBR-19). Washington DC: Author.

Valdés, G. (2001) *Learning and not Learning English: Latino Students in American Schools.* New York: Teachers College Press.

Van Hook, J., and Balistreri, K. S. (2002) Diversity and change in the institutional context of immigrant adaptation: California schools 1985–2000. *Demography* 39, 639–54.

Veltman, C. J. (1983) *Language Shift in the United States.* Berlin: Mouton.

Veltman, C. J. (1988) *The Future of the Spanish Language in the United States.* New York: Hispanic Policy Development Project.

Weinrich, U. (1974) *Languages in Contact.* The Hague: Mouton.

Wiley, T. G. (2000) Continuity and change in the function of language ideologies in the United States. In T. Ricento (ed) *Ideology, Politics, and Language Policies: Focus on English* (pp. 67–85). Amsterdam: John Benjamin's.

Wollenberg, C. (1976) *All Deliberate Speed. Berkeley*: University of California.

Zentella, A. C. (1997) *Growing Up Bilingual.* Oxford: Blackwell.

Chapter 4

The Use of Spanish by Latino Professionals in California

JOSHUA A. FISHMAN, GUADALUPE VALDÉS,
REBECCA CHÁVEZ and WILLIAM PÉREZ

Language Shift and Language Maintenance among Latinos in the United States

According to Fishman (1964), immigrant bilingualism in the United States follows a specific pattern that is common to all immigrant groups and that leads to monolingualism in English by the fourth generation. In the case of Latinos, this pattern of transitional bilingualism leading to language shift is often masked by the continuing arrival of new monolingual Spanish-speaking immigrants into bilingual communities. Unfortunately, as we pointed out in Chapter 3, within the last several years, confusion about the English language proficiency of US Latino populations has been engendered because of the existing ideological climate and because of the activities of several groups and organizations (e.g. US English; English Only) that view Spanish as a threat to English. Members and supporters of these two organizations claim that Hispanics, unlike immigrants in the past, are rejecting the English language.

As we also pointed out in Chapter 3, recent research on language use in Latino communities has made clear that in spite of the influx of monolinguals into Latino communities, the shift toward English among Latinos is unequivocal. Working with 1980 census data, Bills (1989: 26–7), for example, argues that

> there is no evidence in the present study that the Spanish language is being strongly maintained in the United States Southwest. On the contrary, it appears that the Spanish-origin population in the last half of the 20th century is behaving like a "normal" segment of United States society; it seems to be giving up the ethnic language and shifting to English as it becomes exposed to the mainstream of American life. The principal exceptions to this language shift appear to be where there is either isolation from the mainstream or a considerable influx of Spanish speakers from Mexico.

54

More recently Bills *et al.* (1995) concluded that distance from the border (perhaps because of the considerable influx of Spanish speakers from Mexico) contributes to the process of Spanish language maintenance and shift in an important, though secondary, way. Locations closer to the border favor maintenance, while distance from the border favors shift. The authors maintain, however, that even in cities close to the border, the highest predictor of language shift is education. Only when education is partialed out does distance from the border emerge as a nontrivial, but second-order, predictor of language maintenance.

To examine the degree to which direct instruction in a heritage language can reverse or retard the process of language change and language shift and to develop policies on heritage language programs, we carried out a survey of highly educated Latino professionals including doctors, lawyers, college professors, elected and appointed officials, and successful businessmen. We expected that the survey would provide information about the perceived needs for Spanish by professionals, many of whom primarily use English in their professional and personal lives. By conducting such a survey, we hoped to identify the role that Spanish has played in their lives, the kinds of functions that Spanish has or might have had in their lives, the views that they have about their existing proficiencies, the kinds of Spanish instruction that would have been useful to them, and the kinds of Spanish instruction that they would recommend for both secondary and postsecondary institutions in California. We hypothesized that goals currently viewed as essential in heritage language instruction by educational institutions will not be what these individuals identify as most important. The survey instrument contained a battery of questions focusing on the role of Spanish in their lives, their need for Spanish in professional and personal settings, their concern about stigmatized and contact features in their own speech and in that of other Spanish speakers in California, their perceptions of register differences and their importance professionally, and their views about ways in which direct instruction might assist them in efforts to develop or rebuild their own Spanish language competencies.

The Survey of Latino Professionals

A sample of Latino professionals were drawn randomly from lists of such professionals in California. Professionals were identified using lists of professional groups, including professors in the California State University system, professors in the University of California system, judges, lawyers, doctors, teachers, elected and appointed officials, and businesspersons. In the case of doctors, a list of Latino doctors practicing in California was purchased from the American Medical Association (AMA). In the case of lawyers, a list of Latino surnamed lawyers was purchased from the La Raza Lawyers Association. A list of Latino businesspersons was obtained from the *Journal of Hispanic Business*. Names of elected and appointed officials were drawn from the 2000 directory of Latino officials by rank and county obtained from the National Association of Latino Elected and Appointed Officials (NALEO). Names of judges were obtained from a directory of Minority Judges that included listings of judges by ethnicity. Lists of University of California (UC) and California State University (CSU) faculty were compiled from departmental Web sites at each of the California institutions. Finally, high school teachers from public schools were identified by contacting principals and assistant principals at California high schools in 58 counties so that they could recommend or refer individuals who fit our criteria.

A total of 200 individuals were drawn from the lists obtained to adequately sample the various professional groups both in counties whose population was below and above the state median Latino population. In selecting individuals from the identified lists, we sought to select approximately equal numbers of individuals from 8 occupational professional groups and 2 Hispanic population density strata (counties with a Hispanic population at or above the state median and counties with a Hispanic population below the state median). Two samples totaling 200 individuals were drawn for each professional group. One hundred individuals were selected from the bottom counties and 100 individuals were selected from the top counties. A total of 218 individuals were surveyed because some of the original respondents declined to be tape recorded. For the purpose of comparability we replaced those individuals who declined to be tape recorded with people who agreed to be tape recorded so that we could closely listen to and take note of their answers on the open-ended questions.

A telephone survey instrument was developed by project personnel, and versions of the instrument were pretested. Questions covered demographic information (place of birth, country of origin, age of arrival), sociolinguistic information (patterns of English and Spanish use, education, formal study of Spanish, self-evaluation of proficiencies), views about the need for Spanish in professional life, efforts made to improve Spanish, and attitudes toward varieties of Spanish. The survey instrument is included in Appendix A.

The telephone survey of language use was carried out among selected individuals from April to August 2000. After the interviewing process was completed a team of researcher assistants transcribed all 200 tapes. The tapes and transcriptions were checked for accuracy by individuals who had not transcribed the particular tape being reviewed. After all interviews were transcribed they were coded for further analysis. An extensive code book was created during the coding phase. Each interview transcript was coded by two research assistants. A third research assistant checked for reliability among coders. After all 200 interviews were completely coded

Table 4.1 Participant highest level of education

	Frequency	*Percent*
Multiple, postgraduate	3	1.5
PhD/MD	69	34.5
JD	50	25.0
MA/MS/MBA	15	7.5
BA/BS	42	21.0
Some college/ AA	13	6.5
High school/ GED	7	3.5
Eleventh grade	1	.5
Total	200	100.0

and checked for reliability, two identical databases were created and information was entered twice, once into each database. The two databases were then compared for consistency. Any inconsistencies were then reentered and a final database was created and used for statistical analyses presented here.

Personal and professional characteristics of Latino professionals surveyed

A total of 200 individuals, 25 from each of the 7 professions comprised the sample described in this study. The eight professions selected represented business, academia (California State University and University of California faculty members), education (certified secondary-level teachers), medicine (doctors), law (judges and attorneys), and elected officials.

Table 4.1 indicates that participants in this study were highly educated. Approximately one-third of all respondents (34.5%) reported having at least a PhD or an MD. One-fourth of all respondents (25%) had received at least a law degree. Although there was one individual with less than a high school degree, 89.5% of all respondents had at least a 4-year college degree. Finally three individuals reported having multiple postgraduate degrees.

Nativity

Table 4.2 indicates that about one-third (32%) of all respondents are foreign born. The majority of those born outside of the United (47%) arrived before the age of 10. Only 5% of respondents arrived after the age of 30.

Table 4.2 Respondents' place of birth

	Frequency	Percent
Born outside United States	64	32.0
Born inside United States	136	68.0
Total	200	100.0
Age of arrival for foreign born		
1–10	30	47.7
11–20	17	27.1
21–30	13	20.7
31+	3	4.8
Total	63	100.0

Age

Overall, interview participants were predominantly middle-aged. As Table 4.3 indicates, most respondents were between the ages of 31 and 60. Thirty-one percent were between the ages of 41 and 50 while 30% were between the ages of 51 and 60. Thus, 74% of all respondents were 41 years of age or older.

Parent place of birth

Almost two-fifths (40.5%) of all respondents had a mother or a father born in Mexico while about one-fifth (17%) of respondents' mothers and fathers (21%) were born in a Latin American country other than Mexico. Overall, almost three-fifths of all respondents had foreign-born mothers (57.5%) or fathers (61.5%). In addition, slightly more than a third had a

Table 4.3 Respondent's age

Age	Frequency	Percent
71–80	7	3.5
61–70	17	8.5
51–60	60	30.0
41–50	62	31.0
31–40	43	21.5
20–30	9	4.5
Total	198	99.0

mother (35.5%) or a father (33.5%) born in the Southwest while the remaining had mothers and fathers born elsewhere in the United States (see Table 4.4).

Although the vast majority of respondents reported having at least a 4-year college degree, Table 4.4 indicates that most respondents came predominantly from households with low levels of parental educational attainment. Almost 43% of respondents had mothers with only an elementary school education. Similarly, 36% had fathers with only an elementary school education. Seventy-eight percent of all mothers and 71% of all fathers had less than a postsecondary education. About half of all mothers (50.8%) and fathers (47%) attended school outside the United States.

Childhood Spanish language use

To better understand changing patterns of Spanish language use, respondents were asked about their Spanish language use during childhood. Table 4.5 indicates that 55% of all respondents reported always speaking Spanish at home during childhood. This is in contrast to the 9% that reported never speaking Spanish at home during childhood. Of those that spoke Spanish growing up, 25% reported speaking it with their fathers while only 6% reported speaking it with their mother.

Spanish language instruction

According to Table 4.6, 67% of all respondents reported studying Spanish in high school. Of these, one-third studied Spanish for 4 years, one-fourth studied Spanish for 3 years and one-third studied it for 2 years. Of the 200 respondents, only about half (54.7%) reported studying Spanish in college. Seventy-five of the 200 respondents (78.9%) reported studying Spanish between one and four semesters. Most respondents (84.3%) reported not having any type of in-service training in Spanish. About half (54%) of all respondents reported understanding Spanish like a native, but only 44% report speaking Spanish like a native. Thirty-nine percent reported understanding Spanish and 44% reported speaking Spanish fairly well. Only 7% reported understanding Spanish and 13% reported speaking Spanish very little.

Current Spanish language use at home

Table 4.7 presents information regarding current Spanish language use among surveyed professionals. Fourteen percent reported always using Spanish at home. About one of four professionals (25%) reported rarely using Spanish at home while 17% reported never using Spanish at home. Of those reporting any use of Spanish at home, about half (55%) reported

Table 4.4 Parent place of birth and educational attainment

	Frequency	*Percent*
Mother		
Place of birth		
Mexico	81	40.5
US Southwest	71	35.5
Other Latin America, not Mexico	34	17.0
Other US	13	6.5
Unknown	1	0.5
Total	200	100.0
Educational attainment		
Postsecondary school	43	21.8
Secondary school	59	29.9
Elementary school	84	42.6
No schooling	11	5.6
Total	197	100.0
Father		
Place of birth		
Mexico	81	40.5
US Southwest	67	33.5
Other Latin America, not Mexico	42	21.0
Other US	7	3.5
Unknown	3	1.5
Total	200	100.0
Educational attainment		
Postsecondary school	57	29.4
Secondary school	49	25.3
Elementary school	69	35.6
No schooling	19	9.8
Total	194	100.0

speaking Spanish with their spouse. Sixteen percent of respondents reported speaking Spanish with their children, the second most frequent group. Spanish use with other family members and friends was considerably low. In response to questions regarding the reading and writing of Spanish, few professionals reported always reading (2.5%) or writing

Table 4.5 Spanish language use during childhood

	Frequency	*Percent*
1. How often respondent spoke Spanish during childhood at home?		
Always	111	55.5
Often	26	13.0
Sometimes	26	13.0
Rarely	20	10.0
Never	17	8.5
Total	200	100.0
2. With whom did you speak Spanish during childhood?		
Childhood usage with father	46	25.4
Childhood usage with grandparents	39	21.5
Childhood usage with brother	31	17.1
Childhood usage with family friends	31	17.1
Childhood usage with mother	11	6.1
Childhood usage with uncles	8	4.4
Childhood usage with friends	7	3.9
Childhood usage with cousins	5	2.8
Childhood usage with sister	2	1.1
Childhood usage with aunts	1	0.6
Total	181	100.0

(2.0%) Spanish at home. About a fourth (25.5%) reported rarely reading Spanish while 24% reported never reading Spanish at home. About one-third of all respondents (36.0%) reported rarely writing Spanish at home, while another one-third (29.5%) reported never writing Spanish at home.

Spanish language use at work

Table 4.8 indicates that 76% of all surveyed professionals speak Spanish at work at least sometimes while 32% reported speaking Spanish often, and 11% report always speaking Spanish at work. Of those reporting speaking Spanish at work, 65% reported using Spanish to make others feel comfortable. Few professionals reported using Spanish with co-workers for work-related purposes (9.6%), for giving presentations (5.9%), to communicate with clients (5.3%), or to translate oral (1.6%) or written language (1.1%).

Table 4.6 Spanish language instruction

	Frequency	Percent
1. Spanish study in High School		
Yes	119	66.9
No	59	33.1
Total	178	100.0
2. Years studied Spanish in High school		
4	35	29.4
3.5	1	0.8
3	30	25.2
2	40	33.6
1	13	10.9
Total	119	100.0
3. Spanish study in College?		
Yes	95	54.7
No	77	45.3
Total	172	100.0
4. Semesters studied Spanish in College		
9+	4	4.2
5–8	16	16.8
1–4	75	78.9
Total	95	100.0
5. Attended in-service training in Spanish		
Yes	31	15.7
No	167	84.3
Total	198	100.0
6. Understand Spanish		
Like a native	108	54.0
Fairly well	78	39.0
Very little	14	7.0
Total	200	100.0
7. Speak Spanish		
Like a native	87	43.5
Fairly well	87	43.5
Very little	25	12.5
Not at all	1	0.5
Total	200	100.0

Table 4.7 Current Spanish language use at home

	Frequency	*Percent*
1. Current use of Spanish at home		
Always	27	13.6
Often	43	21.6
Sometimes	45	22.6
Rarely	51	25.6
Never	33	16.6
Total	199	100.0
2. With whom do you currently speak Spanish?		
Current use with spouse	88	55.0
Current use with children	25	15.6
Current use with house guests	13	8.1
Current use with father	10	6.3
Current use with mother	8	5.0
Current use with friends	5	3.1
Current use with sister	3	1.9
Current use with grandchildren	3	1.9
Current use with brother	2	1.3
Current use with family friends	2	1.3
Current use with grandparents	1	0.6
Total	160	100.0
3. Read Spanish at home		
Always	5	2.5
Often	32	16.0
Sometimes	65	32.5
Rarely	51	25.5
Never	47	23.5
Total	200	100.0
4. Write Spanish at home		
Always	4	2.0
Often	23	11.5
Sometimes	42	21.0
Rarely	72	36.0
Never	59	29.5
Total	200	100.0

Table 4.8 Spanish language use at work

	Frequency	Percent
1. Speak Spanish at work		
Always	21	10.5
Often	63	31.5
Sometimes	68	34.0
Rarely	36	18.0
Never	12	6.0
Total	200	100.0
2. With whom do you speak Spanish at work?		
Use Spanish at work to make others feel comfortable	122	64.9
Use Spanish at work with coworkers/support staff for work-related purposes	18	9.6
Use Spanish at work by using presentational language, e.g. giving planned or unplanned presentations in front of more than one individual	11	5.9
Use Spanish at work with clients, customers, patients, students, etc.	10	5.3
Do not use Spanish at work owing to lack of fluency	9	4.8
Do not use Spanish at work, although fluent, because not necessary for job functions	7	3.7
Use Spanish at work to practice with whomever	4	2.1
Use Spanish at work to translate orally	3	1.6
Use Spanish at work to write professionally	2	1.1
Use Spanish at work to translate written language	2	1.1
Total	188	100.0

Table 4.9 indicates that 43% of all respondents speak Spanish with monolingual Spanish clients often or always, whereas 19% report never doing so. Similarly, 40% reported speaking Spanish with bilingual clients often or always, while 8% reported never doing so. Forty percent reported never speaking Spanish with monolingual Spanish-speaking colleagues while 10% report always doing so. In contrast to Spanish use with monolingual Spanish-speaking colleagues, only 13% reported never speaking Spanish with bilingual colleagues while 35% reported doing so at least sometimes. Finally, almost 50% reported needing to use Spanish every day, while another 29% reported needing to do so once or twice a week. Only 5% reported needing to use Spanish once or twice a year.

Table 4.9 Frequency of Spanish language use at work

	Frequency	*Percent*
1. Speaks Spanish with monolingual Spanish clients, patients, students, or constituents at work		
Always	32	17.0
Often	48	25.5
Sometimes	51	27.1
Rarely	22	11.7
Never	35	18.6
Total	188	100.0
2. Speaks Spanish with bilingual clients, patients, students, or constituents at work		
Always	19	10.2
Often	55	29.4
Sometimes	67	35.8
Rarely	31	16.6
Never	15	8.0
Total	187	100.0
3. Speaks Spanish with monolingual Spanish employees, support staff, or colleagues		
Always	18	9.6
Often	33	17.6
Sometimes	35	18.6
Rarely	26	13.8
Never	76	40.4
Total	188	100.0
4. Speaks Spanish with bilingual employees, support staff, or colleagues		
Always	8	4.3
Often	57	30.3
Sometimes	75	39.9
Rarely	24	12.8
Never	24	12.8
Total	188	100.0

(Continued)

Table 4.9 (*Continued*)

	Frequency	*Percent*
5. How frequently respondent needs to use Spanish at work		
Every day	92	49.2
Once or twice a week	55	29.4
Once or twice a month	30	16.0
Once or twice a year	10	5.3
Total	187	100.0

Table 4.10 reveals that Latino professionals rarely if ever read professional material in Spanish. Twenty-eight percent reported rarely reading professional material in Spanish while another 30% never did so. Only 3% reported always reading professional material in Spanish. Similarly, 33% reported never writing professional material in Spanish while another 28% sometimes did so. Only 1% reported always writing professional material in Spanish.

Table 4.10 Spanish language professional material reading and writing

	Frequency	*Percent*
1. Reads professional material in Spanish		
Always	6	3.2
Often	21	11.2
Sometimes	53	28.2
Rarely	52	27.7
Never	56	29.8
Total	188	100.0
2. Writes professional material in Spanish		
Always	2	1.1
Often	27	14.4
Sometimes	44	23.5
Rarely	53	28.3
Never	61	32.6
Total	187	100.0

Table 4.11 Workplace language use attitudes

	Frequency	*Percent*
1. Interest in improving Spanish		
Yes	163	81.5
No	37	18.5
Total	200	100.0
2. Speaking Spanish at work makes respondent feel more effective professionally		
Always	107	57.2
Often	41	21.9
Sometimes	24	12.8
Rarely	10	5.3
Never	5	2.7
Total	187	100.0
3. Speaking Spanish would improve professional effectiveness		
Sometimes	3	27.3
Rarely	4	36.4
Never	4	36.4
Total	11	100.0

Interest in improving Spanish

An overwhelming majority of professionals interviewed reported having an interest in improving their Spanish. Table 4.11 indicates that 82% wanted to improve their Spanish while 57% feel that speaking Spanish at work made them feel more effective professionally. No respondent, however, felt that speaking Spanish would improve their professional effectiveness while 27% reported sometimes. Over two-thirds (72.8%) feel that speaking Spanish would only rarely or never improve professional effectiveness.

Attitudes toward different varieties of Spanish

Table 4.12 indicates that most Latino professionals surveyed feel that the best Spanish is spoken in Mexico (33.7%). Seventeen percent felt that no place has a best spoken Spanish while a similar percentage (16.1%) did not identify a particular place or country where the best Spanish is spoken.

Table 4.12 Where is the best Spanish spoken/written?

	Frequency	*Percent*
1. Where is the best Spanish Spoken?		
Mexico	65	33.7
No best – place best spoken	33	17.1
No country listed/No answer – place best spoken	31	16.1
Spain	28	14.5
Many countries listed	15	7.8
Columbia	11	5.7
Argentina	3	1.6
Peru	2	1.0
Puerto Rico	2	1.0
Venezuela	1	0.5
Chile	1	0.5
Costa Rica	1	0.5
Total	193	100.0
2. Where is the best Spanish written?		
No country listed/No answer – place best written	52	26.7
Mexico	43	22.1
Spain	41	21.0
No best – place best written	28	14.4
Many countries listed – place best written	17	8.7
Columbia	5	2.6
Argentina	3	1.5
Chile	3	1.5
Venezuela	1	0.5
Puerto Rico	1	0.5
Costa Rica	1	0.5
Total	195	100.0

Fifteen percent thought that best Spanish is spoken in Spain. On the other hand most professionals (26.7%) did not list a place or country where the best Spanish is written while 22% listed Mexico as the place where the best Spanish is written followed by Spain (21%).

Attitudes toward the teaching of heritage language courses

Table 4.13 indicates that more than 81% of Latino professionals felt that heritage language courses should be offered while 16% felt that no such classes should be offered. Of those who thought such classes should be offered, 31% thought that Mexican Spanish should be taught. Twenty percent thought that U.S. Spanish spoken by minority groups should be taught while a similar proportion (17.8%) felt that general, basic, core grammar Spanish should be taught. Eighty percent thought that these varieties should be taught to all Latinos, while 16% thought that it should be taught to everyone interested, including Latinos and non-Latinos. Only 3% felt that they should be taught to Mexican Americans only. An overwhelming majority (93.5%) felt that that the literature of their stated Spanish variety should be taught to heritage speakers, and a similar majority thought that it should be taught to all Latinos (86%).

Recommendations on the teaching of heritage languages

When asked about their recommendations for the teaching of heritage language courses, Latino professionals had a wide range of suggestions. Table 4.14 summarizes the most often mentioned recommendations. The most frequent suggestion, reported by one-fourth (23.7%) of all respondents, was that the teaching of heritage language should also include making cultural/historical connections. Thirteen percent of respondents mentioned the use of real-life activities to increase student interest. Twelve percent felt that other topics such as legal, medical, or business terms should be taught in Spanish. Finally, among the most often cited recommendations, 11% thought that there needs to be concrete outcomes and placement levels for heritage classes.

To summarize, the descriptive tables above illustrate an alarming trend regarding heritage language maintenance among Latino professionals in California; they are losing their heritage language. One-third of our sample was foreign-born, half of whom came to the United States before the age of 10. Another third of all respondents are US-born children of immigrants whose parents are native speakers of Spanish. Nevertheless, the use of Spanish language among these professionals steadily declines over time. During childhood, 55% of respondents reported always speaking Spanish, mostly with fathers and grandparents. When asked about their current use of Spanish at home, only 14% reported always speaking it, mostly with their spouse or children. Also, whereas 54% reported understanding Spanish like a native, a lower percentage (44%) reported speaking it like a native. Only 19% reported reading Spanish always or often and 14% reported writing it at home either always or often.

Table 4.13 Should heritage courses be taught?

	Frequency	Percent
1. Should special Spanish classes specifically designed for heritage speakers be offered?		
Yes	161	81.3
Maybe	6	3.0
No	31	15.7
Total	198	100.0
2. What variety should be taught?		
Mexican Spanish	48	30.6
US Spanish spoken by minority groups	31	19.7
General, basic, core grammar Spanish	28	17.8
More than one variety	11	7.0
Central American/Latin American Spanish	10	6.4
Castilian/Peninsular Spanish	8	5.1
Technical/Specialized register related to occupations	6	3.8
Combination of many types without limiting students to one	6	3.8
Whatever Spanish teacher is capable	4	2.5
Colloquialisms, dichos, regionalism	2	1.3
Teacher should be sensitive to student needs and not privilege a group	2	1.3
Slang/Calo/Pochismo/Ranchero	1	0.6
Total	157	100.0
3. To whom should these varieties be taught?		
Teach it to all Latinos	122	80.3
Teach it to everyone interested: Latinos and non-Latinos	25	16.4
Teach it to Mexican Americans only	5	3.3
Total	152	100.0
4. Should literature in stated variety be taught to heritage speakers?		
Yes	144	93.5
No	10	6.5
Total	154	100.0

(*Continued*)

Table 4.13 (*Continued*)

	Frequency	Percent
5. To whom should these varieties of literature be taught?		
Teach the literature to all Latinos	123	86.0
Teach the literature to everyone interested: Latinos and non-Latinos	19	13.3
Teach the literature to Mexican Americans only	1	0.7
Total	143	100.0

Although we do not know all the reasons for the decline in enrollment in Spanish language instruction, the trend is very clear – lower enrollments over time. Whereas 67% of respondents studied Spanish in High School, 55% studied Spanish in college and only 16% have received postcollege in-service training in Spanish. Also, whereas 29% studied 4 years of Spanish in high school, only 21% percent studied the equivalent number of years in college.

At work 11% reported speaking Spanish always but mostly to make others feel comfortable. About half of the respondents reported needing to use Spanish at work every day but the frequency of their Spanish use appears to be very low. Whereas Spanish use with monolingual clients always is 17%, this percentage decreases to 10% with bilingual clients. Similarly, Spanish use with monolingual colleagues always is 10% and decreases to 4% with bilingual colleagues. Only 3% of professionals reported always reading professional material in Spanish and 1% reported always writing professional material in Spanish. Although respondents reported a decline in Spanish use at home and at work, the overwhelming majority wanted to improve their Spanish. Many believed that Spanish classes specially designed for heritage speakers should be offered to all those interested. Among the most popular recommendations for such programs was the use of cultural and historical connections to the language. Thus, although language shift seems to be well under way, Latino professionals in California maintained very positive attitudes toward Spanish and its maintenance among heritage speakers. To further study this dynamic using more advanced statistical techniques, we conducted a series of cross tabulation and regression analyses to predict various language use patterns and attitudes.

Spanish Use by Nativity Levels

Use with monolingual Spanish-speaking clients at work

Given that all of our respondents have acquired Spanish as a first language, their use of the language at work still remains unknown. Is it a

Table 4.14 Recommendations

	Frequency	Percent
1. Make cultural/historical connections; show relevance and significance of language to students in heritage classes	45	23.7
2. Use real-life activities, make it interesting and valuable for students' heritage classes	25	13.2
3. Teach other subjects and/or terms in Spanish: legal/medical/business for heritage classes	22	11.6
4. Need to have concrete outcomes/placement levels for heritage classes	21	11.1
5. Do not teach rules of grammar; they are impractical for heritage classes	14	7.4
6. Get qualified teachers who know the language for heritage classes	11	5.8
7. Spanish focus needs to start at an earlier age, before high school	11	5.8
8. Focus on practical conversation for local needs in heritage classes	8	4.2
9. Teach Spanish as a profitable skill; translating is a skill that travels in heritage classes	6	3.2
10. Proper grammar instruction is important in heritage classes	5	2.6
11. Do not teach Spanish; it is English that needs to be emphasized	4	2.1
12. Teach Spanish of diplomacy, the Spanish needed for success in heritage classes	4	2.1
13. Literature is important to include in heritage classes	3	1.6
14. Focus on good/correct writing in heritage classes	3	1.6
15. Focus on global conversation for nonlocal/international needs in heritage classes	2	1.1
16. Teach practical vocabulary to meet everyday/work needs in heritage classes	2	1.1
17. Teach vocabulary to conduct international/business work conversation in heritage classes	2	1.1
18. Teach them to think analytically in Spanish, challenge them in heritage classes	2	1.1
Total	190	100.0

Table 4.15 Spanish speaking at work with monolingual clients by nativity

Nativity	N	Mean
Native of native US born	52	1.56
Native of foreign born	75	2.20
Foreign of foreign born	60	2.50

0 = never; 1 = rarely; 2 = sometimes; 3 = often; 4 = always.

professional asset or hindrance and is it greatly used or infrequently? On the whole, Table 4.15 indicates that such use with monolingual Spanish speaking clients averages out to sometimes (a mean of 2.1 on a 5-point "never" to "always" scale), but varies significantly both by nativity and occupation. The nativity variation noted is in accord with that repeatedly reported in four decades of research on Latinos (third generation [i.e. native of native US born] respondents doing so significantly least often and first generation [i.e. foreign of foreign born] respondents doing so most often, with native US of foreign-born second generation) falling closer to the first than to the third.

Far less expected are the significant occupational differences noted in Table 4.16. Doctors, lawyers, and school teachers speak Spanish with monolingual clients *most often* while business people, college professors (both CSU and UC), and judges do so *least frequently*. Politicians (holding elected offices) are in the middle of this range. The differences noted are obviously due both to the nature of the work involved (doctors, lawyers, and school teachers are most urgently in need of immediate effective communication with their clienteles) as well as with the demographic differences

Table 4.16 Spanish speaking at work with monolingual clients by occupation

Occupation	N	Mean
CSU professor	22	1.41
Business	22	1.55
UC professor	24	1.63
Judge	24	1.83
Politician	22	2.32
Lawyer	25	2.36
Teacher	24	2.50
Doctor	25	3.12

0 = never; 1 = rarely; 2 = sometimes; 3 = often; 4 = always.

(e.g. the respective proportions of "native of native" among them) that characterize the professional subsamples studied. Why Hispanic business people, judges, and college professors are so much less likely than others to accommodate to Spanish monolinguals is less obvious and would merit follow-up to see if it can be replicated. The Nativity × Occupation interaction (i.e. do some nativity groups within some occupational groups claim to perform differently with respect to frequency of speaking in Spanish to monolingual clients) is not statistically significant.

Use of Spanish with bilingual work-related clients

On the whole, the use of Spanish with bilingual clients at work is slightly less than we have found it to be with monolingual interlocutors in that setting, although it is probably not significant. Surprisingly, such usage among certain categories of native of native US-born respondents is actually higher with bilinguals than with monolinguals. This increase is particularly noticeable in connection with native of native US-born doctors, business people, and both categories of professors. There seems to be a special dynamic here, in selected occupational groups, between nativity and occupational language use. Particularly those occupations that were below average for use of Spanish at work with monolingual clients (the native of native US-born contingents) now report increased use of Spanish at work with bilingual clients, sometimes to levels even above those claimed by respondents of foreign or mixed nativity. This special dynamic results in not only the significant nativity group and occupational group differences that we reported earlier, but also in a significant interaction between nativity and occupation as shown by Table 4.17.

This means that whereas nativity and occupation regularly make a difference in the extent to which Spanish is used with bilingual clients at work (roughly along the lines that we have discussed earlier for monolingual clients) there are certain occupations and certain nativity groups in which it makes a particular difference (even more so than among others). As a result, insofar as using Spanish with bilingual clients at work is

Table 4.17 Spanish speaking at work with bilingual clients by profession and nativity

Source	F	P
Occupation	4.54	0.00
Nativity	4.32	0.02
Occupation × Nativity	1.87	0.03

R squared = 0.30 (adjusted R squared = 0.20).

Table 4.18 Spanish speaking at work with bilingual clients by occupation

Occupation	N	Mean
Judge	24	1.29
Business	21	1.81
Lawyer	25	2.20
CSU professor	22	2.23
Politician	22	2.23
Teacher	24	2.33
UC professor	24	2.46
Doctor	25	2.76

0 = never; 1 = rarely; 2 = sometimes; 3 = often; 4 = always.

concerned, judges and business people alone now occupy the low end of the spectrum and all the other occupational groups are clustered together at the high end, with doctors at the very top (see Table 4.18). Overall, the nativity groups line up as before (first generation most, third generation least) and gender, once again, makes little if any difference.

Use of Spanish with monolingual colleagues, employees, and support staff

If the mean self-reported use of Spanish with clients, whether monolingual or bilingual, was roughly in the score-range of sometimes (i.e. 2.0+), this self-reported usage now drops to rarely (i.e. 1.0+) when we turn to monolingual colleagues as shown in Table 4.19. This represents a substantial decline. There still remains a significant nativity of respondent effect in this connection, the generations assuming the usual order that we have encountered before, with foreign of foreign respondents still using Spanish (as noted before) significantly more often than the others do. This is particularly the case when interacting with monolingual employees for female respondents (and therefore, for the first time, there is almost a significant interaction between sex of respondent and generation of respondent [$p = 0.09$]). For both sexes the foreign of foreign respondents are particularly prone to using more Spanish with monolingual colleagues. Indeed, they do so at the same relative frequency as they did with monolingual clients, without any falling off whatsoever as is more generally the case. Of course, this raises the possibility of the existence of particular subsets of monolingual colleagues who are most likely to involve female (but not only female) foreign-born respondents. Perhaps such interlocutors (e.g. foreign-born maids and foreign-born gardeners) disproportionately affect

Table 4.19 Spanish speaking at work with monolingual colleagues by sex and nativity

Sex	Nativity	N	Mean
Male	Foreign of foreign born	47	1.74
	Native of foreign born	49	1.43
	Native of native US born	39	1.13
	Total	135	1.45
Female	Foreign of foreign born	13	2.46
	Native of foreign born	26	0.96
	Native of native US born	13	0.92
	Total	52	1.33
Total	Foreign of foreign born	60	1.90
	Native of foreign born	75	1.27
	Native of native US born	52	1.08
	Total	187	1.42

0 = never; 1 = rarely; 2 = sometimes; 3 = often; 4 = always.

self-reported use of Spanish with monolingual colleagues among foreign-born professionals in general and among foreign-born female respondents in particular.

As before, Table 4.20 reveals a significant difference between occupational groups in connection with use of Spanish with monolingual colleagues. Judges and lawyers fall at the low usage end of the distribution

Table 4.20 Spanish speaking at work with monolingual colleagues by occupation

Occupation	N	Mean
Judge	24	0.75
Lawyer	25	0.88
Teacher	24	1.38
Politician	22	1.45
Doctor	25	1.52
CSU professor	22	1.55
UC professor	24	1.63
Business	22	2.32

0 = never; 1 = rarely; 2 = sometimes; 3 = often; 4 = always.

(even below rarely), while business people now wind up at the high end (mid-sometimes). Later on, we will review our findings as to changing occupational patterns in average use of Spanish as work interlocutors change (from monolingual to bilingual). At this point it may suffice to point out that the alignment across nativity group has remained rather constant (being significantly high for foreign of foreign respondents and low for and native of native). Furthermore, although gender of respondent has generally not been a significant determinant of frequency of Spanish use at work, nor has the monolinguality/bilinguality of the interlocutor, the role of occupational grouping has tended to be a more variable one, depending, in part, on nativity of respondent and on bilinguality of interlocutor.

Use of Spanish at work with bilingual colleagues

Once again, the level of reported use of Spanish is somewhat lower for bilingual colleagues than we saw it to be for monolingual ones. Once again the nativity groups differ significantly (and in the expected direction) from one another, but this time the occupational groups do not differ from each other. Nor is there a significant interaction between nativity and occupation. Nor do the gender groups differ significantly from one another, although, once again, female respondents of foreign nativity score highest of all of our respondents when interacting with bilingual colleagues,. (Nevertheless, the overall interaction between gender and nativity is not significant.) Thus, all in all, with the reported Spanish use level with bilingual colleagues down pretty much across the board, the overall decreased variance in claimed usage of Spanish leaves the nativity of our respondents as the only significant predictor of use of Spanish with bilingual colleagues.

Important as it is to realize that our respondents' use of spoken Spanish at work usually varies by profession and by interlocutor's nativity, it is also instructive to note that whenever such differences do appear, it is the judges who most frequently wind up among those with the lowest usage while doctors, lawyers, and teachers most frequently are among those with the highest (see Table 4.21).

Reading Spanish for professional purposes

Thus far we have concentrated on spoken Spanish at work, considering two types (monolingual and bilingual) of interlocutors and two types of work relationships, clients and colleagues. We now switch our attention to claimed professional reading in Spanish. As we might expect from the fact that most people read less frequently than they speak, Table 4.22 reveals that reading in Spanish is less frequently claimed than speaking in Spanish. Whereas the relative frequency of speaking averages out to a sometimes, reading, on the other hand, averages out to a high-rarely. Nevertheless,

Table 4.21 Review of occupational differences in speaking Spanish at work across interlocutor monolinguality/bilinguality categories

	Monolingual clients	*Bilingual clients*	*Monolingual colleagues*	*Bilingual colleagues*
High	Doctors	Doctors	Business	None
	Lawyers	Lawyers		
	Teachers	Teachers		
		All others not listed below		
Low	Business	Judges	Judges	None
	Judges	Business	Lawyers	
	UC/CSU professors			

there is still sufficient variance in the reading claims for several significant differences to obtain, namely, between the occupational groups and between the nativity groups, as well as a significant Occupation × Nativity interaction. Considering first the differences between occupational groups, lawyers and teachers now score lowest (essentially never) while UC and CSU professors score highest (though only with a high rarely). Keeping in mind that the professors do not include any teachers of secondary-school Spanish in their ranks, their somewhat high scores for professional reading might be expected as a reflection of the professional roles and interests. Nevertheless, one should keep in mind that, all in all, even their average claim for professional reading in Spanish is actually only in the rarely

Table 4.22 Reading of professional material in Spanish by occupation

Occupation	N	*Mean*
Lawyer	25	0.80
Teacher	24	0.88
Doctor	25	1.12
Judge	24	1.17
Business	22	1.36
Politician	22	1.45
UC professor	24	1.79
CSU professor	22	1.95

0 = never; 1 = rarely; 2 = sometimes; 3 = often; 4 = always.

Table 4.23 Reading of professional material in Spanish by occupation and nativity

Occupation	Nativity	Mean
Business	Foreign of foreign born	2.25
	Native of foreign born	0.33
	Native of native US born	0.33
CSU professor	Foreign of foreign born	2.17
	Native of foreign born	1.78
	Native of native US born	2.00
UC professor	Foreign of foreign born	1.44
	Native of foreign born	2.17
	Native of native US born	1.89
Doctor	Foreign of foreign born	1.33
	Native of foreign born	1.00
	Native of native US born	0.75
Judge	Foreign of foreign born	1.67
	Native of foreign born	0.92
	Native of native US born	1.38
Lawyer	Foreign of foreign born	0.67
	Native of foreign born	1.09
	Native of native US born	0.50
Politician	Foreign of foreign born	1.50
	Native of foreign born	1.77
	Native of native US born	0.60
Teacher	Foreign of foreign born	0.88
	Native of foreign born	1.18
	Native of native US born	0.20

0 = never; 1 = rarely; 2 = sometimes; 3 = often; 4 = always.

range. The professional reading in Spanish claimed by lawyers and teachers, at the low end of the occupational grouping, averages out in the high never category.

As for the nativity groups, they once more line up overall in the expected direction. However, there are departures from this expectation (i.e. that foreign of foreign born should claim to read most and native of native US born should claim to read least). Table 4.23 shows that among CSU professors the native of native US-born respondents read Spanish much more than would be expected. This is also the case among UC professors, but it also obtains for their native of foreign-born faculty members as well. Indeed, the native of foreign-born respondents score higher than expected for several other occupational groups as well (for UC professors, lawyers, politicians, and teachers), just as do the native of native US-born respondents for judges. There is no apparent system to these departures, which bring about a significant Occupation × Nativity interaction, so that all we can conclude for the moment is that although the nativity groups do align themselves overall as expected with respect to professional reading, there are several instances in which the native of foreign-born and the native of native US-born respondents read more Spanish than would otherwise be expected on the basis of nativity alone. Certain professions do seem to be associated with more Spanish reading among native-born respondents than do others. What is cause here and what is effect we cannot determine (neither here nor anywhere else in our data).

Although gender does not in and of itself, or in interaction with occupation or nativity, show a significant relationship to professional reading, women on the whole read somewhat more than do men, doing so in the mid-rarely range. Male occupational reading in Spanish is abysmally low, bordering on none for native of native US-born respondents. This otherwise quite sad finding must be viewed in the more general context of lower literacy practices among monolingual Anglo professionals than is the norm assumed to be operative among their Western European counterparts (Fishman *et al.*, 1985).

Writing Spanish among California Hispanic professionals

If reading Spanish is far less common than speaking Spanish among Hispanic professionals in California, then writing Spanish is the least common of all. Table 4.24 reveals that the overall average for writing Spanish with reference to their work falls in the low-rarely range. Nevertheless, there is still significant variation among the occupational groups, among the nativity groups and, finally, a significant Occupation × Nativity interaction as well. Judges score significantly lower on writing Spanish than do all other occupational groups (followed closely by politicians), while UC professors score significantly higher (followed closely by CSU professors). Writing Spanish seems to be largely an academic pursuit among the professionals we surveyed.

Furthermore, in connection with writing professional material in Spanish, the nativity groups on the one hand and the gender groups on the other line up, all in all, in the progression we have come to expect from our previous consideration of reading in Spanish. Even more so than before, Table 4.25 shows that the mean for native of native US-born respondents

Table 4.24 Writing of professional material in Spanish by occupation

Occupation	N	Mean
Judge	24	0.63
Politician	22	0.82
Business	22	1.14
Lawyer	24	1.38
Doctor	25	1.40
Teacher	24	1.42
CSU professor	22	1.50
UC professor	24	1.54

0 = never; 1 = rarely; 2 = sometimes; 3 = often; 4 = always.

now falls to the high never range, while the mean for foreign of foreign-born respondents only ascends to the mid-rarely range.

It should also be pointed out that whereas gender is once more not a main effect in connection with writing professional material in Spanish, it is almost one ($p = 0.09$), indicative of a slight female superiority vis-à-vis writing Spanish in the work context that they do not claim with respect to the lion's share of our analyses either of speaking or of reading in that context. However, the fact that our female sample is so small (only 51, i.e. only 40% as large as our male sample of 135) militates strongly against any of the findings dealing with gender actually reaching the required level of significance ($p = 0.05$) employed elsewhere throughout this chapter. Nevertheless, in each generation (nativity grouping) women claim more professional writing in Spanish than do men (Table 4.26).

Before turning to more attitudinal data pertaining to (Chicano) Spanish, it might merit mentioning the implications of younger generations, and particularly women and those in academic professions, excelling in literacy claims. Throughout the world this has been observed as a sign of the rise of an indigenous intelligentsia. The presence of such an intelligentsia might bespeak a potential for ethnolinguistic mobilization and politicization that

Table 4.25 Writing of professional material in Spanish by nativity

Nativity	N	Mean
Native of native US born	52	0.83
Native of foreign born	74	1.20
Foreign of foreign born	60	1.63

0 = never; 1 = rarely; 2 = sometimes; 3 = often; 4 = always.

Table 4.26 Writing of professional material in Spanish by sex and nativity

Sex	Nativity	N	Mean
Male	Foreign of foreign born	47	1.55
	Native of foreign born	49	1.06
	Native of native US born	39	0.79
	Total	135	1.16
Female	Foreign of foreign born	13	1.92
	Native of foreign born	25	1.48
	Native of native US born	13	0.92
	Total	51	1.45
Total	Foreign of foreign born	60	1.63
	Native of foreign born	74	1.20
	Native of native US born	52	0.83
	Total	186	1.24

has hitherto been noticeably lacking among Hispanics in the United States, including the Southwest (Fishman, 1972). On the other hand, it could be an instance of sound desirability response in the context of nostalgia.

Claiming Spanish to be needed at work

All of our data thus far, derived as it is from self-report, involves an unmeasured modicum of social desirability error variance. When we ask subjects to report on the extent to which they need Spanish at work, the influence of level of social desirability on individual responses is likely to rise. One can recognize the "need" for Spanish at work without being able to speak, read, or write it there at all. Similarly, mastery of the aforementioned basic skills in the workplace does not guarantee in any way a favorable view toward using them there. So far our analyses reveal that it is not often used in the workplace. Our query as to the frequency of needing Spanish at work yielded both an occupational and a nativity main effect, that is, both of these population characteristics independently influenced the responses obtained as to the frequency of need reported.

As for the occupational arena, doctors and also teachers report a significantly more frequent need for Spanish at work, at a mid to high sometimes level, and politicians (and runner-up: CSU professors) report the least need of this kind (at a high rarely level). The nativity order of frequency of needing Spanish at work places native of native US-born respondents below (high rarely) either of the other nativity groups (mid-sometimes). Gender per se (or even in interaction with nativity) seems to be of little, if any, importance insofar as claims to need Spanish at work are concerned.

Of course frequency of need is a very diffuse dimension to rate. When our respondents were asked more concretely "the rate at which Spanish is an aid to professional effectiveness," not only did occupation and nativity yield significant differences, but the interaction between occupation and nativity was also significant. Once more, doctors report the significantly highest relative frequency of finding Spanish to be an aid at work (with teachers only a shade away) and CSU professors report the significantly lowest rate of finding Spanish to be an aid at work (with business folk immediately ahead of them). These findings point to a rough general agreement between frequency of need at work and frequency of finding Spanish to be an aid at work. In addition, the nativity groups line up vis-à-vis finding Spanish to be an aid at work just as they did for frequency of use at work.

An even more massively attitudinal variable deals with whether respondents have an "interest in improving their Spanish" (now, in their adult years, and with work and possibly family responsibilities). Once again we discover from Table 4.27 a significant occupation effect (teachers and judges report a significantly high interest in improving their Spanish and those in business and doctors a significantly low interest along these lines) and a significant nativity effect from Table 4.28, revealing the inverse order to that which obtained for rate of use, i.e. foreign of foreign showing a significantly lower interest in improving their Spanish (63%) than do both Native-born groups (88% and 92%). However, this inverse order (which may primarily reflect degree of mastery) may also capture some aspects of the younger (US-born) generations' conviction that better Spanish is advantageous at

Table 4.27 Interest in improving Spanish by occupation

Occupation	N	Mean
Business	25	0.60
Doctor	25	0.64
Politician	25	0.80
CSU professor	25	0.84
UC professor	25	0.84
Lawyer	25	0.88
Judge	25	0.96
Teacher	25	0.96

0 = no; 1 = yes.

Table 4.28 Interest in improving Spanish by nativity

Nativity	N	Mean
Foreign of foreign born	62	0.63
Native of foreign born	77	0.88
Native of native US born	60	0.92

$0 = $ no; $1 = $ yes.

work. These two overtly attitudinal replies (interest in improving and frequency of need) agree more with each other than either of them does with declared use. Over all, interest in improving one's Spanish is quite high among most of our respondents but, once more, gender per se appears to play no substantive role, whether separately or in interaction with occupation or nativity. We will look at this topic again, by means of a different analytic method, in a later section.

Table 4.29 below shows us the extent to which all of the use variables are related to one another and to the perception that Spanish is an aid at work. The latter is quite unrelated to the former. This is not because interest in improving one's Spanish is an isolate that has no relationship to other matters. It correlates 0.27 with self-identification as a Chicano, –0.40 with childhood use with aunts, –0.46 with childhood use with cousins (as well as negative use with all members of all of one's childhood family and friends) and, finally, –0.42 with foreign birth. Seemingly, we are dealing here with an aspect of the reethnification and relinguification of Chicanos who have experienced a childhood marked by anglification and estrangement from family and friends insofar as the latter were Spanish speakers. Our question as to interest in improving their Spanish "hit them where it hurts" and this undeniably colors their views of Spanish for Native Speakers (SNS) programs.

Table 4.29 Matrix of intercorrelations between claimed use/need of Spanish at work and interest in improving Spanish

	I	II	III	IV	V
I. Speaks at work with monolingual clients	–	.13	0.32**	0.48**	–0.02
II. Use Spanish in work related reading		–	0.52**	0.20**	–0.01
III. Use Spanish in work related writing			–	0.32**	0.02
IV. Spanish is an aid at work				–	0.13
V. Interest in improving own Spanish					–

$**p < 0.05$ for two-tailed test.

Where is the best Spanish spoken?

Attitudes toward "Mexicanness in Speech"

Since there is no consensual, nonpartisan, and nonpejorative name for Mexican-American Spanish, we sought to determine our respondents' attitudes toward the variety most probably and most generally used in their home and neighborhood settings, via a post hoc weighing of their responses. We did this by imposing our own scale of closeness to Mexican Spanish on the responses of the respondents. We weighed responses that referred to varieties of local Spanish, Southwest Spanish, Chicano Spanish or Mexican Spanish as highest (or closeness to Mexican Spanish), and those that referred to Peninsular Spanish as lowest (or furthest from Mexican Spanish). Claims that favored any other New World variety of Spanish, or that claimed that "all varieties are equal and there is no best," were awarded intermediate scores respectively, but lower than that for Mexican Spanish and higher than that for Peninsular Spanish. This question was scored in two ways, one less focused on a place response than on the degree of certainty with the response given. The latter scoring resulted in more score variance (and, therefore, in more significant between-group differences) than did the former and, therefore, we will attend only to that scoring here (Mexicanness of response [re where/what is the "best Spanish" spoken]).

As it has so many times before, nativity yielded (nearly) significant differences ($p = 0.06$). Table 4.30 shows that the responses of the native-born

Table 4.30 Location indicated for where the best Spanish is spoken by sex and nativity

Sex	Nativity	N	Mean
Male	Foreign of foreign born	49	2.59
	Native of foreign born	50	3.18
	Native of native US born	44	2.64
	Total	143	2.81
Female	Foreign of foreign born	13	2.54
	Native of foreign born	26	3.62
	Native of native US born	16	2.88
	Total	55	3.15
Total	Foreign of foreign born	62	2.58
	Native of foreign born	76	3.33
	Native of native US born	60	2.70
	Total	198	2.90

0 = Spain; 1 = refuses to answer question; 2 = any other country *not* Mexico mentioned; 3 = some general statement about any country; 4 = speaks about literacy, educated variety, New World variety; 5 = Mexico.

Table 4.31 Location indicated for where the best Spanish is spoken by occupation and nativity

Occupation	Nativity	Mean
Business	Foreign of foreign born	2.71
	Native of foreign born	2.33
	Native of native US born	3.86
CSU professor	Foreign of foreign born	3.17
	Native of foreign born	3.22
	Native of native US born	2.60
UC professor	Foreign of foreign born	1.78
	Native of foreign born	4.00
	Native of native US born	2.90
Doctor	Foreign of foreign born	2.00
	Native of foreign born	1.44
	Native of native US born	4.00
Judge	Foreign of foreign born	2.67
	Native of foreign born	3.64
	Native of native US born	2.75
Lawyer	Foreign of foreign born	3.33
	Native of foreign born	3.00
	Native of native US born	2.75
Politician	Foreign of foreign born	4.25
	Native of foreign born	4.39
	Native of native US born	0.71
Teacher	Foreign of foreign born	2.25
	Native of foreign born	3.55
	Native of native US born	2.50

0 = Spain; 1 = refuses to answer question; 2 = any other country *not* Mexico mentioned; 3 = some general statement about any country; 4 = speaks about literacy, educated variety, New World variety; 5 = Mexico.

generations yielded the highest Mexicanness scores, with the native of foreign-born scoring highest of all. There is also a significant nativity by occupation interaction with respect to the "where best Spanish is spoken" continuum as demonstrated by Table 4.31. In every occupational group one or another of the US-born generations (usually the native of foreign [or mixed] generation) scores highest vis-à-vis the Mexicanness of their choice of where the best Spanish is spoken. This is a noteworthy difference in nativity line-up with respect to the one we observed initially in connection with active Spanish language use, where the native-born generations continually scored lowest.

Mexicanness of response pertaining to where Spanish is best written

When it comes to written Spanish the overall Mexicanness score drops precipitously and the average opinion moves far toward the South American or even the Peninsular norm. Actually, because of the decreased response variance, none of the major demographic groupings that we have repeatedly reviewed in this chapter (gender, nativity, and occupation) are associated with significant between-group differences (see Table 4.32). Occupation comes closest in this respect ($p = 0.08$), vis-à-vis Mexicanness of response, with doctors, lawyers, and judges gravitating furthest in the peninsular direction and UC professors, politicians, and teachers being at the other extreme. All in all, the occupational groups are consistently far less Mexican in their preference for written Spanish than they were with respect to spoken Spanish, although on the whole the difference between them falls just short of significance ($p = 0.08$).

Perhaps most noteworthy, all in all, is that the preference for Mexicanness is highest in connection with Spanish speech (the mode of communication with which all of our subjects have greatest familiarity), whereas it is at its lowest in connection with written Spanish (a mode of communication

Table 4.32 Occupational differences in Mexicanness of where/what Spanish is written best

Occupation	N	Mean
Doctor	25	1.32
Lawyer	25	1.64
Judge	25	1.76
CSU professor	25	2.48
Business	25	2.56
UC professor	25	2.68
Politician	25	2.84
Teacher	25	2.84

0 = Spain; 1 = refuses to answer question; 2 = any other country *not* Mexico mentioned; 3 = some general statement about any country; 4 = speaks about literacy, educated variety, New World variety; 5 = Mexico.

with which our subjects are, on the whole, far less familiar). In connection with speech, Mexicanness is deemed desirable; in connection with writing (and, perhaps, in connection with exposure to the printed word as well), Mexicanness is deemed rather undesirable and norms believed to be associated with the literary centers of the Hispanic world abroad are preferred – in theory even if not much in implementation. These two findings cannot but be crucial for all those who are interested in community support for Spanish heritage language instruction in the United States.

We will return to the question of where in the world Spanish is best spoken and written (in the opinion of our respondents) further on in a methodologically different section below.

Analysis Using Multiple Correlation Method

Findings were arrived at via a multiple correlation method (unforced, stepwise forward selection procedure[henceforth, multiple correlation]).

Spanish at work

Our interest in Hispanic professionals is at least twofold. Having selected them on the basis of their work, we are naturally interested in how Spanish is related to their work. In addition, given their status in Hispanic society, we are interested in the attitudes and opinions regarding Spanish that these actual or potential community leaders express. In conjunction with the first-mentioned area of interest we now take another methodological tack than we have taken thus far. Instead of probing the importance of specific respondent characteristics (nativity, gender, occupation, etc.), we now ask ourselves: "What other information do we have in our total data set that can contribute maximally and yet parsimoniously to a nonredundant explanation of respondent attitudes and use claims with respect to their using Spanish at work? As Table 4.33 reveals, there are 20 responses in all – of the hundreds if not thousands that we collected – that are of any cumulative use in reaching the highest possible degree of parsimonious clarification of this question. In addition, however, a brief aside may be in order to provide a commonsense understanding of this statistical analysis approach to highly multivariate data.

Our analytic question is not only what is the best single correlate with any given dependent variable (in the present case, "Does respondent speak Spanish at work?"), but also whether there are other variables in our data that, when taken together with the best single correlate, will yield an even better multiple correlation with that same dependent variable. Such other variables must have certain characteristics if they are to perform in this fashion, e.g. they must each *correlate more with the dependent variable than they do with each other*. Only under such circumstances will each successive variable account for some previously unexplained part of the variance in

Table 4.33 How often respondent speaks Spanish at work?

Step entered	Predictor	Correlation with dependent variable	R	R^2	Adjusted R^2
1	How frequently respondent needs to use Spanish at work? Scale: 0 = once or twice a year; 1 = once or twice a month; 2 = once or twice a week; 3 = everyday	0.52	0.52	0.27	0.27
2	How well respondent speaks Spanish? Scale: 0 = not at all; 1 = very little; 2 = fairly well; 3 = like a native	0.45	0.61	0.38	0.37
3	Variety of Spanish that should be taught in the heritage classes. Scale: 1 = standard Spanish; 0 = otherwise	−0.17	0.64	0.41	0.40
4	Should special Spanish classes be designed for native speakers of Spanish? Scale: 1 = gives personal response for why classes should or should not be offered; 0 = otherwise	0.11	0.66	0.43	0.42
5	Spanish variety that should be taught in the heritage classes. Scale: 1 = one variety, so as not to confuse students; 0 = otherwise	−0.11	0.67	0.45	0.44
6	Ever participated in an in-service training for your profession in Spanish. Scale: 0 = no; 1 = yes	0.23	0.68	0.47	0.45
7	Knowledge of the term *regional variety*. Scale: 0 = does not know and asks for clarification of the term; 1 = knows what regional variety is and answers without needing to clarify the term	−0.17	0.69	0.48	0.46
8	Respondent identified as doctor. Scale: 1 = doctor; 0 = otherwise	0.25	0.71	0.50	0.48
9	Respondent identified as lawyer. Scale: 1 = lawyer; 0 = otherwise	0.09	0.72	0.52	0.50

(Continued)

Table 4.33 (Continued)

Step entered	Predictor	Correlation with dependent variable	R	R²	Adjusted R²
10	Where is the best Spanish written? Scale: 1 = Mexico; 0 = otherwise	0.20	0.74	0.54	0.52
11	County average family size in 2002	0.16	0.75	0.56	0.53
12	Mother place of birth. Scale: 1 = Midwest; 0 = otherwise	−0.18	0.75	0.57	0.54
13	Father place of birth. Scale: 1 = Northeast; 0 = otherwise	−0.03	0.76	0.58	0.55
14	Recommendation for heritage classes. Scale: 1 = teaching vocabulary for international business settings; 0 = otherwise	0.01	0.77	0.59	0.55
15	General Spanish should be taught in heritage classes. Scale: 1 = yes; 0 = otherwise	−0.08	0.77	0.60	0.56
16	Current Spanish use with relatives? Scale: 1 = yes; 0 = otherwise	0.16	0.78	0.60	0.57
17	US Spanish variety should be taught in heritage classes. Scale: 1 = yes; 0 = otherwise	−0.03	0.78	0.61	0.58
18	Father place of birth. Scale: 1 = Miami, Florida; 0 = otherwise	−0.15	0.79	0.62	0.58
19	Should heritage classes have concrete set of outcomes for students? Scale: 1 = yes, 0 = otherwise	0.01	0.79	0.63	0.59
20	Mean difference of language use at home as a child and as an adult. Scale: 0 = never; 1 = rarely; 2 = sometimes; 3 = often; 4 = always	0.15	0.80	0.64	0.60

Dependent variable: Speaking of Spanish at work. Scale: 0 = never; 1 = rarely; 2 = sometimes; 3 = often; 4 = always.

the dependent variable and the sum of all of these separate partial portions of the dependent variable will (if, indeed, variables exist with the characteristics indicated by the italicized phrase above), therefore, cumulate to more than the original best correlation of any single variable with the dependent variable. This process of bit-by-bit accumulation can be noted in the fourth column (labeled R) of the table, and the last entry in that column indicates the total multiple correlation arrived at. Clearly, by the time the 20th variable enters into the explanation of the dependent variable, the total correlation with that variable (0.80) is definitely higher than the correlation originally obtained from the highest single correlate (0.52) alone.

The first interesting finding is that CLAIMS as to the frequency of speaking Spanish at work positively related to the frequency of the claimed need (Step 1) to speak Spanish at work (see column 3 labeled "Correlation with dependent variable"). It is also positively related to how well the respondent believes he/she speaks Spanish (Step 2). It is negatively related to favoring a focus on standard Peninsular Spanish in SNS classes (Step 3), to giving a personally referenced reason for favoring or rejecting SNS classes (Step 4), to supporting the teaching of more than one Spanish variety in heritage classes (Step 5), to having participated in a Spanish in-service training (Step 6), and not knowing what the term *regional variety* means (Step 7). Being a doctor is also associated with higher levels of Spanish speaking at work (Step 8), as well as being a lawyer (Step 9), indicating that the best written Spanish is the Mexican variety (Step 10), residing in a county with a higher county-average family size (Step 11), and not having a mother born in the Midwest (Step 12) nor a father born in the Northeast (Step 13). The final set of predictors of Spanish speaking at work include indicating that heritage students should be taught vocabulary for international business settings (Step 14), not supporting the teaching of general Spanish in heritage classes (Step 15), current Spanish use with relatives (Step 16), not indicating that US Spanish variety should be taught to heritage students (Step 17), not having a father born in Miami, Florida (Step 18), supporting the use of concrete outcomes for heritage students (Step 19), and having similar levels of Spanish use as an adult compared to childhood use (Step 20). This cluster of only 20 responses, of the hundreds of others that could have turned up, best predict the claimed "frequency of Spanish at work" criterion (dependent variable). It adds up to a meaningful portrait and to an improved multiple correlation of 0.80, a value that indicates (see R squared column) that we have accounted for just slightly over half of the variation in claimed frequency of speaking Spanish. The procedure, therefore, justifies itself on three grounds: its parsimony, its meaningfulness, and its improvement from the first step to the last.

In many respects, the above thumb-nail sketch both agrees with and differs from the one that appears in conjunction with how often respondents claim that they "need to use Spanish" at work (Table 4.34). In this

Table 4.34 How frequently does the respondent *need to use* Spanish at work?

Step entered	Predictor	Correlation with dependent variable	R	R^2	Adjusted R^2
1	Conviction behind what variety of Spanish should be taught in heritage classes. Scale: 0 = no opinion does not answer; 1 = begrudgingly states answer; 2 = states answer firmly without hesitation; 3 = Mexican variety	0.27	0.27	0.07	0.07
2	Mother's schooling. Scale: 0 = no location of schooling; 1 = in the United States; 2 = outside of the United States	0.25	0.37	0.13	0.12
3	Variety that should be taught in heritage classes should be general, not any specific type of Spanish. Scale: 1 = yes; 0 = otherwise	−0.25	0.43	0.19	0.18
4	Spanish writing at home. Scale: 0 = never; 1 = rarely; 2 = sometimes; 3 = often; 4 = always	0.25	0.47	0.22	0.21
5	Teaching recommendation for heritage classes. Scale: 1 = teach Spanish for diplomacy; 0 = otherwise	−0.16	0.50	0.25	0.23
6	Respondent identified as doctor. Scale: 1 = doctor; 0 = otherwise	0.21	0.53	0.28	0.26
7	To whom should x variety of Spanish literature be taught? Scale: 0 = Mexican Americans; 1 = Latinos; 2 = anyone who wants to read x variety of Spanish literature	0.09	0.55	0.30	0.28
8	Should special heritage classes be offered for native speakers of Spanish? Scale: 0 = no; 1 = maybe; 2 = yes	0.15	0.57	0.32	0.29
9	Where is the best Spanish spoken? Scale: 1 = Costa Rica; 0 = otherwise	−0.08	0.58	0.34	0.31
10	To whom do you speak Spanish the most? Scale: 0 = does not expand or give reference; 1 = never; 2 = depends; 3 = up until school age and then only at home during school; 4 = always with everyone	−0.03	0.60	0.36	0.33

(Continued)

Table 4.34 (Continued)

Step entered	Predictor	Correlation with dependent variable	R	R^2	Adjusted R^2
11	Additional regional variety that should be taught in heritage classes? Scale: 1 = did not give additional variety; 0 = gave additional variety	−0.14	0.61	0.38	0.34
12	Mother's schooling: Scale: 0 = a location was given; 1 = no location was given	−0.07	0.63	0.39	0.35
13	Respondent identified as politician. Scale: 1 = politician; 0 = otherwise	−0.19	0.64	0.40	0.36
14	Highest degree completed/received. Scale: 1 = first grade; 2 = second grade; 3 = third grade; 4 = fourth grade; 5 = fifth grade; 6 = sixth grade; 7 = seventh grade; 8 = eighth grade; 9 = ninth grade; 10 = 10th grade; 11 = 11th grade; 12 = high school/GED; 13 = some college/AA; 14 = BA/BS; 15 = MA/MS/MBA; 16 = JD; 17 = PhD/MD	0.03	0.65	0.42	0.38
15	Where is the best Spanish written? Scale: 0 = does not mention many places; 1 = mentions many places, does not give one location	−0.10	0.66	0.44	0.39

Dependent variable: How frequently do you need to use Spanish at work? Scale: 0 = once or twice a year; 1 = once or twice a month; 2 = once or twice a week; 3 = every day.

case, the single most predictive response ("Conviction as to what kind of Spanish should be taught in SNS classes") reflects not only conviction per se but also the Mexicanness of the preference (Step 1). These respondents, whose mothers' schooling usually occurred outside the United States (Step 2), favor no other kind of Spanish beyond the above-mentioned (Mexicanness) (Step 3). They claim to do a lot of Spanish writing at home (Step 4) and are not interested in having SNS programs that teach Spanish for the purposes of furthering American diplomacy abroad (Step 5). Those respondents who most claim to "need to use Spanish" frequently at work also claim to be doctors (Step 6), they favor teaching their preferred Spanish variety to anyone (Step 7), support the teaching heritage classes (Step 8), and do not believe that the best Spanish is spoken in Costa Rica (Step 9). Finally, claim to need to use Spanish is associated with not having a wide language use (Step 10), supporting the teaching of more than one Spanish variety (Step 11), knowing the schooling of her/his mother (Step 12), not being a politician (Step 13), having higher levels of education (Step 14), and not mentioning many places where the best Spanish is written (Step 15). These 15 responses taken together yield a multiple correlation of 0.66, far above that yielded by the best single correlate with need to use Spanish at work (0.27). Furthermore, no other combination of variables would do as much as these 15 in accounting for the variance in need to use Spanish at work. The variables in this cluster present a portrait of higher education/social status (note the writing of Spanish at home and the occupational concentration in medicine) but yet a strong preference for Mexicanness insofar as language and community are involved.

Interest in improving own Spanish

The issue of improving one's Spanish when one is already an adult professional is a touchy one. Such interest may reflect sorrow, regret, and guilt more than a readiness to follow-through. Nevertheless, it is important to determine to what degree such interest is expressed and, as well as to try to clarify the rationales that come into play in connection with it. All in all, our data yield a total multiple of 0.82 in 23 steps (Table 4.35), which is indicative of a topic worthy of and accessible to further, more focused attention.

The provisional portrait that emerges is one that tends to emphasizes low family use as a child with cousins (Step 1), knowing where father was schooled (Step 2), not self-identifying as foreign-born (Step 3), being born in the Southwest (Step 4), not endorsing the Argentinean variety of Spanish as the best (Step 5), and being of younger age at arrival in the United States for the foreign born (Step 6). Respondents who report wanting to improve their Spanish also feel that it is important to speak Spanish with same-age family members (Step 7), had mother born in the US South (Step 8),

Table 4.35 Which respondents are more interested in improving their Spanish?

Step entered	Predictor	Correlation with dependent variable	R	R^2	Adjusted R^2
1	Persons with whom respondent spoke Spanish as a child. Scale: 1 = cousins; 0 = otherwise	−0.46	0.46	0.21	0.21
2	Location of father's schooling. Scale: 1 = no location mentioned, location unknown/no schooling; 0 = otherwise	−0.19	0.50	0.25	0.25
3	Self-identification. Scale: 1 = foreign born self-identified, question not asked; 0 = otherwise	−0.42	0.54	0.29	0.28
4	Place of birth. Scale: 1 = other United States region not Southwest; 0 = Southwest	−0.17	0.58	0.34	0.32
5	Place where the best Spanish is written. Scale: 1 = Argentina; 0 = otherwise	−0.22	0.61	0.37	0.35
6	Age on arrival for foreign born	−0.41	0.63	0.40	0.38
7	Is it important for Spanish-speaking students to speak Spanish with same-age family members? Scale: 0 = no; 1 = maybe; 2 = yes	0.16	0.66	0.43	0.41
8	Location of mother's schooling. Scale: 1 = US South; 0 = otherwise	0.03	0.67	0.46	0.43
9	Father's place of birth. Scale: 1 = US Northeast; 0 = otherwise	0.07	0.69	0.48	0.45
10	Other regional variety of Spanish that should be taught in heritage classes. Scale: 1 = no other; 0 = mentions another variety	−0.2	0.71	0.50	0.48
11	Mother's place of birth. Scale: 0 = unknown; 1 = other US; 2 = southwest; 3 = Latin America, not Mexico; 4 = Mexico	−0.14	0.72	0.52	0.49
12	Response type as to why x variety of Spanish is written better than any other. Scale: 1 = general response; does not specify why one variety is better than another; 0 = otherwise	−0.02	0.74	0.54	0.51

(Continued)

Table 4.35 (*Continued*)

Step entered	Predictor	Correlation with dependent variable	R	R^2	Adjusted R^2
13	Location of father's schooling. Scale: 1 = Mexico; 0 = otherwise	0.07	0.75	0.56	0.53
14	Respondent's place of birth. Scale: 1 = Mexico; 0 = otherwise	−0.17	0.75	0.57	0.54
15	Father's place of birth. Scale: 1 = Miami, Florida; 0 = otherwise	−0.15	0.77	0.59	0.55
16	Mother's place of birth. Scale: 1 = Northeast; 0 = otherwise	−0.01	0.78	0.60	0.57
17	Additional regional variety should be taught in heritage classes. Scale: 1 = do not teach another variety, more will confuse the students; 0 = otherwise	−0.21	0.78	0.61	0.58
18	Heritage language class recommendation. Scale: 1 = teach vocabulary that will be useful for local everyday needs; 0 = otherwise	−0.05	0.79	0.63	0.59
19	Reason why x country's Spanish variety is written better than anywhere else. Scale: 1 = general response, does not list a certain location over another; 0 = gives specific response	−0.11	0.80	0.64	0.60
20	Respondent's place of birth. Scale: 1 = born in Miami, Florida; 0 = otherwise	0.03	0.81	0.66	0.62
21	Place where the best Spanish is spoken. Scale: 1 = Puerto Rico; 0 = otherwise	0.05	0.82	0.67	0.63
22	Additional regional variety of Spanish should be taught in heritage classes. Scale: 1 = respondent claims question is difficult to understand, does not know what a regional variety is; 0 = answers with ease	−0.03	0.82	0.68	0.64
23	Regional Spanish variety that should be taught in heritage classes. Scale: 1 = other variety, not Mexico or Spain; 0 = otherwise	0.07	0.82	0.68	0.64

Dependent variable: Interested in improving Spanish? 0 = no; 1 = yes.

had a father born in the Northeast (Step 9), do not mention more than one regional variety that should be taught in heritage classes (Step 10), had mothers that were US-born (Step 11), and did not generally express why one type of Spanish variety is written better than any other (Step 12). Furthermore, interest in improving Spanish is associated with having a father that was schooled in Mexico (Step 13), not being born in Mexico (Step 14), not having a father born in Miami/Florida (Step 15), not having a mother born in the Northeast (Step 16), supporting the teaching of several Spanish varieties in heritage classes (Step 17), and not mentioning the teaching of vocabulary that will be useful for everyday needs (Step 18). Finally, interest in improving Spanish is associated with giving a specific response as to why preferred Spanish variety is written better than anywhere else (Step 19), not being born in Miami, Florida (Step 20), mentioning that the best Spanish is spoken in Puerto Rico (Step 21), respondent understands what the term *regional variety* means (Step 22), and supports the teaching varieties of Spanish other than Mexico or Spain varieties (Step 23). This self-portrait contains little that is unusual (perhaps birth of respondents' father in the Northeast qualifies as such and that may imply a curtailment on the use of Spanish during childhood) and we must conclude that the reasons why adult Hispanic professionals become interested in improving their Spanish in their adulthood remain still very largely unexplained, notwithstanding the high multiple correlation attained. These reasons are quite worthy of follow-up (particularly since no predictors related to current Spanish usage are present in the obtained optimal and parsimonious subset).

Mexicanness of where Spanish is best spoken and written

The tendency among a goodly number of our respondents to embrace a Mexican model of best spoken Spanish has been remarked on several times. This tendency toward Mexicanness is constrained when written Spanish is added into the dependent variable (best spoken/written Spanish) by deriving a single total score of Mexicanness on the basis of the independent replies obtained concerning each. The following cumulative multiple correlation identifies the optimal parsimonious subset of respondent characteristics, beliefs, and opinions that go along with variation in the Mexicanness of their total score on the basis of both their written Spanish and spoken Spanish preferences. Since our telephone interviewers reported considerable respondent reluctance or inability to answer (or even to understand) questions concerning the best Spanish of either kind (perhaps indicative of resistance to the widespread downgrading of Mexican Spanish by whatever name) the variance in responses to these questions were correspondingly curtailed, resulting in an inevitable curtailment in our ability to account for that variance. Furthermore, the probable lack of one-dimensionality to total scores based on both spoken and written Spanish will also lower the final multiple correlation that is obtained simply because multiple correlations are optimal when mono-dimensionality obtains in the dependent variable.

According to Table 4.36, the six items that constitute the optimal parsimonious subset of predictors is as follows: Mexicanness of birthplace for both parents (Step 1), the recommendation that SNS classes focus on mastering the Spanish required for responding to local community needs (Step 2), and that the concept of any "additional regional varieties" that might be taught to such students causes either confusion or resistance (Step 3), respondents' mothers' schooling is said to have occurred in the Southwest (Step 4), respondent claims to having themselves studied Spanish in high school (Step 5), and respondent supports teaching of US Spanish varieties in heritage classes (Step 6). As expected, the response variation on this dependent variable is rather modestly accounted for ($R = 0.51$), indicative of the fact that our questions did not capture additional insights into this emotion-ridden aspect of language and ethnic identity, one with considerable relevance for the entire SNS enterprise. Substantively, the optimal and parsimonious subset of best predictors do little more than emphasize Mexicanness of respondents' backgrounds and their emphasis on Spanish instruction so as to better meet community needs and, therefore, reluctance to consider any other varieties of Spanish than the local one.

Attitudes toward SNS per se

It is appropriate that we conclude our discussion with a consideration of two questions dealing directly with the introduction of SNS courses in California high schools and colleges, keeping in mind that we did not specifically design our study in order to answer such questions. The first of these (Table 4.37) deals with the favorableness of opinions toward SNS. The second question (Table 4.38) deals with the complexity or richness of the rationales provided regarding the recommendations that respondents offered concerning courses or emphases that they hoped might be included in SNS programs.

Interestingly enough, Table 4.37 indicates that there are 28 items that constitute the optimal subset of predictors of favoring the offering of heritage classes for native speakers of Spanish. Those who favored SNS tended to explain their views in larger societal terms, rather than in terms of more traditional course content (Step 1), do not believe that the best written Spanish is that of Spain (Step 2), reside in the counties with larger families (probably the counties with larger proportions of Hispanic and other poor families) (Step 3), believe that the best spoken Spanish is Castilian (Step 4), read professional Spanish materials at work (Step 5), do not speak Spanish

Table 4.36 Mexicanness of designating the best spoken – and written – Spanish

Step entered	Predictor	Correlation with dependent variable	R	R^2	Adjusted R^2
1	Parents' birthplace. Scale: 0 = neither parents born in Mexico; 1 = one parent born in Mexico; 2 = both parents born in Mexico	0.29	0.29	0.09	.08
2	Spanish heritage class recommendation. Scale: 1 = conversation skills and vocabulary for local needs and functions; 0 = otherwise	0.18	0.35	0.12	0.12
3	Additional regional varieties that should be taught in heritage classes. Scale: 0 = does not know what regional variety means without clarification; 1 = knows what regional variety means without clarification	−0.22	0.40	0.16	0.15
4	Location of mother's schooling. Scale: 1 = Southwest; 0 = otherwise	0.04	0.45	0.21	0.19
5	Ever studied Spanish in High school. Scale: 0 = no; 1 = yes	0.18	0.48	0.23	0.21
6	Additional regional varieties of Spanish that should be taught in heritage classes. Scale: 1 = US Spanish; 0 = otherwise	0.11	0.51	0.26	0.24

Dependent variable: Location of best spoken and written Spanish toward Mexican variety, range = 0–10.

Table 4.37 Should special heritage classes be offered for native speakers of Spanish in California?

Step entered	Predictor	Correlation with dependent variable	R	R²	Adjusted R²
1	Elaboration type of heritage language class recommendations. Scale: 0 = does not offer recommendations or does not think that classes should be offered; 1 = recommends basic concepts, reading, writing, listening, speaking, grammar; 2 = recommendation includes larger societal implications and benefits, elaborate answer	0.33	0.33	0.11	0.11
2	Place where the best Spanish is written. Scale: 1 = Spain; 0 = otherwise	−0.21	0.39	0.15	0.14
3	County average family size for 2002	0.14	0.42	0.18	0.17
4	Best Spanish variety spoken. Scale: 1 = Castilian; 0 = otherwise	0.07	0.45	0.20	0.19
5	Reading of professional Spanish materials at work. Scale: 0 = never; 1 = rarely; 2 = sometimes; 3 = often; 4 = always	0.14	0.47	0.22	0.20
6	With whom do you currently speak Spanish at home? Scale: 1 = family friend; 0 = otherwise	−0.19	0.50	0.25	0.22
7	With whom do you currently speak Spanish at home? Scale: 1 = friend; 0 = otherwise	0.03	0.52	0.27	0.25
8	Number of semesters studied Spanish in college	−0.09	0.54	0.29	0.26
9	With whom do you currently speak Spanish at home? Scale: 1 = spouse; 0 = otherwise	0.18	0.56	0.32	0.28
10	Activities carried out at work in Spanish. Scale: 1 = speak with whomever comes along to practice; 0 = otherwise	−0.09	0.58	0.35	0.30
11	Variety of place where best Spanish is written. Scale: 0 = Castilian is better; 1 = Castilian is not better, variety from x region is better than Castilian Spanish	−0.14	0.59	0.35	0.31

(Continued)

Table 4.37 (Continued)

Step entered	Predictor	Correlation with dependent variable	R	R^2	Adjusted R^2
12	Reason why in country x variety is best spoken. Scale: 1 = better because not Castilian; 0 = otherwise	−0.06	0.60	0.36	0.32
13	Activities carried out at work in Spanish. Scale: 1 = speak via phone with residents/colleagues in Spanish-speaking countries; 0 = otherwise	0.13	0.62	0.38	0.34
14	Heritage language class recommendation. Scale: 1 = learn Spanish for practical local needs; 0 = otherwise	0.18	0.63	0.40	0.35
15	Conviction behind Spanish variety type that should be taught in heritage classes. Scale: 0 = no opinion, does not answer; 1 = begrudgingly states answer; 2 = states answer firmly without hesitation; 3 = Mexican variety	−0.04	0.65	0.42	0.37
16	Activities carried out at work in Spanish. Scale: 1 = use Spanish to make others feel more comfortable; 0 = otherwise	0.09	0.66	0.43	0.38
17	Additional regional variety of Spanish that should be taught in heritage classes. Scale: 1 = some other variety, Mexico or Spain; 0 = does not mention some other variety	0.05	0.67	0.45	0.40
18	Self-identification type. Scale: 1 = national origin title given; 0 = otherwise	−0.13	0.68	0.46	0.41
19	Additional regional variety that should be taught in heritage classes. Scale: 1 = did not give additional variety; 0 = gave additional variety	0.02	0.69	0.48	0.42
20	Respondent's age	−0.12	0.70	0.49	0.44
21	Spanish use at home. Scale: 1 = Spanish use with younger generations; 0 = otherwise.	−0.03	0.71	0.51	0.45

(Continued)

Table 4.37 (*Continued*)

Step entered	Predictor	Correlation with dependent variable	R	R^2	Adjusted R^2
22	Reason why Spanish variety is spoken better in *x* country than any other. Scale: 0 = refused to respond to question; 1 = gave response but mentioned that they felt inadequate to judge; 2 = gave response with specific location; 3 = gave generalized response about all varieties being equally good; 4 = Mexico	0.11	0.72	0.52	0.46
23	Reason why Spanish variety is written better in *x* country than any other. Scale: 0 = did not answer question 52 so not asked; 1 = gave response but hesitated, felt inadequate to respond; 2 = gave response with specific location; 3 = gave generalized response about all varieties being equally good; 4 = Mexico	0.04	0.73	0.54	0.48
24	Heritage language class recommendation. Scale: 1 = focus on teaching English instead of Spanish; 0 = otherwise	−0.23	0.74	0.55	0.49
25	With whom did you speak Spanish as a child? Scale: 1 = aunt; 0 = otherwise	0.11	0.75	0.56	0.50
26	With whom did you speak Spanish as a child? Scale: 1 = Family friend; 0 = otherwise	−0.02	0.76	0.58	0.51
27	Where is the best Spanish written? Scale: 1 = states best location is just a myth, no best written; 0 = otherwise	0.05	0.77	0.59	0.53
28	Do you read professional materials at work in Spanish? Scale: 0 = no; 1 = yes	0.05	0.78	0.60	0.54

Dependent variable: Should special heritage classes be offered for native speakers of Spanish? Scale: 0 = no; 1 = maybe; 2 = yes.

Table 4.38 Larger societal implications and benefits associated with SNS programs

Step entered	Predictor	Correlation with dependent variable	R	R^2	Adjusted R^2
1	Where is the best Spanish spoken? Scale: 0 = no answer; 1 = begrudgingly answered the question to appease the interviewer; 2 = conditioned their answer by stating they are biased; 3 = stated answer firmly without hesitation	0.22	0.22	0.05	0.04
2	Self-identification. Scale: 1 = Cuban; 0 = otherwise	−0.18	0.28	0.08	0.07
3	Who do you currently speak Spanish with at home? Scale: 1 = with friends at home; 0 = otherwise	−0.17	0.33	0.11	0.10
4	Is it important for students to continue to speak Spanish with older family members? Scale: 0 = no; 1 = depends; 2 = yes	0.17	0.37	0.14	0.12
5	Who do you currently speak Spanish with at home? Scale: 1 = mother; 0 = otherwise	−0.12	0.40	0.16	0.13
6	Where were you born? Scale: 1 = Central America; 0 = otherwise	0.10	0.42	0.18	0.15
7	Why is spoken variety in country x better than anywhere else? Scale: 1 = vocabulary is more extensive/better; 0 = otherwise	−0.06	0.44	0.19	0.17
8	Where is the best Spanish written? Scale: 1 = Spain; 2 = no location; 3 = other, not Spain or Mexico; 4 = Mexico	0.12	0.46	0.21	0.18

Dependent Variable: Complexity and richness of recommendations for what should be taught in heritage classes. Scale: 0 = does not offer up recommendations or does not think that classes should be offered; 1 = recommends basic concepts, reading, writing, listening, speaking, grammar; 2 = recommendation includes larger societal implications and benefits, gives elaborate answer.

at home with family friends (Step 6), but do speak Spanish with friends (Step 7). Supporting the teaching of heritage classes is also associated with having studied Spanish less in college (Step 8), speaking Spanish at home with the spouse (Step 9), not speaking Spanish at work to practice (Step 10), indicating that the Castilian variety is the best written (Step 11), not indicating negative attitudes toward spoken Castilian (Step 12), speaking Spanish at work over the phone with colleagues in Spanish-speaking countries (Step 13), and reporting that Spanish should be learned for practical local needs (Step 14). Furthermore, supporting the teaching of Spanish to heritage students is related to weaker conviction regarding the type of Spanish variety that should be taught (Step 15), reporting using Spanish at work to make others comfortable (Step 16), indicating that additional varieties other than Mexico or Spain should be taught (Step 17), not indicating a national origin identity (Step 18), not stating additional Spanish varieties that should be taught in heritage classes (Step 19), being younger (Step 20), and not using Spanish at home with younger generations (Step 21). Finally, supporting the teaching of Spanish to heritage students is associated with endorsing the Mexican variety of Spanish as being the best spoken (Step 22), best written (Step 23), not indicating that the focus should be on English teaching instead of Spanish (Step 24), speaking Spanish as a child with aunts (Step 25), but not family friends (Step 26), not indicating that there is a best Spanish variety (Step 27), and reading professional materials at work in Spanish (Step 28). All in all, our final multiple is 0.78, indicating that research on this topic has only just begun.

Our ability to answer the second question is only slightly worse and may be suspect in another way. The best subset of predictors, eight in number in this case, zeroes in on those respondents who feel strongly about their SNS Spanish variety choice (Step 1) and those who do not identify as Cuban (Step 2). Such respondents tend not to speak Spanish to their friends when at home (Step 3), but feel that it is important for students to speak Spanish with older family members (Step 4). These respondents also do not speak Spanish at home with their mothers (Step 5), are more likely to be born in Central America (Step 6), do not feel that their preferred spoken Spanish variety has better vocabulary (Step 7), and feel that the best Spanish is spoken in Mexico (Step 8). Curiously absent from both sets of optimal predictors are generational or occupational characteristics. Finally, it should be admitted that some might hold that there is a degree of redundancy between the dependent variable and some of its optimal predictors. That this is not (or not substantially) the case is indicated by the low overall multiple that the optimal subset of predictors yields ($R = 0.46$). It seems clear that there is still much further research that might be needed in this area if it were to be more fully focused on. As it is, our results are quite suggestive insofar as an introductory study, such as the present one, is concerned.

Summary and Conclusions
Reading, writing, and speaking work-related Spanish

(1) We initially examined four demographic variables, which accounted for variance in interlocutor-claimed use of work-related Spanish (speaking, reading, writing) in the following order of significance: occupation of respondent, nativity of respondent, Spanish monolinguality of respondent, and, last of all, gender of respondent.

(2) The claimed level of speaking Spanish with monolingual clients barely reaches the sometimes level and it then remains securely within the rarely level for bilingual interlocutors, whether clients or colleagues, and for both reading and writing work-related Spanish. Judges and lawyers, tied as they are to English texts, usually claim to speak least Spanish, and doctors usually claim to use most. As expected, foreign of foreign respondents generally speak work-related Spanish most often, regardless of interlocutor bilinguality, with native of native US-born respondents generally doing so least frequently. Also as expected, foreign of foreign respondents claim to read and write work-related Spanish most often, native of native US-born respondents *generally* doing so least often. All in all, however, the monolinguality of interlocutors rarely makes much difference with respect to respondent claims as to their work related use of Spanish, and the gender of our subjects rises to significance only in one interaction (involving first-generation foreign of foreign female respondents who score particularly high).

(3) A switchover in some of the above patterns, particularly with respect to nativity of respondents, begins to occur in conjunction with reading and/or writing Spanish. In several occupations native of foreign-born respondents come to the fore and foreign of foreign respondents drop behind.

(4) Spanish as a need/aid for job success *and* interest in improving Spanish The level of claimed need/aid at work is most frequently claimed (at around a low sometimes) by doctors and teachers. Politicians and CSU faculty claim such need/aid least frequently (high rarely). Native of native respondents claim need/aid at work least frequently. However, interest in improving one's Spanish is a substantially different matter. In this connection the switchover effect again comes to the fore and high interest is claimed by judges and native of native US-born respondents more generally. On the whole need/aid for Spanish in connection with success at work, on the one hand, and interest in learning Spanish in adulthood, on the other hand, correlate negatively (−0.13). This may be due to a compensation trend, leading those who accomplished least insofar as childhood/adolescent mastery and use to be concerned now to show most interest, in an effort to recover ground lost. Interest in

improving Spanish is best predicted by a subset of seven variables –
among them never having studied Spanish in high school, belief in the
Mexicanness of best spoken Spanish, and having arrived in the United
States after childhood.

(5) Mexicanness of best Spanish.

In the spoken realm, there can be no doubt as to the widespread preference for a variety of Spanish that is high in Mexicanness. The native
US-born respondents, on the whole and in most occupations, clearly
prefer a Mexican to a Peninsular model for the best spoken Spanish.
However, when it comes to written Spanish a reversal occurs and it
is widely judged to be better to follow a Peninsular model. This may
reflect the written/spoken difference that applies to most languages.
Varieties used in formal education stand closer to an established written model, among which the Peninsular variety has the most prestige
in the Hispanic world. A potential tension between the preference for
high Mexicanness in the spoken variety and low Mexicanness in the
written variety may complicate the adoption of SNS courses, whether
at the level of teacher preparation, student retention, and/or community relations. Via the multiple regression procedure, preference for
the Mexicanness of spoken Spanish was best predicted by an optimal
subset of only six variables, notable among them being Mexicanness
of the birthplace of both parents and recommending both Spanish for
local needs and a US variety of Spanish as priorities for SNS courses.
A preference for Mexicanness of spoken Spanish also appears as a
member of the optimal subset for each of the other three multiple
regressions presented: how often speaks Spanish at work, how often needs Spanish at work, and, finally, interest in improving one's
Spanish.

(6) Special attention is merited in future research for the few contra-
intuitive findings presented in this report, for example (1) the greater-
than-expected work-related reading in Spanish among Native of
foreign born (NF) and Native of native US born (NN) CSU and UC
faculty members and more generally and (2) the inverted order of generational progression for reading and writing in Spanish (i.e. NN > NF
> FF rather than the more common Foreign of foreign born (FF) > NF
> NN). These findings may merely reflect the attitudinal heightening
of a nostalgic nature (noted recurrently since Haugen, 1953) rather than
the beginning of a mobilization on behalf of Spanish among any larger
portion of third-generation Chicano professionals. Finally, it should be
stressed that all of our findings must be considered preliminary and
tentative pending future empirical confirmation and clarification.

(7) Although the more strictly attitudinal dependent variable may remain
the least fully explained (e.g. where Spanish is best spoken or written,
approval of SNS courses, interest in improving one's own Spanish) the

respondents' Mexicanness of either speech or identity (or both) play a role in each of them. Preference for Mexicanness of speech and/or identity is a construct (or construct cluster) that we have just begun to explore.

In spite of the fact that in California Spanish is viewed as a threat to English, it is amply clear from our data that language shift is on-going among Latino professionals. The low sometimes/rarely levels of Spanish speaking, even with monolingual Spanish interlocutors, and the first, to second, to third generational decrease in speaking are both strongly indicative of language shift. Unfortunately, as we will point in Chapters 6, 7, and 8, this trend is fostered by teachers whose texts and methods appear to discourage the community Spanish that the professionals prefer for spoken functions. The suggestions made by the professionals concentrated almost exclusively on Spanish language maintenance (e.g. making cultural/historical connections; showing relevance and significance of language to students' lives, teaching other subjects in Spanish, teaching legal, medical, and business terms in Spanish). Instructional goals guiding instruction for heritage speakers of Spanish at both the high school and the college levels, on the other hand, focused primarily on the teaching of the standard dialect.

References

Bills, G. D. (1989) The US Census of 1980 and Spanish in the Southwest. *International Journal of the Sociology of Language* 79, 11–28.

Bills, G. D., Hernandez-Chavez, E., and Hudson, A. (1995) The geography of language shift: Distance from the Mexican border and Spanish language claiming in the U.S. *International Journal of the Sociology of Language* 114, 9–27.

Fishman, J. A. (1964) Language maintenance and language shift as a field of inquiry. 9, 32–70.

Fishman, J. A., Gertner, M. H., Lowy, E. G., and Milan, W. G. (eds) (1985) *The Rise and Fall of the Ethnic Revival: Perspectives on Language and Ethnicity*. Berlin: Mouton Publishers.

Fishman, J. A., Cooper, R., and Ma, R. (1972) *Bilingualism in the Barrio*. Bloomington, Indiana: Indiana University Publications.

Haugen, E. (1953) *The Norwegian Language in America: A Study in Bilingual Behavior*. Philadelphia: University of Pennsylvania Press.

Chapter 5
The Foreign Language Teaching Profession and the Challenges of Developing Language Resources

GUADALUPE VALDÉS

Educational Institutions and Language Maintenance in California

As was made evident in Chapter 4, the results of our survey of Latino professionals indicate that language shift is ongoing among Latino professionals in California. The low sometimes/rarely levels of Spanish speaking, even with monolingual Spanish interlocutors, and the first-, to second-, to third-generational decrease in speaking are both strongly indicative of language shift. As was also made evident by the survey, 119 individuals or 67% of respondents studied Spanish in high school and 95 individuals or 54% of respondents studied Spanish in college. In making recommendations about the teaching of Spanish as a heritage language, one-fourth (23.7%) of all respondents felt that the teaching of heritage language should also include making cultural/historical connections. Thirteen percent of respondents mentioned the use of real-life activities to increase student interest. Twelve percent felt that other topics such as legal, medical, or business terms should be taught in Spanish. Finally, among the most often cited recommendations, 11% thought that there needs to be concrete outcomes and placement levels for heritage classes.

In the second part of our study, we carried out a survey of current instructional practices used in the teaching of Spanish as a foreign language at the high school and university levels to students who, although educated entirely in English, acquired Spanish at home as their first language. We also carried out visitations and observations of 12 institutions that have implemented special programs for these Spanish-speaking students who are known in the foreign language teaching profession as heritage speakers. As part of our work in answering the study's central questions, we focused on the following subquestions:

- Are current goals guiding existing direct instruction for heritage speakers of Spanish coherent with those of successful Latinos working in a variety of professions in which they have experienced a need for Spanish?

• Are current practices used in the teaching of Spanish as a heritage language coherent with existing theories of individual and societal bilingualism?
• To what degree are present programs successful in achieving their own institutional goals as well as contributing to the maintenance of Spanish?
• What features do heritage programs have to include in order to support heritage language maintenance?
• What kinds of policy recommendations might result in the implementation of educational programs designed to support the development and maintenance of heritage languages in this country?

We present the results of the survey of instructional practices and of our classroom observations in Chapters 6 and 7. In this chapter, we present an overview of the current place of heritage language instruction in American education, with special reference to California.

The place of heritage language instruction in existing programs

In addition to both a community commitment and an individual willingness to maintain and develop Spanish language resources in California, bringing about maintenance and development of high-level, literacy-related proficiencies in Spanish – at least in the near future – will require the direct involvement of existing educational institutions. Within the public education system as it is configured in the United States, students can theoretically be supported in their maintenance and development of home language proficiencies in two types of programs: (1) maintenance bilingual education programs in which Spanish is used as the language of instruction after students have acquired English and (2) foreign language programs in which Spanish is taught as a subject.

Bilingual education programs

In the United States, bilingual education programs are those programs in which minority languages are used in subject matter instruction during the period that students are acquiring English. Bilingual education, while much discussed around the country, is an option actually open to only a small fraction of ELL children, primarily in the first 3 years of schooling. In California, for example, before the passage of Proposition 227, which abolished bilingual education in the state,[1] only 409,874 children of a total of 1,406,166 English language learners were enrolled in bilingual education programs (Rumberger, 1998). Similarly, in other parts of the country, when they exist, bilingual education programs are mainly transitional. They move children quickly into English-only education, usually by third grade.

In California, after the passage of Proposition 227, which prohibited the implementation of bilingual education programs, only children whose parents sign a special waiver may be served by programs in which a non-English language is used. Such children, however, must either be more than 10 years old or spend at least 30 days in English immersion and have needs that will be better served by native language instruction. According to Rosselle (2002), Proposition 227 did not completely eliminate bilingual education, but it greatly decreased the number of students in such programs. From 498,879 students enrolled in bilingual education programs in 1997–1998, only 169,440 enrolled in 1998–1999, 169,929 in 1999–2000, and 167,163 in 2000–2001. Given the current political climate, in which there is an emphasis on the passing of standardized tests in English, it is unlikely that many maintenance bilingual education programs designed to maintain children's Spanish after they have acquired English will be established. The only possible hope for individuals interested in maintaining Spanish as a personal and academic language are programs known as dual-immersion or two-way programs in which Anglophone children and Spanish-speaking children are schooled together using Spanish for 90% of the time and English for 10% of the time at the beginning and slowly shifting these percentages until both languages are used for 50% of the time. Even in such programs the challenge is not simple. Developing high-level academic proficiencies in Spanish as a heritage language through such dual-immersion programs and maintaining the acquired proficiencies throughout a lifetime would, at minimum, require instruction in Spanish from kindergarten through, at least, eighth grade, followed by continued instruction in Spanish during the secondary grades. It is important to emphasize that long-term dual-immersion programs require the willingness of Anglophone parents to school their children with Spanish-speaking beginning English language learners (e.g. newly arrived Latino immigrants) who are perceived to be academically at risk. Given current state politics as well as existing views about the disadvantages of bilingualism and the value of ability grouping in schools, we find it unlikely that a sufficiently large number of Anglophone parents will be willing to have their children participate in such programs. As a result, it is also unlikely that Spanish-medium education can be seen as a solution to the challenge of maintaining Spanish in California.

Foreign language programs

A second and more politically acceptable alternative would involve using the resources of existing foreign language programs to develop literacy-related proficiencies in Spanish after students have acquired literacy in English in elementary programs. In this section that follows, we offer an introduction to foreign language teaching programs in the context of the United States. We describe the language teaching profession and the efforts currently being carried out to address the needs of heritage learners.

The traditional boundaries of the foreign language teaching profession

Traditionally, the foreign language teaching profession in the United States has been concerned with teaching foreign or non-English languages to monolingual speakers of English. Although some school districts provide foreign language classes in elementary school (grades K–5), for most American students, the academic study of foreign languages begins during the middle-school years. At the beginning of seventh grade, students are allowed to enroll in a single elective course, that is, in a class focusing on a noncore area including, for example, art, band, orchestra, cooking, and chorus as well as foreign languages. At some schools, students can choose to study only a commonly taught modern language (e.g. Spanish, French, German). At other schools, the selection of languages includes uncommonly taught languages (Japanese, Russian) and classical languages (Latin). At most schools, students can continue to study the selected language through the eighth grade.

The majority of students who study foreign languages, however, begin the study of Spanish, German, French, Russian, and, more recently, Japanese or Chinese in the ninth grade. Although foreign language study is not required for high school graduation, it is an entrance requirement for some colleges and universities. In California, for example, the campuses of the University of California require 3 years of foreign language study, and the campuses of the California State University system require only 2 years of a foreign language.

At the secondary level, foreign language study is seen as a college-preparatory experience of interest primarily to mainstream, middle-class, English-speaking monolinguals. Students who enroll in foreign language courses are typically academically competent and – even if not particularly interested in becoming proficient in the language studied – interested in obtaining good grades. At most high schools, courses offered in the commonly taught languages (e.g. Spanish), include four full-year courses (e.g. Spanish 1, Spanish 2, Spanish 3, Spanish 4). In addition, one or two courses are offered to prepare students for advanced placement (AP) examinations in either literature or language. A select group of monolingual, English-speaking students who begin the study of a foreign language in middle school or who are highly motivated enroll in AP courses and obtain college credit for foreign language study.

Also, foreign language study can continue or begin at the college and university level. Students who have not studied a foreign language in middle school and high school can enroll in first year and subsequent language courses at the college level. Typically these students do so either for personal enrichment or to meet general education requirements. Many colleges and universities – even those that do not have a foreign language entrance requirement – have a 1- or 2-year foreign language requirement for graduation. At most colleges and universities, language departments administer placement examinations in order to guide students to appropriate courses. The fall 2000 survey of foreign language enrollments in institutions of higher education (Wells, 2004) reveals that among the 2519 institutions responding, Spanish is the language with the highest enrollments, followed by French, German, Italian, American Sign Language, Japanese, Chinese, Latin, and Russian.

The teaching of languages in schools and universities

Two distinct groups of individuals teach foreign languages in schools and colleges/universities. In middle schools and high schools, foreign language instruction is in the hands of credentialed teachers. That is, of teachers who have followed a prescribed program of study in the foreign language as well as in general education courses. To be credentialed by a particular state, teachers typically must fulfill the following requirements: complete that state's prescribed course of study at an accredited institution, pass general subject examinations required of all teachers, pass examinations required in the subject matter to be taught, and for a mandated period of time complete a practicum teaching in middle schools or high schools under the supervision of a credentialed teacher. Most foreign language teachers have either majored or minored in their language in college, and many have had an extensive foreign experience. Nevertheless, given the lifetime challenges of mastering a foreign language, many foreign language teachers do not attain very high levels of proficiency in their foreign language. As Schulz (2000: 5) points out, this lack of adequate teacher proficiency has been a central concern during the past century because "language departments still are hesitant to assess and certify the language proficiency of their majors." Indeed, although current initiatives for certifying the professional competence of teachers (e.g. the National Board for Professional Teaching (NBPTS) World Languages Other than English Standards (2001)) list a standard requiring high-level proficiency in the language to be taught, it is not clear how candidates for National Board Certification will demonstrate such levels of proficiency.

At the postsecondary level, basic language courses (beginning and intermediate language) are taught by young faculty or by full- or part-time lecturers. At colleges/universities with graduate programs, these courses are taught by graduate teaching assistants and often by full- or part-time lecturers as well. The language-teaching staff at colleges and universities have specialized – not in applied linguistics or in language pedagogy – but in the study of literature. Young faculty and lecturers acquire experience in teaching beginning and intermediate language as graduate teaching assistants in their departments. However, as pointed out by Schulz (2000), the preparation of graduate students for teaching language is painfully inadequate. At some institutions, graduate teaching assistants start teaching after only a week's orientation using syllabi and lesson plans developed by the language program coordinator. Some teaching assistants are enthusiastic about teaching and slowly develop a set of effective classroom techniques. For the most part, however, few of these individuals, as teaching assistants, as future lecturers, or as future assistant professors, take on the task of informing themselves about second language acquisition and the intersection of theories of acquisition and classroom instruction.

Traditional foreign language students

Foreign language students in the United States have primarily been fluent speakers of English who have elected to take foreign languages as academic subjects. While it is possible that some of these students have been speakers of languages other than English, up until about 15 years ago,[2] it had not been common for these students to enroll in classes of languages that they already spoke. Italian background students might study Spanish or French. Spanish background students might study Portuguese, and Polish background students might study Russian. For many reasons, it was generally felt that students would not profit from continuing the study of their own ethnic/immigrant languages.[3] Therefore, the traditional foreign language student has been a monolingual, English-speaking student who is expected to move from a state of monolingualism through various stages of incipient bilingualism. Native-like attainment of the foreign language, however, is not expected.

The foreign language teaching profession

According to Kelly (1976), the language teaching profession can be said to have had its beginning 25 centuries ago. The profession has been rooted in traditions associated with the teaching of Latin and other classical languages structured around translation and the methodologies of grammar. Slowly, the modern language teaching profession has moved in search of pedagogies and practices appropriate for developing students' ability to comprehend and/or to produce a language other than the first. According to Kelly (1976: 2), in the teaching of language, "theories have been put forward about every aspect of language teaching, the matter of the course, the methods of transmission, and the media of teaching." Ideas from the study of logic, grammar, rhetoric, philosophy, and later from linguistics and psychology have deeply influenced the teaching of languages. Comparing the linear development of sciences with the cyclical development found in art,

Kelly argues that all teachers, including language teachers, unwittingly rediscover old techniques:

> Whereas artists are willing to seek inspiration from the past, teachers, being cursed with the assumption that their discoveries are necessarily an improvement on what went on before, are reluctant to learn from history. Thus it is that they unwittingly rediscover old techniques by widely different methods of research. (Kelly, 1976: 396)

This same discovery and rediscovery of ideas informing foreign language teaching in the United States is well captured in the recent retrospective summaries of articles published since 1916 in the *Modern Language Journal* (a journal specializing in language learning and teaching). According to Mitchell and Vidal (2001), articles published over this 94-year period make evident that language instruction has been influenced by a set of dichotomous views (e.g. the importance of fluency versus accuracy, the need to teach integrated skills versus separate skills) as well as by various theoretical positions (e.g. contrastive analysis, behaviorism, structural linguistics, and generative linguistics). Among the major mainstream methods listed by Mitchell and Vidal (2001) are (1) the Grammar Translation Method, used in the teaching of Greek and Latin; (2) the Direct Method of teaching language by the direct association of words with actions and objects; (3) the Reading Method, which argues for reading as the principal skill to be acquired by college foreign language learners; and (4) the Audiolingual Method, which derived from the Army Specialized Training Program (ASTP) and involved memorization and pattern drill. This program was implemented during World War II to meet the nation's need for military personnel who could "identify, decode, translate, and interpret strategic messages" (Mitchell & Vidal, 2001: 29). The Audiolingual Method first appeared in the late 1940s and became dominant in the 1960s and 1970s. Focusing primarily on oral language, its theory of language learning was behaviorist. Stimulus, response, and reinforcement were important. The syllabus was organized around key phonological, morphological, and syntactic elements. Contrastive analysis was used for selection of elements, and grammar was taught inductively. Dialogues and drills were used extensively as students responded to stimuli, memorized, repeated, and imitated. Teachers were seen as models of language conducting drills, teaching dialogues, and directing choral responses. The Audiolingual Method was abandoned largely as a result of shifting views about language based on the work of Chomsky (1957, 1959), which argued that language is not merely a process of habit formation, but rather a process of creative construction.

Since the 1970s, members of the profession have moved to the implementation of communicative teaching methods. These varied methods view language as communication and consider the goal of language study as the acquisition of communicative competence. Moreover, they assume that activities involving communication and meaningful tasks will promote learning. Syllabi for communicative courses vary, but generally include lessons on structures and functions and task-based activities. Instructors expect students to play the role of negotiators, contributors, and actors, while instructors are expected to facilitate the communication process, act as participants in communication, and serve as analysts of the communicative needs of students.

Beginning in the late 1970s and 1980s, the American Council on the Teaching of Foreign Languages (ACTFL)[4] engaged in extensive efforts to inform and support proficiency-based teaching in the modern foreign languages. Proficiency-based teaching is defined as teaching that results in the development of measurable speaking, listening, reading and writing proficiencies in a foreign language. ACTFL – in consultation with leading scholars around the country and drawing from work carried out by the Foreign Service – developed *ACTFL Proficiency Guidelines* (1982), a document that describes the speaking, listening, reading, and writing proficiencies developed by novice, intermediate, advanced, superior, and distinguished foreign language learners. ACTFL also developed the *Oral Proficiency Interview* (OPI), an assessment procedure for foreign language learners that is currently used widely by the profession to determine the levels of fluency and accuracy attained by language learners. Overall, the proficiency movement, *ACTFL Guidelines*, and the OPI made evident to practitioners around the country that language learning goals had to involve the development of students' ability to use the target language.

In 1996, ACTFL added to its work on proficiency-based language teaching by becoming involved in the development of the *Standards for Foreign Language Learning* (ACTFL, 1996). The *Standards* were part of the national standards-setting movement that focused on the core academic subjects (mathematics, history, English).[5] Members of most of the associations of language professionals in the country were involved in writing the *Standards* (i.e. American Council on Teachers of Russian, American Classical League, American Association of Teachers of Spanish, American Association of Teachers of German, American Association of Teachers of Italian, American Association of Teachers of French, Joint National Committee for Languages, Central States Conference on the Teaching of Foreign Languages). The five goals that serve as the organizing framework for the foreign language Standards are (1) communicate in languages other than English, (2) gain knowledge and understanding of other cultures, (3) connect with other disciplines and acquire information, (4) develop insight into the nature of language and culture, and (5) participate in multilingual communities at home and around the world.

As will be noted, the *Standards* perspective on language learning views language study as achieving the ability to function in the target language. Students who study language are expected to communicate with others, to explore other disciplines using their target language, and to use their acquired language to participate in multilingual communities in this country and abroad. Moreover, students, through their study of language, are expected to learn about culture and the nature of language.

Looking at the last century it is evident that there have been profound changes in the thinking of researchers and practitioners involved in foreign language teaching. However, in spite of strong efforts by professional associations to change the focus and emphasis of language teaching, the day-to-day practice of classroom instruction draws primarily from the traditions of practice. The audiolingual and contrastive analysis theories identified as central to students' second language learning are still present in the language teaching materials used currently. The materials continue to present the same ordered set of grammatical constructions (e.g. in Spanish, ser versus estar, por versus para, the preterite versus the imperfect). New theories about the stages and order of acquisition of structures in a second language conducted by SLA researchers (e.g. that the order of acquisition of particular structures may not be amenable to direct instruction) have had little impact in most classrooms. Many teachers continue to focus primarily on the teaching of grammatical structures using grammar-based syllabi. Other teachers describe themselves as eclectic and report combining grammar–translation with communicative language teaching. Given the very different theories of language and language learning that underlie these two methods, it is highly possible that teachers are not fully aware of the contradictory positions of the two approaches. Conversely, it may be the case that teachers are less concerned about the incompatibility of underlying theories than they are about students' passing required examinations. For example, they may be aware that while members of their department speak eloquently about the importance of communicative skills, they continue to require tests of key grammatical points and structures. In spite of their own positions on second acquisition theory, teachers may see themselves as obligated to prepare their students for the required assessments. Therefore, they may combine methods they know to be fundamentally incompatible.

The traditional foreign language teaching profession in the United States: A summary

The foreign language teaching profession in the United States has traditionally been dedicated to the teaching of non-English languages to monolingual English-speaking students. However, members of the profession have continually struggled against the indifference of the American public toward languages in general. Language teachers have been largely unsuccessful at persuading parents that language study is worth the time that it requires. Moreover, they have had difficulty producing a significant number of young Americans who are functionally proficient in the languages they have studied.

From time to time, particularly during periods of national emergency, various government agencies have paid attention to foreign language learning. During World War II, for example, concern about the availability of language-competent military led to the development of the Army Specialized Training Programs (ASTP) and to the rise of the Audiolingual method. The Sputnik era brought about the passage of the National Defense Act and projects designed to enhance the preparation of foreign language teachers. Currently, in the aftermath of September 11, there is again interest in non-English languages, particularly in the development of heritage language resources. In the section that follows, we describe the new boundaries of the foreign language teaching profession as it endeavors to involve itself in the teaching of immigrant and ethnic languages in this country.

The New Boundaries of the Foreign Language Teaching Profession in the United States

The teaching of heritage languages

In the United States, the term *heritage language student* has recently come to be used broadly by those concerned about the study, maintenance, and revitalization of non-English languages in the United States. For individuals interested in the strengthening of endangered indigenous languages or the maintenance of immigrant languages that are not normally taught in school, the term *heritage language* refers to a language with which individuals have a personal historical connection (Fishman, 2000). It is the historical and personal connection to the language that is salient and not the actual proficiency of individual students. Armenian, for example, would be considered a heritage language for American students of Armenian ancestry even if such students were themselves English-speaking monolinguals. In terms of strengthening and preserving Armenian in this country, such heritage students would be seen as having an important personal connection with the language and an investment in maintaining the language for future generations. Their motivation for studying Armenian would thus contrast significantly with that of typical students of foreign language.

The foreign language teaching profession currently uses the term *heritage student* to refer to a student of language who is raised in a home where a non-English language is spoken. The student may speak or merely understand the heritage language and be to some degree bilingual in English and the heritage language. This is distinct from the scenario described above where individuals work with endangered indigenous languages or immigrant languages that are not regularly taught in school (e.g. Armenian). Moreover, for foreign language teaching professionals, the term refers to a group of young people who are different in important ways from English-speaking monolingual students who have traditionally undertaken the study of foreign languages in American schools and colleges. This difference has to do with actually developed functional proficiencies in the heritage languages.

It is important to point out that within the foreign language teaching profession, the use of the term *heritage speaker* is relatively new. Its use was generalized for the first time in the *Standards for Foreign Language Learning* (ACTFL, 1996). Up until that time, Spanish instructors were the only members of the foreign language teaching profession who had worked with large numbers of students who already understood and spoke the language that they taught. In an attempt to differentiate between this new group of foreign language students and traditional students, the Spanish teaching profession referred to these students as native speakers of Spanish, as quasi-native speakers of Spanish, or as bilingual students. A dissatisfaction with these terms led to increased use of other terms such as *home background* speakers (as used in Australia) and *heritage language speakers* (as used in Canada). Members of the profession in the United States are currently engaged in examining the use of the term *heritage language* as they research the various types of students who have a family background in which a non-English language is/was spoken. Many researchers and practitioners are also engaged in exploring ways to expand approaches, methods, and alter course sequences to meet the diverse needs of the different students.

The effective involvement of the foreign language teaching profession in teaching heritage languages

The effective involvement by the foreign language teaching profession in maintaining and developing the non-English languages currently spoken by immigrants, refugees, and their children will require that the profession expand and broaden its scope beyond the mere recognition of heritage students as more advanced learners of the target language. To serve heritage students' needs, the profession's areas of interest need to extend to include a population of students who may, in fact, be very unlike traditional foreign language learners at the beginning, intermediate, and even advanced levels. As will be discussed below at greater length, this new population of students includes youngsters who have acquired the target language as their first language, students who have acquired two languages simultaneously, and students who have developed excellent receptive abilities in the language but are reluctant to speak.

To respond to these students' needs, members of the foreign language teaching profession must acquire an understanding of societal bilingualism and language contact[6] as well as theories of second dialect acquisition.[7] Instruction for these very different students must be informed by clear views about the nature of bilingualism itself, the controversies surrounding the definition of bilingualism, and the ways in which bilingual individuals use the two languages in their everyday lives. Also, it must be informed by an understanding of the relationship that contact varieties[8] of language have to monolingual varieties of language, and of the best way to retrieve/revitalize a nondominant first language.

Second language acquisition theories, as well as traditions now guiding traditional foreign language instruction have little to say about these students and what they should be taught. Existing research on incipient or developing bilingualism in foreign or second languages is of little relevance to teachers of heritage students. Moreover, views about second language (L2) developmental sequences and second language (L2) proficiency hierarchies can contribute little to the understanding of the instructional needs of this population. Taking on the challenge of maintaining and developing existing language resources among immigrants, refugees, and their children will involve a dramatic shift in focus by the profession. The dimensions of this shift in orientation can perhaps best be appreciated by comparing the characteristics of traditional foreign language students with those of the new target population of immigrant students.

Understanding the profession's new potential student population: A comparison of two different kinds of bilinguals[9]

In discussing the expansion of the foreign language teaching profession's scope and reach, we have suggested that such an expansion will need to be based on a clear understanding of the nature of immigrant bilingualism and how this type of bilingualism compares and contrasts with the type of bilingualism produced by foreign language instruction. In this section, we present a detailed discussion of immigrant bilingualism and endeavor to present a coherent overview of the language characteristics of the profession's new potential student population.

Defining bilingualism

Bilingualism can be defined as the condition of knowing two languages rather than one. The expression "knowing two languages," however, is far from straightforward. A number of scholars (e.g. Bloomfield, 1933, 56) have subscribed to very narrow definitions of the phenomenon: "the native-like control of two languages." From this perspective, only those individuals able to function as native speakers of each of the two languages would be classified as bilingual. Other researchers (e.g. Macnamara, 1967) have favored much broader definitions and define bilingualism as minimal competence in reading, writing, speaking, or listening in a language other than the first. Haugen (1956), on the other hand, defines bilingualism as the condition of knowing two languages rather than one. For Haugen, the key element in the expression "knowing two languages" is the word *two*. What is of interest is not the degree of proficiency developed in each of the two languages, but rather the fact that proficiency has been developed (to whatever degree) in more than one language.

Haugen's definition includes persons who have only limited proficiency in one modality in a second language. For example, a person who studied French in college and retained the ability to read in this language would be considered to have developed a certain degree of bilingualism. Haugen's definition would also include persons who speak, understand, read, and write one language and only speak and understand another. It also includes persons who are speakers of two languages neither of which has a written form.

Students of bilingualism who follow Haugen's broad definition and whose research involves the investigation of bilingualism in minority communities suggest that bilingual abilities are best thought of as falling along a continuum such as that presented in Figure 5.1.

In this figure, different size fonts indicate different language strengths in language A and language B in different bilinguals. A recently arrived immigrant bilingual, for example, might be represented as Ab (dominant in the immigrant language and in the beginning stages of learning English). Similarly, a fourth-generation bilingual could be represented as Ba (dominant in English; however, retaining some proficiency in the immigrant language). In minority language communities all over the world, such different types of bilinguals live together and interact with each other and with monolinguals on a daily basis using one or the other of their two languages.

Monolingual   Monolingual

A   Ab Ab Ab Ab Ab AB aB aB Ba Ba Ba Ba Ba   B

Figure 5.1 A continuum of bilingual speakers

Researchers have difficulty defining bilingualism precisely, as there are many different conditions and situations that bring about the acquisition and use of a language other than the first. In general, students of bilingualism have attempted to answer questions such as the following: How and why do individuals become bilingual? What roles do bilinguals' two languages play in their everyday behavior? What effect does one language have on the other? How can the individual and group bilingualism be described and measured?

Elective versus circumstantial bilingualism

While there is no universal agreement about what key categories or dimensions should be used in the description of bilingualism, most researchers have divided bilinguals into two fundamental categories: (1) elective bilinguals and (2) circumstantial bilinguals.[10]

Elective bilinguals are individuals who choose to become bilingual and who seek out either formal classes or contexts in which they can acquire a foreign language (i.e. a language not spoken ordinarily in the communities in which they live and work). Moreover, elective bilinguals continue to spend the greater part of their time in a society in which their first language is the majority or societal language. The bilingualism of such elective bilinguals has also been referred to as additive bilingualism because these individuals are in a position of adding another language to their overall linguistic competence in a context in which their first language remains the language of greater prestige and dominant usage.

Monolingual English-speaking Americans who learn French in foreign language classes, for example, are elective bilinguals. They remain bilingual by choice even when they travel to French-speaking countries in order to perfect their French. In contrast with circumstantial bilinguals who will be described below, elective bilinguals put themselves in "foreign" settings for the principal purpose of expanding their language ability. They generally do not intend to live in the foreign country permanently and thus have no "real" need to use their new language to survive.

Circumstantial bilinguals, on the other hand, are individuals who, because of their circumstances, find that they must learn another language to survive. As Haugen (1972b) put it, they are individuals whose first language does not suffice to carry out all of their communicative needs. Because of the movement of peoples and/or because of changes in political circumstances (e.g. immigration, conquest, shifting of borders, establishment of postcolonial states), these individuals find themselves in a context in which their ethnic language is not the majority, prestige, or national language. Therefore, to participate economically and politically in the society of which they are a part, such persons must acquire some degree of proficiency in the societal language. Circumstantial bilingualism has been referred to as subtractive bilingualism because the condition of adding the societal language as a second language inevitably leads to a loss of the first language. Because of the strong pressures exerted by the majority society and the lack of prestige of the original language, for these individuals, the condition of bilingualism results in the gradual abandonment of the first language (L1).

American immigrants are, by definition, circumstantial bilinguals. They are forced by circumstances to acquire English, and they do so in a context in which their own first languages have little or no prestige. Whether they acquire English in formal settings (i.e. in voluntary ESL classes) or in natural interactions with English speakers, they are fundamentally different from elective bilinguals, that is, from persons who study foreign languages strictly by choice. While immigrant bilinguals have a choice of not acquiring English, the consequences of their not doing so are much more life-impacting than are decisions made by elective bilinguals when they elect to learn or not to learn a second language.

The fundamental difference between elective and circumstantial bilinguals has to do, then, not just with conditions in which languages are acquired, but also with the relationship between groups of individuals. Elective bilinguals become bilingual as individuals. The group to which they belong has little to do with their decision to become speakers of another language. Circumstantial bilinguals, on the other hand, are generally members of a group of individuals who as a group must become bilingual in order to participate in the society that surrounds them.[11]

Types of bilingual individuals and bilingual communities

Individual circumstantial bilingualism develops within specific contexts and in conjunction with specific experiences. It is the nature of these experiences that results in a particular type of bilingualism and even in the relative strengths of the two languages with regard to each other in different contexts and domains.

In the United States, circumstantial bilingualism is generally the result of language contact due to immigration. This type of bilingualism also developed when English-speaking populations took over certain territories (e.g. tribal lands inhabited by Native Americans, the states of Texas, New Mexico, Arizona, and California). Most American circumstantial bilinguals, therefore, acquire their two languages within the context of a minority or immigrant community of which they are a part. The nature and type of language proficiency that individuals acquire and develop depends on such factors as generational level, age, occupation, opportunity for contact with speakers of English, exposure to English media, etc. While a number of generalizations can be made about immigrant bilinguals at different stages of their residency in the United States, it is also the case that there are many differences in language proficiency between individuals of the same immigrant generation. Differences in functional ability in both the immigrant language and English are found between bilinguals of different generations and between bilinguals of the same generation. The acquisition of English by new immigrants depends both on the nature of the community in which they settle and on the amount of exposure they have to English in their everyday lives. It is possible for first-generation immigrants to become quite fluent in English after a brief period of residence in this country. This is especially the case if they have had previous exposure to the formal study of English before immigrating to the United States. Other factors including the person they marry, where they live, the number of bilinguals and monolinguals that they interact with, etc., will affect their control and comfort in using the new language over the course of their lives. For most first-generation bilinguals who arrive in this country as adults, however, the immigrant language remains dominant.

This is not necessarily the case for second-generation immigrants. Ordinarily, English exerts a strong pressure involving both prestige within the immigrant community and access to the wider community's rewards. It is frequently the case that by the end of their school years, second-generation immigrants develop a greater functional ease in English for dealing with most contexts and domains outside of the home and immediate community. Here again, there can be many differences between individuals of the same generation. Both the retention of the immigrant language and the acquisition of English depend on the opportunities available for use. In diglossic communities,[12] these individuals will have little access to a full repertoire of styles and levels of language. Because the immigrant language tends to become a language of intimacy and informality, their competence in this language may soon be outdistanced by their competence in English.

This same phenomenon, that is, the outdistancing of the immigrant language by English, is observed in the area of literacy. By the end of the school years (even when the first three may have been supported by mother-tongue teaching), most immigrant bilinguals will have developed skills in both reading and writing primarily in English. Again, the impact of the wider society, the lack of opportunities for using the written immigrant language, the limited number of reading materials available in these languages and the like result in English language literacy, rather than in a bilingual or biliterate profile.

The same generalizations made about first- and second-generation bilinguals can be made for third- and fourth-generation bilinguals. Again, there is much variation within generations, and this variation depends on the access to both English and the immigrant language. Numerous factors can influence immigrant language retention as well as loss for different individuals. It is generally the case that by the fourth generation, immigrants become monolingual in English, the language of the majority society.

Working with circumstantial bilinguals in the United States

To work with heritage students, the foreign language teaching profession needs to understand that the new language students are circumstantial, and not elective, bilinguals. Given the complexity of circumstantial bilingualism, these students cannot be easily grouped using one or two key variables/criteria (such as first language learned or language spoken in the home). Individual circumstantial bilingualism can only be understood against the framework of societal bilingualism. That is, by taking into account the place and function of the two languages in the lives of particular groups of bilingual individuals who primarily share with each other the fact that they are not monolingual. The specific experiences of different individuals in using Language A or Language B will directly impact the development of their functional ability in each language, as well as the development of their linguistic competence in both languages. Factors such as the arrival and presence of new immigrants, the background of these persons (e.g. education, social class), the attitude toward these immigrants, and the opportunities for revitalizing the immigrant language play a large role in the retention or loss of this language by individual speakers. Elements such as the presence of other immigrant groups in the same community and the perceived need to use the societal language as a lingua franca will also significantly impact the degree to which community members use this language frequently. The language used for religious practice, for carrying out business transactions, for entertainment (e.g. availability of movies and television in immigrant languages) will also affect the rate of acquisition of the societal language.

It is important to emphasize, however, that many of these and similar elements may be present repeatedly in the community at different times. Particular bilinguals will be affected to a greater or lesser degree depending on their individual circumstances. Thus, one individual might be influenced by the presence of new immigrants in adolescence, be involved in activities that only require English during her twenties, and marry (for the second time) a newly arrived immigrant from the home country. These different factors will be reflected in the relative frequency with which she uses each of the two languages over the course of her life and the facility, which she develops to discuss specific topics in each language.

More important, however, at any given moment, this same bilingual will possess a greater functional ease (not necessarily an awareness of such an ease) in one or the other of her languages, depending on her experience in similar contexts, with similar speakers, with similar topics or similar functions. Indeed, some researchers (Dodson, 1985)[13] have suggested that for any given interaction or function, all bilinguals have a momentarily stronger language. Whether or not it is possible for them to choose to function in that "stronger" language for that particular interaction depends on the circumstances in which they find themselves. While no systematic research on this question has occurred, it seems reasonable to conjecture that most bilinguals could be made aware of which language would provide greater comfort or ease of expression at that moment.[14]

Individual bilingualism that results from the real use of and experience with two languages is highly complex and variable. While on some level, one may be able to generalize about group tendencies, at another level one cannot make assumptions about the relative strengths and proficiencies of a bilingual's two languages on the basis of one or two factors about her background. Factors such as (a) language spoken in the home, (b) age of arrival in the United States, (c) first language spoken, and even (d) language used most frequently may predict little about a bilingual's relative strengths in each language. Two bilinguals, for example, who share each of the above characteristics may, nevertheless, have had experiences and contacts that result in very different strengths and weaknesses (e.g. strategic proficiency, linguistic proficiency, lexical range) in each of their languages.

According to this perspective, a bilingual individual (either circumstantial or elective) is not necessarily an ambilingual (an individual with native and equivalent competency in two languages) but a bilingual of a specific type who can be classified along a continuum. Some bilinguals would possess very high levels of proficiency in both languages in both the written and oral modes. While others would display varying proficiencies in receptive and/or productive skills depending on the circumstances in which they need to use their two languages. In addition, topic, interlocutors, and the nature of the interaction will affect proficiencies in the two languages.

The heritage language as spoken by circumstantial bilinguals

As has been suggested by the discussion above, the very fact that heritage language students are circumstantial bilinguals means that they do not speak their immigrant or heritage languages as though they had been born, raised, and educated in their monolingual countries of origin. Spanish, French, Vietnamese, Armenian, Japanese, or Hebrew are examples of languages that in general are spoken by American immigrants and which (1) have been influenced to some degree by the English language, (2) have responded to pressing needs to talk about new concepts,[15] and (3) reflect patterns of use in vogue at the time of their own or their parents' emigration.

In addition, depending on the educational and social background of the individuals or groups in question, the varieties spoken may mirror rural or working-class norms of usage. These varieties are rarely familiar to the nonnative members of the foreign language teaching profession in this country, while the native-speaking professionals of the same language background view them with contempt.

As compared with the elective bilingual or traditional foreign language learner, heritage students appear to have several strikes against them. Not only does their ability to use the heritage language fluctuate greatly, but also they have not been exposed to the existence of *faux amies* or false cognates and to the dangers of interference. They will thus unknowingly use established English borrowings while speaking their first language, borrowings that are greatly stigmatized among "knowledgeable" elective bilinguals but are totally acceptable in bilingual communities.

Moreover, circumstantial bilinguals may slip up in other obvious ways, as they are not accustomed to the concern for language form present in foreign language professional circles. For example, in the case of Korean or Japanese, an immigrant bilingual may be unaware of important distinctions in the use of honorifics. In the case of Spanish, such an individual may use an archaic form, such as *truje* (archaic form of the preterite tense of the verb *traer* – to bring) or *caiba* (archaic form of the imperfect indicative of the verb *caer* – to fall), long banished from urban and erudite speech. Use of such stigmatized forms or omission of other forms considered obligatory for monolinguals will immediately brand the individual as a marginal, not-quite-native speaker of the language.

Elective bilinguals generally begin the study of a foreign language at zero or close to zero. In comparison, circumstantial bilingual students normally bring with them very sophisticated abilities in the comprehension of spoken language, a broad range of abilities in the production of the oral language, and more limited abilities in the use of the written language in both the receptive and the productive modes. Indeed, as some researchers have argued (e.g. Valdés, 1989), in spite of their superficial limitations in range and level of use, most circumstantial bilinguals would present a very mixed profile were one to attempt to place them in appropriate classes using the *ACTFL Proficiency Guidelines*.

For example, a largely receptive bilingual who has used his ethnic language to communicate primarily with his grandmother could be placed with others considered to be at the intermediate-high level of the listening continuum. A higher placement would not be indicated because of his limited experience in using his heritage language to discuss factual, intellectual topics. However, the choice of intermediate-high would itself make little sense given that, at this level, listening skills refer to the length of the stretches of speech understood and to the fact that these stretches will pertain to different times and places. This bilingual will have had ample experience talking with his grandmother for extended periods of time and overhearing her talk with others, and he will have no trouble distinguishing between time frames and aspects. Moreover, he will be quite capable of getting the point of even the most subtle joke – a function described by the guidelines as being characteristic of the superior level! The fact is that the circumstantial bilingual simply does not fit either the profession's generally accepted generic descriptions of language proficiency or their underlying assumptions. The descriptions were developed for a very different kind of bilingual.

In summary, what this discussion of the characteristics of the heritage language of immigrant students has sought to point out is that (1) the varieties of ethnic languages spoken by these students cannot be measured fairly by comparing them against the educated monolingual norm and (2) the level of proficiency of these students is not captured in foreign language proficiency descriptions, such as *ACTFL Proficiency Guidelines* and their attendant assessment procedure, the OPI, which were developed for use with elective bilinguals. For the profession, the population of circumstantial bilingual immigrant students presents a new challenge. What needs to be understood clearly is that these individuals are not like the newly arrived educated native speakers who often crowd foreign language departments at the graduate level. They are native speakers of a very special type with very special needs.

Pedagogical challenges of maintaining and developing heritage language resources

In many countries throughout the world, minority languages have been taught in formal classroom settings under different conditions: (a) they have been taught by members of minority communities themselves either after school or on the weekend; (b) they have been taught during the school day or after school by personnel directly contracted by the school district for that purpose; and (c) they have been taught as regular school subjects. In attempting to respond to the pedagogical challenges surrounding the maintenance and development of heritage languages, the foreign language teaching profession may be able to obtain important information about effective and ineffective approaches to teaching by examining the effectiveness of pedagogical strategies already is use in the teaching of minority languages in majority settings.

Instruction in minority languages offered by linguistic minority communities themselves has had as its purpose maintaining or reviving the mother-tongue skills of students who have already acquired the wider societal language. In general, only groups who have strong feelings about maintaining the ethnic-language abilities of their children offer classes or programs to students of varying degrees of bilinguality. In addition, such schools offer instruction in culture, including religious/traditional customs, ceremonies, and texts. Examples of such groups and programs include Chinese, Korean, Armenian, Japanese, and Greek Saturday schools and after-school programs in the United States.[16] Language instruction in such programs frequently assumes that students have oral skills developed by using the language with family members and concentrates on developing reading and writing abilities in the language in question. Studies of the teaching practices used in these programs with students at different levels of proficiency as well as the outcomes of instruction would provide important insights about heritage language maintenance and development for the foreign language teaching profession.

Instruction carried out by school personnel (by either regular or specially contracted teachers) in after-school programs has been offered as a first step in responding to communities' concern about the status and long-term viability of one or several ethnic or heritage languages. In Canada, for example, a number of provincial governments set up such programs. At some schools, courses were open both to students who spoke or understood the ethnic or heritage language as well as to students who had no background whatsoever in the ethnic language. Research on the outcomes and the specific methodologies and pedagogies used in these efforts – beyond those conducted by Cummins (1984) and Danesi (1986) would be particularly useful for foreign language educators in the United States who hope to bring together heritage and nonheritage learners. As Danesi (1986: 3) points out, most research carried out on the teaching and learning of ancestral languages in Canadian schools has focused on the acquisition of English and has been guided by the following questions: (a) What effects do heritage language programs have on the learning of the dominant language(s)? and (b) How do heritage language programs affect overall academic performance and cognitive development? While interesting, this research does not contribute to our knowledge about the maintenance and development of heritage languages.

Situating heritage languages within the academic establishment has also entailed efforts that do not involve classroom instruction. In some cases, communities have been successful in positioning their languages as core or examination subjects within the curriculum. For example, the Korean community in the United States played an important role in establishing a Korean SAT II examination. This examination allows students to present their knowledge of a language that is uncommonly taught in the United States as evidence of academic achievement. Similarly, the Navajo community in New Mexico was successful in having the Navajo language accepted as one of the languages with which students could meet the University of New Mexico's language requirement. The careful study of both of these efforts would shed much light on the language background of students who do well on such examinations and on the kinds of proficiencies that can be measured successfully. Finally, members of one minority group (i.e. Spanish-speaking Latinos in the United States) have – over a period of many years – enrolled in Spanish foreign language classes to fulfill college entrance requirements in high school and graduation requirements in college.

Heritage language classes and Spanish language maintenance

Until the mid-1970s, foreign language teaching professionals exclusively taught Spanish to monolingual Anglophones. However, beginning in the mid-1970s, the increasing number of Spanish speakers entering the country significantly affected the Spanish-teaching profession at both the secondary and the postsecondary levels. College- and university-level faculty who had experience in teaching Spanish as a foreign language (FL) have had to open their doors to students who, in some cases, were more fluent in the language than they were, but who could not talk about the language using the terminology used in the teaching of traditional grammar. Individuals involved in teaching such students Spanish in the classroom setting quickly discovered that these young people had a very difficult time learning grammar rules taught to FL students. Not only did they become confused by explanations of aspects of the language that they already knew (e.g. the difference between *ser* and *estar*), but they also refused to confine themselves to the limited vocabulary of the textbook. Because many Latino students who made it to college had been schooled exclusively in English, they had no experience in reading and writing in Spanish. Worst of all, they were often speakers of stigmatized varieties of Spanish (e.g. rural Mexican Spanish, rural Puerto Rican Spanish). There were no textbooks on the market that could adequately deal with the "problem," and there was little agreement among Spanish-teaching professionals (most of whom had been trained in literature) about what to do and how. The consensus, reflected in the textbooks of that period (e.g. Baker, 1966; Barker, 1972), was that bilingual hispanophone students were in need of remediation, of techniques and pedagogies that would help undo the damage that had been done at home.

More recently, secondary school Spanish teachers have faced an even more difficult situation. Their enrollment includes traditional FL students (anglophone monolingual students), second- and third-generation bilingual Latinos and Chicanos who are largely English-dominant, and newly arrived Latino students who speak little or no English and who have been schooled to a greater or lesser degree in Spanish in their home countries. For many of these latter students, the Spanish language class is the only non-ESL, core academic subject that they are taking. The remaining part of their day is filled with physical education, electives such as drawing and cooking, and several study halls.

Currently, according to a survey of college and university FL departments conducted by the Modern Language Association (MLA; Goldberg *et al.*, 2004), Spanish heritage language classes are offered at 24% of 772 colleges and universities offering majors and advanced courses in Spanish. According to a survey conducted by the National Foreign Language Center (NFLC) and the American Association of Teachers of Spanish and Portuguese (AATSP; Ingold *et al.*, 2002), however, only 18% of 146 campus responding have implemented special courses for heritage speakers. At the secondary level, the percentage is much smaller. According to a survey of FL instruction in elementary and secondary schools conducted in 1997 (Rhodes & Branaman, 1999), 9% of secondary schools in the country currently offer Spanish heritage language programs.

The teaching of Spanish to Spanish-speaking bilinguals, however, is not a new area of interest. Indeed as Valdés-Fallis and Teschner (1977) discovered when they put together a bibliography on the subject, interest and concern about how to teach Spanish to students who already spoke the language had been present in educational circles since the 1930s. It would be accurate to say, however, that in spite of the long-standing interest in this question, it was only in the late 1970s and early 1980s that teaching Spanish to the Spanish speaking as an academic subject became more widely known. At that time, increasing enrollment at state colleges and universities by nontraditional students (particularly Chicanos and Puerto Ricans) led to a realization that existing practices were inappropriate. A number of articles appeared in the late 1970s and early 1980s that attempted to define the field by discussing the difference between FL and native language (NL) instruction (Valdés, 1981), the implications of the study of linguistic differences for the teaching of Spanish to bilingual students (Floyd, 1981; Guitart, 1981; Solé, 1981), concerns and questions surrounding the teaching of the prestige or standard variety (Valdés-Fallis, 1976, 1978; Valdés 1981), and implications for teacher preparation (García-Moya, 1981; Valdés,1980). A number of articles also appeared that described classroom practices and shared suggestions about what to teach and how. Attention was given to the teaching of grammar (Alonso de Lozano, 1981; Lozano, 1981;), spelling (Staczek & Aid, 1981; Valdés-Fallis, 1975), reading and writing (Faltis, 1981, 1984; Teschner, 1981; Villareal, 1981), syllabus design (Feliciano, 1981; Gonzales-Berry, 1981; Orrantia, 1981; Stovall, 1981), and testing and assessment (Barkin, 1981; Ziegler, 1981). Most of these articles appeared in a single collection (Valdés *et al.*, 1981), and included material produced by participants at an NEH summer institute that took place in 1978.

Also during this period, much activity in the field centered around the production of textbooks to be used in teaching bilingual students (e.g. Burunat & Starcevic, 1983; de la Portilla & Varela, 1978; Mejías & Garza-Swan, 1981; Miguélez & Sandoval, 1987; Quintanilla & Silman, 1978; and Valdés & Teschner, 1978, 1984, 1993, 1999, 2002). Practitioners, especially at the university level, settled into what appeared to be comfortable teaching patterns using a variety of readily available materials.

By the late 1980s, however, it became clear that the problems surrounding the teaching of Spanish to bilingual speakers had not been solved. Few materials were available for the secondary level, and younger college faculty, trained primarily in Peninsular and Latin American literature, found themselves facing the same problems that others had faced a decade before. The profession had changed as well. The emphasis in FL teaching had shifted away from grammar-based instruction to a proficiency orientation, and there was much confusion about the right kinds of instruction and assessment. By the late 1980s and early 1990s articles began to appear that examined old issues in new ways or that posed new questions, for example, the use of the oral proficiency interview with bilingual students (Valdés, 1989); the question of dialect and standard (Hidalgo, 1987, 1993; Politzer, 1993); the role of FL teachers in teaching bilingual students (Merino *et al.*, 1993); the relationship between theory and practice (Merino & Samaniego, 1993); and the role of the FL teaching profession in maintaining minority languages (Valdés, 1992). Again, much attention has been given to describing instructional practices (e.g. Faltis & DeVillar, 1993; Gorman, 1993; Hocker, 1993; Roca, 1990) and to curriculum development (e.g. D'Ambruoso, 1993; Quintanar-Sarellana *et al.*, 1993; and Samaniego *et al.*, 1993).

Beginning in the late 1990s and continuing today, professional activities focusing on the teaching of heritage languages have increased enormously. The AATSP initiated its *Professional Development Series Handbooks for Teachers K–16* with its first volume 1 *Spanish for Native Speakers* (AATSP, 2000). The National Foreign Language Center (NFLC) in cooperation with the AATSP developed a language-based resource *Recursos para la Enseñanza y el Aprendizaje de las Culturas Hispanas* (REACH; http://www.nflc.org/REACH/) for teachers of Spanish to heritage speakers. The NFLC also developed *LangNet*, a searchable database that includes Spanish and contains numerous resources for the teaching of heritage languages. In collaboration with AATSP, NFLC also conducted a survey of Spanish language programs for native speakers (Ingold *et al.*, 2002). The Center for Applied Linguistics and NFLC launched the Alliance for the Advancement of Heritage Languages (http://www.cal.org/heritage/). The Alliance sponsored two national conferences in 1999 and 2002 on the teaching of heritage languages in which many members of the Spanish teaching profession participated. The first conference led to the publication of the volume *Heritage Languages in America* (Peyton *et al.*, 2001) in which much attention was given to the teaching of uncommonly taught languages as well as to the publication of a special issue of the *Bilingual Research Journal* focusing on heritage languages (Wiley & Valdés, 2000). The second conference led to the publication of report on research priorities on the teaching of heritage languages entitled *Directions in Research: Intergenerational Transmission of Heritage Languages* (Campbell & Christian, 2003).

In addition, a number of conferences and workshops focusing on the teaching of Spanish as a heritage language have been held around the country. In 1998, UCLA hosted an NEH-sponsored summer institute on the teaching of Spanish to heritage speakers that included a total of 30 secondary-school teachers. Participants in the workshop have produced a document entitled *Spanish for Native Speakers (SNS) Education: the State of the Field* making recommendations on program design, teacher preparation, and policy development (Fischer, 2004). The document is available at http://www.cal.org/heritage/sns/sns-fieldrpt.htm. New Mexico State University hosts an annual summer conference on the teaching of Spanish to heritage speakers. Multiple ERIC digests have been produced on a variety of topics, including selecting materials for Spanish heritage speakers (Winke, 2002), Spanish bilingual students in higher education, learning strategies of Spanish heritage language speakers (Hancock, 2002), and developing dual proficiency (Lewelling & Peyton, 1999). These and numerous other online resources are listed and described in Roca *et al.* (2001). The Alliance Web site at the Center for Applied Linguistics (http://www.cal.org/heritage/resources/) includes listings of online, print, and video resources.

Collections of articles in edited books and journals focusing on the teaching of Spanish as a heritage language continue to appear. For example, *Mi lengua* (Roca & Colombi, 2003) includes a range of articles on such topics as student characteristics (Carreira, 2003), revitalization versus eradication of students' varieties of Spanish (Bernal-Enrìquez & Hernandez Chavez, 2003), language attitudes (Beckstead & Toribio, 2003), and theoretical principles guiding the teaching of Spanish to heritage speakers (Lynch, 2003).

In comparison to other heritage languages (e.g. Arabic, Farsi) and even languages that are taught more commonly, like Chinese and Japanese, the teaching of Spanish to heritage speakers is well established within secondary and postsecondary programs. However, while much has been written about Spanish heritage programs, there is a great deal that we do not know about the role of schools in language maintenance and language shift, about ways of measuring progress in the reacquisition or revitalization of heritage languages, and about the most important differences between L1 and L2 learners. The scholars (e.g. Macías, Wong Fillmore, Wiley, Hornberger, LoBianco) who contributed to the research agenda created at the second national heritage conference stated in Campbell and Christian (2003) that we need to understand the external pressures that heritage speakers are subjected to in this country, the ways in which language ideologies interact with particular pedagogical goals, and the ways in which measurement procedures can engage both community and academic norms. In establishing research directions for the study of intergenerational transmission of heritage languages, Campbell and Christian (2003) point out that numerous questions must be attended to by the research community if the formal educational system is to succeed in its efforts to maintain heritage languages.

The study presented in this book addresses a number of the issues listed in Campbell and Christian's research agenda. In Chapter 4, we examined the degree to which Latino professionals in California have maintained Spanish in their personal and professional lives and the perceived outcome of the study of regular Spanish taught as a foreign language for these Latino professionals during their secondary and postsecondary educational experience. In the following chapter, we present the results of our study of current practices in California secondary institutions.

Notes

1. For a discussion and rebuttal of the arguments presented against bilingual education during the Proposition 227 campaign in California, the reader is referred to Krashen (1999).
2. Within the past 15 years, bilingual Spanish-speaking minority students have enrolled in Spanish language classes in increasingly large numbers. Responses to this enrollment by the profession at the secondary and postsecondary levels will be discussed later.
3. In the Canadian context, the term *heritage languages* is used to refer to non-English and non-French languages spoken by immigrants in Canada. In this work, I use the terms *immigrant*, *ethnic*, and *heritage* languages interchangeably. For an early discussion of problems surrounding the enrollment of immigrant students in classes in their original languages, the reader is referred to Brault (1964).
4. The American Council on the Teaching of Foreign Languages is a national organization dedicated to the improvement and expansion of the teaching and learning of all languages at all levels of instruction. Founded in 1967 by the Modern Language Association, it is the only organization representing teachers of foreign languages and dedicated to fostering and promoting non-English language study in the United States.
5. The education standards movement began in 1983 with the publication of *A Nation at Risk* and continues to the present. The report, prompted by the Secretary of Education, led to the creation of the National Council on Education Standards and Testing (NCEST), an entity that began the development of bipartisan national standards and testing for K–12 education. In 1994, President Clinton signed the Goals 2000: Educate America Act, creating a special council to certify national and state content and performance standards, opportunity-to-learn standards, and state assessments.
6. Languages are said by Weinreich (1974) to be "in contact" when they are used alternately by the same speakers. More recently, Appel and Muysken (1987) have adjusted this definition and speak of two languages being in contact when through force of circumstances speakers of one language must interact with speakers of another in the course of their everyday lives. Such contact, Appel and Muysken argue, inevitably leads to the condition of bilingualism.
7. Theories of second dialect learning are concerned with the acquisition of standard or normative varieties of the same language by speakers of nonprestige varieties. Work in second dialect learning, for example, has been carried out with speakers of African American varieties of English in this country.

8. A contact variety of a language is a variety spoken by bilingual speakers of that language. Varieties of Spanish spoken, for example, by bilingual Basque speakers would be influenced to some degree by speakers' knowledge of Basque and would be considered contact varieties of Spanish. Similarly, varieties of French spoken by bilingual Breton/French speakers would be considered contact varieties of French, and it would be expected that certain features would reflect the speakers' knowledge of these two languages.

9. The discussion in this section draws extensively from Valdés (1992).

10. The terms *circumstantial bilingualism* and *elective bilingualism* are proposed here instead of the terms *natural* and *elite/academic bilingualism* that have been used by others (e.g. Baetens-Beardsmore, 1982; Skutnabb-Kangas, 1981; and Bratt Paulston, 1977).

11. It is important to note that the categories *elective bilingual* versus *circumstantial bilinguals*, while helpful, are not always mutually exclusive. For example, an individual whose circumstances demand that she acquire a second a language may choose or elect to study this language in a formal setting. Similarly, an elective bilingual may decide to reside permanently in a setting wherein she is forced by circumstances to acquire levels of language not within her school-developed range. These distinctions, however, are useful for differentiating between two very different circumstances under which individuals initially come into contact with a language other than their first.

12. Diglossic communities are those in which one language or one variety of language is used for all formal (high) functions (e.g. interacting with official agencies, the presentation of formal speeches, the education of children) and the other language or variety is used for all informal (low) functions. In American immigrant communities, it is generally the case that English is considered appropriate for formal exchanges (political rallies, business meetings, announcements, sermons, lectures, etc.) and the immigrant language is used within the home and community. As a result, US-born persons of immigrant background will seldom have the opportunity to hear the immigrant language used for the high or formal functions. Thus (except for radio and television where available in immigrant languages) they will have no models for this register of language and will not develop this level of language.

13. Dodson employs the term *preferred language* for what has been termed here the language of greater functional ease. He defines preferred as follows: "It is therefore proposed that the term *preferred language* be used to denote that language in which a bilingual, whether developing or developed, finds it easier to make individual utterances in discrete areas of experience at any given moment."

14. This does not mean that most bilinguals would readily admit to such limitations. Indeed, among certain groups of bilinguals, the pretense that *both* of their languages are equally strong is maintained even in the face of glaring evidence to the contrary. Awareness of a *preferred language*, however, would simply involve a momentary sense that the other language (the one not currently being spoken) provides one with greater ease or expressive range.

15. Cultural contact results in exposure to new concepts for which immigrants may not have a word in their original language. In some cases, the term does in fact exist, but is unknown to them. In other cases, the new language and the new culture forces them to make distinctions not previously apparent to them before the contact took place. For example, as pointed out in Chapter 3, Spanish-speaking immigrants believe that there is a lexical "gap" in their Spanish when they encounter the distinction that English makes between *crown*

and *wreath* or *solder* and *weld*. The borrowing *weldear* is a result of such a perception.
16. For a listing and description of such programs, the reader is referred to Fishman and Markham (1979) and Fishman (1966, 1985).

References

Alonso de Lozano, L. (1981) Enseñanza del subjuntivo a hispanohablantes. In G. Valdés, A. G. Lozano, and R. Garcia-Moya (eds) *Teaching Spanish to the Hispanic Bilingual: Issues, Aims, and Methods* (pp. 140–145). New York: Teachers College Press.

American Council on the Teaching of Foreign Languages (1996) *Standards for Foreign Language Learning; Preparing for the 21st Century*. Yonkers, NY: National Standards in Education Project.

Appel, R., and Muysken, P. (1987) *Language Contact and Bilingualism*. London: Edward Arnold.

Author. (2000) *Spanish for Native Speakers. Professional Development Series Handbook for Teachers K-16*. Fort Worth: American Association of Teachers of Spanish and Portuguese and Harcourt Brace.

Baker, P. (1966) *Español para los hispanos*. Skokie, IL: National Textbook.

Barker, M. E. (1972) *Español para el bilingüe*. Skokie, IL: National Textbook.

Barkin, F. (1981) Evaluating linguistic proficiency: The case of teachers in bilingual programs. In G. Valdés, A. G. Lozano, and R. García-Moya (eds) *Teaching Spanish to the Hispanic Bilingual: Issues, Aims, and Methods* (pp. 215–34). New York: Teachers College Press.

Beckstead, K., and Toribio, A. J. (2003) Minority perspectives on language: Mexican and Mexican-American adolescents' attitudes toward Spanish and English. In A. Roca and M. C. Colombi (eds) *Mi lengua: Spanish as a Heritage Language in the United States* (pp. 154–69). Washington, DC: Georgetown University Press.

Bernal-Enríquez, Y., and Hernández Chávez, E. (2003) La enseñanza del español en Nuevo México: "Revitalización o erradicación de la variedad chicana." In A. Roca and M. C. Colombi (eds) *Mi lengua: Spanish as a Heritage Language in the United States* (pp. 96–119). Washington, DC: Georgetown University Press.

Bloomfield, L. (1933) *Language*. New York: Henry Holt.

Burunat, S., and Starcevic, E. (1983) *El español y su estructura*. New York: Holt Rinehard & Winston.

Campbell, R. N., and Christian, D. (2003) Directions in research: Intergenerational transmission of heritage languages. *Heritage Language Journal* 1 (1), 1–44.

Carreira, M. M. (2003) Profiles of SNS students in the twenty-first century: Pedagogical implications of the changing demographics and social status of U.S. Hispanics. In A. Roca and C. Colombi (eds) *Mi lengua: Spanish as a Heritage Language in the United States; Research and Practice* (pp. 51–77). Washington, DC: Georgetown University Press.

Chomsky, N. (1957) *Syntactic Structures*. The Hague: Mouton.

Chomsky, N. (1959) Review of verbal behavior by B. F. Skinner. *Language* 35, 26–58.

Cummins, J. (ed) (1984) *Heritage Languages in Canada: Research Perspectives*. Ottawa: Ontario Institute for Studies in Education.

D'Ambruoso, L. (1993) Spanish for Spanish speakers: A curriculum. In B. J. Merino, H. T. Trueba, and F. A. Samaniego (eds) *Language and Culture in Learning: Teaching Spanish to Native Speakers of Spanish* (pp. 203–207). London: Falmer Press.

Danesi, M. (1986) *Teaching a Heritage Language to Dialect-speaking Students*. Ontario: Ontario Institute for Studies in Education.

de la Portilla, M., and Varela, B. (1978) *Mejora tu español: Lectura y redacción para bilingües*. New York: Regents.

Dodson, C. J. (1985) Second language acquisition and bilingual development: A theoretical framework. *Journal of Multilingual and Multicultural Development* 5(6), 325–46.

Faltis, C. J. (1981) Teaching Spanish writing to bilingual college students. *NABE Journal* 6, 93–106.

Faltis, C. J. (1984) Reading and writing in Spanish for bilingual college students: What's taught at school and what's used in the community. *The Bilingual Review (La Revista Bilingüe)* 11, 21–32.

Faltis, C. J., and DeVillar, R. A. (1993) Effective computer uses for teaching Spanish to bilingual native speakers: A socioacademic perspective. In B. J. Merino, H. T. Trueba and F. A. Samaniego (eds) *Language and Culture in Learning: Teaching Spanish to Native Speakers of Spanish* (pp. 160–169). London: Falmer Press.

Feliciano, W. (1981) Design for a two-semester course for Puerto Rican students. In G. Valdés, A. G. Lozano, and R. García-Moya (eds) *Teaching Spanish to the Hispanic Bilingual: Issues, Aims, and Methods* (pp. 196–210). New York: Teachers College Press.

Fishman, J. A. (2000) From theory to practice (and vice versa): Review, reconsideration and reiteration. In J. A. Fishman (ed) *Can Threatened Languages Be Saved?* (pp. 451–83). Clevedon: Multilingual Matters.

Fischer, L. (2004, August 24) Spanish for native speakers (SNS) education; The state of the field. On WWW at http://www.cal.org./hertiage/sns/sns-fieldrpt.htm. Accessed 24.8.2004.

Floyd, M. B. (1981) Language variation in southwest Spanish and its relation to pedagogical issues. In G. Valdés, A. G. Lozano, and R. García-Moya (eds) *Teaching Spanish to the Hispanic Bilingual: Issues, Aims, and Methods* (pp. 30–45). New York: Teachers College Press.

García-Moya, R. (1981) Teaching Spanish to Spanish speakers: Some consideration for the preparation of teachers. In G. Valdés, A. G. Lozano, and R. García-Moya (eds) *Teaching Spanish to the Hispanic Bilingual: Issues, Aims, and Methods* (pp. 59–68). New York: Teachers College Press.

Goldberg, D., Lusin, N., and Welles, E. B. (2004) Successful college and university foreign language programs 1995–99: Part 2. *ADFL Bulletin* 35 (2/3), 27–70.

Gonzales-Berry, E. (1981) Basic Spanish for native speakers: A rationale and course outline. In G. Valdés, A. G. Lozano, and R. García-Moya (eds) *Teaching Spanish to the Hispanic Bilingual: Issues, Aims, and Methods* (pp. 178–87). New York: Teachers College Press.

Gorman, S. (1993) Using elements of cooperative learning in the communicative foreign language classroom. In B. J. Merino, H. T. Trueba, and F. A. Samaniego (eds) *Language and Culture in Learning: Teaching Spanish to Native Speakers of Spanish* (pp. 144–52). London: Falmer.

Guitart, J. (1981). The pronunciation of Puerto Rican Spanish in the mainland: Theoretical and pedagogical considerations. In G. Valdés, A. G. Lozano, and R. García-Moya (eds) *Teaching Spanish to the Hispanic Bilingual: Issues, Aims, and Methods* (pp. 46–58). New York: Teachers College Press.

Hancock, Z., and ERIC Clearinghouse on Languages and Linguistics Washington DC. (2002) *Heritage Spanish Speakers' Language Learning Strategies*. ERIC Digest (No. EDO-FL-02-06). District of Columbia.

Haugen, E. (1956) *Bilingualism in the Americas: A Bibliography and Research Guide*. Vol. 26. University, Alabama: University of Alabama Press.

Haugen, E. (1972b) Language and immigration. In A. Dil (ed) *The Ecology of Language* (pp. 1–36). Stanford, CA: Stanford University Press.

Hidalgo, M. (1987) On the question of "Standard" vs. "Dialect": Implications for teaching Hispanic college students. *Hispanic Journal of the Behavioral Sciences* 9 (4), 375–95.

Hidalgo, M. (1993) The teaching of Spanish to bilingual Spanish speakers: A problem of inequality. In B. Merino, H. T. Truega, and F. A. Samaniego (eds) *Language and Culture in Learning; Teaching Spanish to Native Speakers of Spanish*. Vol. 82–93. London: Falmer.

Hocker, B. C. (1993). Folk art in the classroom. In B. J. Merino, H. T. Trueba, and F. A. Samaniego (eds) *Language and Culture in Learning: Teaching Spanish to Native Speakers of Spanish* (pp. 153–59). London: Falmer.

Ingold, C., Rivers, W., Tesser, C. C., and Ashby, E. (2002) Report on the NFLC/AATSP survey of Spanish language programs for native speakers. *Hispania* 85 (2), 324–29.

Kelly, L. G. (1976) *Twenty-five Centuries of Language Teaching*. Rowley, MI: Newbury House.

Lewelling, V., and Peyton, J. K. (1999) *Spanish for Native Speakers: Developing Dual Language Proficiency*. Washington, DC: Eric Clearinghouse on Languages and Linguistics.

Lozano, A. G. (1981) A modern view of teaching grammar. In G. Valdés, A. G. Lozano, and R. García-Moya (eds) *Teaching Spanish to the Hispanic Bilingual: Issues, Aims, and Methods* (pp. 81–90). New York: Teachers College Press.

Lynch, A. (2003) Toward a theory of heritage language acquisition. In A. Roca and C. Colombi (eds) *Mi lengua: Spanish as a Heritage Language in the United States; Research and Practice* (pp. 25–50). Washington, DC: Georgetown University Press.

Macnamara, J. (1967) The linguistic independence of bilinguals. *Journal of Verbal Learning and Verbal Behavior* 6, 729–36.

Mejías, H., and Garza-Swan, G. (1981) *Nuestro español*. New York: Macmillan.

Merino, B. J., and Samaniego, F. A. (1993) Language acquisition theory and classroom practices in the teaching of Spanish to the native Spanish speaker. In B. J. Merino, H. T. Trueba, and F. A. Samaniego (eds) *Language and Culture in Learning: Teaching Spanish to Native Speakers of Spanish*. London: Falmer Press.

Merino, B. J., Trueba, H. T., and Samaniego, F. A. (eds) (1993) *Language and Culture in Learning: Teaching Spanish to Native Speakers of Spanish*. London: Falmer.

Miguélez, A., and Sandoval, M. (1987) *Jauja: Método inegral de español para bilingües*. Englewood Cliffs, NJ: Prentice Hall.

Mitchell, C. B., and Vidal, K. E. (2001) Weighing the ways of the flow: Twentieth century language instruction. *Modern Language Journal* 85 (1), 26–38.

National Board for Professional Teaching Standards (2001) *BPTS World Languages other than English Standards*. Arlington, VA: National Board for Professional Teaching Standards.

Orrantia, D. (1981) Spanish for native speakers: A proposed first-year syllabus. In G. Valdés, A. G. Lozano, and R. García-Moya (eds) *Teaching Spanish to the Hispanic Bilingual: Issues, Aims, and Methods* (pp. 169–177). New York: Teachers College Press.

Peyton, J. K., Ranard, D. A., and McGinnis, S. (eds) (2001) *Heritage Languages in America*. Washington, DC: Center for Applied Linguistics/Delta Systems.

Politzer, R. L. (1993) A researcher's reflections on bridging dialect and second language learning: Discussion of problems and solutions. In B. J. Merino, H. T. Trueba, and F. A. Samaniego (eds) *Language and Culture in Learning: Teaching Spanish to Native Speakers of Spanish* (pp. 45–57). London: Falmer.

Quintanar-Sarellana, R., Huebner, T., and Jensen, A. (1993) Tapping a natural resource: Language minority students as foreign language tutors. In B. J. Merino, H. T. Trueba, and F. A. Samaniego (eds) *Language and Culture in Learning: Teaching Spanish to Native Speakers of Spanish* (pp. 208–21). London: Falmer.

Quintanilla, G. C., and Silman, J. (1978) *Español: Lo esencial para el bilingüe.* Washington, DC: University Press of America.

Rhodes, H. C., and Branaman, L. E. (1999) Foreign language instruction in the United States: A national survey of elementary and secondary schools. Arlington, VA: Center for Applied Linguistics and Delta Systems.

Roca, A. (1990) Teaching Spanish to the bilingual college student in Miami. In J. J. Bergen (ed) *Spanish in the United States: Sociolinguistic Issues* (pp. 127–36). Georgetown: Georgetown University Press.

Roca, A., and Colombi, M. C. (eds) (2003) *Mi lengua: Spanish as a Heritage Language in the United States.* Washington, DC: Georgetown University Press.

Roca, A., Marcos, K., and Winke, P. (2001) *Resources for Teaching Spanish to Spanish Speakers: An Online Resource Collection.* Washington, DC: Eric Clearinghouse for Languages and Linguistics.

Rosselle, C. (2002) Dismantling bilingual education implementing English immersions; The California initiative. On WWW at http://www.bu.edu/polisci/CROSSELL/Dismantling%20Bilingal%Education,%20July%202002.pdf. Accessed 15.12.2004.

Rumberger, R. W. (1998) California LEP enrollment growth rate falls. *UC LMRI Newsletter* 8, 1–2.

Samaniego, F. A., Merino, M. J., and Fellows for Español Para Triunfar (1993) Using expert teacher knowledge to develop curriculum for native Spanish-speaking secondary students. In B. J. Merino, H. T. Trueba, and F. A. Samaniego (eds) *Language and Culture in Learning: Teaching Spanish to Native Speakers of Spanish* (pp. 222–58). London: Falmer.

Schulz, R. A. (2000) Foreign language teacher development: MLJ perspectives – 1916–1999. *Modern Language Journal* 84 (iv), 495–522.

Solé, Y. (1981) Consideraciones pedagógicas en la enseñanza del español a estudiantes bilingües. In G. Valdés, A. G. Lozano, and R. García-Moya (eds) *Teaching Spanish to the Hispanic Bilingual: Issues, Aims, and Methods* (pp. 21–29). New York: Teachers College Press.

Staczek, J. J., and Aid, F. M. (1981) Hortografia Himortal: Spelling problems among bilingual students. In G. Valdés, A. G. Lozano, and R. García-Moya (eds) *Teaching Spanish to the Hispanic Bilingual: Issues, Aims, and Methods* (pp. 146–56). New York: Teachers College Press.

Stovall, M. (1981) Spanish for the native speaker: A syllabus. In G. Valdés, A. G. Lozano, and R. García-Moya (eds) *Teaching Spanish to the Hispanic Bilingual: Issues, Aims, and Methods* (pp. 188–95). New York: Teachers College Press.

Teschner, R. V. (1981) Spanish for native speakers: Evaluating twenty-five Chicano compositions in a first-year course. In G. Valdés, A. G. Lozano, and R. García-Moya (eds) *Teaching Spanish to the Hispanic Bilingual: Issues, Aims, and Methods* (pp. 115–39). New York: Teachers College Press.

Valdés, G. (1980) Teaching ethnic languages in the United States: Implications for curriculum and faculty development. *ADFL Bulletin* 11(3), 31–34.

Valdés, G. (1981) Pedagogical implications of teaching Spanish to the Spanish-speaking in the United States. In G. Valdés, A. G. Lozano, and R. García-Moya (eds) *Teaching Spanish to the Hispanic Bilingual: Issues, Aims, and Methods* (pp. 3–20). New York: Teachers College Press.

Valdés, G. (1989) Testing bilingual proficiency for specialized occupations: Issues and implications. In B. R. Gifford (ed) *Test Policy and Test Performance: Education, Language and Culture* (pp. 207–29). Boston: Kluwer Academic.

Valdés, G. (1992) The role of the foreign language teaching profession in maintaining non-English languages in the United States. In H. Byrnes (ed) *Languages for a Multicultural World in Transition: 1993 Northeast Conference Reports* (pp. 29–71). Skokie, IL: National Textbook.

Valdés, G., Lozano, A. G., and Garcia-Moya, R. (eds) (1981) *Teaching Spanish to the Hispanic Bilingual: Issues, Aims, and Methods*. New York: Teachers College Press.

Valdés, G., and Teschner, R. V. (1978) *Español escrito: Curso para hispanohablantes bilingües* (1st ed.). New York: Scribners.

Valdés, G., and Teschner, R. V. (1984) *Español escrito: Curso para hispanohablantes bilingües* (2nd ed.). New York: MacMillan.

Valdés, G., and Teschner, R. V. (1993) *Español escrito: Curso para hispanohablantes bilingües* (3rd ed.). New York: Prentice Hall.

Valdés, G., and Teschner, R. V. (1999) *Español escrito: Curso para hispanohablantes bilingües* (4th ed.). New York: Prentice Hall.

Valdés, G., and Teschner, R. V. (2002) *Español escrito: Curso para hispanohablantes bilingües* (5th ed.). New York: Prentice Hall.

Valdés-Fallis, G. (1975) Teaching Spanish to the Spanish-speaking: Classroom strategies. *System* 3(1), 54–62.

Valdés-Fallis, G. (1976, December) Language development versus the teaching of the standard language. *Lektos*, pp. 20–32.

Valdés-Fallis, G. (1978) A comprehensive approach to the teaching of Spanish to bilingual Spanish-speaking students. *Modern Language Journal* 43 (3), 101–10.

Valdés-Fallis, G., and Teschner, R. V. (1977) *Spanish for the Spanish-speaking: A Descriptive Bibliography of Materials*. Austin, TX: National Educational Laboratory.

Villareal, H. (1981) Reading and Spanish for native speakers. In G. Valdés, A. G. Lozano, and R. García-Moya (eds) *Teaching Spanish to the Hispanic Bilingual: Issues, Aims, and Methods* (pp. 157–68). New York: Teachers College Press.

Wells, E. (2004) Foreign language enrollments in United States institutions of higher education, Fall 2002. *ADFL Bulletin* 35 (2), 1–20.

Wiley, T. G. and Valdés, G. (eds) (2000) Special issue on heritage languages. *Bilingual Research Journal* 24 (4).

Winke, P., Stafford, C., and ERIC Clearinghouse on Languages and Linguistics Washington, DC (2002) *Selecting Materials to Teach Spanish to Spanish Speakers*. ERIC Digest (No. EDO-FL-02-03). District of Columbia: ERIC Clearinghouse on Languages and Linguistics. On WWW at http://www.cal.org/ericcll/DIGEST. Accessed 12.12.2005.

Ziegler, J. (1981) Guidelines for the construction of a Spanish placement examination for the Spanish-dominant Spanish-English bilingual. In G. Valdés, A. G. Lozano, and R. García-Moya (eds) *Teaching Spanish to the Hispanic Bilingual: Issues, Aims, and Methods* (pp. 211–14). New York: Teachers College Press.

Chapter 6

Secondary Spanish Heritage Programs in California

GUADALUPE VALDÉS, JOSHUA A. FISHMAN, REBECCA CHÁVEZ and WILLIAM PÉREZ

To gather information about current practices in the teaching of Spanish as a heritage language in California high schools and in California colleges/ universities, a mail survey of heritage program characteristics was conducted during the 2001–2002 academic year. This chapter presents (1) the results of the survey of instructional practices used in the teaching of Spanish to heritage students in California in secondary institutions and (2) the results of a more extensive study involving observations of heritage programs at six high schools.

Part I: The Survey of Instructional Practices in Secondary Heritage Programs in California
The survey instrument

As we pointed out in Chapter 5, *The Survey of Instructional Practices in Secondary and Post-Secondary Spanish Heritage Programs in California* was designed to answer the following questions:

- Do current programs focus primarily on achieving traditional institutional academic goals or do they also focus on contributing to the maintenance of Spanish?
- Do heritage programs include instruction that supports Spanish language maintenance?
- Are current goals guiding existing direct instruction for heritage speakers of Spanish coherent with those of successful Latinos working in a variety of professions in which they have experienced a need for Spanish?

Project personnel developed and pilot tested the survey instrument with selected members of the profession known for their work in the teaching of Spanish as a heritage language. The instrument targeted language department heads and/or individuals in charge of heritage programs at both the high school and college/university levels. The various sections of the survey requested information about the institution, the institution's full Spanish language program, courses designed for heritage students, placement procedures, curriculum objectives, materials, teaching practices, outcomes, and instructors' language backgrounds and preparation.

Respondents chose one version of Sections 3–9 of the questionnaire if their institution had a special program or special classes for heritage students and another if it did not.

Secondary school participants

The Bay Area Foreign Language Project (BAFLP), an organization that has conducted a number of surveys of foreign language instruction in the state of California, provided the project with the list of secondary schools used in selecting secondary school participants. The BAFLP list contained approximately 300 high schools that had reported implementing Spanish heritage programs. In selecting the high-school sample, we used the total list of 300 high schools obtained from BAFLP and randomly selected approximately equal numbers of schools from two Hispanic population density strata (counties with a Hispanic population at or above the state mean and counties with a Hispanic population below the state mean). The total sample of selected high schools included 173 schools.

Data collection

In early November 2001, surveys with self-addressed and pre-stamped return envelopes were mailed to 173 high-school Spanish language department lead teachers/chairpersons. In early December 2001, we sent a postcard reminder to institutions that had not yet responded. In addition, project staff phoned and sent e-mail reminders during the months of December and January. Duplicate packets were sent out in a number of cases, where individuals had not received or misplaced the original survey mailed to them. Five individuals elected to complete the survey over the telephone. By the middle of March 2002, a total of 52 responses were received. The total response rate was 30%.

In the sections that follow, we describe the results of our survey on current practices in teaching heritage students at the secondary level in California. We included data on only 48 of the 52 schools that offer heritage language instruction in Spanish. The four schools indicating that they no longer offer these programs are not discussed below.

Secondary school findings

Demographic profile of sample

Of the 52 high schools responding, 4 schools reported the termination of their heritage language program owing to a decline in heritage speakers attending their school, lack of support from the school administration, and problems finding teachers capable and willing to teach heritage student classes. Of the 52 high schools, 25 were from counties with Latino populations above the state mean, and 27 were from counties below the state mean. Sixteen programs began before 1990, and 32 programs were established after 1990.

Of the 48 high schools responding to the survey, 76% have an enrollment of 1000–3000 students. Heritage students (i.e. students that speak Spanish at home) are less than half of the total Spanish language enrollment in 73% of the responding high schools. Only 10.4% of high schools offering heritage language courses report that heritage students make up more than three-fourths of the students enrolled in Spanish language classes.

Number of Spanish language courses offered for heritage students

The number of classes offered for heritage students varied. As Table 6.1 shows, 94% of responding high schools reported that they offer first-year Spanish for heritage speakers, and 83% report offering second-year Spanish for heritage speakers. Third- and fourth-year classes are available at, respectively, 33% and 25% of the high schools responding.

Unfortunately, given the wording of our question, it is difficult to determine the exact levels of the classes offered. A first-year course designed for students who speak the language at home ordinarily assumes proficiencies not expected of regular first-year foreign language students. From this perspective, *first-year* is a term used to communicate that a course is to be taken first in an ordered sequence of courses. Similarly, *second-year* is one taken second in the ordered sequence, a *third-year* course is taken third and so forth. Having not made clear the use of these terms in the questionnaire, we

Table 6.1 Courses offered for heritage students at the secondary level

Levels	Percent (No. of programs)
1. What level(s) and type(s) of courses does your institution currently offer for heritage students?	
First-year Spanish for heritage speakers	93.8 (48)
Second-year Spanish for heritage speakers	83.3 (48)
Third-year Spanish for heritage speakers	33.3 (48)
Fourth-year Spanish for heritage speakers	25.0 (48)

have no information about respondents' understanding of them. Moreover, because we did not ask about the relation of heritage courses to regular foreign language courses, we have no information about whether third- and fourth-year courses for heritage speakers enrolled only heritage students or whether such courses combined both groups of students. What we can say is that the majority of programs for heritage students at respond- ing institutions (83%) are indeed *programs*, that is, they include at least two courses. We can also say that at 89% of the institutions that reported offering heritage classes recommend that students enroll in advanced placement (AP) Spanish (Language) after completing the sequence designed for them, and 68% recommend that students take AP Spanish (Literature).

Placement procedures

Placement procedures for heritage students at the high-school level pri- marily involve advisors or counselors. Seventy-one percent of institutions reported that students transfer into heritage courses at the recommenda- tion of a teacher, and 63% reported that students self-select classes on the basis of their personal assessment of their Spanish language proficiency. As is illustrated in Table 6.2, only 23% of responding high schools require that *all* students (regular foreign language students and heritage students) take a general placement examination before enrolling in the Spanish language program. Of the high schools reporting use of a general examination, 100% stated that the writing sections of the general examination were the most useful in identifying heritage students. Reading comprehension and oral interviews were also considered to be useful by more than 50% of respon- dents.

Table 6.2 Placement procedures

Procedure	High schools offering heritage programs
	Percent (No. of programs)
1. How are students placed in the course(s) designed for heritage students?	
Placed by advisors & counselors	93.8 (48)
Self-select	62.5 (48)
Transfer at recommendation of teacher	70.8 (48)
General Placement Examination	22.9 (48)
Language Survey	33.3 (48)
Placement or teacher interview	12.5 (48)
Outside assessment	6.3 (48)

Use of special placement examination for heritage speakers
As compared to the very small number of schools reporting the use of a *general* examination for all students (heritage and regular foreign language), 33% of high schools reported using a *special* placement examination for heritage speakers (Table 6.3).

As was the case for institutions offering a general examination, 100% of the 16 total respondents offering a specially designed placement examination for heritage students agreed that writing is useful for measuring the proficiency of heritage speakers. Table 6.3 shows that students' proficiency in writing on a personal topic was found to be a more effective measure by a much larger number of responding high schools (100%) than was writing on nonpersonal topics (19%). This choice may reflect an assumption about

Table 6.3 Special placement examination for heritage students

	High schools offering heritage programs
	Percent (No. of programs)
1. Does your department offer a specially designed placement examination for heritage students? Yes	33.3 (48)
2. What aspects of language proficiency does the special examination for heritage students measure?	
Identification/production of specific grammatical forms	56.3 (16)
Writing on personal topics	100.0 (16)
Reading informative material	43.8 (16)
Knowledge of grammatical terminology	37.5 (16)
Participation in an interview	56.3 (16)
Ability to correct stigmatized (nonstandard) features	25.0 (16)
Writing on nonpersonal topics	18.8 (16)
Ability to translate from English to Spanish	18.8 (16)
Ability to translate from Spanish to English	18.8 (16)
Reading (literature)	43.8 (16)
Listening to a conversation	31.3 (16)
Ability to make presentations	18.8 (16)
Listening to extended oral presentations	18.8 (16)

heritage students' limited experience in writing, or it may simply be that, because the foreign language teaching profession has not focused as extensively on written language as compared to oral language, secondary school teachers may have limited interest in measuring the different proficiencies displayed in personal versus academic writing.

While the literature describing the bilingualism of Latino communities in the United States suggests that members of these communities have strong receptive proficiencies in Spanish even when their productive proficiencies are limited, school personnel who design special placement examinations do not appear to focus on receptive competence. Only 31% measure conversational listening, and 19% measure listening to extended presentations.

The more frequent use of oral interviews by 56% of schools that designed examinations for heritage students and the limited use (19%) of measures of students' ability to make extended presentations may simply reflect the profession's tendency to use oral interviews to measure productive language proficiency. This use might also reflect school personnel's exposure to heritage students that are either newly arrived immigrants with limited schooling and thus little experience in using presentational language or second/third-generation immigrants who, while they may speak to their parents, have had limited opportunities to use presentational language.

In keeping with language professionals' background in traditional grammar, identification/production of specific grammatical forms were used by 56% of respondents, 38% measured students knowledge of grammatical terminology, and 25% examined students' ability to correct stigmatized (nonstandard) features. It is important to note also that the use of a productive measure of written language (i.e. writing on personal topics) may reflect similar concerns about correctness. Since we did not ask about the scoring of written language samples, we have no information about the degree to which contact features (use of calques and borrowings), disfluencies not part of any Spanish language variety (e.g. past participle regularization, omission of verbal clitic), or the presence of nonstandard features typical of many regional varieties of Spanish (e.g. *haiga, truje*) might influence perceptions of students' overall proficiency in Spanish.

Curriculum objectives

In the case of curriculum objectives, survey respondents were asked to rate a list of 15 objectives as important for foreign language students, important for heritage students, and important for both. The list included objectives appropriate to the four common instructional goals described by Valdés (1995) as (1) the acquisition of a standard dialect, (2) the transfer of reading and writing abilities across languages, (3) the expansion of bilingual range, and (4) the maintenance of immigrant and other heritage languages.

Table 6.4 shows the objectives checked as "important for heritage students" by the high-school respondents. Of the three objectives rated as very important by more than 50% of respondents, two of them, "Identify and correct anglicisms, archaisms and other dialectal or nonstandard forms in their writing" and "Identify and correct anglicisms, archaisms and other dialectal, or nonstandard forms in their speaking," are directly related to Goal 1 (the acquisition of a standard dialect). The other objective rated as very important, "Comprehend written materials on specialized business or professional topics," involves both Goal 3 (the expansion of bilingual range) and Goal 2 (the transfer of reading and writing abilities across languages). However, it is also consistent with a focus on Goal 4 (the maintenance of immigrant or heritage languages).

Of the next three objectives (ranked as fourth, fifth, and sixth in Table 4), two objectives, "Write narrative, informative, and persuasive essays directed to a group of unknown readers" and "Comprehend and read with ease written materials such as novels, short stories, editorials, web materials," focus on the development of reading and writing. The other objective, "Study other disciplines using Spanish (e.g. history, geography, science)," could be considered consistent, with a focus on language maintenance or with the expansion of bilingual range. Less than 10% of respondents were concerned with developing students' ability to spell correctly and to use the oral language in interpersonal or presentational modes. Only 4% of respondents considered that familiarity with the cultures of Spanish-speaking countries was an important goal of heritage language instruction.

Instructional practices

To explore the kinds of teaching practices used in the teaching of heritage students, we presented respondents with a list of practices common in foreign language teaching at both the elementary and more advanced levels. They were asked to rate each practice as effective, not effective, or not attempted with heritage language students. Table 6.5 lists the teaching practices ranked as effective by respondents.

As will be noted from Table 6.5, more than 90% of high-school respondents used individual research and writing projects with heritage students and found that the practice of having students write and revise composition drafts in order to correct errors was effective. The high ranking of these two practices suggests that developing presentational skills in the written language and editing written language for errors and flaws are a strong focus of high-school heritage language instruction. However, concern with language correctness also seems to be a consistent theme across all practices considered effective. Of the 10 practices rated as effective by more than 65% of respondents, 8 practices support the acquisition of the standard dialect, and only 2 practices, "Instruction on the ways that language varies geographically and socially" and "Web research projects by

Table 6.4 Curriculum objectives

Objectives	High schools offering heritage programs
	Percent (No. of programs)
For the entire sequence of courses, how important are the following learning objectives for heritage speakers?	
Language maintenance goals	
1. Comprehend written materials on specialized business or professional topics	50.0 (48)
2. Study other disciplines using Spanish (e.g. history, geography, science)	41.7 (48)
3. Develop a broad vocabulary useful in business and professions	29.2 (48)
4. Understand and interpret extended oral presentations and information available through mass media	27.1 (48)
5. Participate in everyday face-to-face interactions using appropriate levels of Spanish	6.3 (48)
6. Demonstrate familiarity with the cultures of Spanish-speaking countries	4.2 (48)
Expansion of bilingual range goals	
7. Make oral presentations in front of an audience using appropriate levels of Spanish	6.3 (48)
Transfer of reading and writing goals	
8. Write narrative, informative, and persuasive essays directed to a group of unknown readers	45.8 (48)
9. Comprehend and read with ease written materials such as novels, short stories, editorials, Web materials	37.5 (48)
10. Write informal notes and personal letters	12.5 (48)
Acquisition of standard dialect goals	
11. Identify and correct anglicisms, archaisms, and other dialectal or nonstandard forms in their writing	58.3 (48)
12. Identify and correct anglicisms, archaisms, and other dialectal or nonstandard forms in their speaking	50.0 (48)
13. Use and understand grammatical terminology	16.7 (48)
14. Use the written accent	14.6 (48)
15. Spell correctly	8.3 (48)

Table 6.5 Instructional practices

Instructional practice	High schools offering heritage programs
	Percent (No. of programs)
Which of the following teaching practices have you used effectively with heritage learners of Spanish?	
Language maintenance goals	
1. Instruction on the ways that language varies geographically and socially	77.1 (48)
2. Projects involving ethnographic research in communities by students	39.6 (48)
Expansion of bilingual range goals	
3. Web research projects by students	66.7 (48)
4. Frequent in-class listening comprehension activities of extended length	62.5 (48)
5. Analysis of language and style appropriate for different types of published texts	56.3 (48)
6. Oral presentation language/conversation	29.2 (48)
Transfer of reading and writing goals	
7. Individual research/writing projects	91.7 (48)
8. Peer editing of compositions	68.8 (48)
9. Reading of significantly longer assignments	68.8 (48)
10. Group research/writing projects	60.4 (48)
Acquisition of standard dialect goals	
11. Drafting, writing, and rewriting of compositions by students	91.7 (48)
12. Direct study of vocabulary	87.5 (48)
13. Correction of selected common errors by teacher in front of the whole class	83.3 (48)
14. Grammar explanations	81.3 (48)
15. Dictation	70.8 (48)
16. Oral practice of particular grammatical structures	64.6 (48)
17. Instruction that teaches grammar only by pulling out and commenting on particular forms	54.2 (48)
18. Other – Productive skills	20.8 (48)
19. Other – Passive skills	14.6 (48)

students," do not directly support this instructional goal. More than 80% claimed to engage effectively in the direct teaching of vocabulary, in the correction of student errors, and in explaining grammar.

Responses to the question on teaching practices suggests that, when teaching heritage students, high school Spanish teachers use a broad range of practices traditionally used in foreign language teaching, including those used with beginning students, for example, "Oral practice of particular grammatical structures" (64% of respondent), "grammar explanations" (81% of respondents), and "Frequent in-class listening comprehension activities of extended length" (63%). They also consider that practices normally used with more advanced foreign language students such as individual writing and revising (92%), peer editing (69%), and group research and writing projects (60%) can also be used effectively with heritage learners.

Text materials

The question that focused on instructional materials used in the instruction of heritage students asked respondents to write the titles or descriptions of materials currently used in their sequences for heritage learners. Six sets of parallel blank lines were provided so that respondents could write in course numbers and, across from them, the titles of books used. Many respondents listed several titles for a single course, and others listed only one title for each course.

At the high-school level, a total of 40 individuals listed a single title; 27 individuals offered a second title; 13 persons listed a third title; and only 3 persons listed a fourth title. Table 6.6 includes the frequency with which each of the 88 total textbooks listed was reported as used by persons responding to the question. Textbooks have been classified as (1) written for heritage learners, (2) written for both heritage learners and foreign language learners, and (3) written for foreign language learners. In classifying the books, even though a number of texts that have been written for foreign language learners can be adapted for use with heritage students, we classified as intended for both only those textbooks originally written for both groups of students (e.g. *Palabra abierta*) or those supplemented by a workbook or by other supplementary materials for heritage speakers (e.g. *Ven conmigo*).

As will be noted in Table 6.6, textbooks written for heritage learners were listed by 69% of the high-school respondents. Three of these textbooks (*Nuestro mundo, Mundo 21, Español para hispanohablantes,* and *Español escrito*) were written for the college level. *Tu mundo, Encuentros,* and *Sendas literarias* were specifically written for the secondary-school level. The most widely used textbook from this group was *Sendas literarias* (listed 19 times), which uses a literature-based approach for the teaching of reading, grammar, and writing. Six textbooks written for both groups of students or including a

Table 6.6 Books used in the instruction of heritage speakers

	High schools offering heritage programs	
Books listed by intended audience	*Count*	*Percent*
Heritage students		
Entre mundos: An integrated approach for the native speaker		
Mundo 21: Edición alternativa	3	3.5
Nuestro mundo: Curso para hispanohablantes	9	10.6
Nuevos destinos: español para hispanohablantes		
Tu mundo: Curso para hispanohablantes	8	9.4
Avanzando: Gramática española y lectura		
Español para el hispanohablante	2	2.4
La lengua que heredamos: Curso de español para bilingües	2	2.4
Encuentros	7	8.2
Sendas literarias	19	22.4
Español escrito: Curso para hispanohablantes bilingües	5	5.9
Nuevos mundos: Lectura, cultura y comunicación: Curso de español para estudiantes bilingües		
Galería de arte y vida level 4	1	1.2
Tesoro literario	1	1.2
Subtotal	57	67.1
Both heritage and foreign language students		
Palabra abierta		
Avanzando: Gramática española y lectura	1	1.2
Aproximaciones al estudio de la literatura hispánica	1	1.2
Literatura moderna hispánica-An anthology	2	2.4
Dímelo tú!		
Ven conmigo	1	1.2
Subtotal	5	5.9
Foreign language students		
Dime uno, dos, tres	6	7.1
Pasos y puentes	1	1.2

(Continued)

Table 6.6 (*Continued*)

	High schools offering heritage programs	
Books listed by intended audience	*Count*	*Percent*
Voces y vistas	1	1.2
AP Spanish: A guide for the language course	3	3.5
Esencial repaso	1	1.2
Una vez más: Repaso detallado de las estructuras gramaticales del idioma de español	1	1.2
Claro que sí!		
Punto de vista		
Abriendo paso	4	4.7
Galeria de arte y vida level 4	3	3.5
Composición: Proceso y síntesis		
Encuentros maravillosos: Gramática a través de la literatura	2	2.4
Fonética y fonología		
Tesoro literario	1	1.2
Subtotal	23	27.1
Total	88	100.0

supplement for heritage learners were listed. Two of the listed textbooks focus on the teaching of literature, an area traditionally assumed to be appropriate for more advanced study.

A total of eight texts written for traditional foreign language learners were listed by 23 high-school respondents. One of these texts, *AP Spanish: A guide for the language course*, is a highly specialized test preparation manual. Other texts mentioned frequently include *Dime* (listed 6 times), *Abriendo paso* (listed 4 times), and *Galería de arte y vida* (listed 3 times).

Satisfaction with existing program

Individuals responding to the survey were asked whether they were satisfied with the outcomes of their heritage language program. Four blank lines were provided so that respondents could list two areas with which they were particularly satisfied and list two areas in which they felt the program needed to improve.

As will be noted in Table 6.7, 75% of high-school respondents reported being satisfied with students' achievement as measured by course examinations or by success in subsequent courses. A total of 57% of respondents

Table 6.7 Program satisfaction

	High schools
Area	*Percent (No. of programs)*
1. Are you satisfied with the achievement of students in the heritage language program, as measured by course examinations and/or by success in subsequent courses?	
Yes	75.0 (48)
2. Program areas of particular satisfaction (areas)	
Skill-based response	56.5 (46)
Program-based response	56.5 (46)
Student-based response	10.8 (46)
3. Program areas of particular satisfaction (specific items)	
Subsequent class success	52.2 (46)
Reading	39.1 (46)
Writing	17.4 (46)
Cultural/historical themes	15.2 (46)
Vocabulary/orthography	10.9 (46)
Speaking	8.7 (46)
Individual benefits	8.7 (46)
Grammar	6.5 (46)
Multimedia/technology	4.3 (46)
Inclusion ELL/ESL	4.3 (46)
Standard language	0.0 (48)

listed a *skill-based area* with which they were satisfied. A *skill-based response* would generally state that they noticed their students vocabularies improved, or their correct usage of standard Spanish, or students' improvement in written composition and analytical skills. Another 57% of respondents provided what was classified as a *program-based response*. Such responses disclosed satisfaction with the structure of their program, for example, "the integration of technology into the classroom," "overall enrollment up in Spanish classes," "integration of ESL students in AP Language and Literature course," "Spanish speakers stay with the course program," and the addition of "new books/materials to expand literature used in classes." Only 11% of informants offered a *student-based response*, which included claims such as students' being proud of their heritage, or the observation that students acquire self-esteem as their awareness of who they are and the value of their contributions is realized.

Table 6.7 also presents the frequency in which respondents mentioned specific program or skill areas. A *subsequent class success response* was given by 52% of respondents. These responses claimed satisfaction with students' success in subsequent courses. For example, stating that the majority of students go on and get 4 or 5 on the AP test, that students receive high honors in Golden State examination, that a large percentage of students go on to higher-level courses and continue to study in college, and that students increase language development (that) leads to improvement in other subjects, that is, English. A number of respondents specifically mentioned being satisfied with students' improvement in reading (39%), in writing (17%), knowledge of cultural historical themes (15%), and knowledge of vocabulary, spelling, and orthography (11%). Very few high-school respondents listed grammar (7%) or standard language (0%) as areas with which they were satisfied.

Areas needing improvement

Table 6.8, shows the areas in which improvement was thought to be needed by high-school respondents. Sixty percent of individuals listed school logistics issues as the key area that required improvement (e.g. varied levels of classes, better scheduling). Areas seen as requiring improvement included both programmatic issues and proficiency/skill outcomes. In terms of proficiency/skill outcomes, 32% of informants listed writing/vocabulary, spelling as needing improvement. More than 25% of respondents rated programmatic issues such as offering varied class levels, placement examination, and improved materials as needing attention.

Faculty characteristics

All respondents were asked how many faculty taught in the Spanish language program. This number was not to include faculty teaching literature or linguistics. The questionnaire also asked for the total number of instructors teaching in the heritage program. It then asked the respondent to identify the number of instructors in the heritage program that fell into the following groups: (1) US Latinos who grew up with Spanish at home, (2) US Latinos who grew up in non–Spanish-speaking families, (3) Latinos who grew up and were educated in Spanish-speaking countries, and (4) non-Latinos who grew up in non–Spanish-speaking families.

At the high-school level, the number of faculty teaching in heritage Spanish programs within the 48 high schools with heritage programs varied. Table 6.9 shows that 42% of these institutions had 3–5 faculty members, and 44% had 6–10 faculty teaching Spanish. However, faculty involved in the teaching of the heritage sequence numbered 2 or fewer in 67% of high schools responding, and 23% of responding high schools noted 3–5 faculty.

Table 6.8 Areas in which improvement is needed

	High schools
Area	*Percent* *(No. of programs)*
1. Program areas that need improvement (areas)	
School/logistics issue	59.6 (47)
Student performance issue	36.2 (47)
Different foci of classes issue	31.9 (47)
2. Program areas that need improvement (specific items)	
Writing/vocabulary, spelling	31.9 (47)
Offer varied levels of classes	27.7 (47)
Placement examination	25.5 (47)
Improved materials	25.5 (47)
Text analysis skills	19.1 (47)
Student motivation, interests	17.0 (47)
Articulation with the community	10.6 (47)
Standard language	8.5 (47)
Offer classes for students with low levels of literacy	4.3 (47)
No improvement necessary	2.1 (47)
Start program for heritage speakers	N/A

The language background of instructors involved in the teaching of heritage languages also varied. When asked to estimate the percentage of instructors who fell into the four categories listed above, 43% of respondents reported that the majority of their instructors are US Latinos who grew up with Spanish at home. However, 29% of institutions stated that heritage language instructors include Latinos who grew up in other Spanish-speaking countries and 22% responded that non-Latino teachers who acquired Spanish as a second language are also teaching in their heritage programs. Only 3% of institutions reported that their heritage language faculty includes US Latinos raised as English monolinguals.

Preparation of lead instructor

To obtain a more complete picture of heritage instructors' professional training, respondents were also asked to report on the preparation of the person considered the lead instructor in the heritage program. Given our familiarity with the limited training in teaching heritage languages available for secondary teachers, a condition that has necessitated

Table 6.9 Instructor characteristics

Characteristic	High school Percent (No. of programs)
1. Number of instructors teaching Spanish language	
2 or fewer	8.4
3–5	41.7
6–10	43.8
11 or more	6.0
Total	100.0 (48)
2. Total number of instructors in heritage program	
2 or fewer	66.7
3–5	23.0
6–10	8.4
11 or more	2.1
Total	100.0 (48)
3. Mean percentage of instructors who teach heritage students who fall into the following categories?	
US Latinos who grew up with Spanish at home	43.3 (48)
US Latinos who grew up in non–Spanish-speaking families	3.3 (48)
Latinos who grew up and were educated in Spanish-speaking countries	28.7 (48)
Non-Latinos who grew up in non–Spanish-speaking families	21.5 (48)

the organization of nationwide projects and workshops (Fischer, 2004; Potowski, 2003), we expected that most individuals would disclose that they had learned to teach by teaching. Respondents reporting that their institutions offered heritage courses were asked to describe the preparation of their lead instructor by checking all appropriate descriptive statements from a list of 10 alternatives. Descriptive statements about preparation included such alternatives as "Took special course(s) on teaching heritage students as part of a teaching certificate program" and "Attended summer workshop(s) on the teaching of heritage speakers."

As expected, Table 6.10 reveals that 77% of lead instructors learned on the job by teaching heritage learners, 58% attended sessions on teaching heritage learners at professional conferences, and 50% carried out extensive

Table 6.10 Lead instructor preparation

Preparation type	High schools offering heritage programs
	Percent (No. of programs)
1. What types of preparation for teaching heritage speakers has the *lead instructor* in the heritage sequence received?	
Learned on the job by teaching heritage learners	77.1 (48)
Attended sessions on the teaching of heritage speakers at professional conferences	58.3 (48)
Carried out extensive individual reading on the teaching of heritage speakers	50.0 (48)
Attended summer workshop(s) on the teaching of heritage speakers	47.9 (48)
Visited heritage language classes at nearby schools or colleges	37.5 (48)
Took special course(s) on teaching heritage students as part of a teaching certificate program	33.3 (48)
Taught a course or courses for heritage students as part of graduate teaching assistant responsibilities	20.8 (48)
Based on living experience	14.6 (48)
Based on educational experience	10.4 (48)
Took special course(s) on teaching heritage students as part of graduate teaching-assistant training	10.4 (48)
Became member of listserv focusing on the teaching of heritage speakers	8.3 (48)

individual reading on the teaching of heritage students. Thirty-three percent of respondents claimed that they took special courses on teaching heritage students as part of a teaching certificate program. This response suggests that more preservice, foreign language, teacher preparation programs may be including instruction on heritage languages in their programs. However, since no state offers heritage language certification or endorsement for secondary teachers (Potowski, 2003), we find it unlikely that a 33% of lead teachers would have had the opportunity to enroll in such courses. We conjecture that teachers who took preservice courses on Latinos in general or on English language learners of Spanish-speaking backgrounds as part of their general teacher education may have counted such courses as related to the of teaching of heritage learners even though these courses did not cover methodologies specific to teaching Spanish to such students.

Discussion

Survey results indicate that high school heritage language programs vary considerably. Some programs have been in existence since the early 1980s and others have begun only recently. Sequences of courses intended for heritage students also vary. Some institutions describe a 4-year sequence and others report a single course. Placement in heritage courses is primarily carried out by advisors and counselors, but when placement examinations are used, respondents indicate that they measure students' ability to identify and produce specific grammatical forms. Overall, responses to the survey suggest that heritage programs primarily focus on achieving traditional institutional academic goals. Both high-school and college/university respondents reported satisfaction with subsequent course achievement, success in course examinations, as well as satisfaction with the development of reading and writing skills by heritage students. We found no evidence to suggest that high schools offering heritage programs see themselves as engaged in the process of language maintenance. Instructional goals and instructional practices ranked most highly by all high-school respondents are closely aligned with the teaching of the standard dialect (e.g. correcting anglicisms, archaisms, and other nonstandard forms in students' oral and written language, teaching grammatical terminology, and teaching spelling).

Limitations of quantitative data

The mail survey response rate of 30% is low. Thus, the generalizability of our findings to nonrespondent programs may be limited. However, our response rate is similar to mail survey response rates found in the survey methodology literature (Church, 1993; Fox *et al.*, 1989; James & Bolstein, 1992; Kaplowitz *et al.*, 2004). For example in their study, Fox *et al.* (1989) found through meta-analysis that return rates for surveys with no monetary incentive averaged 34%. Our results showed that early respondents did not differ from late responders, suggesting that even nonresponders would have distributed themselves very much like the responders. Nevertheless, caution should be exercised and the results should be considered tentative.

Finally, what was not clear from responses to the survey was the kinds of changes that might need to occur in order for existing Spanish language heritage programs in California to respond to this country's present and future economic and security needs. As the recommendations put forth by secondary-school-level participants in the NEH summer institute in

Spanish for Native Speakers (SNS) Education: The State of the Field (Fisher, 2004) make evident, promoting a language-proficient society will require changes in teacher preparation, classroom instruction, student assessment, and state and school policies. Survey responses indicate that in order for Spanish heritage language instruction to inform the teaching of other heritage languages in this country, much more needs to be done in examining the strengths and weaknesses of existing heritage language programs.

Part II. A Closer View: A Qualitative Study of Selected Secondary Spanish Heritage Programs

In at attempt to obtain a more nuanced view of the ways in which formal education programs might support the expansion and maintenance of Spanish as a heritage language in California, we studied six high schools that responded to our survey. It was our expectation that by visiting classes and by carrying out face-to face interviews with faculty involved in teaching heritage learners, we would learn more about specific goals of Spanish heritage courses and about practices that have been found particularly effective in developing the language resources of heritage speakers.

Selection of institutions studied

The selection of high schools studied was made using the register of survey respondents for both high schools and colleges. Using survey responses about program histories, we first compiled an initial list of early programs (established before 1984), programs in existence for a considerable period of time (established between 1985 and 1994), and recently established programs (established after 1995). This initial list was then subdivided into institutions with low, medium, and high Latino enrollment.

The original list of 48 schools that reported having established heritage programs was used to randomly select the last few schools drawn. School personnel were then contacted and asked if they would allow us to visit for a day or two in order to study their heritage course offerings more closely. All high schools initially contacted consented to our visit; however, scheduling conflicts resulted in our replacing two schools initially selected with similar schools from our randomized list.

To carry out our more detailed study of heritage programs, we spent one full day at each secondary and postsecondary institution, often observing three to four classes and interviewing teachers/lecturers and coordinators/heads of the programs. We were able to visit a full spectrum of long-established, well-established, and more recently established programs at institutions that had low and high heritage speaker enrollments.

However, we recognize that our short visits to each school were not extensive enough to allow us to fully appreciate the strengths of each of these programs. What the visits did allow us to do was to invite six individuals and their colleagues who had responded to our survey to share with us more extensive answers to the questions that we had asked in multiple-choice and fill-in-the-blank formats. It also allowed us to examine their views of their students' proficiencies, and to learn more about what they considered to be successful and unsuccessful pedagogies, and textbooks.

In interviewing persons involved in the teaching of Spanish as a heritage language at the six high schools, we addressed the following topics:

- Program history
- Students' language proficiency
- Courses available
- Placement in courses
- Objectives of program
- Textbooks and other materials used
- Teaching practices effective and ineffective
- What was working and what they wanted to change
- Recommendations for other schools considering starting a heritage program
- Views about the relationship between heritage language programs and the Spanish language needs of Latino professionals in California

It is important for us to emphasize that in obtaining permission to carry out our visits and interviews, we agreed that all information obtained during our visits would be kept confidential. We further agreed that individual privacy would be maintained in all published and written data resulting from the study. For that reason, we refer to the institutions visited, for example, as High School A, using letters A through F for each of the six high schools.

Characteristics of high schools visited

The high schools selected for further study include the institutions listed in Table 6.11. As will be noted from Table 6.11, two high schools (High Schools A and B) had relatively low Latino enrollment, two schools had a Latino enrollment of more than 50% (High Schools C and D) and two schools had a Latino enrollment of more than 90% (High Schools E and F). Two high schools (High School B with relatively low Latino enrollment and High School E with more than 90% Latino enrollment) implemented Spanish heritage language programs before 1985. Two schools with similar high and low enrollment characteristics (High School A with 33% Latino enrollment and High School F with 98% Latino enrollment) implemented programs after 1995. Patterns of program establishment in the schools

Table 6.11 High schools visited

Institution	Total enrollment	Latino enrollment	Program established
High School A	1607	33%	After 1995
High School B	2112	37%	Before 1985
High School C	1895	57%	Between 1985 and 1994
High School D	1715	56%	Between 1985 and 1994
High School E	706	90%	Before 1985
High School F	2959	98%	After 1995

visited directly confirm what respondents to the survey also reported: that Latino enrollment alone has not accounted for the establishment of Spanish heritage language programs in California.

The six schools studied at greater depth are located in different types of communities in California. Table 6.12 provides information about the population characteristics of the geographic area in which each school is located. Table 6.12 also illustrates the ways in which the school settings visited are dissimilar. For example, High School B is located in a geographic area with a population of 26,663 in a county that has a population density of 670 persons per square mile. It is located near a large metropolitan area and has a Hispanic or Latino population of 22%. By comparison, High School C is in a geographic area that has a population of 25,869, but it is located in a county with a population density of only 109 people per square mile. This particular geographic area is 50% Latino. Education characteristics in these two geographic areas are also dissimilar. Only 5% of the adult population in the area in which High School B is located have an education of less than ninth grade. However, in the case of High School C, 16% of the population in the community has an education of less than ninth grade. High School B and C, therefore, are dissimilar schools in that they serve students of very different backgrounds. In addition to being located in communities that vary in terms of degree of urban influence, low employment, and persistent poverty, the six schools also vary in terms of their proximity to the border. High School D, for example, is located directly on the United States–Mexico border, and High School F is located in a rural agricultural area that depends highly on immigrant labor.

Table 6.13 provides data on student achievement at the six schools visited. As will be noted from Table 6.13, High School D, which is located in an area with a high density of population that is 47% Latino, has the highest Academic Performance Index (API) score[1] of the six schools visited. This API score is congruent with the fact that High School D is a specialized magnet school that draws students from a very large metropolitan school

Table 6.12 Community profile for high schools visited

Institution	Population of geographic area	No. of persons in county per square mile	Percentage of Hispanic or Latino population	Percentage of population with less than ninth-grade education
High School A	121,780	1318	21%	7%
High School B	26,663	670	22%	5%
High School C	25,869	109	50%	16%
High School D	3,694,820	2344	47%	19%
High School E	7,525	121	86%	37%
High School F	22,724	214	97.4	43%

Source: US Census Bureau. (2000). Table DP-1 Profile of General Demographic Characteristics 2000.

Table 6.13 Student achievement data

Institution	School API index	English language learners
High School A	631	380
High School B	616	302
High School C	598	360
High School D	766	113
High School E	552	413
High School F	525	1627

Source: California Department of Education http://data1.cde.ca.gov/dataquest/

district. The other five schools are regular public high schools serving particular communities.

The six high-school Spanish heritage programs

As was reported by respondents to the *Survey of Instructional Practices in Secondary and Postsecondary Spanish Heritage Programs*, the high schools visited offer an ordered set of courses for heritage speakers that include at least two levels. As Table 6.14 makes clear, these courses are taught primarily by US Latinos, but also by Anglo-Americans who acquired Spanish as a second language. Only 2 non-US Latinas of the 15 teachers at the six schools are involved in heritage language teaching. At High Schools C, E, and F, Anglo-American teachers serve in the role of primary (or only) teachers of heritage language speakers.

Although all courses are year-long courses, levels and content vary widely across the six schools. For example, at High School D, courses for heritage speakers are called *bilingual Spanish*, not because it is a course taught in two languages, but because the students are considered to be bilingual in Spanish and English. A course labeled SNL1 (Spanish as a Native Language) in Table 6.14, for example, might assume very sophisticated speaking skills on the part of entering students and serve as a pre-AP Spanish language experience. This is the case for SNL1 at High School E. On the other hand, a very similar label and number may also be given to a course designed to serve as a dead-end option for non–college-prep Latinos. At High School A, for example, Native Speaker 1 (NS1) is a remedial course that enrolls both newly arrived immigrant students from Mexico who have low literacy skills as well as second- and third-generation Latinos who, although highly literate in English, have limited literacy skills in Spanish. Both groups of students, because they are seen as noncollege material, do not move beyond NS1. The companion course, NS2, is a college-preparatory course designed for newly arrived immigrant students who have attended *secundaria* or *preparatoria* across the border in Mexico.

Table 6.14 Characteristics of Spanish heritage offerings at high schools visited

	Number of individuals teaching in heritage program	Ethnicity of teaching staff	Courses in heritage program	Average Enrollment
High School A	1	1 US Latino	NS1 (remedial) NS2 (college prep)	20
High School B	3	2 US Latino 1 Latino (non-US)	NS1, NS2 NS3, NS4 NS5, NS6 AP Language AP Literature	38
High School C	1	1 Anglo-American	Bilingual Spanish1 Bilingual Spanish2 Bilingual Spanish3 Bilingual Spanish4 5 (AP Language)	30
High School D	4	2 US Latino 1 Anglo-American	NS1, NS2, NS3 AP Language AP Literature	28
High School E	2	1 Anglo American 1 US Latino	SNL1 (pre-AP) SNL2 (AP Language)	35
High School F	5	1 Anglo-American 3 US Latino 1 Latino (non-US)	NS1, NS2, NS3 AP Language AP Literature	30

At High Schools C and F, newly arrived, highly literate immigrant students are immediately placed in AP language or literature. As a result, regular heritage courses are often given a low priority. At High School F, for example, which has a non-Latino enrollment of only 2%, the regular courses, NS1, NS2, and NS3, are small and intended for students described as *los más pochitos*. That is, for students whose Spanish is characterized by variety of stigmatized contact features. As the program director put it,

> That's for the... that's for the ones, the *más pochitos*. You know. So that they could understand, but they've been schooled mainly in English. They've been schooled in English. Or they've lost the Spanish. And sometimes in a family one will maintain and one will have lost it for... Or that they can understand it maybe but they don't want to speak it? Or that they just test lower when in our writing test. They don't write anything or they write very broken, or they write a small amount. (Program Director, High School F)

At High School F, the faculty teaches many sections of AP language and literature. It is this aspect of the program and the fact that newly arrived Mexican students experience very high levels of success in taking AP examinations that make the teaching staff at High School F the most proud. Much less time and attention, therefore, is given to students, who because they have been educated in English from an early age, are not seen as capable of reaching the required AP levels.

At five of the schools (High Schools A, B, C, D, and E), heritage and nonheritage students are enrolled in both AP language and AP literature. In some schools (High School D), heritage students are the minority in AP courses. At High Schools B, C, and E, however, only two or three nonheritage students enroll as such in AP language and literature. A common factor at all six high schools is that AP classes are primarily populated by the particular group of students that has the highest status.

Enrollment and language requirements vary greatly at the six institutions studied. At High School D, the magnet school, all students are required to take 3 years of a foreign language. Most heritage speakers, therefore, enroll in NS1 and NS2 and AP language. At High School B, on the other hand, students, regardless of actual proficiency, are generally expected to take the courses in order. Freshmen heritage students enroll in NS1 and NS2 and sophomores enroll in NS3 and NS4, and it is only seniors who enroll in AP language. Exceptions were reported, but these appear to be rare.

In sum, classroom observations at six high schools and interviews with teaching staff at each school confirms our interpretation of survey data regarding courses offered for heritage students at the high-school level. The terms *first year* and *second year* used in the survey as well as the actual titles given to courses at different schools do not reveal the complexity of existing Spanish heritage language courses currently offered at the high-school level. Nor do they indicate their relationship to traditional foreign language courses. Programs at each of the schools visited appear to be a product of specific local conditions and expectations, institutional history, majority/minority relations, and personalities and ideologies.

Origin and establishment of heritage language programs

In an attempt to obtain a greater understanding of the local conditions and expectations that surround heritage language programs, we asked all individuals interviewed to share with us the history of the program at their institution. Individuals currently teaching at High Schools A, D, and E had little information about the original perceived need for the program, the activities surrounding the establishment of the program, or administrative responses. Teaching staff at the three other institutions (High Schools B, C, and F), however, were themselves closely involved in the establishment of the programs.

In the case of High School B, the current program coordinator was hired to take on the responsibility of teaching in the program once it was established. He recalled that the program began around 1985 because the Spanish teacher was having problems with the heritage students. At the time, nonheritage students and heritage students were brought together in a special program designed to provide intensive Spanish instruction for nonheritage students and intensive English instruction for newly arrived students. However:

> Nonnative speakers (NNS) always felt threatened by the native speakers (NS) because they weren't fluent. And when I got here it was the end of the program, and the kids didn't want to be with the Anglo kids, and the Anglo's didn't want to be with the Latino Kids anymore... She [the woman who started the program] was frustrated because when she was teaching, the kids would correct her, you don't say it that way, and that's not the way you say it, or that's incorrect. And some of the kids were from [city across the border] and they knew what they were talking about, so she hated that... She never taught the NS, she gave it to an NS teacher... Well, I was that NS teacher, and it was my first job, so of course I would take them, I didn't know what was going on at the time, so I took them like a regular class but all done in Spanish. In other words it was in Spanish for NS, and so I taught them about history and other things to try to stimulate their interest in learning, and more about their background. (Teacher 1, High School B)

At the other two high schools (C and F), the programs were started by Anglo-American women who continue to teach heritage courses themselves. At High School F, the program director redesigned AP language courses so that she could attract newly arrived, educated students from Mexico. She expanded the number of AP courses taught each year, arguing that ESL enrollment and low GPAs should not exclude Spanish-speaking students who could excel in AP Spanish courses. At High School C, the teacher who established the program sought to meet the specific needs of heritage students who were then enrolled in Spanish classes designed for foreign language learners. She recalled that initially it was hard to make the administration understand why it was important to separate students. They worried that separating students was equivalent to tracking. Eventually, however, she was given approval:

> Well, after I did the research I talked to the principal about it and I was given approval to go ahead and make these changes. And I think also that the curriculum committee helped because when they came to observe they really liked the fact that we were dealing with the needs of the students. So, that helped a lot. I got support from them. And, um, of course the teachers in my department are all in favor of it because they know how hard it is to teach a class of beginning level 1 Spanish when you have mixed people in there, you know? You either get a group that's completely bored and like, "I know this already." Or else you go too fast and then you lose the other ones, so it really helps everybody in the department to make special classes for the Spanish speakers. (Teacher, High School C)

Overall, the recollections of three individuals at three different high schools about the conditions that led to the establishment of separate heritage and foreign language classes suggest that the circumstances encountered by these teachers were congruent with those reported in the literature. What has not been reported in the literature extensively is the position of the founder of the program at High School F, who has struggled to expand the AP language and literature programs to provide arriving immigrant students with courses appropriate to their Spanish language academic backgrounds and intellectual development. Program structures at all six high schools that were part of the study, however, suggest that, in California, heritage language teaching has come to be closely identified with AP instruction.

Views of students' proficiency

When asked to describe students' language proficiency, teaching staff interviewed at all six high schools revealed unfavorable views about the varieties of Spanish spoken by students. They also revealed a limited familiarity with bilingualism and language contact. For example, when asked to describe the language proficiency of the students when they enter the program, a teacher at High School D described it as

> "Kitchen Spanish," a colleague's term that I use because I have never heard another term that is more accurate and descriptive at the same time. The students can talk about food and household tasks; they can follow and sometimes participate in the types of conversations that might take place around the dinner table; but they typically do not have command of the academic register in Spanish. Some may lack confidence and be very reluctant to speak in Spanish. They typically understand more than they speak and may be able to read, but have not generally had any instruction in writing. (Teacher, High School D)

Similarly, at the high school in which sections of AP Spanish were increased, the teaching staff made a clear distinction between well-educated Mexican students and students who have been raised in this country. The program coordinator described higher-level students as follows:

> If they come with schooling from Mexico they tend to be OK and they're strong, the vocabularies are really astounding ... The same student who, in English, if you have a conversation seems just kinda little dull, you have the same kind of conversation in Spanish and the student is ... handles complexities and has satire and irony and is very bright and has a sparkle. And a lot of time we don't get to see that, if we don't talk to them in Spanish. It's hard to be charming when you're struggling to find the word. (Program coordinator, High School F)

Another teacher in the program spoke of the students enrolled in her NS1 Spanish classes for heritage speakers.

> Por ejemplo en la clase que tengo, esta del nivel más bajo, tengo estudiantes que hablan perfectamente español en su casa. Hablan español, pero no saben leer ni escribir nada en español. Y también allí en esta clase tengo estudiantes que no hablan nada de español, y que son como tercera generación yo pienso. No hablan nada ... Pero es que en su casa no hablan español, porque ya los papás hablan inglés. Entonces esos muchachitos hablan inglés en casa también. Pero, no se pueden comunicar con la abuelita, o el abuelito, o la tía abuela. No se pueden comunicar. Y este, entienden algunas frases sencillas ellos, nada más.

> *For example in the class that I have, this one that's the lowest level, I have students that speak Spanish perfectly at home. They speak Spanish, but they don't know how to read or write anything in Spanish. I also have in that class students who don't speak any Spanish at all and that are, I think, third-generation. They don't speak at all. At home they don't speak Spanish because*

> *their parents already speak English. Then these youngsters speak English*
> *at home too. But they can't communicate with the grandfather or the grand-*
> *mother or the great aunt. They can't communicate. And, um, they understand*
> *some simple phrases, that's all.*

In spite of her description of her students' limitations, while visiting her
beginning class, we noticed that she conducted instruction entirely in
Spanish. She did not shift to English at any time for exercises or for instructions. Students seemed, to us, perfectly capable of comprehending Spanish.

At High School E, teachers, while pointing out that there was an enor-
mous range of proficiencies in their students, generalized about characteristic problems as follows:

> A huge problem they have is the use of the *b* and the *v*, and it changes
> the whole – and also, like I said before, a huge thing – they have a
> problem with accents. And they don't realize how it will change the
> whole meaning of what you're saying when one little line ... Um, they
> don't realize how much they know and how much they don't know,
> as far as their Spanish goes. (Teacher, High School E)

Descriptions of student proficiencies offered by interviewees were often
imprecise and impressionistic and appear to collapse differences between
written and spoken language:

> But most of them have their background either with their families,
> their relatives, their friends, um their working. Sometimes they work
> in the field, ... they ... their Spanish is not always the best. They use
> a lot of slang sometimes. That I'm trying to change. Or spelling. I'm
> trying to improve on but that's about it. (Teacher, High School C)

The relationship between good Spanish and family background was
commonly mentioned:

> For some students it [language proficiency] is very poor because they
> were born here and they started learning language at home but at
> school they only learned English, and their parents are of low socioeco-
> nomic status so the parents' Spanish is also not very educated because
> sometimes the parents haven't had the opportunity to go to school ei-
> ther. ... Writing for example, expressing ideas, the lower students don't
> have subject-verb agreement, lack of articles, they don't complete their
> words. (Teacher High School B)

From the above description, for example, it was difficult to ascertain
whether the problem of lack of subject-verb agreement was characteristic of written language and inexperience in editing written language, or
whether some students had only partially acquired Spanish. Since, in our
experience, subject-verb agreement in oral production and the ability to

identify ungrammatical sentences in which there is no such agreement is one of the features that distinguishes heritage students from beginning foreign language learners, we were somewhat baffled by this description. We concluded that the teacher's description of *lower students'* Spanish, rather than a precise portrayal, was more an expression of the teacher's beliefs about the "flawed" nature of Spanish produced by these students.

In sum, in talking about students' proficiencies in Spanish, teachers at the six high schools revealed an ability to differentiate between students who had been educated in Spanish (whose dominant language continued to be Spanish) and students who were dominant in English. They also revealed a lack of familiarity with contact varieties of Spanish and with phenomena such as code-switching and borrowing that are characteristic of such language varieties. They tended to view the presence of these features in students' Spanish as problematic.

Placement procedures

At two of the high schools studied (High Schools A and D), placement is conducted by counselors or vice principals. However, interviewee responses about placement procedures at four high schools provided additional information about the use of writing samples in making decisions about placement. Unfortunately, like descriptions of student proficiency, descriptions of scoring criteria used to place students in classes tended to be imprecise. At High School E, for example, a one-page personal essay is used to divide students into AP and non-AP heritage students. The essay is scored by all members of the teaching staff involved in the AP Spanish program. A holistic scoring process is used and students who "write very broken or write a small amount" are placed in lower sections. At High School E, the senior teacher administers both an oral interview and what he calls a written questionnaire.

> We give them a little written questionnaire, you know, what's your name, you know, ¿Cuál es tu dirección, dónde vives, cuántos años llevas aquí, blah blah blah blah blah. And we give it to them in English and Spanish and the first thing we do is to see what side they go to. And then I give them an oral interview and, depending on how they answer – and a lot of times they play little games and you'll ask them in Spanish and they'll answer you in English and they'll say that they don't understand any Spanish but they don't realize that I'm asking them questions in Spanish. So we do a lot of that. (Teacher 1, High School E)

At High School E, the interview and the questionnaire are used to differentiate between heritage and nonheritage students. Because the two heritage classes are sequential, it is not used to place students in one or the other of the two classes. Any evidence of receptive or productive proficiency results in students' being placed in the heritage sequence.

At High School C, the teacher uses a publisher's test as follows:

> All I really need is their composition on the back because their writing sample . . . I can place them from their writing sample. If they write their paragraphs with a lot of spelling errors, verbs used not correctly, no subjunctive or something, then they belong in the beginning level. If they can write really well, a paragraph well written with fewer errors, then I put them in a higher level, I put them in 3, 4, because they already don't need all that basic spelling. And so I, usually they enter either at 1, 2 . . . or 3, 4 is the most. I have put people into 5 right away if they have had a lot of schooling, and [if] their writing is almost perfect I'll put them up to 5 right away. (Teacher, High School C)

When asked how she places students who appear to have characteristics of level 1–2 as well as levels 3–4 and 5, the teacher explained that study skills and motivation were also important.

> But the problem that I have is, the students like in this, the fifth period class; before this one, a lot of those students did not take the 1–2 level. They write better. But they have no skills, study skills, they have no motivational skills. See, its, in my opinion, it's better to start with 1, 2, because that's where I work with the study skills. . . . So in level 1–2, I can teach them the study skills and that's basically . . . what they need more than anything is learn how to study. Don't know how to study at all. And a lot of the kids that are in the fifth period, they never had me for that; they never had Spanish before so they're, that's why it's so difficult I think. I, the more I'm seeing this the more I'm seeing that there's more to just 1–2 than teaching the grammar and the writing. There's also the teaching of how to study. (Teacher, High School C)

The teacher at High School C also commented that because many of the Spanish speakers are afraid to go into the Spanish speaking courses, teachers of regular courses also administer a written test in their courses to Latino students. In those cases, the teacher explains to students that they belong in heritage classes. However, students are not forced out of regular Spanish instruction although they might become bored with class activities.

Finally, at High School B, although the usual procedure is for entering ninth graders to begin at level 1 and then proceed to levels 2 and 3 and onto the AP level, a writing test is also administered by all teachers to find exceptions. The grading of the test was described as follows:

> The teachers give the students a writing sample, and from there they base their decision, on whether they stay first level because you can't even really make a sentence or spell or whatever, and if she sees they

can spell, she will put them in the second level and then that teacher says they're either overqualified for one group, so she will put them in third year level. It's sort of like tracking, so that is the placement. (Teacher 1, High School B)

As will be noted from these descriptions, interviewees were either unable or unwilling to offer concrete depictions of criteria used for grading written placement samples even when asked to expand on their initial portrayals of the grading process. It appears, moreover, that teachers focus primarily on disfluencies, that is, on features including misspellings, flawed syntax (i.e. broken language, limitations in the use of tenses). From the single mention of errors in the response of the teacher at High School C, it is not possible to determine whether contact features or the presence of nonstandard features typical of many regional varieties of Spanish (e.g. *haiga, truje*) resulted in different levels of placement.

Course and program objectives

Teachers at the six high schools were also asked to share with us objectives for courses as well as objectives for the Spanish heritage program as a whole. In responding to our questions, individuals at five of six high schools listed the specific grammatical points they cover:

The 1-2 level has an introduction to Spanish grammar for the students, um, we usually do, we do all the tenses except we don't really go into the subjunctives too much, that's in the next level. But we do, you know, the present, the past, the future, the conditional, . . . commands, present subjunctive is all done in 1 year. For the native speakers, but I also put in all of the cultural things that is not being done in a regular one class. (Teacher, High School C)

Or they offered a description of course content in general:

Course content includes work on sentence structure, paragraph writing, accent marks, and grammar. (Teacher, High School A)

When we pushed them to be more precise, most interviewees struggled to communicate standards of desired performance. A teacher at High School E, for example, referred to levels in the Mexican educational system as norms that he hoped students would reach.

Manipulate Spanish grammar on the par with second or third year *secundaria*, speak, read, and write on par with the second or third year *secundaria*. So the norm would be *secundaria*. (*Uh-huh. Ok, anything else?*) Ah for 2SB probably the norms go up, I want them at *preparatoria* level. Um, we spend a lot of time correcting the common errors, the *b* and the *v*, um, local usages of grammar that are understood but incorrect,

> grammatically speaking. We do spend a lot of time with that. Just a lot of time with just where the accents go – all that kinda stuff that the kids don't get. (Teacher, High School E)

Other individuals simply spoke about the broad goals of heritage language instruction in the lives of students:

> At the end of the program the students should be able to be successful in college. OK? Because it goes for depth. If you can handle depth in one subject you can handle depth in other subjects. (Teacher, High School F)

And

> appreciate their culture, learn a little bit about their language, their Spanish language and . . . appreciate the fine points of learning a language. And raise their self-esteem. (Teacher, High School C)

In one case, an individual sought to combine a very specific course-focused goal to broader objectives:

> The main objective of the program for native speakers is for them to be able to conduct literary analysis in Spanish. They should be able to carry out high-level academic discussions in Spanish. They should be comfortable expressing and supporting their opinions. The goal is AP Spanish Lit, because it serves as a confidence-builder for many kids who would otherwise never take an AP course. It is hoped that the year following AP Lit, students will take one or more related courses, AP history, art, English. (Teacher, High School D)

Finally, at least one individual at each school talked about students' bettering themselves:

> Wanting very much for students to elevate their colloquial Spanish to academic Spanish, the focus of this program is on reading and writing – much more so than the regular Spanish 1 curriculum. (Teacher, High School A)

In terms of the four goals for heritage language instruction (Valdés, 1995) – (1) the acquisition of a standard dialect, (2) the transfer of reading and writing abilities across languages, (3) the expansion of bilingual range, and (4) the maintenance of the heritage language – we conclude that, as was the case for survey respondents, teachers at all six high schools primarily focus on the acquisition of the standard dialect. Of the 15 people observed and/or interviewed, 13 were involved in teaching students grammar or grammatical terminology, correct spelling, and accent placement. However, three or four individuals were much more focused on reading and writing objectives related to the transfer of reading and writing skills, and to objectives related to the maintenance of a heritage language (e.g. the study of culture, development of vocabulary). Finally, three interviewees emphasized that their principal objective went much beyond the study of Spanish. They wanted heritage courses to offer students academic skills that they could later use to be successful in college, and they wanted to increase students' pride and self-esteem.

In sum, the study and program objectives at the six high schools revealed that teachers are primarily focused on just two of the four goals previously identified for heritage language instruction (Valdés, 1995). However, the study also reveals, perhaps, the need to expand the list of these goals to a total of six: (1) the acquisition of a standard dialect, (2) the transfer of reading and writing abilities across languages, (3) the expansion of bilingual range, (4) the maintenance of the heritage language, (5) the development of academic skills, and (6) the increase of students' pride and self-esteem.

Instructional practices

To explore the kinds of teaching practices used in the teaching of heritage students, survey respondents were given a list of practices common in foreign language teaching at both the elementary and more advanced levels. The practices were grouped under the original four instructional goals. They were asked to rate each practice as effective, not effective, or not attempted with heritage language students. Interviews and observations of 15 teachers at six high schools provided many more details about instructional practices relating to some of the originally identified four goals, as well as practices supporting the expansion of the original list to six goals for instruction.

Table 6.15 provides a list of seven goals: the expanded list of six goals and a seventh goal focused on AP preparation. It also lists specific instructional practices observed under each goal. It is important to emphasize that, on this list, instructional practices are grouped under the specific objectives described by the teachers.

As will be noted in Table 6.15, Goal 1, which includes instructional practices aimed at maintaining language beyond the school setting, was modified as "Language and Culture Maintenance." The modification includes pedagogies aimed at helping students to become aware of Latin-American/Spanish traditions (High School C) and to develop an identification with cultural practices outside their immediate family and community context. For several teachers, activities centering on this goal included having students engage in the analysis of contemporary protest songs (Teacher 2, High School B) and in the examination and production of artistic products (Teacher, High School C).

Table 6.15 Observed and described teaching practices and classroom activities listed under six instructional goals

Goal	Activities/practices
1. Language (culture) maintenance	Reading of legends (Maya, Aztec, Latin America, Spain) Study of Latin American countries Analysis of contemporary songs of protest Study of vocabulary drawn from songs of protest Examination of artistic products Involvement in artistic production
2. Expansion of bilingual range	Direct study of vocabulary
3. Transfer of reading and writing	In-class diary and journal writing Sharing of diary writing with whole class Peer editing of compositions Group research/writing projects Mini-lessons on grammatical "problems" found in compositions Extensive reading (free voluntary reading) Intensive reading (assigned reading) Retelling of reading
4. Acquisition of standard dialect	Drafting, writing, and rewriting of compositions by students to correct errors Study of spelling Study of rules for placing accents Grammar explanations and exercises • Study of verb conjugations in different tenses • Identification of various tenses in texts • Using particular tenses in diary entries • Oral and written drills on particular grammatical structures • Use of workbooks with grammar and spelling exercises Correction of selected common errors by teacher in front of the whole class Form-focused instruction (instruction that teaches grammar by commenting on particular forms in texts)
5. AP preparation	Literature AP • Instruction providing context and background for works of literature • Reading of works of literature • Silent individual reading • In-class reading aloud • Literary analysis and discussion

(Continued)

Table 6.15 (*Continued*)

Goal	Activities/practices

	• Viewing of video versions of works of literature
	• Fill-in-the-blank responses to readings
	• Study of metrics (rhyme schemes in poetry)
	• In-depth discussion of literary vocabulary (tropes, figures of speech)
	• Writing in literature journals (response to works read)
	• Writing of summaries on works of literature
	Language AP
	  • Listening comprehension based on AP materials
	  • Instruction on essay organization
	  • Vocabulary review
	Oral presentations based on picture sequences

6. General academic skills	Extensive reading Exercises to develop strategies for memorizing vocabulary Frequent in-class listening comprehension activities to develop focus and attention Development of public-speaking skills – individual and group presentations Writing exercises to develop writing fluency
7. Community building and increasing self-esteem	Classroom exercises and activities to teach mutual respect

As will also be noted in Table 6.15, in comparison to other goals, very little attention was given to Goal 2, the expansion of bilingual range, per se. One or two individuals mentioned the need for expanding the vocabulary of heritage students. Overall, teachers did not display an understanding of their students as bilingual individuals who might be either English or Spanish dominant. Moreover, they did not appear to be familiar with the literature on heritage language students or with the *ACTFL Foreign Language Standards*, that is, with material that might have led them to develop pedagogies designed to expand students' strengths in areas in which they were limited.

The listing of practices in Table 6.15 makes clear that most instructional practices were centered around (1) the transfer of reading and writing, (2) the acquisition of the standard dialect, and (3) the preparation of students for the AP examinations in Spanish literature and language. Some of the practices used in the teaching of reading and writing (e.g. diary and journal writing) are typical of those used in English language arts courses. Others are typical of those used with students of Spanish as a foreign language (e.g. study of verb conjugations, error correction, grammatical explanations.) All practices used in AP classes are also utilized with foreign language students who prepare for these examinations.

Included in the listing of practices in Table 6.15 are a number of activities and classroom practices that merit more extensive discussion because of the unique characteristics of heritage language students. These include (1) the language used in instruction, (2) the direct teaching of grammar, (3) extensive reading, (4) attention given to general academic skills, and (5) the building of community and increasing self-esteem.

Language used in instruction

Except for an occasional response in English to particular students or a rule generalization in a grammar class (High School E), all instruction we observed occurred in Spanish. Students were expected to respond in Spanish. However, during class discussions, when students could not immediately access a required word or phrase, they often switched momentarily into English. In some classes, the teacher or other students would provide the needed language, but, in others, attention was directed to the ideas being exchanged, and no attempt was made to recast the student's English utterance in Spanish.

The direct teaching of grammar

The direct teaching of grammar appears to be central to heritage language instruction at the high-school level. The study of grammar is embedded in course syllabi and course objectives as part of the core curriculum that students must cover. In all cases, this core consists of topics traditionally presented to foreign language learners (e.g. verb tenses, direct and indirect object pronouns, contrasts between preterite and imperfect). For AP language classes, attention is given to the grammar points to be tested on the examination itself. The amount of time devoted to grammar explanations and grammar exercises, however, varies widely. For example, Teacher 1 at High School D, who teaches heritage students, no longer teaches grammar directly as an end in itself. She commented that she found that students made the same errors in their writing after direct instruction in grammar as before. She now waits until students have completed several writing assignments to address common errors.

The senior teacher at High School E, however, still believes strongly in teaching grammar:

> A lot of people say, you know, good 'ol grammar like we got when we were kids, you're not supposed to do that any more. Well, I found that no, it works quite well. And do you do it inductively or deductively? Pick a day. I'll do it. [laughter] I mean, it depends on the group and that kind of stuff. (Teacher 1, High School E)

Our observation of this teacher's classes revealed that this teacher continues to use materials produced for foreign language learners to teach direct and indirect objects, verb conjugations, and tenses to heritage learners. The teacher does not build on students' implicit grammar systems but assumes that, like foreign language learners, heritage learners must begin, for example, by memorizing verb endings.

Teacher 2 at High School B, who was a heritage learner herself, has a very different position on the teaching of grammar to heritage speakers. Speaking about her own experience in studying Spanish, she recalled:

> Well when I first started, I liked it because I thought oh I know Spanish and it will be easy, but when I took it at the college level, I realized it was actually so much harder for me a native speaker than a nonnative speaker learning Spanish for the first time. I knew Spanish already, it was like the information had been placed in my head but I didn't know where I'd gotten it from, so when I started studying it, the grammar, oh my I thought I was going to go crazy, I used to cry because I didn't get the accents, and I couldn't hear the stress . . . It was a terrible time with it. (Teacher 2, High School B)

Asked about what her students would be able to do after they finished her class, she responded:

> Um, they will be able to . . . gosh . . . write more effectively, speak more fluently, definitely read a lot better. They will definitely be able to have some understanding of accents, some understanding of the structure of preterite and subjunctive tense. I don't think they will every really get it though. I try to go more in depth with them and explain the structure, I mean they know that it is in the past, and they know how to conjugate the words correctly, but when I try to do the preterite chart with them as I call it, I did the *yo tu, él, ustedes*, they were like what are you doing? I know what I'm doing already why are you trying to complicate it for me? I felt so helpless and hopeless, because my other foreign students are like oh yeah we understand that, because they got it last year in Year 1 with the present tense, and they've seen the chart already so they know how to conjugate the words with the right endings. They know what it means to conjugate.

As a heritage learner who had experienced frustration because her teachers were not aware of the difference between knowledge of a grammatical meta-language and knowledge based on an implicit, unconscious grammar, Teacher 2 was very aware that pedagogies used with nonspeakers of the language can confuse heritage speakers.

> And as a native speaker you don't know that [what it means to conjugate], and when I was thrown into a third-year class at the high-school

level my junior year because second year was too easy and one of my fellow students asked me hey how do you conjugate this, and I was like what is conjugate? I'd never heard of that word before. You know conjugate, *hablar yo hablo*. I was like, OK, give me a sentence, give me a sentence. And they were like, how do you say this? And I'd get it, like perfect, because I'd know what everything meant. And that is how I see my students, who are like, why are you complicating things for me?

In sum, at all six high schools visited, we observed the teaching of grammar to heritage language learners. Teachers taught grammar using materials and exercises normally used with foreign language learners, sometimes with a few adaptations. Except for Teacher 2 at High School B, no one mentioned challenges or difficulties in using traditional foreign language pedagogies with heritage students. We suspect that difficulties experienced by students – because they are seen as being less prepared academically than foreign language students – are attributed to deficient study habits or lack of motivation rather than to inappropriate teaching practices.

Extensive reading

We identified extensive reading as one of the practices recently proposed in foreign language instruction (Day and Bamford, 1998) that appeared to be quite successful with heritage language learners. Two of the teachers of a total of 15 (Program coordinator, High School F, and Teacher 2, High School D) use extensive reading in their classes. Teacher 2, High School D, requires 50 pages a week of voluntary free reading, on which she then holds individual conferences with students. She views this as essential to students' becoming good readers in Spanish. The program coordinator at High School F, by comparison, views reading as important, not only in AP language and literature but in building students' study skills across a lifetime.

And I – the idea is that – I push reading, reading and this gets out. I have kids from other classes, kids, a whole bunch of students will come in and ask for books and then they'll want to go on to *Los de abajo* You know that's a really good book – it's not on AP reading list but it's a book that a lot of students like, especially boys. It's exciting. We read *Vianey Desmundo*, which is like a novel. You know, a lot of different books that I just have, *Pepita Jiménez* and things like that, that I think teenagers might like. So I push those and kids come in and I think that helps coz they get the idea of reading, so when they go into AP literature it's not like "Oh we have to read a whole book?" There's a kind of a little base. And we could do that more. We could do that more. We just need more books. (Program coordinator, High School F)

This particular teacher uses extensive reading in her ESL classes with the same students she teaches in AP Spanish courses. She wants students to "see reading as a pastime, as a hobby, as a desirable thing." She sees herself as working to get students away from television and believes that teachers can actually have an influence on young people.

> Yes. Its real common, every year I just brainwash them and by the end of the year, *oh yo casi nunca miro tele* "I almost never watch TV." And it's almost a point of pride where at the beginning it's "yeah I watch a lot of TV and I'm proud of it" – where it becomes a thing that you do behind closed doors in shame and watching TV. But you know you can, they do believe adults. It's not true that adults can't convince students. (Program coordinator, High School F)

For this teacher, reading is the most important academic skill that students can acquire. She sees it as the secret to future success and achievement and is willing to spend, not only class-time, but her own funds to collect hundreds of volumes of adolescent fiction in both English and Spanish to attract students to reading. In observing the eagerness with which students in this program borrowed books from the teachers' library, and in examining the extended book reports produced by such students, we conclude that a broader implementation and study of extensive reading as a means of providing heritage students with a quantity of rich language input in both colloquial and academic registers and styles deserves increased attention.

General academic skills

With very few exceptions, teachers at all six high schools expressed concern about the motivation and academic preparation of certain groups of heritage speakers. At some schools (e.g. High School F), the problem students are those arriving from Mexico with little or no schooling. While at other schools (e.g. High Schools C and D), the problem students are second- and third-generation students who, although raised in this country, appeared not to be highly motivated to do well in school. These students are seen as having discipline problems (High School D), short attention spans and low motivation (High School C), have little support at home (High School B), are slow learners (High School B), are unwilling or incapable of doing homework (High School A), and as needing to be entertained (High School A). As a result of these views and concerns, a number of teachers consider it is important to use teaching practices that will help students to develop a higher self-esteem, more confidence in speaking in public, greater fluency in writing, and general study skills. Even though classroom activities carried out with these goals in mind may be very similar to activities carried out in language classrooms in general, we list them separately here because teachers at High Schools B, C, and F identified them specifically as intended to enhance students' academic preparation and study skills more broadly.

Building community and increasing self-esteem

At many high schools in California, heritage language classes bring together newly arrived immigrants and long-time US-identified students together. Because of differences in language backgrounds and life experiences, there are often conflicts between these groups of students.[2] At some high schools (e.g. High Schools A, E, and F) this problem has been solved by placing newly arrived students in AP classes and second- and third-generation students in lower-level heritage classes. At High School B, a school located on the border, Teacher 1 described problems that the school had experienced in attracting teachers to work with heritage speakers. He commented that students do not "have stability at home" because the parents may be on the other side of the border. As a result, students come to school wanting to hang around. For teachers this is a challenge because students appear to be unmotivated. They seem to have no discipline and no study skills, so teachers that expect students "to come in, sit down, and take notes" have a problem. Teacher 1 argues that teachers have to be willing to "break the mold, and inconvenience" themselves. "In order for the kids to get interested ... you have to get out of your shell."

Teacher 1 found himself breaking the mold by having to take time out to build community among students.

> I first got the class at the beginning of the school year. They were all critical of each other, and that is what they see out in the community. And this is what level? This is third level, and they were all judgmental of each other. It was horrible. They were picking on each other. Foul language was rampant in the classroom, and that is one thing I do not tolerate and I just couldn't believe what I was seeing, so I had to develop activities for how was I [going to] attack these kids, and that was how I felt, How do I attack these kids? Because it was on a personal level, and they were getting down and personal and on an emotional level with one another. So then my first two weeks of activities was solely tied into their emotional past, their emotional experiences, value, human dignity, all those things entitled, and it made those kids stop. Because I said to them wait a minute, if you call her *pinche gorda* or whatever, you know that has consequences, maybe not apparently. You think it is funny, but why are you saying that, not so much focusing on what you said, but why are you saying it? What motivates you to say that? Let's talk about you. And I would focus on them and why people are abusive to one another, and it seemed like before they got here it they thought it was OK to say *pinche huey* ... *pinche* whatever. Why are you saying those things? Why are you degrading another human being? And those activities focused, tunneled; you know, gave me a funneling

effect and started getting the kids to respect each other and value each other and be respectful with each other and with me as well. (Teacher 1, High School B)

Teacher 1 recalled that initially students were ruthless and "would comment on each other's Spanish as well." There was a point, however, when he felt that things had changed:

I think that it is inherent in teenagers to be cruel, but the activities that focused, that helped me the most was to analyze it and give everyone an equal platform to value everybody. It was incredible after the activities that I did like death and dying, *abuelita abuelito* and then we had a death last year, of a kid who was drag racing and I brought a picture of him in and the feeling that you felt, and everyone came together and everyone was very sad and went to church and everything... Those were the activities [that] were the best. I would go home and say yes they got it.

To build community, however, he confessed that he had to forget grammar and canonical literature. He had to find literature that students could identify with. He also had to get to students to see that misfortunes were not funny, to identify with others, and to value other human beings. Teacher 1 concluded that heritage students require that teachers create a sense of family and discipline in which everyone is accountable for their actions. After that is in place, "you can do whatever you want and take them anywhere."

Textbooks used

The textbooks used in the six high schools included two books intended for heritage speakers (*Tesoro literario, Español para los hispanos*), two books intended for both heritage and foreign language students (*Avanzando, Aproximaciones*) and a number of books intended for foreign language students (*Dime, Encuentros maravillosos, Pasos y puentes, Leyendas latinoamericanas, Leyendas mexicanas, Leyendas de España, Album*) and miscellaneous texts and workbooks typically used in AP preparation. A number of individuals primarily followed a single text (e.g. *Dime* at High School C, and *Aproximaciones* by Teacher 3 at High School F). Most teachers, however, used sections and readings from a variety of different texts.

When asked about the contents of an ideal textbook for their program and students, teachers listed artwork, history, prewriting activities, more grammar exercises, and readings appropriate for teenagers. There was no mention of a need for books that present grammatical explanations directed specifically at heritage learners, exercises designed to tap into their unconscious grammars, or readings drawing from a variety of disciplines.

Outcomes

When asked about evidence of their program's success, few individuals interviewed gave a precise answer. Two individuals (the program coordinator at High School F and Teacher 1 at High school D) viewed passing rates on the AP examinations as evidence of their students' and their program's effectiveness. Two other teachers (Teacher, High School C, and Teacher 1, High School B) spoke of success in different terms. The teacher at High School C considered herself and her program successful if students improved "either in attentiveness, arriving on time, being ready, doing their best." She expected that if these behaviors were in place, students would achieve both in her classes and in other classes. Teacher 1 at High School B considered himself successful if his students became "lifetime learners" and were "motivated to read more and became very proud of the skills they possess."

We found it interesting that we were given no examples of the progress made by second- and third-generation heritage speakers in terms of language by any of the persons observed and interviewed. However, we found this seeming lack of interest to be consistent with teachers' views about the quality of bilingual students' Spanish as well as their evaluation of these youngsters' academic preparedness. Teachers who described non-AP heritage students as unmotivated, having a short attention span, and unconcerned about grades were naturally delighted when they saw growth and progress in these areas. On the other hand, if teachers simply looked for indicators of growth and progress such as those used with foreign language learners, growth in heritage speakers would be hard to recognize. Such indicators (e.g. ability to list verb endings in particular tenses) might not reveal very much about speakers who have acquired Spanish as a first language. Overall, language teachers appeared to know very little about indicators of growth and progress that might point to outcomes more closely aligned with language maintenance or the development of bilingual range in these young speakers.[3] They were not prepared to look for increased use of the language outside of school or the beginning acquisition of other registers and styles.

Staff characteristics

As we pointed out in Table 6.14, of the 15 individuals observed and interviewed in our study of six high schools, only 3 Anglo-American teachers were involved in heritage language teaching; 10 teachers were Mexican American, and 2 were Latinos raised and educated in Latin American countries. None of the 15 individuals teaching heritage courses received training or preparation in addressing the needs of bilingual learners. One teacher (Program coordinator, High School F) had been exposed to the notion of special classes for heritage speakers through her roommate in college who was a teaching assistant for a heritage course at the college level. Another teacher (Teacher, High School C), when faced with the need to implement separate courses for foreign language and heritage speakers, carried out research by examining available textbooks. Four teachers had been heritage learners in the very high schools in which they were teaching. These individuals, while very sympathetic to the needs and frustrations of their students when studying grammar, had not received the necessary background in the study of bilingualism and language contact that would have helped them make sense of their students' apparent limitations.

Preparing students for life outside of school

When we talked about the study we had conducted of Latino professionals in California and their need for Spanish and asked what they thought their program might do to prepare students for life outside of school, teachers had very little to say. It was very difficult for them to think outside of their own areas of activity. Some suggested that the school run a special set of career preparation workshops or activities, others pointed out that students needed to enter college and then the appropriate professional schools, and a few repeated the usual generalizations about the need for bilingual professionals in a state with a high Spanish-speaking population. One individual (who primarily focused on grammar in his classes) conjectured that reading and writing would be very important for future professionals. Several others concurred with the opinion expressed by Teacher 1, High School B, when we asked in what ways Native Speaker programs should have as their goal the preparation of Latino professionals:

> To be proficient, to be proficient in Spanish, and to just make them feel proud, because a lot of them feel shame for speaking Spanish, make them feel proud of who they are and where they come from, and they are worth twice as more as a monolingual, and make sure they have pride in who they are. And a lot of times, it is easier said than done, a lot of outside forces put them down, and then they start believing it. And these teenage years are so vulnerable, one word can make the difference. (Teacher 1, High School B)

For this teacher, and those who agreed with him, the production of Latino professionals does not primarily involve language. It involves giving students a foundation and a belief in themselves that can help them succeed in whatever they undertake.

For this teacher and others like him, the goals of building community and self-esteem are most important for heritage learners. Nevertheless, these very same teachers in spite of their awareness of the circumstances in which their students live also work in a context in which views of language correctness are a part of their professional identities. Not surprisingly, like others of his colleagues at the six schools, Teacher 1 from High School B was also convinced that his students needed a standard Spanish vocabulary and standard grammar in order to speak correctly.

Tensions, challenges, and recommendations

In concluding our interviews, we asked teachers to talk about tensions and challenges that they continued to encounter. We also asked them to formulate three recommendations for other teachers who were interested in starting heritage programs. As might be expected, in offering recommendations for other teachers, interviewees revealed many of their own concerns as well. In terms of tensions and challenges, teachers mentioned the need for stronger administrative support, the need for more books, and concern about teacher turnover. They also talked about the school's low expectations for heritage students and the struggle they faced in raising money for students who could not afford to pay for AP examinations. At one school, for example, the students themselves raised the funds for the examinations, and, at another, teachers had lobbied the district to contribute five dollars for each student's examination. In making recommendations to other teachers, interviewees emphasized that monolingual (newly arrived) and bilingual students (second- and third-generation) should be separated. They also recommended that programs be allowed to grow slowly and that only experienced teachers be given classes for heritage speakers. Most important, they stressed that teachers need to become familiar with students that they teach. The Anglo-American teacher at High School C emphasized the importance of understanding the difference between students who are heritage students from poor families and ordinary foreign language students:

> They may not remember the grammar point but they are working harder... They need a lot more human element I think. I feel that they – they need to feel love from their teacher and acceptance and expectations. And I – I – they don't; it's not just like you say go home and study and they're gonna go do it. They have to be motivated. And for a non-Spanish speaker you can say, yeah, you gotta go home and study, and they'll probably go home and study, but these kids have responsibilities. They work. They have to take care of other children. They have to take care of family members. They sometimes – they are the only ones who are the [English] speakers in the family. They have to go with mom when she has a doctor's appointment; they gotta go and they gotta talk. I mean, I understand all this. And I feel that if they can just get the opportunity, then they can succeed. And many, many of them do.

For this teacher, as well as for other heritage language teachers, the challenge of working with heritage students in secondary language programs involves factors that go far beyond language. The mix of students in classrooms is one factor, as is the attitude of the teacher toward this group of students. For the teachers most committed to the students, holding students accountable for their actions while recognizing their value to the community as a whole was essential to helping them succeed, not just in Spanish, but in school and in life beyond the Spanish classroom.

Heritage Programs at the High School Level: A Summary

The study of six high-school-level Spanish heritage language programs suggests that an expectation that formal language programs as currently configured can and will contribute to Spanish language maintenance is misguided. Schools do not see their role as providing support for such efforts. Rather, they see themselves as engaged in the teaching of a core curriculum centering on the study of grammar and literature. The most they can aspire to is having students test well on advanced placement examinations designed to offer college credit to traditional students of foreign language who enter college and university departments of foreign language. What is clear is that, in spite of extensive campaigns to change the teaching of foreign languages in this country carried out by professional organizations such as American Council on the Teaching of Foreign Languages (ACTFL) and the American Association of Teachers of Spanish and Portuguese (AATSP), standards-based teaching designed for heritage students is not yet a reality at these six schools. Teachers are not engaged in developing students' interpersonal, interpretive, and presentational communication skills, are not engaged in making connections with other disciplines, nor in making students aware of how first and second languages are acquired and how implicit grammars work. Heritage students are first and foremost high-school students whose success is measured, not by their ability to use Spanish extensively for a variety of purposes, or by the progress they make in expanding their (colloquial and academic) range in two languages, but by their ability to sit quietly in class, to complete assignments, do well on tests and quizzes on aspects of grammar taught to foreign language learners, and, possibly, to speak a variety of Spanish identified by their teachers as the standard. There is a serious disconnect between what counts as success in the high-school context and what those concerned about maintaining heritage languages know is essential for the continued use of those languages over a lifetime.

Notes

1. In the state of California, the Academic Performance Index (API) is calculated on a scale of 200 to 1000 that reflects a school's performance on statewide student assessments including three test components of the Standardized Testing and Reporting (STAR) Programs, as well as the California High School Exit Examination (CAHSEE). The STAR test includes the California Standards Tests (CST),

the California Alternate Performance Assessment (CAPA), and the California Achievement Test (CAT/6) Survey.
2. At many high schools, affiliation with one of two gangs (Norteños and Sureños) is related to recency of arrival. Newly arrived students – whether they join gangs or not – will tend to be sympathetic to Sureños. On the other hand, English-speaking, more acculturated students will be sympathetic to Norteños. Tensions and rivalries between these two groups are often reflected within heritage language classrooms.
3. Teachers' lack of knowledge about language characteristics that might indicate particular types of growth in heritage speakers is directly related to the fact that the study of second-dialect and second-register acquisition is in its infancy in the applied linguistics and the language teaching professions as a whole.

References

Church, A. H. (1993) Estimating the effect of incentives on mail survey response. *Public Opinion Quarterly* 57 (1), 62–79.

Day, R. R., & Bamford, J. (1998) *Extensive Reading in the Second Language Classroom.* Cambridge: Cambridge University Press.

Fischer, L. (2004) Spanish for native speakers (SNS) education: The state of the field. On WWW at http://www.cal.org./hertiage/sns/sns-fieldrpt.htm. Accessed 24.8.2004.

Fox, R. J., Crask, M. R., and Kim, J. (1989) Mail survey response rate: A meta-analysis of selected techniques for inducing response. *Public Opinion Quarterly* 52 (4), 467–91.

James, J. M., and Bolstein, R. (1992) Large monetary incentives and their effect on mail survey response rates. *Public Opinion Quarterly* 56 (4), 442–53.

Kaplowitz, M. D., Hadlock, T. D., and Levine, R. (2004) A comparison of web and mail survey response rates. *Public Opinion Quarterly* 68 (1), 94–101.

Potowski, K. (2003) Chicago's heritage language teacher corps: A model for improving Spanish teacher development. *Hispania* 86 (2), 302–11.

Valdés, G. (1995) The teaching of minority languages as 'foreign' languages: Pedagogical and theoretical challenges. *Modern Language Journal* 79 (3), 299–328.

Chapter 7
Postsecondary Spanish Heritage Programs in California

GUADALUPE VALDÉS, JOSHUA A. FISHMAN, REBECCA
CHÁVEZ and WILLIAM PÉREZ

This chapter presents (1) the results of a survey of instructional practices used in the teaching of Spanish to heritage students in California in post-secondary institutions and (2) the results of the more extensive study involving observations of heritage programs at six colleges/universities in California.

Part I: The Survey of Instructional Practices in Secondary and Postsecondary Spanish Heritage Programs in California

Postsecondary school participants

A list of postsecondary institutions was obtained from the Modern Language Association (MLA), an organization that regularly conducts surveys of foreign language enrollment in institutions of higher education in the United States. The MLA list identified 63 junior colleges, colleges, and universities that had responded affirmatively to questions about heritage program implementation. The schools were identified in a survey the MLA conducted in 2000. We expanded the original list of 63 institutions to include 212 other colleges, universities, and junior colleges listed on the California Department of Education Web site that were not included on the MLA list. We included on our final list all postsecondary institutions that indicated either on their Web site or through further contact via email or phone correspondence that they had a Spanish language program. The final list of postsecondary institutions to which the survey was sent was composed of a total of 173 junior colleges, colleges, and universities.

Data collection

In early November 2001, surveys with self-addressed and prestamped return envelopes were mailed to 173 Spanish language department lead teachers/chairpersons at colleges/universities. In early December 2001, we sent a postcard reminder out to institutions that had not yet responded. In addition, project staff phoned and sent email reminders during the months of December and January. Duplicate packets were sent out in a number of cases. Five individuals elected to complete the survey over the telephone. By the middle of March 2002, responses from a total of 52 colleges/universities had been received. The total response rate was 30%.

In the sections that follow, we describe the results of our survey on current practices in teaching heritage students at the postsecondary level. We include data on practices used in teaching heritage speakers in institutions that offered heritage programs and in institutions that had not instituted such programs.

Demographic profile of sample

Of the 52 postsecondary institutions that completed questionnaires, 35 indicated that they did have heritage language programs/classes for Spanish speakers, and 17 indicated that they did not offer such programs. Of the 52 institutions responding, 33 were from counties with Latino populations above the state mean and 19 were from counties with populations below the state mean.

Of the 35 colleges/universities that offer special or separate courses for heritage students, 16 programs began before 1990, and 19 after 1990. Of the 35 colleges/universities offering special courses in Spanish for heritage students, 43% are small (i.e. 10,000 or less students), 29% are medium sized (10,000–20,000 students), 17% are large (20,000–30,000 students), and 11% are very large (more than 30,000 students). Of the 17 colleges/universities not offering special courses in Spanish for heritage students, 53% are small (i.e. 10,000 or less students), 35% are medium-sized (10,000–20,000 students), 11% are large (20,000–30,000 students), and 0% are very large (more than 30,000 students).

At institutions offering heritage courses, the percentage of heritage students in Spanish language programs varies. However, it is less than one-fourth of the enrollment at 31% of the institutions and less than half of the enrollment at 34% of the 35 institutions. Only 31% of these respondents indicated that heritage student enrollment was greater than half of all students enrolled in the Spanish language program. At 70% of postsecondary institutions without heritage programs, the percentage of heritage students in Spanish language programs also varies. However, it is less than one-fourth of the enrollment at 59% of institutions and less than half of the enrollment at 35% of the 17 institutions. Only 6% of the respondents indicated that they did not have any heritage student enrollment.

Table 7.1 Program levels of colleges/universities offering special courses for heritage students

Level	Percent (No. of programs)
What level(s) and type(s) of courses does your institution currently offer for heritage students?	
First-year Spanish for heritage speakers	45.7 (35)
Second-year Spanish for heritage speakers	57.1 (35)
Composition for heritage speakers	37.1 (35)
Advanced grammar for heritage speakers	40.0 (35)
Oral communication for heritage speakers	20.0 (35)

Number of Spanish language courses offered for heritage students

Colleges and universities offering heritage courses

The total number and the exact levels of courses available for heritage students at postsecondary institutions that offered such courses was also difficult to determine. Table 7.1 shows that 46% of respondents reported offering a first-year Spanish course for heritage students and that 57% of respondents reported offering a second-year course for heritage students. In college/university Spanish departments, *first year* Spanish generally refers to courses that carry a first-year course number (e.g. 1, 101). Moreover, they are generally basic introductory courses usually taken by freshmen. *Second year* courses carry a second-year course number (e.g. 12, 201) and have first-year courses or equivalents as prerequisites. At some institutions (e.g. Stanford University, New Mexico State University), the series of courses designed for heritage students begins at the second-year level. Students' real-life experiences in the language serve as prerequisites to the second-year course rather than enrollment in first-year courses.

Because we did not explain our use of the terms *first year* and *second year* for college-level offerings, we cannot be certain about what respondents meant in checking the options we provided. Interpreting their answers according to the explanation about first- and second-year courses provided earlier, we conclude that 46% of institutions responding offer a course for heritage students that carries a first-year course number and 57% of institutions offer a course that carries a second-year number. We can reach no conclusions, however, about the total number of courses (i.e. semesters, quarters) that make up the heritage sequence or about whether first-year courses are prerequisites to second-year courses at institutions that offer both levels of courses.

We also have many questions about courses beyond the second-year level that were checked by respondents. Again as we did not make clear that our list of courses referred to classes designed exclusively for heritage students, it is not evident whether the 37% of respondents that reported offering composition courses for heritage speakers teach a separate course in composition for such students or whether they simply require heritage students to take a composition course. We have similar concerns about the interpretation of 40% of respondents who claimed to offer advanced grammar for heritage students and 20% of respondents who reported offering oral communication for heritage speakers.

Information about the courses recommended for heritage learners after completing special courses is more easily interpretable. For example, only 18% of respondents reported recommending that students take Spanish conversation courses. This suggests that the majority of responding departments considered heritage students' oral proficiency to be beyond that of conversation courses designed for foreign language learners. Courses in Spanish composition and introductory courses in Spanish literature were recommended by 59% of respondents. This suggests that members of responding departments consider that heritage students need additional work in writing after the sequence for heritage students and that they consider them ready to begin the study of literary texts. Only 32% of respondents consider that heritage students have sufficient preparation to enroll in advanced literature courses in the department.

Colleges and universities not offering heritage courses

In the case of institutions without heritage programs, respondents were asked to check all courses in which heritage learners normally enrolled from a list of typical Spanish department courses. As noted in Table 7.2,

Table 7.2 Program levels of colleges without specialized courses for heritage students

Level	Percent (No. of programs)
At what levels and in which types of courses do heritage students enroll? Which courses combine heritage speakers and traditional foreign language students?	
First-year Spanish	52.9 (17)
Second-year Spanish	70.6 (17)
Writing and composition	52.9 (17)
Advanced grammar	47.1 (17)
Oral communication/conversation	52.9 (17)
Culture and civilization courses	52.9 (17)
Introductory literature courses	52.9 (17)
Advanced literature courses	29.4 (17)

71% of respondents reported that heritage students enroll in second-year Spanish courses. They also reported that students enroll in first-year Spanish (53%), in writing and composition courses (53%), in oral communication/conversation courses (53%), in culture and civilization courses (53%), and in introductory literature courses (53%). Only 29% of respondents reported that heritage students enroll in advanced literature courses in the department.

Placement procedures

Colleges and universities offering heritage courses

Colleges and universities offering heritage courses report that students are placed in heritage courses by advisors and counselors (77%). Students also self-select and enroll in such courses at 74% of institutions responding. Only 31% of departments that offer heritage courses use a general placement examination required of all students taking Spanish for placing heritage students in appropriate courses. At the colleges and universities using a general placement test, only 10 individuals responded to our questions on the usefulness of specific parts of the general examination for the identification of heritage students. Of these 10 respondents, 60% also found the writing sections of the examination to be the most useful. Fifty percent of these same 10 individuals considered sections on grammar and terminology and sections on standard language the most useful for identifying such learners.

Colleges/universities that do not offer heritage programs rarely use a general placement examination intended for placing traditional foreign language learners when attempting to place heritage learners in Spanish classes (Table 7.3). Rather, heritage students are placed in appropriate courses at 82% of these institutions by advisors and counselors. Students also self-select and enroll in Spanish language courses at 71% of institutions responding. In colleges and universities not offering heritage programs, a single individual responded to our questions on the usefulness of specific parts of the general examination for the identification of heritage students. This individual found all parts of the examination equally useful for identifying heritage speakers.

Use of special placement examination for heritage speakers

Colleges and universities offering heritage programs

Only a very small number of colleges and universities offering heritage programs reported using Spanish placement examinations for heritage speakers. Only four respondents (11%) responded affirmatively to our question about the use and design of a special placement examination developed for heritage students (Table 7.4). Of the four persons responding affirmatively to this question, 100% measured students' ability to identify and produce specific grammatical forms. Measures of proficiency

Table 7.3 Placement procedures

Procedure	Colleges offering heritage programs	Colleges not offering heritage programs
	Percent (No. of programs)	Percent (No. of programs)
a. How are students placed in the course(s) designed for heritage students?		
Placed by advisors and counselors	77.1 (35)	
Self-select	74.3 (35)	
Transfer at recommendation of teacher	48.6 (35)	
General placement examination	31.4 (35)	
Language survey	11.4 (35)	
Outside assessment/placement or teacher interview	5.7 (35)	
b. Tell us how heritage students are placed in courses		
Placed by advisors & counselors		82.4 (17)
Self-select		70.6 (17)
Transfer at recommendation of teacher		64.7 (17)
General placement examination		11.8 (17)
Language survey		5.9 (17)

in writing on personal topics, in reading informative material, and in using grammatical terminology were used by 75% of these informants. Measures that involved participation in an oral interview, ability to correct stigmatized forms, and writing on nonpersonal topics were used by 50% of respondents.

The 14 respondents who provided answers to the questions on the specific contents of the general and special placement examinations reflected the profession's concern for correctness and standardness. Writing sections, grammar and terminology and standard language were ranked highest by the 10 individuals using a general placement examination, and identification/production of specific grammatical forms, writing on personal topics, and knowledge of grammatical terminology were considered important measures by the four individuals who used a special language examination. Once again, since we did not ask about the scoring of writing samples, we can only speculate about the degree to which writing measures were used to determine the standardness of students' language.

Table 7.4 Special placement examination for heritage students

	Colleges offering heritage programs
	Percent (No. of programs)
1. Does your department offer a specially designed placement examination for heritage students?	
Yes	11.4 (35)
2. What aspects of language proficiency does the special examination for heritage students measure?	
Identification/production of specific grammatical forms	100.0 (4)
Writing on personal topics	75.0 (4)
Reading informative material	75.0 (4)
Knowledge of grammatical terminology	75.0 (4)
Participation in an interview	50.0 (4)
Ability to correct stigmatized (nonstandard) features	50.0 (4)
Writing on nonpersonal topics	50.0 (4)
Ability to translate from English to Spanish	33.3 (3)
Ability to translate from Spanish to English	33.3 (3)
Reading (literature)	25.0 (4)
Listening to a conversation	25.0 (4)
Ability to make presentations	25.0 (4)
Listening to extended oral presentations	0.0 (4)

Colleges and universities not offering heritage programs

Institutions that did not offer heritage programs did not use a *special* placement examination designed exclusively for heritage students.

Curriculum objectives

In the case of curriculum objectives, mail survey respondents were asked to rate a list of 15 objectives as important for foreign language students, important for heritage students, and important for both. The list included objectives appropriate to the four common instructional goals described by Valdés (1995) as (1) the acquisition of a standard dialect, (2) the transfer of reading and writing abilities across languages, (3) the expansion of bilingual range, and (4) the maintenance of immigrant and other heritage languages.

Table 7.5 Curriculum objectives

Objectives	Colleges offering heritage programs	Colleges not offering heritage programs
	Percent (No. of programs)	Percent (No. of programs)
For the entire sequence of courses, how important are the following learning objectives for heritage speakers?		
Language maintenance goals		
1. Comprehend written materials on specialized business or professional topics	25.7 (35)	29.4 (17)
2. Study other disciplines using Spanish (e.g. history, geography, science)	22.9 (35)	23.5 (17)
3. Develop a broad vocabulary useful in business and professions	17.1 (35)	11.8 (17)
4. Understand and interpret extended oral presentations and information available through mass media	22.9 (35)	17.6 (17)
5. Participate in everyday face-to-face interactions using appropriate levels of Spanish	5.7 (35)	0.0 (17)
6. Demonstrate familiarity with the cultures of Spanish-speaking countries	5.7 (35)	5.9 (17)
Expansion of bilingual range goals		
7. Make oral presentations in front of an audience using appropriate levels of Spanish	11.4 (35)	11.8 (17)
Transfer of reading and writing goals		
8. Write narrative, informative, and persuasive essays directed to a group of unknown readers	20.0 (35)	17.6 (17)
9. Comprehend and read with ease written materials such as novels, short stories, editorials, Web materials	25.7 (35)	17.6 (17)
10. Write informal notes and personal letters	11.4 (35)	11.8 (17)
Acquisition of standard dialect goals		
11. Identify and correct anglicisms, archaisms, and other dialectal or nonstandard forms in their writing	51.4 (35)	41.2 (17)

(Continued)

Table 7.5 *(Continued)*

Objectives	Colleges offering heritage programs	Colleges not offering heritage programs
	Percent (No. of programs)	Percent (No. of programs)
12. Identify and correct anglicisms, archaisms, and other dialectal or nonstandard forms in their speaking	45.7 (35)	41.2 (17)
13. Use and understand grammatical terminology	2.9 (35)	0.0 (17)
14. Use the written accent	11.4 (35)	5.9 (17)
15. Spell correctly	8.6 (35)	0.0 (17)

Colleges and universities offering heritage programs

As shown on Table 7.5, first data column, 51% and 46% of colleges and universities offering heritage programs rated "Identify and correct anglicisms, archaisms and other dialectal or nonstandard forms in their writing" and "Identify and correct anglicisms, archaisms, and other dialectal or nonstandard forms in their speaking" as the most important curriculum objectives for heritage students. Two objectives – "comprehend written materials on specialized business or professional topics" and "comprehend and read with ease written materials such as novels, short stories, editorials, web materials" – were considered important by 26% of respondents. There was little agreement on the remaining objectives. The two objectives on which there was the greatest agreement related to the instructional focus on the acquisition of the standard dialect. The next two most highly rated objectives involve the transfer of reading and writing abilities, the expansion of bilingual range, and quite possibly language maintenance.

Colleges and universities not offering heritage courses

As was the case for the college/university respondents that had implemented heritage programs, respondents that had not implemented such programs rated a list of 15 objectives important for foreign language students, important for heritage students, and important for both. The second data column on Table 7.5 shows the objectives checked as important for heritage students by respondents.

"Identify and correct anglicisms, archaisms, and other dialectal or nonstandard forms in their writing" and "identify and correct anglicisms, archaisms, and other dialectal or nonstandard forms in their speaking" were rated as very important by 41% of informants. One objective –

"comprehend written materials on specialized business or professional topics" – was considered important by 29% of respondents, and 23% rated "study other disciplines using Spanish" as very important for heritage learners. Once again, the two objectives on which there was the greatest agreement related to the instructional goal focusing on the acquisition of the standard dialect.

As Table 7.5 makes clear, there was a clear agreement among respondents at both types of institutions in terms of curricular objectives for heritage students. What this agreement suggests is that views and beliefs about the strengths and weaknesses of heritage students' Spanish are widely shared within the profession.

Instructional practices

To explore the kinds of teaching practices used in the teaching of heritage students, respondents were given a list of practices common in foreign language teaching at both the elementary and more advanced levels. They were asked to rate each practice as effective, not effective, or not attempted with heritage language students. Table 7.6 lists the teaching practices ranked as effective by respondents.

Colleges and universities offering heritage programs

The highest percentage of college/university personnel (97%) at institutions offering heritage programs agreed that "drafting, writing and rewriting of compositions by students in order to correct errors" and "individual research/writing projects" were the most effective in working with heritage language students (Table 7.6, first data column). College/university faculty appear to value both the development of presentational skills in the oral language as well as language correctness. More than 80% of respondents value the use of grammar explanations when working with these students.

Of the 10 practices rated as effective by more than 65% of college respondents, only 3 (direct study of vocabulary, correction of selected common errors in front of the whole class, and oral practice of grammatical structures) can be classified as supporting the acquisition of the standard dialect. The other practices – instruction on the ways that language varies geographically and socially, analysis of language and style appropriate for different types of published texts, Web research projects by students, and reading of significantly longer assignments – support other instructional goals, including language maintenance, expansion of bilingual range, and transfer of reading and writing.

As was the case with curriculum objectives, there is agreement among college/university respondents offering heritage programs about the effectiveness of teaching practices, many of which have traditionally been used in foreign language instruction. Respondents, for example, include direct teaching of vocabulary among the 10 most highly rated practices as

Table 7.6 Instructional practices

Instructional practice	Colleges offering heritage programs	Colleges not offering heritage programs
	Percent (No. of programs)	Percent (No. of programs)
Which of the following teaching practices have you used effectively with heritage learners of Spanish?		
Language maintenance goals		
1. Instruction on the ways that language varies geographically and socially	82.9 (35)	52.9 (17)
2. Projects involving ethnographic research in communities by students	25.7 (35)	17.6 (17)
Expansion of bilingual range goals		
3. Web research projects by students	71.4 (35)	41.2 (17)
4. Frequent in-class listening comprehension activities of extended length	28.6 (35)	64.7 (17)
5. Analysis of language and style appropriate for different types of published texts	80.0 (35)	64.7 (17)
6. Oral presentation language/conversation	20.0 (35)	17.6 (17)
Transfer of reading and writing goals		
7. Individual research/writing projects	97.1 (35)	82.4 (17)
8. Peer editing of compositions	62.9 (35)	47.1 (17)
9. Reading of significantly longer assignments	68.6 (35)	76.5 (17)
10. Group research/writing projects	51.4 (35)	35.3 (17)
Acquisition of standard dialect goals		
11. Drafting, writing, and rewriting of compositions by students	97.1 (35)	94.1 (17)
12. Direct study of vocabulary	71.4 (35)	76.5 (17)
13. Correction of selected common errors by teacher in front of the whole class	77.1 (35)	70.6 (17)
14. Grammar explanations	82.9 (35)	82.4 (17)
15. Dictation	60.0 (35)	70.6 (17)
16. Oral practice of particular grammatical structures	68.6 (35)	76.5 (17)

(Continued)

Table 7.6 Instructional practices *(Continued)*

Instructional practice	Colleges offering heritage programs	Colleges not offering heritage programs
	Percent (No. of programs)	Percent (No. of programs)
17. Instruction that teaches grammar only by pulling out and commenting on particular forms	62.9 (35)	41.2 (17)
18. Other – Productive skills	14.3 (35)	17.6 (17)
19. Other – Passive skills	14.3 (35)	5.9 (17)

well as grammar explanation and correction of common errors in front of the whole class. These data once again suggest the existence of profession-wide agreement about the types of practices that support specific curricular goals. Because the primary goal of instruction appears to be the acquisition of the standard dialect, teaching practices coherent with this goal are highly rated as well. It is important to note that four practices considered effective by more than 65% of respondents also support the transfer of reading and writing, the expansion of bilingual range, and language maintenance.

Colleges and universities not offering heritage programs

In terms of the list of teaching practices common in foreign language teaching at the elementary, intermediate, and advanced levels, responding colleges/universities without heritage programs also rated each practice as effective, not effective, or not attempted with heritage students. Table 6, second data column, shows the percentage of respondents that rated particular practices as effective.

The highest percent of college/university personnel at institutions without heritage programs (94%) agreed that drafting, writing and rewriting of compositions by students to correct errors was effective in working with heritage language learners. The same group agreed by 84% that individual research/writing projects worked with heritage language learners. More than 80% of respondents also value the use of grammar explanations when working with these students.

Of the 10 practices rated as effective by more than 65% of respondents, 7 practices can be classified as supporting the acquisition of the standard dialect. While 3 practices – "reading of significantly longer assignments," "analysis of language and style appropriate for different types of published texts," and "frequent in-class listening comprehension activities of extended length" – support other instructional goals, including expansion of bilingual range and transfer of reading and writing abilities.

There is agreement between the two groups of college/university respondents in terms of the effectiveness of particular teaching practices, most of which have traditionally been used in foreign language instruction. For example, both groups include direct teaching of vocabulary among the 10 most highly rated practices as well as grammar explanation and correction of common errors in front of the whole class. These data point, once again, to the existence of profession-wide agreement about the types of practices that support specific curricular goals. Since both groups of respondents report that the primary goal of instruction for heritage students is the acquisition of the standard dialect, it is not surprising that they also report the effective use of teaching practices coherent with this goal.

Text materials

The question that focused on instructional materials used in the instruction of heritage students asked respondents to write the titles or descriptions of materials currently used in their sequences for heritage learners. Six sets of parallel blank lines were provided so that respondents could write in course numbers and, across from them, the titles of books used. Many respondents listed several titles for a single course, and others listed only one title for each course.

Colleges and universities offering heritage programs

In listing textbooks used in courses for heritage programs, a total of 29 of the 35 college/university respondents listed one title, 15 individuals listed two titles, 8 individuals listed three titles, and 2 respondents listed four titles. Table 7.7, first data column, includes the frequency with which each of the 51 textbooks was listed.

Textbooks written for heritage learners were listed by 80% of the college/university respondents that offer heritage programs. The most commonly listed titles include *La lengua que heredamos: Curso de español para bilingües* (listed 14 times), *Nuestro mundo: curso para hispanohablantes* (listed 8 times), and *Nuevos mundos: Lectura, cultura y comunicación* (listed 6 times). Only three texts intended for both heritage and foreign language students were listed. One of these texts, *Avanzando: Gramática española y lectura*, was listed 6 times. Only two texts written for foreign language learners were listed.

Colleges and universities not offering heritage programs

Respondents from colleges and universities not offering heritage programs listed a total of 10 textbooks. One textbook intended for heritage learners, *Nuevos destinos: Español para hispanohablantes*, was listed 2 times. Two books intended for both heritage and foreign language students were listed. Of these two texts, *Avanzando*, was listed 2 times. Two texts intended for foreign language learners were listed. Of these texts, *Claro que sí* was listed by 4 respondents.

Table 7.7 Books used in the instruction of heritage speakers

Books listed by intended audience	Colleges offering heritage programs		Colleges not offering heritage programs	
	Count	Percent	Count	Percent
Heritage students				
Entre mundos: An integrated approach for the native speaker	3	5.9		
Mundo 21: Edición alternativa	8	15.7		
Nuestro mundo: Curso para hispanohablantes	1	2.0		
Nuevos destinos: español para hispanohablantes	1	2.0	2	20.0
Tu mundo: Curso para hispanohablantes				
Avanzando: Gramática española y lectura	2	3.9		
Español para el hispanohablante	4	7.8		
La lengua que heredamos: Curso de español para bilingües	14	27.5		
Encuentros				
Sendas literarias				
Español escrito: Curso para hispanohablantes bilingües	2	3.9		
Nuevos mundos: Lectura, cultura y comunicación: Curso de español para estudiantes bilingües	6	11.8		
Galería de arte y vida level 4				
Tesoro literario				
Subtotal	41	80.4	2	20.0
Both heritage and foreign language students				
Palabra abierta	1	2.0		
Avanzando: Gramática española y lectura	6	11.8	2	20.0
Aproximaciones al estudio de la literatura hispánica	1	2.0		

(Continued)

Table 7.7 (*Continued*)

Books listed by intended audience	Colleges offering heritage programs		Colleges not offering heritage programs	
	Count	*Percent*	*Count*	*Percent*
Literatura moderna hispánica-An anthology				
¡Dímelo tú!			1	10.0
Ven conmigo				
Subtotal	8	15.7	3	30.0
Foreign language students				
Dime uno, dos, tres				
Pasos y puentes				
Voces y vistas			4	40.0
AP Spanish: A guide for the language course				
Esencial repaso				
Una vez más: Repaso detallado de las estructuras gramaticales del idioma de español				
¡Claro que sí!			1	10.0
Punto de vista	1	2.0		
Abriendo paso				
Galería de arte y vida level 4				
Composición: Proceso y síntesis	1	2.0		
Encuentros maravillosos: Gramática a través de la literatura				
Fonética y fonología				
Tesoro literario				
Subtotal	2	3.9	5	50.0
Total	51	100.0	10	100.0

Satisfaction with existing program

Individuals responding to the survey were asked whether they were satisfied with the outcomes of their heritage language program. Four blank lines were provided so that respondents could list two areas with which they were particularly satisfied and two areas in which they felt the program needed to improve.

Colleges and universities offering heritage programs

In colleges and universities offering heritage programs, 80% of respondents stated that they were satisfied with the achievement of students in heritage programs (Table 7.8). A total of 71% of respondents listed a

Table 7.8 Program satisfaction

Area	*Colleges offering heritage programs*	*Colleges not offering heritage programs*
	Percent (No. of programs)	*Percent (No. of programs)*
1. Are you satisfied with the achievement of students in the heritage language program, as measured by course examinations and/or by success in subsequent courses?		
Yes	80.0 (35)	41.2 (17)
2. Program areas of particular satisfaction (areas)		
Skill-based response	71.4 (35)	41.2 (17)
Program-based response	11.4 (35)	5.9 (17)
Student-based response	28.6 (35)	11.8 (17)
3. Program areas of particular satisfaction (specific items)		
Subsequent class success	14.3 (35)	5.9 (17)
Reading	23.3 (35)	41.2 (17)
Writing	42.9 (35)	23.5 (17)
Cultural/historical themes	17.1 (35)	0.0 (17)
Vocabulary/orthography	20.0 (35)	0.0 (17)
Speaking	17.1 (35)	29.4 (17)
Individual benefits	25.7 (35)	11.8 (17)
Grammar	11.4 (35)	11.8 (17)
Multimedia/technology	2.9 (35)	0.0 (17)
Inclusion ELL/ESL	0.0 (48)	0.0 (17)
Standard language	20.0 (35)	11.8 (17)

skill-based area with which they were satisfied. A *skill-based response* would generally state that they noticed their students' vocabularies improved or their correct usage of standard Spanish, or students' improvement in written composition and analytical skills. The specific skill area with which they were most satisfied was the development of writing (43%). More than 20% of respondents mentioned being satisfied with reading (23%), vocabulary/orthography (20%), and standard language (20%).

Another 11% of respondents provided what was classified as a program-based response. Such responses disclosed satisfaction with the structure of their program, for example, the integration of technology into the classroom, overall increased enrollment in Spanish classes, integration of students in language and literature courses, Spanish speakers stay with the course program, and the addition of new books/materials to expand literature used in classes. Twenty-nine percent of informants offered a student-based response, which included claims such as students' being proud of their heritage, or the observation that students acquire self-esteem as their awareness of who they are and the value of their contributions is realized.

Table 7.8 also presents the frequency that respondents mentioned specific program or skill areas. A *subsequent class success response* was given by 14% of respondents. These responses claimed satisfaction with students' success in subsequent courses stating, for example, that the majority of students go on to higher-level courses. A number of respondents specifically mentioned being satisfied with students' improvement in reading (23%), in writing (43%), knowledge of cultural historical themes (17%), and knowledge of vocabulary, spelling, and orthography (20%). A small number of respondents listed grammar (11%) and standard language (20%) as areas with which they were satisfied.

Colleges and universities not offering heritage programs

Colleges and universities not offering heritage programs were much less satisfied with program outcomes than their colleagues in institutions offering such programs. Only 41% of informants stated that they were satisfied with student achievement (Table 7.8). The same number of informants (41%) identified skill development as the area with which they were most satisfied. The area of reading was mentioned most frequently by 41% of persons responding to the questionnaire, followed by speaking (29%) and writing (24%). The areas of vocabulary/orthography and cultural/historical themes were not mentioned by this group of individuals.

Areas needing improvement

Colleges and universities offering heritage programs

In terms of areas needing improvement, 57% of respondents from colleges/universities offering heritage programs listed school/logistics

Table 7.9 Areas in which improvement is needed

Area	Colleges offering heritage programs	Colleges not offering heritage programs
	Percent (No. of programs)	Percent (No. of programs)
1. Program areas that need improvement (areas)		
School/logistics issue	57.1 (35)	64.7 (17)
Student performance issue	25.7 (35)	35.3 (17)
Different foci of classes issue	34.3 (35)	23.5 (17)
2. Program areas that need improvement (specific items)		
Writing/vocabulary, spelling	37.1 (35)	29.4 (17)
Offer varied levels of classes	40.0 (35)	23.5 (17)
Placement examination	22.9 (35)	17.6 (17)
Improved materials	22.9 (35)	0.0 (17)
Text analysis skills	8.6 (35)	11.8 (17)
Student motivation, interests	5.7 (35)	11.8 (17)
Articulation with the community	0.0 (17)	0.0 (17)
Standard language	5.7 (35)	5.9 (17)
Offer classes for students with low levels of literacy	2.9 (35)	5.9 (17)
No improvement necessary	5.7 (35)	0.0 (17)
Start program for heritage speakers	N/A	47.1 (17)

issues as needing attention (Table 7.9, first data column). Forty percent of persons responding to the questionnaire listed offering varied levels of classes most frequently, followed by improvement in writing/vocabulary, spelling (27%). Placement examination and improved materials were mentioned by 23% of personnel responding to the questionnaire. As compared to high-school programs, institutions of higher education with heritage programs did not mention articulation with the community.

Colleges and universities not offering heritage programs

Table 7.9, second data column, shows that, as was the case for colleges/universities offering heritage programs, institutions without heritage programs frequently mentioned school/logistics issues as needing improvement (65%). For 47% of these institutions, however, these logistics issues involve starting a program for heritage speakers. This result is not entirely surprising given that only 41% of respondents (Table 7.8) stated that they were satisfied with student achievement.

Faculty characteristics

All respondents were asked how many faculty currently taught in the Spanish language program. This number was not to include faculty teaching literature or linguistics. The questionnaire also asked for the total number of instructors teaching in the heritage program. It then asked the respondent to identify the number of instructors in the heritage program that fell into the following groups: (1) US Latinos who grew up with Spanish at home, (2) US Latinos who grew up in non–Spanish-speaking families, (3) Latinos who grew up and were educated in Spanish-speaking countries, and (4) Non-Latinos who grew up in non–Spanish-speaking families.

Colleges and universities offering heritage programs

The number of instructors involved in teaching language in Spanish departments at institutions offering heritage programs varies. At 46% of the postsecondary institutions that reported active heritage programs, 6–10 individuals are involved in language instruction. At 34% of institutions responding, 11 or more persons teach the Spanish language. Table 7.10 shows the number of language-teaching instructors, the total number of instructors in the heritage program, and the percentage of instructors from each of four language background groups.

As will be noted from Table 7.10, the number of instructors teaching in heritage programs is small. Fifty-one percent of respondents reported that two instructors or fewer are involved in the heritage program, and 34% stated that three to five individuals were engaged in such instruction. While we used the term *instructor* in our survey, we did not ask whether these individuals were tenure-track or non–tenure-track faculty. Given current patterns of hiring in language programs at the postsecondary level, it is reasonable to conjecture that, except for very small institutions, individuals teaching Spanish language (as opposed to Spanish literature) are non–tenure-track appointments to whom the title of either instructor or lecturer is given.

Table 7.10 also shows the nationality and language background of the persons engaged in the teaching of Spanish as a heritage language. At the college and university levels, the highest percentage of heritage language instructors (54%) are Latinos who grew up and were educated in Spanish-speaking countries. These data suggest that either US Latinos are not as present as non-US Latinos among the instructor ranks in colleges/universities or that they are not selected by their institutions to deliver such instruction. A much smaller percentage of teachers of non-Latino

Table 7.10 Instructor characteristics

Characteristic	Colleges offering heritage programs	Colleges not offering heritage programs
	Percent (No. of programs)	Percent (No. of programs)
1. Number of instructors teaching Spanish language		
2 or fewer	8.6	23.5
3–5	11.4	35.3
6–10	45.7	17.6
11 or more	34.3	23.5
Total	100.0 (35)	100.0 (17)
2. Total number of instructors in heritage program?		
2 or fewer	51.4	N/A
3–5	34.3	N/A
6–10	11.4	N/A
11 or more	2.9	N/A
Total	100.0 (35)	N/A
3. Mean percentage of instructors who teach heritage students that fall into the following categories?		
US Latinos who grew up with Spanish at home	20.0 (35)	21.6 (17)
US Latinos who grew up in non–Spanish-speaking families	1.5 (35)	0.0 (17)
Latinos who grew up and were educated in Spanish-speaking countries	54.1 (35)	40.8 (17)
Non-Latinos who grew up in non–Spanish-speaking families	17.6 (35)	36.6 (17)

backgrounds are engaged in the teaching of Spanish as a heritage language at the college/university levels.

Colleges and universities not offering heritage programs

The number of instructors involved in teaching language in Spanish departments without specialized programs also varied. At 24% of the postsecondary institutions responding, two or fewer individuals are in-volved in language instruction. At 35% of institutions, three to five per-sons teach the Spanish language, and at 18% of institutions, the language-teaching faculty numbers from six to ten. More than 11 faculty members are involved in the language program at 24% of institutions. Table 10 also shows that the highest percentage of language instructors in the de-partment (41%) are Latinos who grew up in Spanish-speaking countries, followed by non-Latinos who grew up in non–Spanish-speaking house-holds (37%), and finally by US Latinos who grew up with Spanish at home (22%).

Preparation of lead instructor

To obtain a more complete picture of heritage instructors' professional training, respondents were also asked to report on the preparation of the person considered the "lead instructor" in the heritage program. Given our familiarity with the limited training in teaching heritage languages avail-able for secondary teachers – a condition that has necessitated the organiza-tion of nationwide projects and workshops (Alliance for the Advancement of Heritage languages; Fischer, 2004; Potowski, 2003) – we expected that most individuals would disclose that they had learned to teach by teach-ing. Respondents reporting that their institutions offered heritage courses were asked to describe the preparation of their lead instructor by check-ing all appropriate descriptive statements from a list of 10 alternatives. Descriptive statements about preparation included such alternatives as "Took special course(s) on teaching heritage students as part of a teaching certificate program" and "Attended summer workshop(s) on the teaching of heritage speakers."

Colleges and universities

Table 7.11 shows the type of preparation received by lead instructors at responding postsecondary institutions. Individuals working with heritage learners have had little formal preparation. Eighty-three percent of persons responding to the survey reported that their lead instructor has learned on the job by teaching heritage learners, 57% reported that the lead instructor carried out extensive reading on the teaching of heritage speakers, and 46% reported that the instructor had attended sessions on the teaching of heritage languages at professional meetings.

We were surprised by the data about the preparation of lead instructors at institutions that offered programs for heritage speakers because, given what appears to be a very modest interest in heritage learners in insti-tutions of higher education around the country (Ingold et al., 2002), 29% of respondents reported that their lead instructor "took a special courses on the teaching of heritage students as part of graduate teaching-assistant

Table 7.11 Lead instructor preparation

Preparation type	High schools offering heritage programs	Colleges offering heritage programs
	Percent (No. of programs)	Percent (No. of programs)
What types of preparation for teaching heritage speakers has the *lead instructor* in the heritage sequence received?		
Learned on the job by teaching heritage learners	77.1 (48)	82.9 (35)
Attended sessions on the teaching of heritage speakers at professional conferences	58.3 (48)	57.1 (35)
Carried out extensive individual reading on the teaching of heritage speakers	50.0 (48)	45.7 (35)
Attended summer workshop(s) on the teaching of heritage speakers	47.9 (48)	28.6 (35)
Visited heritage language classes at nearby schools or colleges	37.5 (48)	25.7 (35)
Took special course(s) on teaching heritage students as part of a teaching certificate program	33.3 (48)	22.9 (35)
Taught a course or courses for heritage students as part of graduate teaching assistant responsibilities	20.8 (48)	11.4 (35)
Based on living experience	14.6 (48)	8.6 (35)
Based on educational experience	10.4 (48)	5.7 (35)
Took special course(s) on teaching heritage students as part of graduate teaching assistant training	10.4 (48)	5.7(35)
Became member of a listserv focusing on the teaching of heritage speakers	8.3 (48)	5.7 (35)

training," and 26% report that they "taught a course or courses for heritage students as part of graduate teaching assistant responsibilities." These responses suggest that there may be a greater availability of heritage programs and graduate training in the teaching of heritage students in Spanish departments than has been documented to date. In addition, it might suggest that respondents saw their general foreign language teaching methods course(s) as also preparing them to teach heritage students.

Discussion

Survey results indicate that at both the high school and college/ university levels, heritage language programs vary considerably. Some programs have been in existence since the early 1980s and others have been established only recently. Sequences of courses intended for heritage students also vary. Some institutions describe a several-year sequence and others report a single course. At the college and university levels, the survey supports the findings of the work conducted by Ingold *et al.* (2002) that heritage programs are unevenly available.

Focus on traditional academic goals

The profile of heritage language instruction in California revealed by the survey suggests that heritage programs primarily focus on achieving traditional institutional academic goals. Heritage programs (sequences of language course or single courses) are described as being part of existing Spanish language and literature programs. College/university respondents reported satisfaction with subsequent course achievement of students and their success in course examinations. Moreover, they were satisfied with the development of reading and writing skills by heritage students.

Language maintenance

We found no evidence to suggest that high schools or colleges and universities offering heritage programs see themselves as engaged in the process of language maintenance. Curriculum goals related to language maintenance (e.g. study other disciplines using Spanish, understand and interpret extended oral presentations and information available through the mass media, and participate in everyday face-to-face interactions using appropriate levels of Spanish) were not ranked as very important by respondents.

Instructional goals guiding existing instruction for heritage speakers of Spanish at both the high school and the college levels are not consistent with the recommendations made on the teaching of heritage languages by successful Latino professionals in response to the telephone survey that was carried out as a part of the larger project (Valdés *et al.*, 2004). The suggestions of these individuals – while varied – focused almost exclusively on Spanish language maintenance (e.g. making cultural/historical connections; showing relevance and significance of language to students' lives; teaching other subjects in Spanish; teaching legal, medical, business terms in Spanish). Conversely, instructional goals and practices that ranked most highly, or were viewed as effective by all college/university respondents, were closely aligned with the teaching of the standard dialect (e.g. correcting anglicisms, archaisms, and other nonstandard forms in students' oral and written language, teaching grammatical terminology, and teaching spelling).

Limitations of the quantitative data

Similar to the High School survey data, the response rate of colleges and universities was also a low 30%, suggesting caution in generalizing to nonrespondent programs. However, as discussed in chapter 6, our response rate is similar to mail survey response rates found in the survey methodology literature (Church, 1993; Fox *et al.*, 1989; James & Bolstein, 1992; Kaplowitz *et al.*, 2004). Fox *et al.* (1989), for example, found that return rates for surveys with no monetary incentive averaged 34% in their meta-analytical study. Similar to the high-school sample, our results showed that college/university early respondents did not differ from late responders, suggesting that even nonresponders would have distributed themselves very much like the responders. Nevertheless, caution should be exercised and the results should be considered tentative.

Furthermore, the survey provides no information about the reasons behind the strong focus on the teaching of the standard dialect by college/university faculty. We can conjecture that such a focus has to do with the preparation normally received by teaching assistants in foreign language departments, but it is not clear why there is a lack of interest in language maintenance and in the use of Spanish outside of the department by heritage learners.

Part II: The Closer Study of Selected Postsecondary Spanish Heritage Programs

In at attempt to obtain a more nuanced view of the ways in which formal education programs might support the expansion and maintenance of Spanish as heritage language in California, we studied six colleges and universities that responded to our survey. It was our expectation that by visiting classes and interviewing faculty involved in teaching heritage learners face-to face, we would learn more about specific goals of Spanish heritage courses and about practices that have been found particularly effective in developing the language resources of heritage speakers.

Selection of institutions studied

As was the case for secondary institutions, the selection of colleges/ universities studied was made using the register of survey respondents for colleges/universities. Using survey responses about program histories, we first compiled an initial list of early college/university programs (established before 1984), programs in existence for a considerable period of time (established between 1985 and 1994), and recently established programs (established after 1995). We then subdivided the initial list into institutions with low, medium, and high Latino enrollment.

The list of 35 college/university respondents that reported established heritage programs was stratified so that our sample would also include 4-year state institutions (California State University campuses and University of California campuses), community colleges, private 4-year liberal arts colleges and universities, and vocational/religious institutions. Compiling the final list of colleges and universities to be visited was complex because some institutions only offered heritage courses during select quarters/semesters rather than the entire academic year. Because we carried out our visitations in the fall quarter, our final selection included four state-supported universities, one private college/university that prepared students for the ministry, and one community college, all of which offered heritage courses during the fall quarter/semester.

To carry out our more detailed study of heritage programs, we spent one full day at each postsecondary institution, often observing two to three classes and interviewing teachers/lecturers and coordinators/heads of the programs. We were able to visit a full spectrum of long-established, well-established, and more recently established programs at institutions that had low and high heritage speaker enrollments. However, we recognize that our short visits to each institution were not extensive enough to allow us to fully appreciate the strengths of each of these programs. As was the case at secondary level institutions, the visits did allow us to invite at least six individuals and their colleagues to share with us more extensive answers to the questions that we had asked in the survey in multiple-choice and fill-in-the-blank format. It also allowed us to examine their views of their students' proficiencies, and to learn more about what they considered to be successful and unsuccessful pedagogies.

In interviewing persons involved in the teaching of Spanish as a heritage language at the six colleges/universities and the six high schools, we addressed the following topics:

- Program history
- Students' language proficiency
- Courses available
- Placement in courses
- Objectives of program
- Textbooks and other materials used
- Teaching practices effective and ineffective
- What was working and what they wanted to change

- Recommendations for other schools considering starting a heritage program
- Views about the relationship between heritage language programs and the Spanish language needs of Latino professionals in California

It is important for us to emphasize that in obtaining permission to carry out our visits and interviews, we agreed that all information obtained during our visits would be kept confidential and that individual privacy would be maintained in all published and written data resulting from the study. For that reason, we refer to the institutions visited as College/University A etc., using letters A through F for each of the six high schools or colleges/universities.

Characteristics of colleges/universities visited

The colleges/universities selected for further study are listed in Table 7.12 below. As will be noted in this table, Colleges/Universities A and B have a low enrollment of Chicano/Latino students, and both of these institutions draw a statewide student body. Nevertheless, College/University A's heritage program was established before 1984. Colleges/Universities C and D have a similar Chicano/Latino enrollment and draw both a regional and local student body. College/University D established heritage courses before 1984 and College/University C established them between 1985 and 1994. Finally, Colleges/Universities E and F – the institutions with Chicano/Latino enrollment of 33% and 42%, respectively – implemented

Table 7.12 Colleges and universities visited

Institution	Type of institution	Latino enrollment	Program established
College/University A	State-supported university	15%	Before 1984
College/University B	State-supported university	10%	Between 1985 and 1994
College/University C	State-supported university	22%	Between 1985 and 1994
College/University D	State-supported university	23%	Before 1984
College/University E	Church- affiliated private college	33%	After 1995
College/University F	Community college	42%	After 1995

heritage courses after 1995 even though College University E enrolls students from the entire state of California, while College/University F enrolls local students exclusively. The percentage of Latino enrollment in postsecondary institutions does not appear to account for the early establishment of heritage language programs in Spanish.

At all colleges and universities visited, classes in Spanish intended for heritage language students were offered in departments of Spanish or in departments of foreign languages. As summarized in Table 7.13, however, very few faculty in these departments are involved in teaching heritage languages. At three institutions, a single individual is responsible for teaching heritage courses. The number of courses offered at these institutions directed at heritage students ranges from a high of three quarters/semesters to a low of one quarter. Enrollment in heritage courses is generally modest at all institutions except for College/University C, which reports an average enrollment of 30–36 students in two or more sections.

Students enrolled in the Spanish language program include first-, second-, third-, and fourth-generation Latinos. The tendency at all institutions is to refer to heritage students as *native speakers* as opposed to other students in the program, who are known as *foreign language learners.*

A close examination of the courses offered at the six postsecondary institutions revealed that, as was evident from responses to the survey, the terms *first year* and *second year* do not adequately describe the levels of heritage courses offered at the postsecondary level or their place in a sequence of courses. For example, the heritage courses offered at College/University F are the fifth and sixth courses in a sequence of six available semester-long courses as presented in Table 7.14.

The first four courses cover introductory and intermediate Spanish and are intended for students beginning their study of Spanish as a foreign language. The fifth and sixth courses – which serve heritage students – cover readings in Spanish and Spanish American literature. It is not clear how many nonheritage students enroll in these courses. No other higher-level Spanish classes are offered.

By comparison, College/University C offers a single, one-semester course entitled "Spanish for Bilingual Students." As shown in Table 7.15, the course is one of five courses listed as lower-division Spanish. The other four courses are intended for beginning and intermediate-level foreign language students. Heritage students who major in Spanish must also enroll in the two upper-division courses designed for heritage students.

We conclude that heritage offerings at different institutions vary widely and can only be compared with great caution, taking into account the following dimensions: (1) total number of semester-long or quarter-long courses designed especially for heritage speakers, (2) number of heritage courses designated as lower-division, (3) number of courses designated as

Table 7.13 Instructors, courses, and typical course enrollment

	Number of individuals teaching in heritage program	Ethnicity of faculty	Courses in heritage program	No. of classes offered per quarter or semester	Typical course enrollment
College/University A	1 coordinator 2 lecturers	3 US Latinas	3 quarters	2	30
College/University B	1 teaching assistant	1 US Latina	1 quarter	1	20
College/University C	2(full-time faculty) 3 (lecturers)	1 US Latina 2 Latina (non-US)	3 semesters	2–3	30–36
College/University D	4 (full-time faculty)	1 US Latina 3 Latino (non-US)	2 semesters	1	25
College/University E	2 (full-time faculty)	1 US Latino 1 Latina (non-US)	2 semesters	1	3–8
College/University F	1 (full-time faculty)	1 Latina (non-US)	2 semesters	1	12–15

Table 7.14 Spanish course offering at College/University F

Courses offered	Sequence	Intended for
Beginning Spanish 1	FL course 1	Foreign language students
Beginning Spanish 2	FL course 2	Foreign language students
Intermediate Spanish 1	FL course 3	Foreign language students
Intermediate Spanish 2	FL course 4	Foreign language students
Literature 1	Heritage course 1	Heritage language students
Literature 2	Heritage course 2	Heritage language students

upper-division, (4) number of heritage courses that count toward major requirements.

Origin and establishment of heritage language programs

As was the case at the six high schools visited, we asked all interviewees at the six postsecondary institutions to tell us about the history of the heritage courses their institutions offer. Faculty interviewed at institutions B, C, E, and F were personally involved in implementing and teaching the first courses. In each of these cases, separate courses were started as a response to particular conditions that made instruction difficult for students, instructors, or both. The program coordinator at institution B, for example, recalled that first-year courses consisted of a three-quarter sequence. However, students at very different levels enrolled in those courses:

> Había gente que era de distintos niveles y entonces funcionaba problemáticamente porque para los anglohablantes era una presencia negativa porque sabían el español. En cambio [en] el nivel muchas veces de gramática etc. fallaban los chicos. Entonces se vio la necesidad de crear

Table 7.15 Spanish course offerings at College/University C

Level	Courses offered	Sequence
Lower division	Beginning Spanish 1	FL course 1
	Beginning Spanish 2	FL course 2
	Intermediate Spanish 1	FL course 3
	Intermediate Spanish 2	FL course 4
	Intermediate Spanish for heritage speakers	Heritage course 1
Upper Division	Composition and grammar 1 for heritage students	Heritage course 2
	Composition and grammar 2 for heritage students	Heritage course 3
	Literature and linguistics courses	Required courses for majors

un curso por un lado para encontrar las necesidades de este grupo y por otro también para separarlos del otro que tienen otra serie de necesidades. Entonces en la primavera hice yo, inventé el curso de [course title], que fuera una secuencia un tanto aparte porque pueden los alumnos venir directamente a ese curso sin pasar ni por lo de primer año ni por los de [course numbers of beginning and intermediate Spanish]. Y desde entonces lo hemos ofrecido cada trimestre. (Program coordinator, College/University B)

There were people that were of different levels and so it functioned problematically, because for the Anglophones it was a negative presence because they knew Spanish. However, at the level of grammar etc. the youngsters would fail. So then the need was seen to create a course on the one hand to find the needs of this group and on the other to separate them from the other[s] who have another series of needs. Then, that spring, I made – I invented – the course [course title] that would be a separate sequence because students can come directly to that course without passing first year or the other [course numbers of beginning and intermediate Spanish]. And from that time, we have offered it every quarter.

Conditions were somewhat different at College/University F. At this institution, courses were created in response to student demand for specially designed courses. The students were supported by the ESL teacher who still teaches part-time in the Spanish department. Even though the individual now teaching the course was involved in designing the first course, she does not take credit for starting the program herself.

At the institutions where interviewees had been the originators of the first courses taught at their institution, they were able to provide us with rich descriptions of the circumstances that led to separating heritage students from "regular" students. They spoke particularly of complaints made by regular students who felt they were not receiving enough attention and of faculty members' perceptions about the inferior quality of heritage students' Spanish. By comparison, faculty members at Colleges/Universities A and D only had some information about the founders of the heritage programs at their institutions. Therefore, they could only speak in very general terms about the particular conditions that might have led to the design of new courses.

Overall, the descriptions given of conditions leading to the implementation of separate heritage courses as well as current views about students' Spanish language proficiency (to be discussed below) are consistent with those observed at the six high schools visited. Mainly, the programs seem to arise as a response to a particular pattern of student enrollment and staffing at a specific point in time. Courses were not implemented because the faculty had a deep theoretical understanding of bilingualism or a deep commitment to maintaining the Spanish language. Nor because they wanted to establish first-rate, state-of-the-art language programs coherent with the most advanced thinking in the language teaching profession.

Views about students' language proficiency

When asked about students' language proficiencies, the lack of success of heritage students in regular foreign language and literature classes, and the reasons for that lack of success, a few respondents linked this lack of success to the educational disadvantages experienced by poor Latinos in general. However, more commonly, responses centered around the quality of Spanish spoken by heritage language students. When asked about the origin of the program; for example, one faculty member from College/University D, one of the oldest programs in the state of California, responded:

> Y la otra razón muy importante [por la cual se tiene el programa para hispanohablantes] es que nos encontramos que los estudiantes hispanohablantes de esta región, aunque se comunican bastante bien en forma verbal, no siempre correctamente pero se comunican bien, tenían muchos problemas serios con la lectura y con la escritura. Entonces pensamos que estas clases le ayudarían a ellos a pulir su español y a tener un español universitario pues porque si van a recibir un título universitario tiene que ser un español universitario. No un español de España no un español de Venezuela ni de México, simplemente un español educado. (Faculty Member 1, College/University D)

> *The other very important reason [for having the heritage program] is that we found that Spanish-speaking students from this region, even though they communicate pretty well orally, not always correctly, but they communicate well, had many serious problems with reading and writing. So we thought that these classes would help them to polish their Spanish and to have a college-level Spanish because if they are going to get a college degree, it has to be a college Spanish. Not the Spanish of Spain, not the Spanish of Venezuela or Mexico, simply an educated Spanish.*

All other individuals interviewed shared this same view but expressed it in different terms. Some justified their position by pointing out the value of good Spanish on the job market:

> so they have had limited exposure to the language and it has been very focused on what goes on in the home, so they need to expand their vocabulary, they need to acknowledge, you know, that there are different varieties of Spanish, they are not very familiar with the formal language, academic language, or the written language, so I feel that they have lots that they are bringing, but it would be great if I could reach a different level in their Spanish skills so they could actually go out and use it in the job market, things like that. (Faculty member, College/University F)

Others spoke of bringing students' skills up to the level of

> standard speech, the prestigious form, the monolithic accepted form of Spanish that is spoken throughout the world. (Faculty member, College/University D)

Still others expressed concern about students' tendency to code-switch and pointed out that code-switching was caused by students' limitations in vocabulary.

At two institutions, both coordinators and teaching staff appeared to focus on writing and spelling limitations:

> And then I have students who have always spoken Spanish at home but you know who've never really had and like bilingual education or any kind of bilingual education that mattered in terms of, in terms of like being able to write Spanish, you know. So, but then they make what we consider, what we consider some of the very common native speaker mistakes. You know, like confusing the *y* with the *ll*. (Coordinator, College/University B)

The concern about writing sometimes extended to text organization (introductions, conclusions, transitions, and central arguments), but often returned to perceived grammatical limitations.

> I, you know, one of the things that's difficult for my students is that they, you know, it's like they don't even know the parts of a sentence, you know what I mean? You ask them for what the parts of a sentence are and, I mean this is just an example, it's like, an extreme example. . . . No. I mean, some of them do and some of them are like huh and then you say the predicate you know the verb you know and then yeah and then they say, "Oh yes I seem to recall that word from when I was in third grade," you know. So, you know, so you know like today for example I don't know if it was in the second class that we had, yeah it was in the second class where we had that example of where the *infinitivo* does not, does not acquire a diphthong right and it was kind of like, you know, maybe a couple of students could say, you know, it doesn't need the *diptongo* because it's an *infinitivo*. And so those words, like, the *infinitivo*, *indicativo*, *subjuntivo* they don't, they don't have it. (Teaching assistant, College/University B)

For 12 of the 14 individuals interviewed at the college and university levels, grammatical competence seemed to involve the knowledge and use of a meta-language to talk about the language:

> The native speakers need more help with writing and basic grammar concepts, for example, what is a noun, verb, direct noun, direct object, the type of word, whether it is a noun verb. (Faculty Member, College/University D)

At other times, however, it was not clear whether interviewees were concerned about students' ability to identify particular grammatical structures or to produce them.

> They should be able to analyze language, and know parts of grammar, tenses of verbs. They usually come to class with no knowledge of subjunctive, conditional. Generally they use them, but cannot identify them, and sometimes they just use them incorrectly, or identify what they are using incorrectly. (Faculty Member, College/University D)

In their discussions of students' language proficiencies, faculty involved in the teaching of heritage language courses at six institutions of higher education shared views about language correction that are common in most departments of foreign languages (Valdés *et al.*, 2003, in press). These views are typical of faculty members trained in the study of literature who have little knowledge of first language acquisition, second language acquisition, bilingualism, language variation, and the like. Many have very conservative views of standardness and correctness that may be, to some degree, the result of their work with second language learners and the profession's emphasis on accuracy.

Placement

Responses to survey questions from the 35 colleges and universities that had implemented heritage programs revealed that at least 77% of the responding institutions had advisors and counselors place students in appropriate level classes. Students also self-select heritage courses in 74% of these institutions. Only 31% of the institutions use a general placement examination intended for all students enrolling in lower-division Spanish courses, and only 11% (4 of 35 institutions) reported using a special placement examination specifically for heritage students. The survey also revealed that institutions using general placement examinations rely primarily on writing on personal topics, reading, and scores on knowledge of grammatical terminology to place students. Institutions using special examinations for heritage students reported basing decisions on students' ability to produce specific grammatical forms, on writing about personal topics, and on reading informative material. Since we did not ask about criteria used to score writing samples, we did not obtain information about the types of language features that influence individuals' judgments and placement decisions. We hoped, therefore, that the close study of six colleges/universities would allow us to obtain additional information about measures used to evaluate the proficiencies of heritage students.

Unfortunately, placement procedures are informal (oral interview, advising, self-selection) at five of the institutions visited. Only College/University B has developed a placement measure. This measure was not shared with us. According to information provided by the teaching assistant then teaching the course, however, the placement examination is referred to as a *pruebita* (a little test) and includes a number of parts:

> There's translation. You know, there's ah there's questions to which they have to respond in Spanish. So we're looking at, you know, what you know, if they know how to use, like verb tenses, you know, if they know how to respond to a question, if they understand the question, if they know how to like reformulate their response with parts of the question. So, for example, you know: "Que harás cuando salgas de clase? or Cuando salga de clase da dasdaddadda." So we're just looking to see what verb tenses they have a handle on, you know, for example. And then, along with that with the *pruebita*, there's a survey, where we ask them, you know. Just like what classes they've taken, what grades they've gotten, why they're taking the class, you know, things like that. Have you taken AP Spanish? What was your score? things like that. (Teaching Assistant, College/University B)

According to the program coordinator, who does not herself teach in the program but supervises placement, the *pruebita* reveals that there are a number of very different levels and backgrounds among the students. There are students who completed *preparatoria* in Mexico and are well prepared in Spanish and less prepared in English. There are also students who are English dominant and who have trouble with writing in Spanish. Currently, with a single-quarter offering, both groups of students are placed in that single course. However, the test does identify less-prepared students who produce nonstandard forms such as *haiga* or *dijieron* as well as the flawed use of written accents.

Even though the placement measure was not shared with us, it appears that, as we conjectured after reviewing the results of the survey, contact features (use of borrowings) as well as nonstandard features typical of many regional varieties of Spanish (e.g. *haiga, truje*) directly influence perceptions about students' proficiency in Spanish at College/University B. Our conjecture is consistent with the views expressed by program personnel when asked to describe students' proficiencies.

Course and program objectives

The *Survey of Instruction Practices in Secondary and Postsecondary Spanish Heritage Programs* also asked respondents to rate a list of objectives as important for foreign language students, important for heritage students, and important for both. The list included objectives appropriate to the four common instructional goals described by Valdés (1995) as (1) the acquisition of a standard dialect, (2) the transfer of reading and writing abilities across languages, (3) the expansion of bilingual range, and (4) the maintenance of immigrant and other heritage languages. When asked what they expected that students would be able to know and do at the end of the heritage class sequence, some interviewees spoke eloquently about the importance of raising students' self-esteem and validating what they know. For example, the faculty member at the community college stated:

> I'm very very interested in raising their self-esteem and validating that they do know a lot and validating that yes they are bilingual already and, you know, these are students who have been usually the ESL learners so they have that stigma attached sometimes, and then sometimes they have it in Spanish too because sometimes they realize that they cannot read a book in Spanish or they cannot write something in Spanish, other than the shopping list, and so they have been in that situation in the two languages. And I'm very interested in just showing them that they can do something about it and they actually have a lot of valuable skills, and don't think that oh they are not up there yet, whatever they bring that is great. So I'm interested in that aspect too. (Faculty Member, College/University F)

Three other individuals also specifically mentioned fostering students' appreciation for what they brought with them, instilling in them a passion for their culture and language, and making them more confident in speaking and writing.

All individuals interviewed, however, also described specific objectives most of which focused on (1) the improvement of students' Spanish overall and (2) teaching students to read and write. The notion of improvement, however, involved a variety of dimensions. For some respondents, improvement involved helping students to carry on conversations with other native speakers, reading books, and writing in Spanish with greater accuracy (e.g. with correct spelling, including the use of written accents). For others, improvement had to do with enlarging students' vocabulary and refining their grammar. Finally, for five individuals interviewed, Spanish instruction for heritage speakers had as its purpose helping students to acquire the tools needed to continue the formal study of Spanish.

> Mi propósito es que los estudiantes tengan las estrategias necesarias para poder seguir avanzando en sus estudios de español. La clase les provee una idea bastante general de la situación latinoamericana, la situación histórica, no solamente la gramática y forma de escribir. Creo que al final de la clase van a tener el deseo de continuar y las herramientas para poder hacerlo. (Lecturer, College/University C)

> *My purpose is that students have the necessary strategies to continue to make progress in their study of Spanish. The class provides them with a fairly general idea of the Latin American situation, the historical situation, not just grammar and the written form. I think that at the end of the class, they are going to have the desire to continue on and the tools to be able to do so.*

Three interviewees were concerned about helping students to acquire additional registers in Spanish:

> When the students complete the classes they will be able to write standard Spanish with eloquence and have an understanding of register of spoken and written Spanish differences. (Faculty, College/University D)

> The focus is on improving the academic language proficiency of the students while fostering an appreciation for the multiple varieties of Spanish that exist. The program seeks to build the practical language skills that the students will need in order to work in the community as well as build their appreciation for and ability in academic forms and discourse in Spanish. (Faculty, College/University C)

And:

> se puede crear una conciencia de orgullo por la lengua porque muchas veces lo que uno se da cuenta muy claramente es que hay un, para usarlo en términos PC, una falta de autoestima en cuanto al español, un sentido de deficiencia de que yo no hablo bien el español, o lo hablo pocho. Esto, entonces de la idea de que lo hablas como lo hablas y lo que tienes que ver es que hay distintos registros en español, igual que en inglés, y tienes que poder cambiar de marcha. Y saber cuándo decir una cosa y a quién, y cuándo no decirla. Y no tener un solo registro. (Coordinator, College/University B)

> *one can create a sense of pride in the language because many times what one finds out clearly is that there is a – to use it in PC terms – a lack of self-esteem with regards to Spanish, a sense of deficit of I don't speak Spanish well or I speak it mixing English with Spanish. This, then from the idea that you speak it like you speak it and that what you have to see is that there are different registers of Spanish, the same as in English, and you have to be able to change pace. And to know when to say something and to whom and when not to say it. And not have just one register.*

Faculty at College/University E, in particular, because they are preparing students for the ministry, sought to develop students' Spanish so that they could work with members of the community on a one-to-one basis as well as to speak in public to deliver the word of God. The development of greater proficiency for heritage speakers, for them, is much more specific and tangible than it tends to be at other institutions.

At all six institutions, at least one individual interviewed (and often all persons interviewed) mentioned grammar as a key element of heritage language instruction, especially when comparing objectives for heritage students with objectives for traditional foreign language students. Grammatical analysis, a greater emphasis on grammar, refining grammar, reviewing grammar, and cleaning up students' language with grammar instruction were repeatedly mentioned as a necessary path to improvement, language growth, and the acquisition of proficiency in the written language. For some individuals, there appeared to be an unspoken tension between goals involving the development of students' self-esteem and their evaluation of the Spanish actually used by their students:

Lo que yo quiero, es que agreguen, si ya hablan el spanglish con sus amigos, y les funciona, está bien, pero me gustaría que no usaran espanglish con alguien que no fuera de su ámbito. (Lecturer, College/University E)

What I want is for them to add (something), if they already speak Spanglish with their friends and it works for them, that's fine, but I would like for them not to use Spanglish with someone who is not from their own locality.

Overall, individuals who had been teaching for a long time (e.g. senior faculty, experienced coordinators) seemed to tiptoe around the clear contradictions that exist between valuing what students bring with them to the classroom and improving their Spanish. As one faculty member stated:

I want them to understand diversity, and I want them to be aware of the fact that the language might be different and also in that I never criticize or I would never want to substitute what they bring, I just expose them to the differences but I always tell them you know what you got is great, keep speaking this type of Spanish that you brought to the class at home because that is OK and that is the appropriate thing in that context. So I don't what to substitute what they are bringing you know; I want to expand on that. (Faculty, College/University F)

In sum, in terms of program objectives, only one program (College/University A) tends to steer away from improvement as such and focuses on the history and culture of Latin America. The objective of the program is

to give them a broader knowledge of their collective and individual history as Latinos. Much of this is done to broaden their horizons and to try to instill in them a passion for the language and the culture that the language is situated in. (Program coordinator, College/University A)

The course and program objectives of the six postsecondary institutions can best be understood by examining their goals and objectives against the list of goals for heritage language instruction that was expanded on the basis of the close study of the six high schools: (1) the acquisition of a standard dialect, (2) the transfer of reading and writing abilities across languages, (3) the expansion of bilingual range, (4) the maintenance of the heritage language, (5) the development of academic skills, and (6) the increase of students' pride and self-esteem.

Interviews with program personnel at postsecondary institutions identified only three of the six total goals guiding heritage language instruction: the acquisition of the standard dialect, the transfer of reading and writing abilities, and the increase of students' pride and self-esteem. It is important to point out, however, that for the majority of interviewees, self-esteem and pride are considered to be directly related to students' use of a normative standard language. There was no mention of expansion of bilingual range, the maintenance of the heritage language, or the development of academic skills in general.

Instructional practices

As was the case with the six secondary institutions studied closely, interviews and observations of heritage language classes at the postsecondary level provided us with information about the ways in which broad instructional goals were implemented on a day-to-day basis. Since we observed only one or two classes at each of the institutions visited during a 1- or, at best, 2-day period, we can only describe the practices we saw and list the practices described to us by interviewees when we specifically asked about effective practices they use. We have no information about whether the described practices are actually implemented or about what happens in classes we observed during the rest of the quarter or semester or even the rest of the week.

Table 7.16 provides an extended list of the goals of heritage language instruction. This list includes both the four goals identified by Valdés (1995) as well as the two new instructional goals (the development of academic skills and the increase of students' pride and self-esteem) identified as a part of this study. In Table 7.16, we have placed instructional practices that we observed or that interviewees described to us as typical of heritage language instruction under each of these six broad goals.

As will be noted in Table 7.16, at the postsecondary level, at the six institutions visited, attention was given primarily to the transfer of reading and writing. All individuals interviewed mentioned reading literature and writing college-level papers as a core focus of the program. Observed classes supported this view, even though particular classes might limit themselves to exercises on the written accent, or peer editing of composition drafts, or in-class reading of single texts.

As Table 7.16 also makes evident, the second area of interest among college-level instructors involved the acquisition of the standard dialect. Again, all individuals interviewed stressed the importance of students' acquiring the standard language and described general practices they had used successfully. Unfortunately, we did not have the opportunity

Table 7.16 Observed and described teaching practices and classroom activities listed under six instructional goals

Goal	Activities/practices
1. Language (culture) maintenance	Reading of or about pre-Columbian works Reading of Latin American history Reading of Latin American literary works Presenting well-known *dichos* Making connections between readings/*dichos* and student experiences Study of oral traditions in indigenous cultures Research projects with presentations on topics of personal interest related to class
2. Expansion of bilingual range	Vocabulary expansion • Identification of new words in dictated passages • Close passage of text read by class, students produce missing words • Examination of words in context when reading
3. Transfer of reading and writing	Spelling • Dictation of passages, including passages from works of literature • In-class correction of dictations • Copying of *refranes* and *dichos* • Completion of spelling exercises in textbook • Practice using the written accent on dictated words • Dictation of individual words • Spelling quizzes Writing • Drafting of full papers of various lengths (multiple drafts required) • Reading of compositions to class Revision of written assignments • Whole-class revision of texts with organization flaws • Whole-class analysis of essay organization Editing of written assignments • Peer editing of compositions (online class) • Pair work to identify errors • Rewriting of composition correcting errors identified by peers or instructor Reading • Reading aloud by teacher to students • Reading aloud by students to the whole class • Reading of text assigned as homework (literature, online news stories) • Discussion of comprehension questions focusing on the reading • Reading aloud in small groups • Close examination of arguments presented in texts

(Continued)

Table 7.16 (*Continued*)

Goal	Activities/practices
4. Acquisition of standard dialect	Grammar explanations and exercises • Presentation of stems and endings for regular present subjunctive verbs • Drill of present subjunctive • Correction of sentences with target structures written on the board by students • Quizzes on grammatical structures covered • Identification of targeted grammatical forms or structures (to express particular meanings) • Written exercises on targeted grammatical forms • Translation • Grammar practice with online exercises designed for foreign language learners • Form-focused instruction using literary texts to illustrate grammatical use Direct teaching of standard dialect • Identification of stigmatized forms (*pos, pa*) • Identification of regional forms (*hacerse la rata*)
5. General academic skills	None observed or described to us
6. Community building and increasing self-esteem	Development of undergraduate tutoring program

of observing such practices. Only one instructor, the teaching assistant at College/University B, presented grammatical structures directly.

Vocabulary expansion involving examination of words in context was observed at four of six campuses. This particular practice was listed under the objective "expansion of bilingual range" because it was the goal of the instructor to add to students' existing vocabularies, rather than to correct or change their existing lexical inventories.

Practices supporting the goal of "language and culture maintenance" were observed and heard described exclusively at College/University A. At this institution, the general objective of the three-course sequence is to give students "a broader knowledge of their collective and individual history as Latinos." For that reason, class time is invested – not in improving students' language – but in having students discover major figures that are considered to be part of their history, for example, Atahualpa, Cuauhtemoc, Sor Juana, Bolívar, Martí. Students write papers and carry out projects relating to the readings, but the focus of this writing is to have students engage deeply with their history and their cultural heritage written in Spanish.

At College/University A, the first course in the series of three concentrates on pre-Columbian history, and students read texts such as the *Populvuh*. In the second course, students read extensively about Latin America. Finally, in the third course, students study a variety of Latin American texts of the last 150 years. At the end the course sequence, students will have read at least 10 classic works, including Pedro Páramo, the writings of Sor Juana Inés de la Cruz, el Lazarillo de Tormes, Fuenteovejuna, and other texts that focus on themes such as hunger, power, and dictatorship.

It is important to point out that although a number of individuals interviewed spoke eloquently about raising students' self-esteem, no specific practices were observed that could be categorized as directed at improving students' self-image. Nor did interviewees specifically describe activities that they believed had been successful in this regard. In the case of community building, a single activity was described to us. This activity is part of the program at a single institution. At this institution, heritage students completing the three-quarter heritage series are eligible to apply for tutor positions in the program. Program tutors meet seven times per quarter with a group of four undergraduates enrolled in the heritage classes. The tutors are trained by the program coordinator, who makes certain that these more senior students know how to answer questions about readings, how to engage students in close discussions about particular questions relating to their own experience, and how to support students in their writing. The tutoring program serves as a special incentive for students who were enrolled in the heritage program to carry out meaningful work in which they continue to use Spanish and creates a close-knit community of Latino students.

Textbooks

Four college/university programs used a total of five textbooks: *Ahora sí*, *La lengua que heredamos*, *Nuevo Mundo*, *Tradición y cambio*, and *Palabra abierta*. Faculty at the two other institutions did not limit themselves to a single book. Instead, they used a variety of supplementary materials and single editions of classic works. All interviewees offered clear opinions about the strengths and weaknesses of the materials they were using or had used. In commenting about components or material that particular textbooks lacked, respondents also gave additional information about their course objectives and about student needs. In Table 7.17, we present comments made about the perceived weaknesses of textbooks in use at each of the six institutions visited.

When asked to describe an ideal textbook, only two individuals responded with extended descriptions. One individual described a comprehensive text that included self-correcting exercises:

> El texto ideal tiene que traer todo lo que es la parte de la enseñanza de la gramática, la escritura, desde la forma más simple hasta la forma más

Table 7.17 Comments made about specific textbooks used at the college/university level

Institution	Textbook(s) used	Comments
College/University A	A variety of classic texts and authors	Faculty do not use Spanish textbooks for heritage speakers because readings are too short or there is no context presented for the readings.
College/University B	Readings from a variety of texts Review of Spanish grammar written for FL students that is now out of print	Faculty do not use textbooks for heritage speakers that are written in Spanish because grammatical explanations are not understood by students.
College/University C	*Nuevo mundo, Tradición y cambio*	Themes in the first text are repetitive. The book needs *dichos*, and history.
College/University D	*La lengua que heredamos*	This text needs more exercises requiring students to analyze syntax. Information in the book is too scattered.
College/University E	*La lengua que heredamos, Palabra abierta*	*Palabra abierta* should be less feminist in orientation.
College/University F	Ahora sí	*Ahora sí* has good topics that students can relate to, but coverage of grammar structure is incomplete. More materials about spelling are needed as well as coverage of relative pronouns and complex sentences.

avanzada con muchos ejercicios para ellos practicar y escribir, porque necesitan los ejercicios con un buen cuaderno de trabajo. Por eso me gustó este texto porque trae un buen cuaderno de trabajo con un índice de respuestas para que los estudiantes se auto corrijan. Si el profesor no puede estar con ellos todo el tiempo ellos pueden, en su casa, hacer su cuaderno de trabajo y auto corregirse y traer sus preguntas o sus dudas a la clase. Así que todos los libros me parecen buenos porque traen bastantes ejercicios. Bastante práctica para que ellos practiquen. (Faculty, College/University D)

The ideal text has to have everything that is part of teaching grammar, writing, from the simplest to the most advanced form with lots of exercises so that they can practice and write, because they need exercises with a good workbook. That's why I liked this text because it has a good workbook, with an index for the answers so that the students can self-correct. If the professor cannot be with them all the time they can, at home, do their workbook and self-correct and bring their questions or doubts to class. So I think all books are good because they have enough exercises. Enough practice so that they can practice.

Other individuals gave much less detail, but imagined a book that would include brief readings to allow students to feel successful from the very beginning of their study of Spanish.

Most instructors reported using supplementary materials that they themselves produced (overheads with grammatical explanations) or commercially available materials such as videos and films. Some require their students to purchase a dictionary; others direct students to the Internet and identify links to materials related to class themes, and still others make copies of favorite readings from other books.

Outcomes

When asked about outcomes, that is, how they know that students have learned something in their classes, most interviewees hesitated momentarily. One individual talked about student grades, reporting that only three or four students received a grade of A or conversely failed the class. Three other interviewees offered examples of specific improvement they had noticed in their students such as better oral communication skills, increased use of accurate written language, or improved reading proficiency. One individual spoke about students' pass rates in the class and another about their enrollment in higher-level courses. Another respondent described student success by depicting the change in student behaviors in detail:

From the point of view of the language I do see a change, throughout the semester. It is hard to measure that change, it is very subjective and it's different for different students, but I definitely see that change and how I can tell is I definitely see in the work that they are doing and in class participation. I mean I've had students who started the semester who are really scared or ashamed to speak Spanish and now they are taking part in classroom discussions. So I can see that they are moving from not speaking Spanish to speaking Spanish. I have students who started the class speaking, trying to speak Spanish but reverting into English very frequently or using English only for the transition words, and you know all of that, and I got them to use Spanish more and more. So it is very hard to measure but I definitely see a change. (Faculty, College/University F)

College/university faculty tend to measure student progress from the standpoint of the program in which they teach. Moreover, they appear to evaluate student outcomes from the perspective of members of the department who will teach heritage students in future courses. In offering evidence of success, they speak of students' having fewer errors and feeling more confident, about students' having greater self-esteem, about their continuing into upper-division courses, and about their being able to use grammatical terminology, to read better, and to improve their writing. All of these outcomes relate to three principal goals: the acquisition of standard language, the transfer of reading and writing abilities, and the development of self-esteem. Once again, college/university faculty made the assumption that when students' Spanish "improves," that is, becomes more normative, their self-esteem will improve as well.

Staff characteristics

As pointed out in Table 7.13, of the 15 individuals involved in the teaching of Spanish as a heritage language, 7 are tenure-track faculty, 7 are full-time lecturers, and 1 is a teaching assistant. Eight individuals are US Latinos, and seven are non-US Latinos (i.e. Latinos who grew up and were educated in Spanish-speaking countries). No non-Latinos are involved in heritage language instruction at the institutions we visited.

None of the individuals currently teaching in college/university heritage programs had received formal training in teaching heritage students. Without exception, they had simply been assigned the classes for heritage students, or they had chosen to teach the classes because of their interest in Latino students. Several of the US Latino faculty identified strongly with their students.

Preparing students for life outside of school

Except for faculty teaching at the private college that trained students for the ministry, all other faculty, lecturers, and teaching assistants have given little thought to the possible relationship between heritage language classes and professional careers. Program and course objectives are viewed from the perspective of departmental course and program requirements. Furthermore, heritage speakers are seen as college or university students who needed to pass those courses to receive credit and to improve their Spanish for further study. When we asked what heritage courses might do differently if they had as one of their objectives preparing students to use the language professionally, one individual pointed out that English was the language that would be needed for professional work in California and not Spanish! Overall, it is difficult for faculty to imagine what they might do differently in their classes that could be useful to future professionals working as doctors, lawyers, nurses, and businessperson. Some individuals spoke about the direct benefit of Spanish courses for future bilingual teachers; but again, this benefit was seen as directly related to developing competence in the standard language.

Tensions, challenges, and recommendations

We asked college/university faculty to talk about tensions and challenges they continue to encounter and to formulate three recommendations for other institutions interested in starting heritage programs. Some of the challenges and tensions described to us relate directly to what is seen as students' poor background in Spanish grammar. At College/University D, for example, faculty complain about students' not being allowed to take Spanish in high school and therefore not knowing "what it means to conjugate a verb" or that "Spanish is a language with a system." Other faculty at this same institution worry about students' not understanding why they do not automatically receive a grade of A in regular Spanish courses where they are mixed with foreign language learners.

At other institutions, faculty are concerned about the need to publicize the heritage program more broadly (College/University C), about obtaining appropriate textbooks (College/University E), and about heritage students' responses to Anglo-American faculty (College/University B). The most serious concern for all faculty was the relationship between different groups of students. Tensions between newly arrived immigrant students who have been educated in Spanish and second- and third-generation students who have been educated only in English are quite serious at the college and university levels. One individual spoke of the prejudices between the two groups of students and emphasized that ideally they should be placed in different courses.

> Pero los pone uno en un mismo salón, afloran toda una serie de prejuicios de un lado y del otro. (Program coordinator, College/ University B)
>
> *But one puts them in the same classroom and a whole series of prejudices emerge from one side and the other.*

In terms of recommendations, individuals interviewed recommended implementing two levels of heritage courses: a first-level heritage course parallel to beginning Spanish for foreign language learners to serve the needs of students who are not literate in Spanish and an intermediate heritage course for more advanced students. They also made several recommendations about the ethnicity of faculty, the teaching of composition courses using extensive models of student writing, the need for faculty to get to know students.

Only one faculty member (Program Coordinator, College/University A) recommended that heritage courses be designed to meet students' needs directly. She also recommended that faculty inform students about the levels of commitment that retaining Spanish and developing the language will take.

> It's important to know who the students are, why they are taking the class: To prepare themselves for literature? To practice Spanish?... If people decide to take the course, and retain their Spanish, they need to know that it will take discipline. That it is not just speaking it but that to widen, learn a larger vocabulary, or to expand your registers/knowledge of Spanish. That this will take some time; it is not just a small decision/process. (Program coordinator, College/University A)

For college and university part-time and adjunct faculty, the challenges of working with heritage students involve factors that go beyond language. They are quite aware of their low status within departments of Spanish and of the insecurity surrounding their jobs. Lecturers understand that they can make few decisions about heritage courses and that their work will be evaluated, in part, by the degree to which students can pass undetected among "regular" students in upper-division courses taught by tenure-track and tenured faculty.

Heritage programs at the college/university level: A summary

The study of six college/university-level Spanish heritage language programs suggests that an expectation that formal language programs as currently configured can and will contribute to Spanish language maintenance is misguided at the postsecondary level also. Colleges and universities do not also see their role as providing support for such efforts. They see themselves as either providing courses through which students fulfill a general education requirement in language or as preparing students who will major in Spanish. As Brecht and Walton (2000) pointed out, curricula in such departments are largely designed to fulfill an imagined vocational and reproductive function, in which faculty members prepare students to become foreign language department faculty like themselves. There is, therefore, a constant preoccupation with language correctness.

At all six colleges/universities visited, interviewees described heritage students' Spanish as deficient. They also spoke of the need for students to "improve" their Spanish by studying traditional grammar. Interestingly, perhaps because of the importance of reading and writing at the college level, much more class time was devoted to reading in the classes we observed than to the direct teaching of traditional grammar. Still, there does appear to be some confusion about practices that can bring about growth in written Spanish at both the text and sentence levels. Many of the practices observed appear to be based on current popular practices in the teaching of English composition (e.g. process writing, peer review, use of multiple drafts). Multiple drafts, however, are used exclusively to correct grammatical and orthographical errors. Little attention is given to text organization, argument structure, and the like.

Only one institution has a program in place where Spanish is used as a medium rather than as the focus of instruction. In this program (College/University A), the exploration of Latin American history is seen as a basis for the continued development of the language acquired at home. Much less direct attention is given to language conventions.

Conclusion: The Study of Selected Heritage Language Programs

The study of six college/university heritage language programs confirmed the findings of the mail survey conducted with 35 colleges/universities that implemented heritage programs. As reported by more than 75% of college/university respondents, the six educational institutions that we visited primarily focused on goals and practices that had as their primary purpose developing students' proficiency in standard Spanish (such as the direct correction of language forms).

Observations and interviews conducted with a total of 14 individuals at the six institutions offered us important additional insights about the common rationale behind these practices. With two exceptions, all 14 individuals interviewed and/or observed had unfavorable views of the Spanish spoken by second- and third-generation speakers of Spanish and by newly arrived immigrants from Mexico who came from rural areas and had little schooling. Interviewees had no knowledge of language variation or bilingualism and of contact and rural varieties of Spanish. Non-US Latinos and US Latinos both described the language proficiency of their students in disapproving terms, often confusing a lack of knowledge of a grammatical meta-language with intellectual and linguistic limitations. The "educated Spanish" of upper-class Spanish-speaking monolinguals was seen as the ideal to which all students should aspire and the primary goal of heritage language instruction. Learning to use the standard language well was assumed to lead directly to growth in pride and self-esteem for Latino students.

Notes

1. Evidence of this growing interest can be seen in the recent work of the Alliance for the Advancement of Heritage Languages carried out by the National Foreign Language Center and the Center for Applied Linguistics (http://www.cal.org/heritage/index.html). Activities sponsored by or directly related to the efforts of the Alliance include three national conferences as well as the establishment of the *Heritage Language Journal* (http://www.heritagelanguages.org/).

References

Brecht, R., and Walton, R. W. (2000) System III: The future of language learning in the United States. In R. D. Lambert and E. Shohamy (eds) *Language Policy and Pedagogy* (pp. 111–27). Philadelphia, PA: Benjamins.

Church, A. H. (1993) Estimating the effect of incentives on mail survey response. *Public Opinion Quarterly* 57 (1), 62–79.

Fischer, L. (2004) Spanish for native speakers (SNS) education: The state of the field. On WWW at http://www.cal.org./hertiage/sns/sns-fieldrpt.htm. Accessed 24.8.2004.

Fox, R. J., Crask, M. R., and Kim, J. (1989) Mail survey response rate: A meta-analysis of selected techniques for inducing response. *Public Opinion Quarterly* 52 (4), 467–91.

Ingold, C., Rivers, W., Tesser, C. C., and Ashby, E. (2002) Report on the NFLC/AATSP survey of Spanish language programs for native speakers. *Hispania* 85 (2), 324–29.

James, J. M., and Bolstein, R. (1992) Large monetary incentives and their effect on mail survey response rates. *Public Opinion Quarterly* 56 (4), 442–53.

Kaplowitz, M. D., Hadlock, T. D., and Levine, R. (2004) A comparison of web and mail survey response rates. *Public Opinion Quarterly* 68 (1), 94–101.

Potowski, K. (2003) Chicago's heritage language teacher corps: A model for improving Spanish teacher development. *Hispania* 86 (2), 302–11.

Valdés, G. (1995) The teaching of minority languages as 'foreign' languages: Pedagogical and theoretical challenges. *Modern Language Journal* 79 (3), 299–328.

Valdés, G., Fishman, J. A., Chávez, R., and Pérez, W. (2004) Language shift among Latino professionals in California. Unpublished manuscript.

Valdés, G., González, S., García, D. L., and Márquez, P. (2003) Language ideology: The case of Spanish in departments of foreign languages. *Anthrophology and Education Quarterly* 34 (1), 3–26.

Valdés, G., González, S., García, D. L., and Márquez, P. (in press). The challenges of maintaining non-English languages through educational institutions. In D. M. Brinton and O. Kagan (eds) *Heritage Language Acquisition: A New Field Emerging* (Vol. 34, pp. 3–26). Mahwah, MJ: Erlbaum.

Chapter 8

The Teaching of Heritage Languages

Lessons from California

GUADALUPE VALDÉS

Introduction

The study of Spanish heritage instruction in California has many implications for the development and maintenance of other heritage languages in the United States and for the establishment of language policies that can support not only the revitalization and maintenance of indigenous and immigrant languages but also the dissemination of theoretical insights and sound pedagogical approaches based on these insights. Our observations of heritage language classrooms and our survey of college/ university and high-school programs suggest that current heritage language instruction involves ad hoc adaptations of foreign-language-teaching approaches that may or may not be appropriate for this particular set of learners. In this chapter, we argue that, in order for post-9/11 efforts aimed at developing existing language resources in this country to be successful,[1] sustained attention must be given to (1) development of theories of heritage language development/reacquisition and (2) examination of the role of language ideologies in the teaching and learning enterprise. We first discuss the development of theories of heritage language development/reacquisition and argue that this development must be based on the investigation of the implicit systems acquired by different types of heritage learners in their nondominant first languages (L1s). We outline a research agenda focusing on questions that need to be examined carefully to develop appropriate pedagogies for heritage speakers. We then introduce the concept of language ideology and examine its role in the teaching of heritage languages. We begin by considering the ways in which language ideologies influence language instruction in departments of Spanish and then describe how these same or similar ideologies might play a role in the teaching of other heritage languages in the United States.

Toward the Development of Theories of Heritage Language Development/Reacquisition

The greatest challenge facing the foreign language profession in teaching heritage learners who elect to maintain or develop their first language (L1) in formal instructional settings is the design of instruction that is not only appropriate for their current and future needs but that is also based on coherent theories of instructed language acquisition for these particular groups of learners. Ideally, pedagogical approaches used with heritage learners would be based on an understanding of the implicit linguistic knowledge systems of heritage speakers and on a familiarity with the processes involved when speakers of such nondominant first languages attempt to develop or reacquire these languages in formal instructional settings. At present, although we have some knowledge of the role of instruction in restructuring the interlanguages of second language (L2) learners,[2] we have no information about the role of formal instruction in restructuring or reshaping the knowledge systems of learners who are in many ways quite different from traditional classroom learners. As government-funded initiatives move forward to ensure the expansion of high-level language resources in a variety of languages that are spoken in ethnic communities in the United States, it is imperative that a clear research agenda on the development and reacquisition of heritage languages be established and systematically carried out to maximize efforts undertaken by both educational institutions and government agencies in increasing essential language resources.

In this section, we briefly review key characteristics of heritage language speakers and outline elements of a research agenda directed at understanding both the development/reacquisition of heritage languages as well as the role of instruction in these processes.

Heritage learners as L1/L2 users

In the last several years, Vivian Cook, a very distinguished researcher in the area of SLA, has made a strong case for the study of what he refers to as *multicompetence* (Cook, 1992, 1996, 2002). He has argued that it is of particular importance for the second language acquisition field to engage in the study of the *L2 user*, an individual who has knowledge of and uses a second language, rather than in the exclusive study of the *L2 learner*, an individual whose task of acquisition is seen as not yet finished. Drawing from research on bilingualism, he points out, moreover, that L2 users are, by definition, different from monolingual speakers. Rejecting the view that the ultimate state of L2 learning is to pass undetected among native speakers, Cook (2002: 9) emphasizes that "the minds, languages and lives of L2 users are different from those of monolinguals," and that "L2 users are not failures because they are different." In suggesting the term *L2 user* and rejecting the designation *bilingual,* Cook (2002: 4) points out that the term has "contradictory definitions and associations in both popular and academic usage."

Recently, Valdés (in press) argued that the term *L2 user* is not entirely appropriate for the description of heritage language learners. Pointing out that the term *L2 user* still tends to emphasize and focus attention primarily on the L2, she proposes the term *L1/L2 user* to describe heritage learners, many of whom acquire the L2 in a combination of naturalistic and instructed settings and continue to use the L1 to some degree in their everyday lives. We use the term *L1/L2 user* interchangeably with the terms *bilingual* and *heritage speaker* in the discussion that follows to emphasize the difference between heritage speakers and second language learners.

Approaches to the study of L1 acquisition

In acquiring their first language, children build an implicit, unconscious system that underlies both the production and comprehension of language. According to innatist theories of L1 acquisition, these unconscious systems are constrained by universal linguistic principles, to which the name Universal Grammar (UG) has been given. Children are thought to be equipped or preprogrammed with these universal principles (UG), and it is this unique biological endowment that allows them to acquire an immensely complex linguistic system in a very short time that goes far beyond the specific grammatical properties present in the language input that surrounds them. Interactionist approaches to the study of first-language acquisition, on the other hand, although concerned about the product of language acquisition, focus instead on the language acquisition process. These latter researchers examine the stages that children go through as they become speakers of the language who can interact appropriately with other speakers of the community because they have acquired all the elements of language, both structure and usage (Clark, 2002). Even though there is disagreement among researchers about both the specific mechanisms involved in L1 acquisition and about ways in which children's systems change over time, researchers agree that, when a particular language has been acquired, speakers of that language have in place an internalized system for that language that includes linguistic knowledge (i.e. knowledge of the sound system, knowledge of the meanings of words, knowledge of syntactic rules) as well as pragmatic knowledge (i.e. knowledge about how to participate in conversations and knowledge about what to say to whom and when).

Acquisition in L1/L2 users

Bilingual acquisition has been defined as "the acquisition of two languages in childhood" (Deuchar and Quay, 2000: 1). There is disagreement among researchers, however, about the precise time in childhood when exposure to the two languages must begin in order to be considered acquisition of two L1s. McLaughlin (1978), for example, defined *simultaneous acquisition* as a situation in which a child is exposed to two languages before the age of 3 and *successive acquisition* as a situation in which exposure to a second language after the age of 3. Other researchers (e.g. DeHouwer, 1995) reserve the term *bilingual language acquisition* to the exposure of a child to two languages within the first month of birth. Exposure to a second language after 1 month up to the age of 2 is described instead as *bilingual second language acquisition* (De Houwer, 1995). Deuchar and Quay (2000: 2) use the term *bilingual acquisition* "to refer to situations where the child is regularly exposed to two languages from birth or during the first year of life."

Romaine (1995), drawing from Harding and Riley (1987), maintains that much of the work on bilingual acquisition has been methodologically flawed and that many studies do not describe the context of acquisition or the age or patterns of exposure to two languages. Romaine classifies types of bilingual families, the acquisition context, and strategies used in exposing children to two languages as presented in Table 8.1.

Unfortunately, as Romaine points out, few studies of bilingual language acquisition studies have been carried out in Type 6 contexts. Thus, we have little information about children who are born and raised in heritage language communities among both monolingual speakers of the heritage language *and* bilingual speakers of the dominant and the heritage language. Immigrant/minority communities are home to speakers of both the immigrant and the societal language. Both newly arrived immigrants and adult native-born individuals may be part of the same family. Children raised in such communities are often part of large extended families in which the original varieties of the heritage language of its members may be converging with other immigrant varieties of the same language present in the community. Recently arrived individuals may be at different stages of acquisition of the societal language, while members of the family who have been in the country for many years might be at various stages of loss or attrition of the heritage language. Children who acquire two languages in such contexts will be exposed to two languages in ways that are quite unlike the exposure experienced by children who are members of families of Types 1–5 listed in Table 8.1. For children of Type 6 families, exposure to one or the other for the two languages may vary significantly, depending on which members of the household are present at particular points in time. Even though there is no consensus about the influence of parental or caretaker speech on bilingual children's language acquisition involving, for example, language mixing, Bialystok (2001) maintains that studies of monolingual language acquisition show that there is a certain influence. She concludes that "the effect is pervasive enough ... to acknowledge that

Table 8.1 Acquisition contexts in bilingual families

Type	Parent's language	Community language	Strategy used
Type 1: One person – one language	Different native languages. Each have some competence in other language.	One parental language is dominant in community.	Each parents speaks own language to child.
Type 2: One language – one environment	Different native languages	One parental language is dominant in community.	Both parents speak nondominant language. Child hears nondominant language outside the home from others.
Type 3: Home language – no community support	Same native language	Parental language is not the dominant language.	Both parents speak nondominant language. Child hears nondominant language outside the home from others.
Type 4: Home language – no community support	Different native languages	Neither parental language is dominant language.	Each parents speaks own language to child.
Type 5: Nonnative parents	Same native language	Parental language is dominant language of the community.	One parent speaks to child in nonnative language.
Type 6: Bilingual parents	Common native language and community language	Sectors of community are also bilingual.	Parents code-switch and mix languages.

the language children hear has a role in shaping the language they will speak" (p. 115).

The knowledge systems of heritage learners

By definition, L1/L2 users have internalized two implicit linguistic knowledge systems, one in each of their languages. Whether they acquired the societal language and the heritage language simultaneously as infants or sequentially as young children or as adolescents, heritage speakers use their two languages on an everyday basis with interlocutors who are both monolingual in each of their two languages as well as bilingual in both languages. Moreover, as Grosjean (1985) and Cook (1997) have argued, L1/L2 users are not two monolinguals in one, but rather specific speaker-hearers who have acquired their two languages in particular contexts and for particular reasons. Viewed from a bilingualist rather than a monolingualist perspective, L1/L2 users have acquired two knowledge systems that they use to carry out their particular communicative needs, needs that may be quite unlike those of monolingual native speakers, who use a single language in all communicative interactions. Oksaar (1997: 9), for example, argues that bilingual individuals may have "not only two or more sets of rule complexes from their languages, regulating their communicative performance, but at least three, the third complex arising from LX," which consists, to a large extent, of items from L1 and L2. Oksaar maintains that LX itself is governed by its own norms of usage.

Also arguing for a bilingualist perspective on L1/L2 users, Grosjean (1997) contends that, at any given moment, bilinguals are in states of activation of their languages and language-processing mechanisms that are either monolingual or bilingual. Depending on the base language used and the interlocutors involved, an L1/L2 user will be either in (1) a monolingual mode in language A, (2) a monolingual mode in language B, or (3) a bilingual mode. While in one or the other of the monolingual modes, the other language is deactivated to some extent and transfer between the two languages is reduced. In the bilingual mode, however, because both languages are active, transfer between the two languages as well as the tendency to code-switch will be evident to a greater degree. Grosjean argues that, since language behavior in different modes most probably reflects how bilinguals process their two languages, research on bilingual competence and performance must take into account language mode.

Unfortunately, as a number of researchers (e.g. Cook, 1997; Mohanty & Perregaux, 1997; Romaine, 1995; Woolard, 1999) have pointed out, bilingualism has generally been seen as anomalous, marginal, and in need of explanation. In spite of the fact that the majority of the populations of the world are bilingual or multilingual, the position that has been taken by many researchers is that the norm for human beings is to know a single language. As Cook points out (1997: 280), "A person who has two languages is strange in some sense, obviously different from the *normal* person. Hence, the questioner looks for the differences caused by this unnatural condition of knowing two or more languages" (italics ours). According to Woolard (1999), until very recently, multiplicity and simultaneity were not part of sociolinguistic theory, and notions of unitary language, as well as notions of bounded, and discrete codes were never problematized. The tendency among many researchers, therefore, has been to propose that "true" or "real" bilinguals are the sum of *two native-speaking monolinguals*. According to this perspective, a true bilingual is expected to be two native speakers in one person.

The notion of the native speaker – especially as applied to bilingual individuals – is neither simple, obvious, nor straightforward (Davis, 1991, 2003). From some perspectives, for example, Coulmas's (1981), only those speakers of a language qualify as potential informants "whose first language it is." According to this view, there is a qualitative difference between a first and second language. Other students of the concept of native speaker take an even more extreme position. Ballmer (1981), for example, argues that bilingual individuals are not native speakers of either of their languages. According to Kramsch (1997: 363), "originally, native speakership was viewed as an uncontroversial privilege of birth. Those who were born into a language were considered its native speakers, with grammatical intuitions that nonnative speakers did not have." Kramsch argues that a closer examination of the concept reveals that it has often been linked to social class and to education. She maintains that the native speaker norm that has been recognized by foreign language departments in United States, for example, is that of "the middle-class, ethnically dominant male citizenry of nation-states" (p. 363). By implication, the language of non – middle-class citizens of such nations has been considered suspect.

Taking a slightly different perspective, Haugen (1970: 225) contends that the native speaker norm, even as a popular concept, is difficult to apply to most bilinguals:

> To be natively competent in two languages would then mean to have had two childhoods, so that all the joys and frustrations of the fundamental period of life could penetrate one's emotional response to the simple words of the language. It would mean to have acquired the skills of reading and writing that go with two separate educational systems such as all literate societies now impose on their adolescents, or the corresponding rigorous forms of initiation and skill development that formed part of all nonliterate societies. It would mean to have two different identities, one looking at the world from one point of view, the other from another; it would mean sharing in the social forms, prejudices, and insights of two cultures. In short, it would mean being two entirely different people.

While absolutely equivalent abilities in two languages are theoretically possible, except for rare geographical and familial accidents, individuals seldom have access to two languages in exactly the same contexts in every domain of interaction. L1/L2 users do not have the opportunity of using two languages to carry out the exact same functions with all individuals with whom they interact or to use their languages intellectually to the same degree. They thus do not develop identical strengths in both languages.

More important, perhaps, is it is not the case that all monolingual native speakers would be successful if measured against the norm of the educated native. It thus makes little sense to use a monolingual native-speaker norm to evaluate the competence of L1/L2 users. As Cook (1997: 294) has argued, it is not clear why we should "ever compare two types of people in terms of a bookkeeping exercise of profit and loss."

A Research Agenda on Heritage Language Development and Reacquisition

To design instruction aimed at developing the unique language strengths of heritage language learners, a systematic research agenda needs to be put in place that can guide the multiple aspects of this research. This agenda must focus not only on the linguistic characteristics of heritage learners, but also on the role of instruction in the development/reacquisition of nondominant L1s. At the minimum, such an agenda must:

(1) Develop language evaluation/assessment procedures that can identify key differences among heritage learners.
(2) Investigate the implicit systems of different types of heritage learners in their nondominant L1s.
(3) Determine the degree of system restructuring that would need to take place in order for heritage speakers at different levels of heritage language proficiency to carry out particular functions in particular settings using appropriate linguistic forms.
(4) Investigate the role of different types of instruction in such restructuring for different types of heritage speakers.
(5) Determine whether pedagogies used to restructure the interlanguages of L2 learners can also be effective for various categories of heritage speakers.

Identifying key differences among heritage learners

Given the complexity of the bilingual experience and the fact that there are few L1/L2 users who are ambilingual, we can hypothesize that there are important differences in the implicit linguistic knowledge systems of various types of L1/L2 users who are grouped under the label *heritage speakers* in an academic context. A research agenda designed to support theories of the development/reacquisition of heritage languages that are acquired as L1 by these users, therefore, needs to begin by developing procedures for examining similarities and differences among individual heritage speakers of the same language as well as between categories of heritage speakers of different languages. These procedures must ultimately lead to the development of typologies of heritage speakers that are potentially important for classroom instruction. What are needed are typologies that go beyond traditional generational categorizations (first-, second-, and third-generation) of immigrant speakers that are commonly used in sociolinguistic research as well as beyond other categorizations that focus on recency of arrival, schooling, and access to the standard language (e.g. Valdés, 1995). For pedagogical purposes, useful classifications should be able to provide information about the linguistic proficiencies of heritage speakers, about the characteristics of their underlying implicit knowledge systems, and about the differences among heritage speakers of the same generation and background.

The development of proficiency assessment procedures

A starting point for establishing general typologies of heritage speakers of different types will require the development of proficiency assessments of various types that will allow researchers to compare and contrast various types of speakers along a variety of dimensions. Such procedures must be capable of providing information about the range of functions that can be successfully carried out by different speakers in different contexts as well as information about the linguistic characteristics of the various registers present in the language repertories of individual L1/L2 users. A resulting language proficiency scale might, for example, resemble that used by Hallamaa (1998: 72–74) in his study of endangered languages.[3] Hallamaa's scale includes the following 11 categories:

(1) Speaks eloquently and knowledgeably.
(2) Speaks fluently, prefers language for most interactions.
(3) Speaks fluently but prefers another language.
(4) Speaks with "minor" flaws, including careless or uncertain words, grammar simplifications, limited vocabulary, use of unassimilated loan words.
(5) Speaks a little. Makes "serious" grammatical errors. Tends to revert to other language when encountering difficulties.
(6) Understands the language well but is not able to or does not speak it.
(7) Understands some. Can understand topic of conversations carried out around him.
(8) Understands standard set of questions and commands. May have had instruction in this language as a foreign language.
(9) Understands at least two dozen words in the language.
(10) Understands half a dozen words in the language.
(11) Does not understand the language.

As will be noted, this set of categories, while not entirely satisfactory, is structured so that differences between various types of L1/L2 users can be identified. For Hallamaa's purpose, which was the creation of community profiles for potentially endangered languages, it was important to identify numbers and ages of speakers who were eloquent and knowledgeable and other types of speakers ranging from those who still preferred L1 to those who no longer had receptive proficiencies in the language.

To provide adequate instruction for heritage speakers, it will be important to determine not only speaking fluency in general, but also the number of registers and varieties produced and understood as well as levels of literacy developed in the heritage language. One might imagine, for example, categorizing knowledgeable and eloquent heritage speakers as:

(1) Biliterate, eloquent and knowledgeable speakers of *domestic and academic registers*[4]
(2) Monoliterate (or biliterate), eloquent and knowledgeable speakers of a *domestic register* in an *urban/prestige variety* of the language
(3) Monoliterate (or biliterate), eloquent and knowledgeable speakers of a *domestic register* in a *rural/nonprestige variety* of the language
(4) Monoliterate (or biliterate), eloquent and knowledgeable speakers of a *domestic register* in a *contact variety* of the language

Other fluent speakers might be identified in similar ways:

(5) Monoliterate (or biliterate) fluent speakers of a *domestic register* in an urban (or rural or contact) variety of the language *who still prefer that language*
(6) Monolinterate (or biliterate) fluent speakers of a *domestic register* in urban (or rural or contact) variety of the language *who prefer the other language*

In the case of speakers who produce "flawed" language, the categorization of these speakers might take into account the possible sources of the identified flaws. For example:

(7) Hesitant speakers of flawed language. Speech suggests *incomplete acquisition* of obligatory categories and/or limited vocabulary
(8) Hesitant speakers of flawed language. Speech suggests *language attrition*

Fine-grained categorizations such as these – while detailed – are a necessary preliminary to the detailed study of both inter- and intraheritage learner variation in the various subsystems of their nondominant language. Assessment procedures might adapt or draw directly from methodologies used in the study of fossilization in L2 learners (Han, 2003) and include oral and written proficiency tests, dialect- and register-sensitive cloze procedures (Gibbons & Ramirez, 2004), and grammaticality/acceptability judgments. A focus on the linguistic forms frequently examined by L2 researchers might be especially useful in comparing L1/L2 users with L2 learners and in examining the role of instruction in the development/reacquisition of heritage languages in classroom contexts.

What is clear is that, in order to understand the knowledge systems of L1/L2 users, an analytical model is needed that is capable not only of "tracing changes in relative L1 competence over time, after immigrants have arrived in the L2 environment" (Kenny, 1996: 6), but also of providing information about the *communal language* to which they have been exposed as well as the *I-Language* (an individual speaker's idiolect; Mufwene, 2001). A speaker who has been raised in a community within which the communal language is a contact variety of that language, for example, will produce speech that may appear flawed from the perspective of an urban or prestige monolingual variety. Such "flawed" speech, however, might nevertheless be generated by a fully acquired linguistic system that has not undergone attrition. As Kenny (1996) argues, in understanding language loss or attrition, researchers must go beyond a structural approach that is limited to the identification and analysis of linguistic elements that appear to be either different or missing when compared to the speech of normative L1 speakers. In immigrant communities, the various incoming varieties of the heritage language may have converged to produce a new dialect through processes involving accommodation, the development of interdialectalisms, leveling, and simplification (Penny, 2000). The resulting communal language may have undergone a series of both downward and upward changes through the imitation of the features used by high-prestige speakers as well as those used by less privileged speakers who nevertheless enjoy covert prestige. Features that were stigmatized in the original home country, for example, may spread among speakers who need particular "street credibility" (Penny, 2000: 69). In addition, through its contact with the dominant language, the communal language may have also undergone contact-induced language change (Thomason, 2001; Thomason & Kaufman, 1988) through lexical and structural borrowing. Finally, changes may have taken place in the communal language that, while originating in the monolingual environment, may have been accelerated because of contact with the dominant language.[5]

In sum, carrying out research on L1/L2 users designed to inform instruction in their heritage language will require that researchers attend carefully to questions such as those raised by Grosjean (1998), more recently recalled by Wei (2000: 481–82), and adapted here to apply to heritage speakers:

- Which languages (and language skills) have been acquired by heritage speakers?
- When and how was the heritage language acquired?
- Was the cultural context of acquiring the heritage and the societal language the same or different?

- What has been the pattern of heritage language use?
- What is the relationship between the heritage speaker's two languages?
- Are one or several languages still being acquired?
- Is the heritage speaker in the process of restructuring (maybe losing) a language or language skill because of a change of linguistic environment?
- Has a certain language stability been reached?
- Which languages (and language skills) are used currently, in what context, for what purpose, and to what extent?
- What is the heritage speaker's proficiency in each of the four skills of listening, speaking, reading, and writing in each language?
- What is the heritage speaker's proficiency in various dialects, registers, or styles of each language?
- How often and for how long is the bilingual in a monolingual mode (i.e. when one language is active) and in a bilingual mode (i.e. when both languages are active)?
- When in a bilingual mode, how much code-switching and borrowing takes place?
- What is the heritage speaker's age, sex, socioeconomic and educational status, etc.

Valid and effective formal instruction for heritage learners must be based on measurement and assessment procedures that attend carefully to these questions. What needs to be determined in understanding the role of instruction in developing or maintaining heritage languages is whether heritage students – by formally studying their L1s – are involved in one or more of the following processes:[6]

(1) the acquisition of incompletely acquired features of the L1 as a "second" language;
(2) first language (re)acquisition involving features that have undergone attrition;
(3) the acquisition of a second dialect (D2 acquisition);
(4) the development of discourse skills in the written and oral language, including the acquisition of academic registers and styles (R2 acquisition); and/or
(5) the acquisition of literacy.

Silva-Corvalán (2003a, 2003b), for example, reports on the Spanish of young children in Los Angeles who at school age have not yet acquired the complete tense, aspect, and mood system of Spanish. She argues that, without school support, such children will not completely acquire the linguistic system of the language as used by normative L1 speakers because of limited access to Spanish language input. For Silva-Corvalán, the extended intensive contact with the societal language in the school context appears to interrupt the normal process of L1 acquisition in later childhood. Children move through the same stages of acquisition but at a slower rate and, once the L2 becomes dominant, their use of the L1 decrease significantly. According to Silva-Corvalán, as a result of a lack of input and fewer opportunities for using the L1, children who grow up in contexts in which one of their two languages is limited in use will not fully acquire the subsystems of the language that are acquired by youngsters in monolingual settings at an early age. In her work on the Spanish of Los Angeles, Silva-Corvalán (1994) maintains that the Spanish of third-generation speakers who have grown up in this country is characterized by a reduced range of styles as a result of either language attrition or incomplete acquisition. She notes that the use of Spanish in Los Angeles appears to be much less frequent among both second- and third-generation speakers in the home domain.

The use of a simplified verb system as well as the uneven control of the heritage language (often made evident by the constant use of pauses, hesitations, and fillers) may not, however, indicate that the language has been incompletely acquired by a heritage speaker. What will not be immediately clear from superficial assessments, however, is whether flawed production is due to interrupted acquisition, individual language attrition, or "full" acquisition of a contact variety of the heritage language that is now quite different from the varieties of the heritage language originally brought to the community. A theory of instruction supporting the development or reacquisition of a nondominant L1 for such learners will require an understanding of how and whether the implicit systems of speakers who have incompletely acquired the heritage language, speakers whose heritage language has undergone attrition, and speakers of a heritage language that has undergone extensive change are alike or different. What needs to be explored is how these different systems – if they *are* different – might be reshaped by formal instruction. In the case of incomplete acquisition, the instructional problem to be solved might involve, for example, the full acquisition of tense, aspect, and mood in the L1. Instructional approaches might, therefore, include second-language methodologies used in the teaching of both the oral and written language to L2 learners.

In the case of language attrition (the erosion, decay, contraction, or obsolescence of a language), the process of reacquisition might be quite different. Much attention, therefore, must be given to the study of suspected language attrition among heritage learners. What needs to be understood is both the process and the speed of attrition in individuals who are members of particular communities as well as the subsystems that undergo attrition. In a foundational article on language attrition, Anderson (1982) argues that language attrition researchers must take into account comprehension and production, uses of both oral and written language, traditional linguistic levels (i.e. phonology, morphology, syntax) as well as functions, domains of use, and discourse competencies of the speakers in question. Anderson maintains that for each linguistic feature examined, researchers much have what he terms a *baseline comparison*; that is, they must have two types of normative data: (1) the normal use of particular features by fully competent speakers and (2) the use of the features by the individuals being studied *before* they underwent language attrition. Anderson emphasizes that a distinction must be made between *dysfunctional attrition*, which causes a reduction in communication, and *cosmetic attrition*, which involves the reduction of features that are socially valued but does not interfere with communication.

Unfortunately, diagnosing attrition and distinguishing attrition from incomplete acquisition as well as from full acquisition of a contact variety of a language on the basis of language assessment procedures is not simple. The same features listed by Anderson to signal attrition (use of analytic versus synthetic structures, use of lexical borrowings, convergence of syntactic form, cognate transfer, literal translation) are also indicative of three very different types of conditions (incomplete acquisition, individual language attrition, or use of a communal contact variety that has undergone convergence and reduction). In the case of language attrition, the instructional problem to be solved is one of either reacquisition of the subsystems that have undergone attrition and/or the reversal of ongoing attrition of particular subsystems/features. One can conjecture that if attrition is caused by a removal from "the type and quantity of linguistic input and linguistic interaction necessary to maintain the full lexical, phonological, morphological, and syntactic distinctions that are made by fluent competent speakers of this language" (Anderson, 1982: 91), reversal of attrition would need to involve rich input and intensive interaction typical of monolingual linguistic environments. Without evidence to the contrary, one could not conclude that direct forms- or form-focused instruction or other typical pedagogies used in L2 instruction would be particularly beneficial in the process of reacquisition or reversal of attrition. This is, however, an empirical question, and one which can only be answered by examining the effects of different types of instruction designed to reverse attrition in a category of students who have been carefully identified as having undergone attrition in their heritage language.

For the heritage speaker who has fully acquired a communal language that has undergone extensive changes through its contact with other varieties of the same language and with the dominant language, the instructional problem to be solved is quite different. If the goal is for such speakers to acquire the normative monolingual variety through formal instruction, what needs to be understood is the process of D2 acquisition. These heritage speakers are not involved in acquiring parts of a system that have been incompletely acquired, nor are they involved in reacquiring subsystems that have been lost. In this case, heritage speakers are involved in acquiring an *additional* variety of the same language. What they must learn is which features of the communal language do and do not correspond to the features of the normative monolingual varieties of the language. A possible theory of D2 acquisition, for example, might parallel theories of L2 acquisition and propose that in acquiring D2s, learners move through a set of interdialect grammars until they reach the desired end state. In addition, if the goal of heritage language instruction is also for these D2 learners to develop reading and writing skills, literacy instruction would ideally be based on an understanding of the differences and similarities between literacy acquisition in a D2 and literacy acquisition in both a first and a second language.

If the goal of heritage language instruction for heritage speakers who are acquiring a D2 is also for them to extend their repertoires to include styles and registers of the heritage language appropriate for communicating in academic or professional settings, instruction must be based on an understanding of the acquisition of additional registers by *monolingual* speakers who have not had access to contexts in which these particular registers are used. The instructional problem to be solved in this case is the acquisition of additional registers (R2 acquisition), that is, a set of discourse practices that are directly tied to values and norms of a particular social group (Gee, 1990). As Gee has also pointed out, however, particular discourse practices are difficult to acquire in classroom settings because learners may have little or no access to speakers who use these particular specialized registers. In attempting to add such higher registers of their heritage language to their repertoires, L1/L2 users may attempt to imitate these registers by transferring and adapting features of similar registers from their L2. A possible theory of R2 acquisition might, therefore, parallel theories of L2 and D2 acquisition and propose, as Valdés and Gioffrion-Vinci (1998) did, that in acquiring second or additional registers and dialects, learners move through a set of interregisters before they reach the desired end state. Clearly, to develop adequate and effective instruction of heritage learners whose goal it is to acquire additional varieties and registers of the heritage language, careful research must be carried out on the process of D2 and R2 acquisition in naturalistic settings as well as on the effects of different types of instruction on both of these processes.

A final category of heritage speakers – in addition to those who have incompletely acquired the language, those whose language has undergone attrition, and those who speak a contact variety of the language – includes L1/L2 users who cannot or will not speak the heritage language although they are able to participate in interpersonal, face-to-face communication with bilingual individuals who speak to them in this language. These passive L1/L2 users exhibit strong receptive proficiencies in their heritage language, which, while limited, still exceed the receptive proficiencies acquired by beginning and even intermediate learners of a foreign language. At the minimum, receptive L1/L2 users offer evidence of having acquired what Clark (2003) refers to as C-representations, that is, a system of representations for comprehension of the language that allows them to parse the stream of speech into meaningful units. How this system is related to the productive system in the L1 and to the receptive and productive systems in the L2 is of central importance to the development of pedagogical approaches for developing the existing proficiencies of such speakers in a classroom setting. A theory of heritage language growth/development for such individuals must be based on a better understanding of comprehension and production grammars (Swain *et al.*, 1974). We need to understand (1) how and why these two types of knowledge systems develop independently, (2) how comprehension and production grammars are related, (3) whether the presence of comprehension grammars supports the acquisition of production grammars in specific ways, and (4) whether these individuals are more similar to L2 learners than to L1 speakers.

Unfortunately for educators, a single group of heritage learners enrolling in a heritage language class will in most cases include students who are quite dissimilar from each other and who are involved in very different processes of L1 reacquisition/development. Some language educators and researchers, moreover, are not entirely persuaded that heritage learners are fundamentally different from intermediate and advanced second language (L2) learners. They maintain that, because both groups produce comparable "errors", the implicit L1 systems of heritage learners must be similar to the transitional L2 systems of L2 learners. They therefore conclude that the same approaches to language instruction will be successful.

Indeed, what is evident from working with heritage language learners is that they are both like and unlike traditional L2 learners. As compared to L2 learners, heritage learners exhibit a broad range of receptive and productive competences in both the L1 and the L2. Some heritage students, however, while displaying some limitations when compared to educated native speakers of the same age, have highly developed productive and receptive proficiency in their L1 and, in some ways, appear to be similar to advanced L2 learners. As has been made evident by recent work on advanced L2 learners (Byrnes, 2002; Byrnes & Maxim, 2003, Leaver & Shekhtman, 2002) these learners (referred to by Byrnes (2002) as AL2 learners are individuals who have full access to the mechanical aspects of the language, who can produce various correct structures to express the same idea, and but need to acquire a more sophisticated repertoire of ways to persuade, convince, and carry out communicative tasks to interact with educated native-speakers, transact business in foreign contexts, and use the written language professionally. This description also seems to fit the

Russian and Spanish-speaking heritage speakers examined by Angelelli and Leaver (2002: 197–8) who point out that these students:

> ... typically perform well in Interpersonal mode (direct oral or written communication between two persons) but less well in Interpretive (mediated communication via print and broadcast materials) and Presentation (oral or written communication for an audience without immediate possibilities of personal interaction) modes, as described in the National Foreign Language Standards (ACTFL, 1999).

Agreeing with Valdés and Gioffrion-Vinci (1998) that heritage students need to acquire a broad repertoire of registers and genres, Angelelli and Leaver maintain that similar pedagogical approaches can be used with both groups of students. Such approaches include those described by Byrnes and Maxim (2004) and Kern (2004) as utilized by the New London Group (1996) with native English speakers – often with members of stigmatized minority groups – who are seen to be in need of acquiring "a set of discourse practices, oral and written, connected with the standard dialect of English" (Gee, 1990). This particular approach to literacy studies focuses specifically on the discursive nature of knowledge construction by engaging in genre studies. For researchers interested in examining the process of R2 (second register) or G2 (second genre) acquisition, the focus on the development of genres, styles and registers by L2 learners and by heritage learners offer exciting possibilities for investigating the differences in rate of acquisition, stages of acquisition, and ultimate attainment of registers and genres of these two groups of learners. It is evident, however, that much research needs to be done on the similarities and differences between the implicit systems of advanced language learners and heritage speakers of various types, before it can be assumed that the processes of R2 (second register) or G2 (second genre) acquisition will be similar in L2 learners and L1/L2 users.

The study of ultimate attainment of L2s is fundamental to SLA researchers for theoretical purposes and to applied linguists as they seek to develop not only descriptive rubrics of language proficiency that go beyond existing Foreign Service Institute's (FSI) scales but also to define levels of what Byrnes *et al.* (2002: 25) have referred to as "advancedness" among L2 learners. Ultimate attainment, moreover, continues to be important within debates about the critical period in L2 acquisition, which, in the United States, have become part of the political debates over bilingual education. Educators can gain much from an increased understanding of the kinds of language pedagogies that can improve proficiencies in both the written and the oral language in students who have already achieved fluent, functional proficiencies in an L2 but who may wish to develop a broader range of registers and styles. Similarly, they can gain much from the study of the development of high-level proficiencies in two languages by interpreters of language minority origin who were able to develop such proficiencies in communities in which the functional specialization of languages provided little access to a range of oral and written texts and interactions.

In sum, the study of heritage learners raises a number of important theoretical issues for researchers seeking to understand the human language faculty. These questions include:

- What issues are raised about the process of L1 acquisition by the acquisition of strong receptive versus productive grammars in heritage learners?
- What accounts for the acquisition of receptive versus productive competence in heritage learners?
- Can comprehension grammars (as opposed to productive grammars) be used to develop the L1?
- How can the different sources of "flawed" language production (interlanguages, interdialects, and interregisters) in the L1s of heritage learners be identified?
- How does the "flawed" language production of heritage learners compare with that of L2 learners.
- How do monolingual L1 speakers acquire a range of registers and genres in their L1?
- What is the order of acquisition of particular features of second registers (R2s) by L1 speakers?
- How do monolingual L1 speakers acquire a D2?
- What is the order of acquisition of particular features in a D2 by L1 speakers?
- Are notions of interdialect or interregister useful in describing the acquisition of additional registers and dialects of L1 by heritage learners?
- What can formal classroom instruction accomplish for heritage learners?
  - Are there types of instruction that can reverse language attrition?
  - What types of instruction can result in the acquisition of a range of registers and styles?

The implementation of a research agenda

The research agenda that we have outlined above was designed to suggest that the development of heritage language resources, if it is to be undertaken successfully, will require the careful and systematic investigation of different types of heritage learners and of the effect of various types of instruction on the development/reacquisition of their heritage language. National investments in the simple adaptation of pedagogies currently used with L2 learners are based on unfounded assumptions about the restructuring of the implicit systems of such learners and may be largely unsuccessful on a long-term basis. As Hidalgo (1993) noted, direct instruction on normative structures appears to lead to very limited changes in the language used by heritage students for everyday communication. Retreating from the position she expressed in Hidalgo (1987), she describes her previous practice as attempting to correct the three most noticeable morphosyntactic characteristics of the "nonstandard structures heard from immigrants from the countryside"(1987: 88). She concludes (1993: 80) that

> Given that correction implies criticism of that which is perceived as erroneous or mistaken, the reaction of the Mexican-American students is confusion, shame, or contained anger, since this correction reminds the individual of the speech of their grandparents, their parents, their older siblings, and all those people who they most love. The sporadic and asystematic correction of an adult implies, then, humiliation by what is one's own, contempt for what is authentic, disdain for the legitimacy of the dialect or idiolect.

Hidalgo concludes that the acquisition of standard forms is a slow process that is "subjected to a number of social and cultural variables that do not depend on the individual" (p. 89). She argues that professors of Spanish working with heritage speakers

> should not expect their students to attain a quasi-literate mastery of their mother tongue because the educational system has not offered them opportunities galore to educate themselves in their own language. (p. 89)

As government-funded programs move forward to promote the expansion of high-level ethnic/heritage language resources in the United States, it is imperative that careful and valid evaluations of current efforts in teaching heritage languages be carried out at the same time that a long-term research initiative is established to support our understanding of the role of instruction on the development/reacquisition of such languages.

Ideologies of Language and the Teaching of Heritage Languages in the United States[7]

The second greatest challenge facing the foreign language profession in teaching heritage language learners is the impact of the language ideologies of language professionals on the teaching/learning enterprise. In this section, we begin with a discussion of language ideology as a system of ideas about social and linguistic relationships that reproduce and legitimate the social order. We proceed to a description of departments of Spanish, their faculty, and their students and argue that established institutional foreign language programs – although involved in a nonhegemonic practice, the teaching of non-English languages – are nevertheless working in concert with deeply held American ideologies and beliefs about language. In the case of heritage languages, we argue that these unexamined beliefs can result in the alienation and marginalization of L1/L2 users even in those departments that have implemented heritage language programs.

Defining ideology

The term *ideology* is one that evokes a number of contradictory responses among scholars of very different backgrounds and persuasions. As Geertz (1973) has pointed out, the term has itself been ideologized. It is difficult to find neutral or nonevaluative definitions of the term, and scholars (e.g. Gee, 1990: 24) who attempt to define the term refer to difficulties of charting an uncertain path among "treacherous rocks" and "hazardous reefs" that are a product of the highly contentious issues that are involved in its definition.

Woolard (1998), in her overview of definitions of ideology, identifies four general strands or themes that recur in current writing. The first strand takes the perspective that ideology is ideational and conceptual and involves beliefs and ideas. According to this view, ideology is not necessarily conscious, and it may not involve a system of thought. Ideology is, rather, lived relations, which Eagleton (1991: 18) describes as "a particular organization of signifying practices which goes to constitute human beings as social subjects and which produces the lived relations by which such subjects are connected to the dominant relations of production in society." The second strand views ideology as dependent on material conditions and particular social position. For some individuals, this second strand leads to a third perspective, that is, the conceptualization of ideology as ideas and belief systems directed at and engaged in a struggle to maintain or acquire power. The fourth strand views distortion, error, and illusion as central to the conceptualization of ideology. From this perspective, ideology involves cognitive distortions that depart from scientific objectivity.

Thompson (1984) views ideology as linked to the process of sustaining societal asymmetries. He identifies two distinct conceptualizations of ideology that emerge from the literature. One conceptualization he labels as purely neutral or descriptive. The other conceptualization, one that is focused on asymmetrical relations of power, he refers to as the negative conceptualization. Thompson speaks of the neutral conceptualization as referring in general to systems of thought or belief systems. He speaks of the negative perspective as the critical conception of ideology. Agreeing with Thompson that the principal difference between conceptualizations of ideology involves neutral versus negative views of the term, Woolard (1998) suggests that even the most seemingly neutral uses of the word connote disapprobation, and for that reason some scholars prefer more neutral expressions such as culture, worldview, and belief.

The study of language ideology

In making an argument for the study of language ideology, Woolard (1998: 3) offers the following definition of the term: "Representations, whether explicit or implicit, that construe the intersection of language and human beings in a social world." Arguing that ideologies of language are not about language alone, Woolard (p. 3) insists that they enact ties of language to identity and underpin "the very notion of person and the social group, as well as such fundamental social institutions as religious ritual, child socialization, gender relations, the nation-state, schooling, and law." She cites other definitions of language ideology, including Rumsey (1990: 346), who defines the concept as "shared bodies of commonsense notions about the nature of language in the world"; Silverstein (1979: 193), who defines it as "sets of beliefs about language articulated by users as a rationalization or justification of perceived language structure and use"; Heath (1989: 53), who views language ideology as "self-evident ideas and objectives a group holds concerning roles of language in the social experiences of members as they contribute to the expression of the group"; and Irvine (1989: 255), who considers language ideology to be "the cultural system of ideas about social and linguistics relationships, together with their loading of moral and political interests."

Citing Eagleton (1991: 19), who points out that "ideology creates and acts in a social world while it masquerades as a description of that world," Woolard and the researchers who work in this tradition agree with Thompson (1990) that ideology and social relations are mutually constitutive. They consider that the study of language ideologies is important because it allows us to understand how such ideologies mediate meanings for social purposes, how everyday interactions in institutional settings reproduce and legitimate the social order, and how deeper messages about how the world operates are co-constructed and conveyed.

Language ideology and the ideology of nationalism

The relationship between language and nationalism has been a matter of controversy. As Stavenhagen (1990) points out, nations can be seen as objective facts, that is, as entities that bring together large numbers of people who share common objective traits such as language, religion, history, customs, and values. They can also be seen as expressions of a common consciousness and a common will to exist as a nation. For some scholars (e.g. Gellner, 1983), it is this common consciousness, this nationalism, this sense of imagined membership in a wider community as described by Anderson (1991) that gives rise to nations. In many cases, intellectual elites have been successful in creating such a nationalistic consciousness by manipulating language as an instrument in the expression of a national essence. As Safran (1999) argues, however, language itself is not a sufficient ingredient of nationalism. Nations have not been created because groups have been conscious of speaking a common language. Rather, languages as symbols of nationhood have become important once nations have come into being.

According to Bourdieu (1982/1995), the making of a nation, moreover, necessitates the creation of a "standard" language that is then legitimized as the normalized language and imposed on its citizens. Bourdieu (1995: 45–46) further argues that domination of the nonspeakers of the national language is exerted through a variety of mechanisms and institutions. In order for one mode of expression among others (a particular language in the case of bilingualism, a particular use of language in the case of a society divided into classes) to impose itself as the only legitimate one, the linguistic market has to be unified and the different dialects (of class, region, or ethnic group) have to be measured practically against the legitimate language or usage. Integration into a single "linguistic community," which is a product of the political domination that is endlessly reproduced by institutions capable of imposing universal recognition of the dominant language is the condition for the establishment of relations of linguistic domination. The educational system plays an important role in both the legitimization of particular ways of speaking and the devaluing of popular or regional modes of expression. Interestingly, speakers of dominated languages or dialects collaborate in the destruction of what Bourdieu (1982/1995: 49) called their "instruments of expression" because they believe that accepting the hierarchy of linguistic practices will increase their value on the educational market and lead to economic advantages. It is not the case that individuals are coerced directly into accepting a common or standard language. It is rather that they form a complicity with dispositions that are inculcated subtly and slowly through suggestions and even through insignificant moments of everyday life. As Thompson (1995) points out, for Bourdieu, speakers of nonofficial languages or varieties betray their acceptance of the negative evaluation system that views them as inferior. Calling this phenomenon "symbolic power" or "symbolic violence," Bourdieu maintains that its success depends on those dominated sharing the same set of beliefs about the value and legitimacy of modes of speech considered to be correct and appropriate by the powerful members of the society.

Recent work on the study of language in bureaucratic settings has focused on the ways in which language ideologies and practices constitute and reproduce the ideological hegemony of the state (e.g. Schieffelin et al., 1998). According to Phillips (1998), this new orientation owes much to recent interest on the nation as a sociocultural phenomenon. Nationness itself has been problematized. Phillips argues for increased attention to the ways in which nation-imagining ideologies are shared across institutions and nations. Pointing out that the ideology of one state, one nation is transnational, she contends that it is important to discover how various local communities and institutional settings articulate with broader processes.

We agree with Phillips that some institutional settings (e.g. educational settings, media production enterprises) are centrally involved in the production of state hegemony. In the case of multilingual, multiethnic nations in which nationalist ideologies are strongly centered around monolingualism, we contend that such institutional settings play an important role in transmitting the kinds of dispositions that Bourdieu (1982/1995) argues will result in abandonment of the original instruments of expression or modes of speech by the dominated. In such multilingual nations, these dispositions support a shift to the national language by the speakers of nonofficial languages. What this suggests is that Woolard (1998) is correct when she points out that the understanding of both language maintenance and language shift requires more than the traditional sociopsychological study of individual attitudes or the macrosociological study of events. It requires the examination of the inculcation of hegemonic beliefs about both monolingualism and bilingualism as they are encountered in seemingly neutral and even counterhegemonic activities and practices.

Ideologies of bilingualism and monolingualism in the United States

Popular beliefs about bilingualism in the American context are part of a linguistic culture/ideology that considers monolingualism in English to be "the crowning attribute of citizenship" (Jordan, 1921: 35). However, a mapping (Wetherell & Potter, 1992) of the popular *and* scholarly discourse on bilingualism reveals a multilayered set of themes that contribute directly to a version of reality where monolingualism is viewed as the normal and ideal human condition while bilingualism is seen as profoundly suspect.

The popular ideological discourse on bilingualism reflects not only a strong nationalistic philosophy that directly condemns the publicly supported use of non-English languages, but also a set of related beliefs that view bilingualism of indigenous and immigrant groups as problematic. Embedded in this discourse are strong beliefs about the dangers of early bilingualism, about the problems of language contamination, and about the negative effects of bilingualism on individuals. It is a complex discourse strongly influenced by research carried out on IQ at the turn of the century and by current debates about the education of minority children (Crawford, 1992). In addition, derogatory terms referring to the contact varieties of non-English languages spoken by bilingual individuals (e.g.

Spanglish, Finglish, Chinglish) are used casually in the everyday talk of both monolingual speakers of English *and* even by speakers of those varieties who have internalized the widespread monolingualist perspective. The use of such terms implies that these varieties are corrupt and inferior mixtures of two languages and not legitimate and rule-governed ways of speaking.

Interestingly, the scholarly discourse on bilinguals and bilingualism continues to feed existing popular negative views about the phenomenon. Recent scholarly books on bilingualism (e.g. Hamers & Blanc, 2000; Romaine, 1995) provide extensive overviews of the limitations of research on topics such as the cognitive consequences of bilingualism and intelligence. Themes such as "bilingualism as a psychological and/or social handicap," and "bilingualism as deviant and in need of explanation" (Woolard, 1999) are as present today in scholarly discussions in fields such as psychology, sociology, and education as they were in the early part of the 20th century. Even within the linguistic study of bilingualism, the theme of "bilingualism as linguistic handicap" is consistently reflected in descriptions of (1) "interference" between bilingual speakers' two languages, (2) in concern about "fossilization" in the L2 acquisition literature, and (3) in examinations of the types of "language mixing" that can be brought about as a result of extended contact between two languages (Thomason, 2001). Moreover, the contemporary literature on contact varieties of language (e.g. US Spanish) makes frequent references to "imperfect learning" (Thomason, 2001) and "incompletely acquired" forms (Silva-Corvalán, 1994). Similarly, the themes of "semilingualism" and "limited bilingualism" (Cummins, 1973, 1979, 1981; Cummins & Gulustan, 1974) have been firmly established within the educational sphere and the discourse of both researchers and practitioners. Within this sphere, what Mohanty and Perregaux (1997) have referred to as the monolingual bias and Cook (1997) has called the monolingualist perspective has resulted in the widespread acceptance of the container view of bilingualism (Martin-Jones & Romaine, 1987). Within this view, an adult bilingual is measured against the supposedly full container of the adult monolingual, and a bilingual child is compared with the partially filled container of the monolingual child. Only "balanced" bilinguals, who have native-like proficiency in each language, are considered to be "full" or "real" bilinguals. By this definition, individuals who grow up in bilingual communities, who use two languages in their everyday lives for different purposes, but who are not two monlinguals in one are referred to as pseudo-bilinguals.

Ideologies of monolingualism are reflected in the very use of the term *bilingual*. As Haugen (1970) pointed out, the term is used around the world to cover a variety of phenomena that have little in common with each other except that they are perceived as problematic. For example, in school settings within the United States the term *bilingual* is used to refer to non – English-speaking children. However, *bilingual* within these settings is a euphemism for poor, disadvantaged, or newly arrived immigrant children who are, in fact, *monolingual* speakers of their immigrant language.

Departments of Foreign Languages in American Universities

Academic departments, "despite their temporal shifts of character and their institutional and national diversity," share "recognizable identities and particular cultural attributes" (Becher, 1989: 22). Academic tribes focus on particular areas of knowledge and follow traditions and customs into which they were socialized as young apprentices. Within departments and within academic disciplines, much importance is given to boundary maintenance:

> Disciplinary communities which are convergent and tightly knit in terms of their fundamental ideologies, their common values, their shared judgments of quality, their awareness of belonging to a unique tradition – in short, their fraternal sense of nationhood – are likely to occupy intellectual territories with well defined external boundaries. What is more, when the patriotic feelings within a discipline run high, deviations from the common cultural norms will be penalized and attempts to modify them from the outside will be rejected. Any systematic questioning of the accepted disciplinary ideology will be seen as heresy and may be punished by expulsion. (Becher, 1989: 37)

Moreover, within academic departments, there are well-established hierarchies and a constant ranking of individuals, subspecialties, reputations, publications, and the like that position particular individuals within the hierarchy.

Departments of foreign languages in particular occupy a unique space in American universities. Faculty in these departments are engaged in carrying out intellectual work in "foreign" languages in a society that has been largely indifferent to and, at times, antagonistic toward the study and teaching of all non-English languages. Interestingly, however, the primary business of academic departments of foreign languages in American universities is not the teaching of language but the teaching of literature. For most faculty, the teaching of language – although necessary because of the support that it provides graduate teaching assistants – is an area to which they give very little attention. As Bourdieu (1988) has pointed out, the structure of university fields tends to reflect the structure of the fields of power. As a result, foreign language departments and their faculty rarely enjoy the cultural prestige accorded to the faculties of law, medicine, or science within their colleges and universities. Foreign language faculty, therefore, must often struggle against the stereotypical view of themselves as mere teachers of French, German, or Spanish whose primary function is to provide language instruction to undergraduates.

In departments of foreign languages, in addition to the normal hierarchies of power based on subject matter specialization that are found in other academic departments, special power structures are developed that center around language. In particular, these hierarchies reflect the special value given to what is termed native-speaking ability. Faculty and students who are *native* speakers of the target language – that is, who learned the language of the department as a mother tongue – are often considered by members of the profession to be inherently superior to faculty and students who are *nonnative* – that is who have acquired the target language as a foreign or second language.

The case of Spanish language departments

Spanish language departments are directly involved in both the teaching of the Spanish language in the United States and in the production of Spanish language majors who enter the secondary teaching profession. They are also involved in the preparation of masters and doctoral students who will become faculty members at institutions of higher education. As is the case in other academic departments, students in Spanish departments are socialized to accept well-established hierarchies and constant rankings of individuals. This process of socialization results in shared common values and judgments of quality that center, to a great degree, around dominant definitions of appropriate and correct language. We maintain that these deeply established and unquestioned ideologies account for the attitudes toward heritage students' Spanish that we encountered when interviewing faculty members at 12 California institutions.

The process of socialization that takes place in Spanish departments has much to do with the fact that the faculty is made up primarily of individuals from two very different backgrounds: (1) native speakers of Spanish raised in Spain or Latin America and (2) Americans who acquired Spanish as a foreign language. In some highly factionalized departments, these very different cultural and linguistic backgrounds create a context within which language itself can become one more weapon in an arsenal of powerful implements of war. Present-day discussions of Spanish in the United States in departments of Spanish are influenced directly by long-term anxieties about language change. Even though apprehensions about good and bad Spanish are frequently centered primarily around contact with English, everyday descriptions of the language spoken by new immigrants in the United States that are often heard in departments of Spanish include a listing of features (*haiga, truje, vénganos*) that are considered to be part of *la norma rural*, rather than *la norma culta*, as well as examples of lexical uses characteristic of particular regions (*chueco, guajolote*).

In some cases, native speakers of peninsular Spanish may take the position that their own linguistic abilities are superior to those of their Latin

American colleagues who are thought to speak a less pure and less au-
thentic Spanish. They may recommend that their students travel to Spain
to immerse themselves in the best Spanish and suggest that study in Latin
America is less desirable. Latin Americans, on the other hand, together with
their peninsular counterparts may sit in judgment of the language abilities
of their American colleagues who acquired Spanish as a foreign language.
In some departments, so-called *near-native* ability in the target language
is not enough. The underlying belief is that only those persons who have
grown up in the original culture and who have learned the language in
the course of primary socialization can truly understand both the foreign
literature and its culture.[8] The situation becomes even more complex when
one considers the place of ethnic/heritage language speakers in Spanish
departments. That is, second-, third-, or even fourth-generation members
of immigrant families who are American-born (e.g. Mexican-Americans
and Puerto Ricans) and who have developed their Spanish competencies
in their homes and communities as well as in the American academy. There
is often much hesitation about hiring such individuals in Spanish departments because they are thought to speak the wrong kind of language. What
is often not mentioned is that their class backgrounds clash directly with
those of faculty members who were raised in middle-class circumstances
in foreign countries.[9]

In addition to traditional L2 students, many Spanish departments also
enroll significant numbers of students from Latin America and Spain at the
graduate level. Many such students are older than their American counterparts and have extensive experiences in the areas of writing and publishing. More recently, as our survey of colleges and universities indicates,
an increasing number of bilingual US Latinos have entered departments
of Spanish at both the graduate and the undergraduate levels. The cultural
and linguistic differences among students and faculty manifest themselves
in a variety of ways and are reflected in the everyday interactions of individuals within the department. In particular, they are revealed in the work
carried out with heritage students in both secondary and postsecondary
institutions.

As we pointed out in Chapter 5, the increased presence of US Latinos
in Spanish departments has led to special courses for heritage speakers.
For concerned Spanish-language – teaching professionals, the question
is how to further develop the language abilities of heritage students at
both the secondary and undergraduate levels when they appear not to
have achieved sustained written and oral fluency in academic registers of
Spanish. Our study of heritage courses and programs in California revealed
that there is little consensus about what pedagogies work and what do not
work with such students, but that there is almost complete agreement
about the goals of such instruction – the acquisition of the standard dialect. Secondary school teachers and faculty at postsecondary institutions

share similar views about varieties of Spanish brought into the classroom by heritage students and are especially concerned about language contamination. They share a strong belief in the teaching of a grammatical metalanguage and in the power of that acquired knowledge to transform both the identities and the self-images of heritage students.

Spanish-speaking intellectuals and departments of Spanish

We hypothesize that the hurdles facing departments of Spanish in working with heritage students has to do not only with the culture of the discipline and its perspective on correct Spanish, but also with the experiences of many members of those departments when confronted by the reality of the place of Latinos in the United States. The experiences of faculty members and students raised in the upper-middle classes in Spain or Latin America are different in many ways from those of newly arrived poor immigrants of Mexican origin. Within the university setting, such individuals enjoy a privileged status as intellectuals. Outside the university, however, in spite of their class background, Spaniards and Latin Americans are often perceived by Anglo-Americans to be no better than their working-class counterparts.

Over time, Spanish-speaking intellectuals inevitably become aware of existing negative attitudes toward both the Spanish language and toward Latino immigrants in this country. Moreover, these intellectuals soon discover that they have received an ethnoracial classification of "Latino" or "Hispanic," which is foreign to their experience. As we have pointed out in this chapter and as a number of scholars have recently pointed out (e.g. Gracia, 2000; Mendieta, 2000; Mignolo, 2000; Rodriguez, 2000; Schutte, 2000), in Latin America, "race" is social-racial as opposed to a genealogical construction that involves a number of variables, including both class and skin color. Therefore, many Spaniards and Latin Americans reject being classified as members of a "nonwhite" racial group that includes individuals with whom they would not have been grouped in their countries of origin. Like the early *Californios*, they see themselves as *gente de razón*, who have very little in common with their working-class US Latino students who are the children of dark-skinned *mestizo* immigrants.

In terms of language, members of Spanish department faculties, because they work with the language itself, are more aware of their own Spanish use and that of others than are most US Latinos. Engaged as they are in the study and teaching of great works, they have clear notions about the skilled use of language. Moreover, because of their disciplinary training and frame of reference and because they work directly with Anglophone students who are learning Spanish, they have strong beliefs about appropriate language use. For example, a recent study of language ideologies within a Spanish language department conducted by Valdés *et al.* (2003, in press) revealed the existence of a set of beliefs about language constructed around the notion of the monolingual, educated native speaker. The discourse surrounding the notion of the *monolingual*, educated native speaker permeated all seemingly neutral departmental interactions and resulted in a clear departmental hierarchy in which monolingual native speakers had the highest status and US Latinos were considered marginal. There was a fear of language transfer and contamination, of diminished strengths in one language if another was used well, and a sense of loss of native-speaker legitimacy if English was spoken too well.

Views toward the Spanish spoken by US Latinos in the department were strongly negative, and upper-middle-class individuals tended to emphasize the differences between themselves and working-class immigrants in this country. Moreover, the term *bilingual* was used narrowly to describe rare instances of equivalent proficiencies in two languages or employed as a dismissing euphemism for US Latinos. Everyday interactions in the department transmitted consistent messages to students (e.g. the behavior of upper-class Spanish-speaking monolinguals was seen as the ideal to which all students should aspire).

The fear of language transfer and contamination and of diminished strengths was evident especially in the discourse of members of the department from Spain and Latin America who had been in this country for many years. They understood that, after a long period in the United States, their lives had permanently changed. Many knew that they would not return to their countries of origin. For these individuals, Spanish took on a special significance. In many cases, they experienced a special sadness and perhaps the singular fear of the pervasive presence of the dominant language in their lives that is typical of intellectuals who have abandoned their homeland. As Sarduy explains in his essay, *Exiliado de sí mismo*, being deprived of one's native land is not primarily a physical deprivation of scents, colors, and sounds, but rather

> El verdadero salto es lingüístico: dejar el idioma – a veces él nos va dejando.... Muchos de los grandes escritores actuales, y de mis amigos, han dado ese salto, que es para mí el ejemplo mismo de la voluntad y del coraje: Semprún, Bianciotti, Arrabal, Maner; otros, al contrario, se han ido hundiendo cada vez más en el pasado del habla, como si quisieran con ese hundimiento, con ese regreso al origen, compensar la lejanía física. (Sarduy: 57)

> *The true leap is a linguistic one: abandoning the language – at times it slowly abandons us. ... Many of today's great writers, and of my friends, have made that leap which is for me an example of will and courage: Semprún, Bianciotti, Arrabal, Maner; others, on the contrary, have descended more deeply into the past each time as if they wanted with that descent, with that return to the beginning, to compensate for a physical distance.* (My translation)[10]

Members of Spanish department faculty, like other exiled intellectuals to whom language is important, fear the slow attrition of their Spanish. They notice when words do not come quickly to mind, and they are hesitant to use expressions that might sound foreign or old-fashioned to their original compatriots. Individual faculty members, moreover, may not know that they share such fears with other colleagues. They may silently worry that, because they are no longer exposed in the same way to the multiple voices engaged in scholarly conversations in the Spanish-speaking world, they might no longer be able to address the "heteroglot voices" that provided the background for their own voice (Bakhtin, 1981).

In sum, an examination of Spanish language departments suggests that the departments are settings in which expatriate intellectuals, although they "picked up roots in an orderly manner" (Malkki, 1997: 62) before moving to the foreign soil, are nevertheless aware of their uprootedness and displacement. While acknowledging this, they might not have embraced the nation-imagining beliefs of US society and its ideologies of monolingualism. Moreover, their own response to imposed and unfamiliar racialized and classed identities often results in both conscious and unconscious attempts to differentiate themselves from working-class Latino immigrants. Their preoccupation with Spanish leads them to embrace not only the ideologies of language that are part of the preoccupation with unity and fragmentation, but also values that echo the traditional views and beliefs of US society within which bilingualism – especially that developed in homes and communities by immigrant populations – is profoundly suspect.

Given the climate found in departments of Spanish – a climate that is deeply rooted in ideologies of *unidad del lenguaje* and that is influenced by the surrounding political environment – we were not surprised at the responses we received to our questions about heritage speakers or about the primary focus of both college/university and high programs on the teaching of the standard language. High-school teachers and college and university faculty are products of these departments, and their focus is on producing speakers of standard Spanish who can pass undetected in traditional Spanish language programs originally designed for L2 learners. We are not optimistic about the ability of Spanish departments to develop language programs for heritage language speakers that will lead to the lifelong maintenance and use of the language for both professional and personal purposes among Latino youngsters in California or in the United States.

The Teaching of Heritage Languages: National Challenges

As we pointed out in the introduction and in Chapter 5, within the last several years there has been an increasing interest in the teaching of heritage languages not only from language-teaching professionals but also from other educators committed to the maintenance of non-English languages in this country. For the first time, individuals who teach both commonly and less commonly taught languages at both the secondary and postsecondary levels have come into contact with individuals who through immersion programs, dual immersion programs, and community-based language schools and programs are working to develop the next generation's proficiencies in both indigenous and immigrant languages. For the first time also, professionals engaged in the teaching of such languages as Spanish and French have found themselves in conversations with teachers of what Gambhir (2001) referred to as the "truly less commonly taught languages" such as Bengali, Zulu, and Khmer.

For non-English languages in the United States, these are times of possibility. Indeed, the events of September 11, tragic as they were, once again brought to the nation's attention the strategic importance of what have ordinarily been referred to as "foreign" languages. Many of us are hopeful that the newly organized initiative on heritage languages will be able to play an important role not only in establishing language policies that can support the revitalization and maintenance of indigenous and immigrant languages but also in disseminating theoretical insights and pedagogical approaches across very different languages that nevertheless share a common current societal context.

Encouraging as these new initiatives are, heritage-language-maintenance initiatives continue to face a number of serious challenges. Many communities must still establish new programs, find suitable materials, identify teachers, and obtain necessary funding and support. Other more established groups, on the other hand, must make demands on high schools and universities for the implementation of language programs in "new" languages. For still others, the main goal is to obtain legitimacy. To do so, they must demand such things as national standardized examinations that will allow their youngsters to receive credit for proficiencies developed both in and out of school. What is clear is that, in spite of Fishman's (1991) cautionary statements about the limitations of educational institutions in reversing language shift, many individuals – including newly funded national defense grantees – continue to see educational institutions as a very large part of the solution. It is reassuring to believe that once languages have become part of established programs and once the study of these languages receives academic credit, most of the battles to develop language resources will be over. Not surprisingly, the role of educational institutions in transmitting deep societal values is seldom examined.

Our research suggests that the very same ideologies that we have described in Spanish language departments in California are present in other established university language departments dedicated to the study of both commonly and uncommonly taught languages. We conjecture, moreover, that such ideologies will also be commonplace as new programs in the truly uncommonly taught languages are implemented. Such ideologies will continue to be present for a number of different reasons. First, most language departments are primarily made up of individuals who were raised in areas of the world where the language was the dominant and/or national language. They may have very little knowledge or understanding of societal bilingualism and a deep commitment to the languages and literatures that they teach. As a result, much attention will be given to "protecting" the language from contamination from the English that surrounds them and to providing a model of a standard target language free of vulgar colloquialisms and popular jargon. Language practices, moreover, will be colored by a nationalist aesthetic (Thomas, 1991) that is concerned with the characteristic features of the original national language and culture. As Haugen (1972b: 2) pointed out when speaking of immigrant languages in America,

> Each language has parted from the strict purity of its native form and has taken elements from American English. Each language has been forced to adapt itself to new conditions, and thereby gives us a vivid picture of the immigrant's struggle for a position within the new nation and his gradual accommodation to its demands.

> The usual attitude to this phenomenon, among both lay and learned, has been one of scorn or amusement. The educated foreigner has regarded the lingo of his American compatriots as debased and vulgar, and has struggled against that "demoralizing" influence of his American environment as best he could.

A second reason for the continued presence of the ideologies of monolingualism in foreign language departments has to do with the idealized native speaker norm that we described earlier and that is central to the activities of the foreign language profession as a whole, with job descriptions that advertise for native and near-native proficiency, and with the persistent monolingualism of many foreign language faculty who have not themselves become bilingual in English and their home language. The idealization of the native speaker norm among such language professionals interacts in important ways with notions of standardness and linguistic purism.

Finally, as Haugen (1972a: 9) again tells us as he speaks of the pressures that all bilinguals experience in keeping their two codes separate,

> The pressure to maintain separate codes is greatest in the case of sophisticated circles using the highest prestige forms of a standard language. A French-English bilingual who is a writer or university professor is under great pressure to keep each of his languages pure, i.e., free from code convergence.

Foreign-language – teaching professionals who are committed to the maintenance and teaching of their languages may unfortunately become individuals who are intolerant of varieties of language used by heritage speakers because they have little understanding of language contact and bilingualism. Fear of contamination and erosion in their own languages may contribute to the scorn that they direct against American bilinguals who, unlike these professionals, may be second- or third-generation speakers of the heritage language.

Beliefs about language held by members of non – English-language teaching departments – especially among the less commonly taught languages – have not yet been explored at great length. For many language groups, the experience of immigration is a new one, and there is little information available about the characteristics of the language varieties of children raised in bilingual homes in this country. As the newly organized initiative on heritage languages moves forward, it will be important to examine not only practices and policies designed to support the revitalization and maintenance of indigenous and immigrant languages but also the shared commonsense notions about language correctness and purity held by language-teaching professionals as well as the role that institutional settings play in transmitting the kinds of dispositions that Bourdieu (1982/1995) argues will result in the abandonment of the original instruments of expression by speakers of minority languages. The teaching and study of heritage languages may not be successful if we are not able to address unexamined but very central challenges to heritage language maintenance and development among second- and third-generation American bilinguals.

The effective involvement by the foreign language teaching profession in maintaining and developing the non-English languages currently spoken by immigrants, refugees, and their children will require that the profession expand and broaden its scope very much beyond the mere recognition of heritage students as more advanced learners of the "target" language. To serve heritage students' needs, the profession's areas of interest need to extend to include a population of students who are very unlike traditional foreign language learners at the beginning, intermediate, and even advanced levels.

The results of our study of the teaching of Spanish as a heritage language in California suggests that, in order to respond to these students' needs, members of the foreign language teaching profession and government agencies charged with building capacity in strategic languages by developing the proficiencies of heritage learners must acquire an understanding of societal bilingualism and language contact as well as of theories of second dialect/second register acquisition. Instruction for these very different students must be informed by clear views about the nature of bilingualism itself, the controversies surrounding definitions of bilingualism and the ways in which bilingual individuals use two languages in their everyday lives. It must also be informed by an understanding of the relationship that contact varieties of language have to monolingual varieties of language and of the best way to retrieve/revitalize a nondominant first language.

As was pointed out by the high-school teachers participating in the ACTFL/Hunter College initiative (Webb & Miller, 2000) in their *Statement of Shared Goals and Fundamental Beliefs* (pp. 83–85), teachers of heritage languages should (1) "understand how complex heritage learners are," (2) "acquire the sociolinguistic foundations that enable them to be respectful of language origins and ever-evolving language varieties, dialects, registers, and styles that students bring with them to class and build upon them," and (3) "help students to recognize the uses and purposes of their heritage language both in their immediate environment and in a global society."

Notes

1. The Center for the Advanced Study of Language (http://www.casl.umd. edu/), for example, focuses on enhancing the ability of Americans to understand and speak other languages at high levels of proficiency. In identifying language needs and resources, a briefing paper (June 2004) identified ethnic language communities as one available source of language expertise.
2. For a recent very thorough discussion of this topic, the reader is directed to Han (2004).
3. Hallamaa (1998) carries out the evaluation process by posting questions to informants about their proficiencies as well as by directly observing their speaking ability. Because Hallamaa's purpose is to create a profile for particular communities, much attention is given to the age of informants.
4. The terms *domestic* and *academic register* are used by Gibbons and Ramirez (2004) to refer to registers used at home by minority speakers and to registers used for more complex and public uses.
5. Gutierrez (2003), for example, argues that, in Spanish, the innovative use of *estar* in domains previously occupied by *ser* had its origin in a monolingual context but is advancing at a faster rate in bilingual communities in the United States.
6. The discussion on this topic draws extensively from Valdés (in press).
7. Parts of this presentation appear in Valdés *et al.* (2003) and Valdés *et al.* (in press).
8. Recently much attention has been given to the construct of native speaking ability as it is used in departments of foreign languages in this country. The reader is referred to Eoyang, (1999), Kramsch (1999), Maier (1999), Valdés (1998), and Tesser (1999).
9. Valdés (1991) offers an interesting description of the place of majorities and minorities in foreign language departments.
10. I am indebted to Jerónimo Arellano, a doctoral student in Spanish and Portuguese at Stanford University for pointing out the significance of this essay in the context of the study of bilingualism.

References

ACTFL (1999) *Standards for Foreign Language Learning; Preparing for the 21st Century*. Yonkers, NY: National Standards in Education Project.

Anderson, R. W. (1982) Determining the linguistic attributes of language attrition. In R. D. Lambert and B. F. Freed (eds) *The Loss of Language Skills* (pp. 83–118). Rowley, MA: Newbury House.

Anderson, B. (1991) *Imagined Communities*. New York: Verso.

Angelelli, C., and Leaver, B. L. (2002) Heritage speakers as learners at the superior level: Differences and similarities between Spanish and Russian student populations. In B. L. Leaver and B. Shekhtman (eds) *Developing Professional-level Language Proficiency* (pp. 197–218). Cambridge: Cambridge University Press.

Bakhtin, M. M. (1981) Discourse in the novel. In M. Holquist (ed.) *The Dialogic Imagination* (pp. 259–422). Austin: University of Texas Press.

Ballmer, T. T. (1981) A typology of native speakers. In F. Coulmas (ed) *A Festschrift for Native Speaker* (pp. 51–67). The Hague: Mouton.

Becher, T. (1989) *Academic Tribes and Territories: Intellectual Enquiry and the Cultures of Disciplines*. Milton Keynes: Open University Press.

Bialystok, E. (2001) *Bilingualism in Development: Language, Literacy, and Cognition*. Cambridge: Cambridge University Press.

Bourdieu, P. (1982/1995) *Language and Symbolic Power*. Cambridge, MA: Harvard University Press.

Bourdieu, P. (1988) *Homo Academicus*. Stanford, CA: Stanford University Press.

Byrnes, H. (2002) Toward academic-level foreign langauge abilities: Reconsidering foundational assumptions, expanding pedagogical options. In B. L. Leaver and B. Shekhtman (eds) *Developing Professional-level Language Proficiency* (pp. 34–76). Cambridge: Cambridge University Press.

Byrnes, H., and Maxim, H. (eds) (2004) *Advanced Foreign Language Learning: A Challenge to College Programs*. Boston, MA: Thompson/Heinle.

Clark, E. V. (2003) *First Language Acquisition*. London: Cambridge.

Cook, V. (1992) Evidence for multi-competence. *Language Learning* 42 (4), 557–91.

Cook, V. (1996) Competence and multi-competence. In G. Brown, K. Malmkjaer, and J. Williams (eds) *Performance and Competence in Second Language Acquisition* (pp. 57–69). Cambridge: Cambridge University Press.

Cook, V. (1997) The consequences of bilingualism and cognitive processing. In A. M. B. de Groot and J. F. Kroll (eds) *Tutorials in Bilingualism : Psycholinguistic Perspectives* (pp. 279–99). Mahwah, NJ: Erlbaum.

Cook, V. (2002) Background of the L2 user. In V. Cook (ed) *Portraits of the L2 User* (pp. 1–28). Clevedon: Multilingual Matters.

Coulmas, F. (1981) *A Festschrift for Native Speaker*. The Hague: Mouton.

Crawford, J. (ed) (1992a) *Language loyalties: A Source Book on the Official English Controversy*. Chicago: University of Chicago Press.

Crawford, J. (1992b) *Hold Your Tongue: Bilingualism and the Politics of English Only*. Reading, MA: Addison Wesley.

Cummins, J. (1973) A theoretical perspective on the relationship between bilingualism and thought. *Working Papers on Bilingualism* 1, 1–9.

Cummins, J., and Gulustan, M. (1974) Some effects of bilingualism on cognitive functioning. In S. T. Carey (ed) *Bilingualism, Biculturalism and Education*. Edmonton: University of Alberta Press.

Cummins, J. (1979) Linguistic interdependence and the educational development of bilingual children. *Review of Educational Research* 49, 222–51.

Cummins, J. (1981) The role of primary language development in promoting educational success for language minority students. In California State Department of Education Office of Bilingual Bicultural Education (ed) *Schooling and Language*

Minority Students: A Theoretical Framework (pp. 3–49). Los Angeles: California State University, Evaluation Dissemination and Assessment Center.

Davis, A. (1991) *The Native Speaker in Applied Linguistics.* Edinburgh: Edinburgh University Press.

Davis, A. (2003) *The Native Speaker: Myth and Reality.* Clevedon: Multilingual Matters.

DeHouwer, A. (1995) Bilingual language acquisition. In P. Fletcher and B. MacWhinney (eds) *Handbook of Child Language* (pp. 219–50). Oxford: Blackwell.

Deuchar, M., and Quay, S. (2000) *Bilingual Acquisition: Theoretical Implications of a Case Study.* Oxford: Oxford University Press.

Eagleton, T. (1991) *Ideology: An Introduction.* London: Verso.

Eoyang, E. (1999) The worldliness of the English language: A lingua franca past and future. *ADFL Bulletin* 31 (1), 26–32.

Fishman, J. A. (1991) *Reversing Language Shift.* Clevedon: Multilingual Matters.

Gambhir, S. (2001) Truly less commonly taught languages and heritage language learners in the United States. In J. K. Peyton, D. A. Ranard, and S. McGinnis (eds) *Heritage Languages in America* (pp. 207–28). Washington, DC: Center for Applied Linguistics/Delta Systems.

Gee, J. (1990) *Social Linguistics and Literacies: Ideology in Discourses.* London: Falmer.

Geertz, C. (1964/1973) Ideology as a cultural system. In *The Interpretation of Culture* (pp. 194–233). New York: Basic Books.

Gellner, E. (1983) *Nations and Nationalism.* Oxford: Blackwell.

Gibbons, J., and Ramirez, E. (2004) *Maintaining a Minority Language: A Case Study of Hispanic Teenagers.* Clevedon: Multilingual Matters.

Gracia, J. J. E. (2000) Affirmative action for Hispanics? yes and no. In J. J. E. Gracia and P. De Greiff (eds) *Hispanics/Latinos in the United States* (pp. 201–21). New York: Routledge.

Grosjean, F. (1985) The bilingual as a competent but specific speaker-hearer. *Journal of Multilingual Multicultural Development* 6, 467–77.

Grosjean, F. (1997) Processing mixed language: Issues findings and models. In A. M. De Groot and J. F. Kroll (eds) *Tutorials in Bilingualism* (pp. 225–54). Mahwah, NJ: Erlbaum.

Grosjean, F. (1998) Studying bilinguals: Methodological and conceptual issues. *Bilingualism: Language and Cognition* 1, 131–49.

Hallamaa, P. (1998) Endangered languages: methodology, reality and social advocacy. In J. Niemi, T. Odlin and J. Heikkinen (eds) *Language Contact, Variation, and Change* (pp. 70–97). Joensuu, Finland: University of Joensuu.

Hamers, J. F., and Blanc, M. H. A. (2000) *Bilinguality and Bilingualism* (2nd edn). Cambridge: Cambridge University Press.

Han, Z. (2003) *Fossilization in Adult Second Language Acquisition.* Clevedon: Multilingual Matters.

Harding, E., and Riley, P. (1987) *The Bilingual Family.* New York: Cambridge.

Haugen, E. (1970) On the meaning of bilingual competence. In R. Jakobson and S. Kawamoto (eds) *Studies in General and Oriental Linguistics: Presented to Shiro Hattori on the Occasion of his Sixtieth Birthday* (pp. 221–29). Tokyo: TEC.

Haugen, E. (1972a) Active methods and modern aids in the teaching of foreign languages. In R. Filipovic (ed) *Papers from the Tenth Congress of the Federation Internationale des Professeurs de Langues Vivants* (pp. 1–14). London: Oxford University Press.

Haugen, E. (1972b) Language and immigration. In A. Dil (ed), *The Ecology of Language* (pp. 1–36). Stanford, CA: Stanford University Press.

Heath, S. B. (1989) Language ideology. In *International encyclopedia of communications* (pp. 393–95). Oxford: Oxford University Press.

Hidalgo, M. (1987) On the question of "Standard" vs. "Dialect": Implications for teaching Hispanic college students. *Hispanic Journal of the Behavioral Sciences* 9(4), 375–395.

Hidalgo, M. (1993) The teaching of Spanish to bilingual Spanish speakers: A problem of inequality. In B. Merino, H. T. Truega, and F. A. Samaniego (eds) *Language and Culture in Learning: Teaching Spanish to Native Speakers of Spanish* (Vol. 82–93). London: Falmer.

Irvine, J. T. (1989) When talk isn't cheap: Language and political economy. *American Ethnologist* 16, 248–67.

Jordan, R. H. (1921) Retention of foreign language in the home. *Journal of Educational Research* 3, 35–42.

Kenny, K. D. (1996) *Language Loss and the Crisis of Cognition: Between Socio- and Psycholinguistics*. Berlin: Mouton de Gruyter.

Kern, R. G. (2003) Literacy and advanced foreign language learning: Rethinking the curriculum. In H. Byrnes and H. H. Maxim (eds) *Advanced Foreign Language Learning: A Challenge to College Programs* (pp. 2–18). Boston: Thomson.

Kramsch, C. (1997) The privilege of the nonnative speaker. *Publications of the Modern Language Association*, 112 (3), 359–69.

Leaver, B. L., and Shekhtman, B. (eds) (2002) *Developing Professional-level Language Proficiency*. Cambridge: Cambridge University Press.

Malkki, L. H. (1997) The rooting of peoples and the territorialization of national identity among scholars and refugees. In A. Gupta and J. Ferguson (eds) *Culture, Power, Place: Explorations in Critical Anthropology* (Vol. 52–74). Durham: Duke University Press.

Martin-Jones, M., and Romaine, S. (1987) Semilingualism: A half-baked theory of communicative competence. *Applied Linguistics* 7 (1), 26–38.

McLaughlin, B. (1978) *Second-language Acquisition in Childhood*. Hillsdale, NJ: Erlbaum.

Mendieta, E. (2000) The making of new peoples: Hispanizing race. In J. J. E. Gracia and P. De Greiff (eds) *Hispanics/Latinos in the United States* (pp. 45–59). New York: Routledge.

Mignolo, W. D. (2000) Hispanics/Latinos (and Latino studies) in the colonial horizon of modernity. In J. J. E. Gracia and P. De Greiff (eds) *Hispanics/Latinos in the United States* (pp. 99–124). New York: Routledge.

Mohanty, A. K., and Perregaux, C. (1997) Language acquisition and bilingualism. In J. W. Berry, P. R. Dasen, and T. S. Saraswathi (eds) *Handbook of Cross-Cultural Psychology: Basic Processes and Human Development* (Vol. 2, pp. 217–53). Boston: Allyn and Bacon.

Mufwene, S. S. (2001) *The Ecology of Language Evolution*. Cambridge: Cambridge University Press.

Oksaar, E. (1997) Social networks, communicative acts and the multilingual individual. In E. H. Jahr (ed) *Language Change: Advances in Historical Sociolinguistics* (pp. 3–19). Berlin: Mouton de Gruyter.

Penny, R. (2000) *Variation and Change in Spanish*. Cambridge: Cambridge University Press.

Phillips, S. U. (1998) Language ideologies in institutions of power: A commentary. In B. B. Schieffelin, K. A. Woolard, and P. V. Kroskrity (eds) *Language Ideologies: Practice and Theory* (pp. 211–25). New York: Oxford.

Rodriguez, C. (2000) *Changing Race: Latinos, the Census and the History of Ethnicity in the United States*. New York: New York University Press.

Romaine, S. (1995) *Bilingualism* (2nd edn). Oxford: Blackwell.

Rumsey, A. (1990) Wording, meaning and linguistic ideology. *American Anthropologist* 92, 346–61.

Safran, W. (1999) Nationalism. In J. A. Fishman (ed) *Handbook of Language and Ethnicity* (pp. 77–93). New York: Oxford.

Schieffelin, B. B., Woolard, K. A., and Kroskrity, P. V. (eds) (1998) *Language Ideologies: Practice and Theory*. New York: Oxford University Press.

Schutte, O. (2000) Negotiating Latina identities. In J. J. E. Gracia and P. De Greiff (eds) *Hispanics/Latinos in the United States* (pp. 61–75). New York: Routledge.

Silva-Corvalán, C. (1994) *Language Contact and Change: Spanish in Los Angeles*. New York: Oxford University Press.

Silva-Corvalán, C. (2003a) Narrating in English and Spanish: Story telling in the words of a 5-year-old bilingual. *Revista Internacional de Lingüística Iberoamericana* 1 (2), 35–58.

Silva-Corvalán, C. (2003b) El español en Los Angeles: Adquisición incompleta o desgaste linguistico? On WWW at http://cvc.cervantes.es/obref/espanol_eeuu/bilingue/csilva.htm. Accessed 5.11.2004.

Silverstein, M. (1979) Language structure and linguistic ideology. In P. R. Clyne, W. F. Hanks, and C. L. Hofbauer (eds) *The Elements: A Parasession on Linguistic Units and Levels* (pp. 193–247). Chicago: Chicago Linguistic Society.

Stavenhagen, R. (1990) *The Ethnic Question: Conflicts, Development, and Human Rights*. Tokyo: United Nations University Press.

Swain, M., Dumas, G., and Naiman, N. (1974) Alternatives to spontaneous speech: Elicited translation and imitation as indicators of second language competence. *Working Papers on Bilingualism* 3, 68–79.

Thomas, G. (1991) *Linguistic Purism*. London: Longman.

Thomason, S. G. (2001) *Language Contact: An Introduction*. Washington DC: Georgetown University Press.

Thomason, S. G. and Kaufman, T. (1988) *Language Contact, Creolization, and Genetic Linguistics*. Berkeley: University of California Press.

Thompson, J. B. (1984) *Studies in the Theory of Ideology*. Berkeley: University of California Press.

Thompson, J. B. (1990) *Ideology and Modern Culture*. Stanford: Stanford University Press.

Thompson, J. B. (1995) Editor's introduction. In J. B. Thompson (ed) *Language and Symbolic Power* (pp. 1–34). Cambridge MA: Harvard University Press.

Valdés, G. (1995) The teaching of minority languages as 'foreign' languages: Pedagogical and theoretical challenges. *Modern Language Journal* 79 (3), 299–328.

Valdés, G., and Geoffrion-Vinci, M. (1998) Chicano Spanish: The problem of the 'underdeveloped' code in bilingual repertoires. *Modern Language Journal* 82 (4), 473–501.

Webb, J. B., and Miller, B. L. (eds) (2000) *Teaching Heritage Learners: Voices from the Classroom*. Yonkers, NY: American Council on the Teaching of Foreign Languages.

Wei, L. (2000) *The Bilingualism Reader*. London: Routledge.

Wetherell, M., and Potter, J. (1992) *Mapping the Language of Racism: Discourse and the Ligitimation of Exploitation*. New York: Columbia University Press.

Woolard, K. A. (1998) Introduction: Language ideology as a field of inquiry. In B. B. Schieffelin, K. A. Woolard, and P. A. Kroskrity (eds) *Language Ideologies: Practice and Theory* (pp. 3–47). New York: Oxford University Press.

Woolard, K. A. (1999) Simultaneity and bivalency as strategies in bilingualism. *Journal of Linguistic Anthropology* 8 (1), 3–29.

Chapter 9

Imagining Linguistic Pluralism in the United States

JOSHUA A. FISHMAN

The Impossible Dream?

Is the entire notion of "happy pluralism," where two or more ethno-linguistic groups coexist amically within one polity, a contradiction in terms? An illusion of romantics and others not too securely anchored in modern reality? Maybe so, but that was not the view of Otto Bauer (1881–1937; 1907/2000), nor of Horace Kallen (1882–1974; 1998) nor of Nathan Birnbaum (1864–1937; see Fishman, 1982), and it is not today the view of Lottie Guinier (2002), nor of Michael Walzer (1997) or Will Kymlicka (1995). Nevertheless, there is no gainsaying the fact that the majority of American social scientists, social philosophers, and social commentators today have either never heard of the concept or, if they have, are dubious, critical, or downright negative toward it, often not realizing that it has such deep roots, and overwhelmingly positive ones at that, both abroad and here. Examine the collections of early 19th-century "letters sent home" by immigrants to America (Lepore 2000), first those from Norway, Germany, and the Netherlands and, later, those from Italy, Poland, and Russia), and the topic of reestablishing sociocultural continuity, and of doing so on an intergenerationally reliable basis, is discussed again and again. Examine the uninterrupted and ongoing efforts to build institutions of language and culture maintenance (schools, churches, periodicals, choruses, reading circles, summer camps, theaters, kindergartens and nursery groups, radio [and now TV] stations, orchestras, etc.) in the New World. Visit the endless archival collections devoted to documenting accomplishments – many of them still ongoing and vibrant – in LOTEs (languages other than English) and you cannot but come away convinced that these languages were and are labors of love for millions upon millions of Americans of all generations. How can all of this be overlooked and brushed away or consigned to the shadows and the dustbins of our public life? Indeed, something is amiss here, for there is a steep price to pay for peripheralizing such matters and that price has both internal and external ramifications, touching on individual health and happiness on the

273

one hand, and on national well-being and international relations on the other.

Myths and Realities

Our myths mirror our dreams, but myths are collective creations (perhaps not unlike Jung's collective unconscious), whereas the relevance of dreams is typically individual. Why do we have a myth that George Washington, "the father of our country," admitted to chopping down his father's favorite cherry tree, because he "just couldn't tell a lie" (seemingly a greater moral lapse than chopping down the tree to begin with)? Probably, because we need the reassurance that our country is built on an honorable and moral foundation. But is it true? Who knows? But whether or not it is actually true is far less important, and would tell us far less about America's self-image, than does *why we so want it to be true*. Another such myth is that our "Pilgrim Fathers," having left England because of religious persecution, subsequently also left the Netherlands (where they had all resettled prior to departing for the perilous New World) because they did not want their children to become exclusively Dutch speaking. Is this true? I have never found this frequently recited tale in any first-rate history of the United States or of early British settlements in the New World. It would be interesting to discover *where* this myth (if that is what it is) hails from and *when* it arose, but it is doubly interesting to ponder *why* it arose and why it has persisted in popular folklore. Certainly it legitimizes the centrality of English in the American experience, but it can be interpreted to also legitimize concerns about the protection of all immigrant-based mother tongues, that is, those of non-Anglophones as well.

In the latter case, why aren't language rights enshrined in the American Constitution? Why does the Constitution (and its added amendments) show such great concern for individual rights, such as "civil rights," but not for collective rights, such as "language rights"? Why does this particular "dream" of the Pilgrims remain unrealized and unrecognized, whereas their other dream, freedom of religion, remains so firmly in place that even a war with much of the Moslem world has failed to detract from its luster, notwithstanding the group basis of its realization? Is the lack of language protection just an oversight or a matter of deeper historical significance? Why can butterflies and minnows be protected by law, but ravaged languages remain without recourse? Who really needs butterflies or minnows anyway (Garcia, 1991)? These are not meant to be rhetorical questions. To answer them seriously (at least as seriously as many other stable, democratic, and modern states have done) requires us to step back from current American reality into its past and into its "What ifs."

What Were the Founding Fathers Thinking About, If Not Language?

Just as naively as Moslem children attending public schools in France recite the obligatory lessons about "Our ancestors the Gauls," so American children, whether white, black, brown, or yellow all refer to the same "Pilgrim Fathers" and to the same "Founding Fathers" of the Republic. The kinship term is intended metaphorically, of course, to indicate empathy and acceptance: regardless of our particular mothers (mother tongues) we are all united via a single set of fathers (fatherland). However, when we stop to examine what these fathers had to say about the plurality of languages, which was even then apparent to all who would but look, we find that they said little or nothing about it. How could such a group of well-read, well-intentioned, and otherwise well-attuned-to-the-times individuals have overlooked something so momentous as protecting the ethnic (actually, ethnoreligious) and ethnolinguistic diversity of the new land that they were establishing on these shores? If we search through the entire extant corpus of the minutes of their meetings, as well as their speeches, writings for periodicals and books, and their diaries, letters, and notes, we must conclude that language and languages were simply not on their minds.

Why is that? They were certainly aware that the Catholics in New England consisted very largely of French speakers, that Anibaptist Pietists in Pennsylvania were overwhelmingly speakers of one regional variety of German (later to be called Pennsylvania Dutch, Pennsylvania German, or "Pensylfawnisch"), that the Indians that were then still very near at hand were not speakers (certainly not native speakers) of English, as neither were the Swedes, the Dutch, or the Jews (whether Ashkenazi or Sephardi) scattered throughout the middle Atlantic states. In fact, about 25% of the total population of the colonies spoke a LOTE in 1790 (Lepore, 2002) and, therefore, could not easily have been overlooked. However, using an Old Testament approach to human failings, the Founding Fathers often satisfied themselves with negative pronouncements or prohibitions ("Thou shalt not....") and "Congress shall make no law regarding...") in order to curtail undesired behaviors, rather than voicing positive pronouncements, with respect to languages, religions, and interethnic affairs. English too gave way to this approach. There was no requirement as to English anywhere in the Federal statutes (even though the future President would have to be American-born, he did not necessarily have to be English-speaking), because to do otherwise, that is, to actually require English in order to hold any office might infringe on freedom of speech, press, and/or religion.

Some have speculated that this innocence of concerns pertaining to language was a carryover from Britain's lack of an English Academy (to parallel the famous French academy [1635] already well past the completion of its first century) or even an official or standard English dictionary, but I am not at all convinced that this speculation (about which there is a very meager written record, to say the least) tells the whole story, even were it to be true. This lack of interest in putting English on a pedestal also continued after the revolution, as America's first lexicographer Noah Webster (1758–1842) quickly discovered, to his chagrin, when he tried in vain to solicit congressional support for his fond plans to establish a governmentally "linked" or recognized "Academy of Federal English" (Webster, 1802). Indeed, the lack of constitutional provision for the conduct of education further weakened any chance that Congress might legislate on the language of education in the newly established republic. Why did the Founding Fathers launch what they hoped would become a model for democracy without a single explicit mention of language and certainly without any mention of support for either English or LOTEs? What in the world were these folks thinking about that resulted in such a huge blindspot (judging by the social theory that later developed and became dominant throughout much of Europe and, indeed, most of the world)?

The Intellectual World of Our "Fathers"

Our forefathers were mostly well educated, as befitted men of their enterprise, property, and aspirations. We find references in their works to the political and social theory and theorists of classical Greece and Rome and to those of late medieval and early modern Britain, France, and the German lands (there being no Germany per se until past the mid-point of the 19th century). Religion was much on their minds, particularly the lessons to be learned from the painful attempts of England and France, during past centuries and also during their own lifetimes, to favor, regulate, sponsor, assist, and require one religion or another, prohibiting or downgrading all others. Even the very existence of God was a troublesome intellectual and moral issue, one that preoccupied them sufficiently to want to keep God out of governmental business, authority, or responsibility. This is not to say that they were avowed atheists, but many of them were deists, skeptics, or agnostics. When they thought or spoke of religion it is fair to say that they only had the varieties of Western Christianity in mind, and even their few references to Judaism were exclusively biblical (i.e. to the so-called Old Testament) rather than to any postbiblical beliefs, observances, rabbinic opinions, or philosophical writings well known to scholars in Christian Europe.

What is amazing is that in this entire exquisite body of speculation and reflection there is nothing or almost nothing about language or languages. Neither Voltaire nor Montesque, nor Rousseau, nor any of the other famous Pensee were at all interested in language issues, although social and political issues in general interested them greatly, both as philosophers and *hommes d'action.* We *should* be surprised at this gap in their imagination, curiosity, and knowledge, but we are not, because we have come to take it for granted that our Founding Fathers reflected deeply on most aspects of human behavior, human rights, and governmental concerns more specifically. But their general praiseworthiness only increases our puzzlement rather than assuage it. Why should such a well-educated group of minds, equal in brain power, originality curiosity, and goodwill to any group of thinkers and statesmen anywhere in the Western world at their time have had such a remarkable blindspot, and, what is more, why should a similar blindspot have existed also among the vast majority of British and French thinkers of that same time? I would like to suggest that it was the nature of the Zeitgeist of the time in the ethnolinguistically consolidating "state into nationality" intellectual circles to conceive of social reality exactly in this manner, believing firmly that the true condition of society was "postethnic" and, therefore, inevitably monolingual and monocultural within national borders.

18th-Century France's Political Philosophy

The leading philosophers of "France" and "the French people" wrote as if a united and homogeneous France were consensually an eternal, natural, and preordained verity. There were still indigenous minorities aplenty in France then, just as there are today, but it was the received wisdom of the time that these were useless, "non–state-building" entities that were already dead or dying. French may not then even have been widely spoken in France, particularly in the south, east, north, and west of the realm (i.e. at any distance from Paris), but even before the French Revolution ruled that the regional languages were null, void, and illegal, they were considered to be mere dialects and *patois* (*pawlike* means of communication used by those who lived their lives at a subhuman level), disregarded because those languages were symbolic of speech communities that constantly ignored the Center's insistence on rendering all laws and acts into French and that, therefore, they *deserved* to be roundly ignored by the Center in turn.

In the 18th century, "France" had finally come into being, fully and proudly coalesced and unified, and it was a glory to behold: the strongest and most cultured (or, in its own eyes, the "only cultured") state in Europe! Not the least of its "achievements" was to leave all its regional particularities behind and to follow the one and only "la belle France" into yet unimagined heights of greatness and goodness. It was this set of widely shared underlying postethnic and uniformational assumptions that liberated the "philosophes" to ponder the nature of social and economic issues; of law, crime, and punishment; of government; and the nature of man and their respective duties and obligations toward each other (Lough 1982), precisely as if no minority peoples and languages even existed. Of course, they were profoundly mistaken. To the exasperation of France and the consternation of its minorities to this very day, the true state of affairs is and was very different (viz. the recent protest [January 27, 2004] of a Breton member of European Parliament's "Culture Committee," after a 17-year-old Breton schoolgirl had completed the first week of a hunger strike against the French government's decision to cut its already inadequate 2004 budget for minority education. This act could not go unnoticed by the European Union.

> [T]he French government continually seeks our assistance in the European Parliament in opposing the hegemony of the English language, yet here we now have that government showing rank disrespect for the regional and minority languages within its own state. There is no point to start talking about diversity in Europe unless that diversity is respected within its respective member states. The decrease offered this year to regional languages clearly means that there is no will to support Basque, Breton, Catalan or Occitan in France. (Bos Sole & Hicks, 2004)

With the wisdom of hindsight we can say today that defining minorities out of existence and ignoring them in intellectual or governmental discourse does not make them so and even postpone the cause of unity. But Jefferson, Franklin, Adams, and other avid readers of French thought in mid- to late-18th-century America could not have had any independent knowledge on this matter and proceeded on the assumption that France was indeed the monoethnic and monolingual entity that its blindspot enabled it to pretend it was then, and that it continues to pretend it is to this very day.

Mid-18th-Century Great Britain

Matters were neither better nor different across the channel from France. England's leaders had already come to the position that any discussion of Scots, Irish, or Welsh was totally passé. They were merely vestigial ruins of prehistoric entities long gone from the arenas of public life and thought. The struggles against the Center there, in the century prior to the American Revolution, never addressed the minorities issue as an issue of cultural democracy, even if the debate was entered into by individuals who themselves stemmed from those areas but had been reethnized into the British mainstream. The residual problems of the regions in which those groups resided were considered to be merely of a practical nature and greater religious tolerance, economic opportunity, and, particularly, more attention to the needy would not only ameliorate all of them but further unity and harmony as well. Statesmen and thinkers, therefore, had no need to address the issues of cultural pluralism for the nation and cultural self-determination for the regions. The notion of good government could be speculated about almost as if it were the continuation of a discourse with the ancient Greeks and Romans (who also recognized no minority cultures or languages). The cities of Ireland and Welsh were English preserves established through the labor of dispossessed, impoverished, illiterate and woefully ignorant peasants from the countryside. Even if one granted that these were injustices, and not all were about to do so, the theory of good government (its structure, its goals, its dramatis personae, its raison d'etre, etc.) could proceed without coming to grips with such minority affairs, neither ab initio nor even at all. England appeared to its ruling classes to be a fully unified state and its peoples were or would soon be of one stock, and the better the state functioned the sooner that highly desired state of affairs would come to pass. No appreciation for what was being overlooked or surpressed could be gained from the literature of the time.

State nationalities (rather than nationality states) were not only the established but also the desired "order of things" in Western Europe. Spain too was a proud member of the "Western Club," its regional minorities too being roundly ignored and a unified, centralized Castillian state was the only reality or option whose thought and culture reached the literate outside world. The opposite order (in which preexisting nations created states for their own defense and development) was considered to be an inversion of nature, indeed, "unnatural," and none of the great Spanish (or British, French, and German) philosophers had a good word to say on its behalf. Our Founding Fathers found nothing in their pursuit of "the best European literature" that could have made even the wisest or most sensitive among them believe or suspect otherwise than that "polity creates culture," that is, the progression of events experienced or foreseen by the great Western European monarchies.

It was the stability of the state's central apparatus – its coin, its royal family, its weights and measures, its governing bodies, its roads, its police and military services, its laws, its customs and celebrations, etc. – that was thought to ultimately fashion a single nation out of a mixture of people of differing provenance and to convince them that they not only belonged together but that they were one by fate, by experience, and by preference. That the Founding Fathers opted for democracy ("a democratic republic") was revolution enough for them and we cannot fault them that they did not entertain and apply to the American setting the opposite sequence of events (namely that "culture creates polity") via which a people creates its political arrangements to defend its preexisting authenticity and its specialness. No such progression was recognized in 18th-century West (or, more accurately, in the pre–French Revolution West) and, therefore, the Founding Fathers and whatever *primum mobilae* they provided for the new republic, simply lacked the conceptual tools for aspiring toward governmentally supported cultural pluralism, cultural democracy, cultural stewardship, and minority

representation in the very workings of state-sponsored bodies, their processes, and their budgetary perquisites.

Different ideas of "freedom" and "liberty" did exist, of course, and did
so primarily among the Anglo immigrants, from whom most of our Founding Fathers came (Fischer, 2004). New England Puritans pursued "ordered
liberty," or community self-government, which could impose substantial
restrictions on individual freedom of action or conscience. Southern cav-
aliers believed in "hegemonic liberty," in which liberty was a jealously
guarded aristocratic privilege that entitled some to rule the lives of others.
By contrast, Delaware Valley Quakers subscribed to "reciprocal liberty," in
which every person was recognized as a fellow child of God, entitled to
self-determination and freedom of conscience. Finally, the largest group of
Anglo immigrants, the borderlanders, often called Scottish–Irish, adhered
to "natural liberty," a visceral defense of self and clan. German-Americans
sought a freedom that would allow them to establish their own way of life
in security and peace, fundamentally a desire to be left alone by government (Postrel, 2004). Several of the above could have metamorphosed into
something broader than self-interest appeal for cultural pluralism, individual or collective, but none of them did. They were each too weighed down
by their pre-American struggles for life, law, and acceptance to take the
next logical step into cultural pluralism, not only as a liberty but as a right.

Another Place, Another Time

Not only was Eastern Europe (east of the Rhine) far different than the
contemporary Western European intellectual scene that we have just briefly
described above, but, within a century later, even Western Europe itself was
profoundly changed. England could no longer pretend that the Irish were
gone and done with (although Britain had done all it could to kill them
off or drive them away during the state-manipulated famines of the prior
century), nor that the Welsh were soon to expire, or that the Scots were
simply good and frugal English folk with a funny accent. Not only did
Spain increasingly recognize the obvious, namely that its larger minorities
(Catalans, Basques, Galicians, and Asturians) were there to stay and that
they would make demands on the Central authorities forever and a day,
but even the French too were forced to seek some accommodation (or, at
least, to plan arriving at an understanding with the Bretons, Occitans, and
Alsatians) in the foreseeable future. The tide of nationalism ("the principle
of nationalities") that Napoleon had both unleashed and fostered from the
Pyrenees to the sands of Egypt engulfed all that stood in its way and the last
multiethnic empires (those of Austro-Hungary, Russia, and the Ottomans)
made several grudging concessions to it and were ultimately destroyed by
it in the early 20th-century's Great War. An American president, Woodrow
Wilson, was so impressed by the justice of the "principle of nationalities"

that he utilized it as a guiding principle for dismembering the Central Powers who had lost that war (although there is no evidence that he also planned to foster it in the West of Europe or in the United States itself – "Physician, heal thyself!").

But what if the United States had been established just then, a mere century and a quarter after its true founding? Its Founding Fathers would have read Herder galore, and Kautsky, and Massarik and Vuk Karadzic, and the spokespersons for Greece, for Poland, for the Ukraine, for the Jews, Turks, etc., etc. They might still have utilized the slogan "E pluribus unum" but they would have been just as concerned for "pluribus et union," that is for the protection of *pluribus* as for the achievement of *unum*. The "many" can coexist with the "one," as Belgium, Switzerland, Singapore, India, the Philippines and various other democratic settings amply reveal.

Cultural Pluralism in the United States

With the massive central, eastern, and southern European immigrations to the United States during the last quarter of the 19th century and the first quarter of the 20th, attempts began to be made to harmoniously combine the Western and the Eastern approaches to language and ethnicity under some sort of single governmental umbrella. However, precisely because of the massiveness of the inflow from "less favored points of origin," the rejection of immigrants (which previously had a "Know Nothing" anti-Catholic bite to it) was generalized into calls for antihyphenization as a whole. The latter soon led to anti-immigration legislation and to the imposition of quotas that were particularly aimed at restricting potential immigrants from non-"Western" countries of origin. The quotas were aimed at limiting the small pool of permitted newcomers to the proportions of individuals from their countries of origin in the US population in 1790, when the American population was overwhelmingly English, Irish, Scottish, and German. These were all countries of origin from which few immigrants could be expected at that time, immediately after the Great War, so that even the tiny quotas established for them frequently went unfilled. In addition, the Great War and its aftermath fostered a hue and cry over German language maintenance in the United States. A rash of prohibitory legislation, at the state (and sometimes at the City) level, beginning before the War and continuing into the 1920s, were aimed specifically at denying its public or institutional use (actually, the use of *any* foreign "vernacular," classical tongues being magnanimously exempted in view of the fact that no immigrants claimed to speak them and, furthermore, in view of the fact that they had religious uses that the State [or the states] could not easily tamper with).

It required a Supreme Court ruling (*Meyer vs. Nebraska*, 1923) to find such legislation unconstitutional, both because children belonged to their parents, not to the state (and the parents, therefore, had sole jurisdiction over which language(s) should be used as medium(media) of instruction for their children), and because language teaching was an old and honorable profession, and the state, therefore, should not interfere with the livelihoods of those who engaged in it. During the hearings various justices also rejected Nebraska's claim that early and prolonged exposure to a foreign language affected the brains and hearts of the young and made it impossible for them subsequently to grow up to be true Americans, or that any other palpable danger to public peace and safety existed that might justify any prohibition such as that which Nebraska had instituted.

The Magna Carta

The Supreme Court's ruling in Meyer vs. Nebraska has been grandiloquently referred to as "the Magna Carta of language rights in the USA." Unfortunately, this is not the case and calling it so is not only incorrect but reveals a profound misunderstanding of what the Magna Carta really was. The Magna Carta, in 1215, did not merely reign in the powers of King John but it granted specific rights, powers, and privileges to the nobles, knights, and barons who were at odds with him. Prohibiting the states from adopting exclusionary legislation with respect to the languages of instruction for the young is by no means the same as adopting a supportive substantive policy in the language area. The court's ruling in Meyer vs. Nebraska, rather than being a Magna Carta, is actually in the long tradition of the Supreme Court's actions concerning religion. Those provisions merely say that the Congress shall take no action concerning "the establishment of religion," without expressing any opinion as to whether religion is good, bad, or indifferent. Similarly, in Meyer vs. Nebraska, the Court merely said that Nebraska could not prohibit the use of foreign vernaculars in education, but it did not really express any view as to whether such use was good, bad, or indifferent. Moreover, in its religion rulings the Court itself is continuing a practice that derives from the sad history of the religious wars and persecutions in Western Europe in the 17th and 18th centuries and from the views of social and moral philosophers as to how those evils could best be avoided in the future. In the ruling on Meyer vs. Nebraska it is less clear just what experiential body of historical or legal evidence relative to the role of non-State languages, either in Europe or in America, the Court was drawing upon. Thus, the latter opinion leaves the United States essentially without a substantive language policy, and a "no-policy policy" inevitably benefits the status quo of English as lingua franca, rather than protecting the future of community-based LOTEs as desiderata of America's national interest. For that goal to be reached, a proactive and substantive approach to cultural and linguistic pluralism is essential.

The National Interest

It has been frequently observed that the theory of democracy has more to say about *how* government proceeds and *who has access* to these processes, than about any substantive goals or products that democracy fosters. Thus, we cannot guarantee that all democracies will institute a separation between church and state. Indeed, there is no such guarantee in most democratic settings around the world (e.g. England and Sweden have State Churches, as do most democracies in the non-Western world, where Orthodox Christianity [Greece], Islam [Algeria], and Hinduism [India] are not only dominant but state supported, protected, or "established"), although freedom of religion (or irreligion) is almost universally a democratic guarantee and is even guaranteed in many states ("polities") with State religions. But "freedom of..." provisos are not fully substantive either. If LOTEs are to become relatively stabilized in America's future then they must come to be regarded as in the national interest in positive and substantive terms, like the preservation of our fresh air, oil reserves, forests, streams, plants, and animal life (and, indeed, of the rights to the very land itself that makes their continued existence possible).

The preservation of national monuments, historical buildings, and scenic wonders are "self-evidently" in the public interest, even for those who never lay eyes on them. So is the support of registered charities, which explains why we grant our residents tax exemptions for supporting them (even religious charities, religious buildings, and religious bodies per se, thereby raising the taxes for the irreligious). There are substantive laws that specially protect Indian "nations" and their sacred places, streams, and mountains against thieves and souvenir hunters (this protection being paid for from the tax revenues from "pale-faces"). We subsidize farms (particularly small farms that are fast becoming vanishing species, utilizing the taxes paid by urban dwellers as well), the mailing of periodicals at lower-than-usual rates (both to foster literacy and a free press, utilizing tax funds that are also paid by all those who get their news on the Web), we subsidize the health of the elderly (at the expense of the tax-paying young), we regulate pure food and drug laws (at the expense of individuals who oppose any governmental tampering with their food), public safety (at the expense of those who need no protection), public transportation (utilizing the tax revenues that are also collected from owners of private vehicles), and public education (taxing even those who have no children or whose children receive their education from private and church schools), etc. Couldn't LOTE institutions (neighborhood centers, schools, media centers, cultural centers, etc.) be given special recognition as being in the public interest at least as much as some of the foregoing? Of course they could, if we would but notice them.

Personality Principle, Organizational Principle, and Territorial Principle

If LOTE-speaking community resources are to be supported in the national interest, what are the operative units that will be recognized for this purpose: individuals, organizations, or communities. If every individual who meets certain requirements can qualify for recognition (as is the case under the Americans with Disabilities Act or the Social Security Act), this would require a much larger and more expensive support apparatus, since individuals frequently move and require "recognition" and assistance for the purposes of the Act, wherever they may be. But there is even a more valid reason why individual speakers of LOTEs are not necessarily the best support units for maximizing the vitality and longevity of the LOTEs themselves. Languages are basically means of social communication and they require a social setting for their proper development even within individuals. One such social setting may be nonprofit and organizational in nature. There are many American precedents for such an approach. The Peace Corp is one such organizational setting and the Red Cross is another, the Neighborhood Crime Watch is still another, the Community Garden Club or the Community Library Association are yet others, and the Young Farmers of America is still another. Note that not all of the foregoing were federally initiated and that some involve no governmental funds at any level. We must not confuse public support with governmental auspices no matter how often that may (initially) be the case.

Organizations that qualify under the provisions of the Act receive support for activities that are in accord with the purposes of the Act. Support for LOTEs might very well be on an organizational basis, the organizations themselves applying for available support. This approach to LOTE maintenance has been followed abroad in Ireland, Friesland, the Basque region, and in the United States by SPCAs, local art museums, the Bureau of Indian Affairs, etc. Organizations require supervision or certification, of course, but they are much more likely to stay put and can also build into their operation a degree of intergenerational continuity, which is very desirable for the maintenance of language resources. Finally, an even larger context for LOTEs is that which exists where the territorial principal obtains. This principal has long been utilized for Romansh support in Switzerland, for the support of "scheduled languages" in India, for the support of Sorbian in Germany, etc. It may be amenable to American practices, because it assumes a central authority that supports various local ventures, but, of course, it needs to be protected from political maneuverings and needs to be set up as an ongoing principle of government, perhaps with its own cabinet-level secretary. The late, lamented Office of Bilingual Education and Minority Language Affaires might have developed into something like this – since school districts are territorial – but it was done in before it could mature by those who were arrayed against it and who would have undercut it eventually, come what may, because of the undeservedly bad press that bilingual education had faced from the 1980s on. Of course, the territorial principle and the organizational principle can be combined, organizations within districts being budget-oriented toward their particular district rather than necessarily toward national headquarters.

Perhaps a personal anecdote would be pardoned at this juncture. As a 10-year-old, I once accompanied my father for a walk through the neighborhood on a lovely spring evening. We passed the local public school, already closed at that hour, and I was surprised to note my father's interest in it. How many pupils did it serve? What proportion of them were Jewish? How many teachers? What proportion of them were Jewish. From how far around did the pupils come each day? etc. Finally, he turned to me and said, "You know, there is no good reason why the school board couldn't let Yiddish speakers use the school after regular hours for courses and activities related to their particular culture that they want. If the board would pay the teachers something for two hours a day every afternoon during the regular school year, that wouldn't come to very much at all, and only those who were interested need attend. They could get a certificate in recognition of their participation, if they did well, and might even get a few credits toward graduation. Why shouldn't the school board do that for us?"

The memory of my father's words, so forlorn at the time that he uttered them (forlorn even though he believed that the neighboring German and Italian parents would also be interested in organizing something along these lines in conjunction with other nearby schools), always reawakens in my mind when I note the Mandarin, Korean, Vietnamese, Arabic, French, and Spanish opportunities, roughly along those very same lines, now available in the Palo Alto/Stanford area. In addition, there are also Mandarin and Spanish immersion schools (oversubscribed and with a long waiting list) in the same area, totally operated by public funds. My father, a self-educated Social Democrat in accord with the pre–World War I Austro-Hungarian model, would hardly be able to believe it – or the Australian efforts in Sydney and Melbourne precisely along these lines – were he alive today.

I do not recommend this administrative or that administrative approach to the problem of proper units of recognition for publicly subsidized pluralism, *nor should such steps begin and end with the school*. What I do maintain is that subsidized cultural pluralism at the neighborhood level could be implemented were there the necessary will and understanding to do so. Both the sidestreams and the mainstream need to be involved in converting this from a pipedream into a reality. Balkanization, fratricide, or social conflict, on the one hand, and decreased gross national product, on the other, are not really consequences to be worried about, as has been empirically demonstrated innumerable times (most recently and quantitatively in Fishman, 2003) as has their groundlessness, relative to the real dangers of extirpation and alienation under the benevolent hucksterism of the "Greater American co-Prosperity Sphere," are patent for all to see who care to look. The blessings of subsidized sidestream community life in the languages pertaining to such life are worth ever so much more than the televisions, automobiles, and computers that are presumably the compensation package for the surrender of cultural democracy. No such either–or option (i.e. either alienation from the mainstream or participation in subsidized neighborhood cultural pluralism) exists, however, and if there were such a real democracy, a cultural democracy, it would let communities choose on an informed basis just how they would prefer to live their lives. Life is far more symbiotic and combinatorial than are the suspicious ideologies of the mainstream.

The Special Case of Spanish

A plea for subsidized cultural pluralism at this stage in American sociopolitical reality, or a plea for at least imagining such cannot proceed without singling out the Spanish case. Had similar discussions been held in the late 18th or early 19th century, they could not have proceeded without considering the special cases of the Franco-Americans. In the mid–19th century they would particularly have needed to consider the Hiberno-Americans; in the late 19th century the German-Americans; and in the early 20th, the Southern and Eastern Europeans. Today, it is crucial that Hispano-Americans be drawn into the debate, rather than having its decisions dumped upon them unawares. It should come as no surprise that in an overwhelmingly Protestant nation there will be a confluence of Catholicism (both Western and Eastern) and the history of debate in connection with subsidized cultural pluralism. Catholics and non-Christians provide the lion's share of our current (and probably of our most likely future) immigration, whether from the New World or the Old. As such, subsidized pluralism will inevitably rise and fall in accord with their appreciation and understanding of it. The Church's century-long flight from its immigrant roots and its headlong pursuit of Americanism "pure and simple" would be a factor requiring special consideration under any circumstances.

This is doubly the case given that Hispanics are, at one and the same time, not only overwhelmingly Catholic but overwhelmingly "newcomers": (first- and second-generation Americans) for whom subsidized cultural pluralism would make a big difference during their early accompanying Americanization. The settlement pattern of incoming and recently arrived Hispanics is also one that favors their candidacy for subsidized cultural pluralism. They are sufficient in numbers and in demographic concentration to make assisting their language and culture maintenance a tactically parsimonious undertaking. They are often sufficiently "intact" culturally and linguistically to constitute concentrated and intergenerationally continuous communities. They are not likely to melt away, both because they are often a visible (i.e. a racially constructed) minority and because their continued arrival fosters their long-term recognizability. Finally, having largely arrived in the United States in the period since governmental assistance has been made available (often both via legislation and by court order) to poverty pockets of the limited-English-speaking, they have built fewer voluntary cultural, educational, political, and self-help neighborhood institutions of their own than have other and older immigrant groups to the United States. On a smaller scale, similar benefits would accrue to Chinese, Japanese, Korean, Thai, Pacific Islander, Arabic-speaking (Lebanese, Palestinian, Egyptian, Jordanian, Saudi, Iraqi, etc.), Indian, and Pakistani newcomers. We must not wait until these all melt into the landscape linguistically and attitudinally, even if it is more difficult for them to do just that because of racist America's reaction to their darker skin color.

An approach that would not make Hispanics stand out on the one hand, and definitely include them too on the other , is what is called for here. Each of the successive immigration waves that have hit our shores roughly at 50-year intervals since the very founding of the Republic have brought us gifts of great worth. May the Hispanics be the ones that finally help us launch subsidized ethnocultural and ethnolinguistic pluralism wherever it can take root and flourish. If this approach is not implemented soon and in favorable environments, then Spanish too, like French and German before it in the USA, will "go down the tubes," propelled by alienation, de-ethnization and delinguification. If we cannot stabilize Spanish on an intergenerational basis (so that it does not constantly depend on transfusions from new immigrants), at a time when the federal government is issuing calls daily for native Spanish speakers that can help with the war effort, then we cannot do it at all. Another great national resource and an incomparable reservoir of identity, creativity and self-knowledge will have been lost to all of us as individuals, not to mention the incomparable loss to our national well-being.

Summary

The lack of protected ethnolinguistic pluralism in the United States is a by-product of its peculiar settlement history and its intellectual parentage. Organized and publicly supported language planning on behalf of sidestream languages, cultures, and societies would be a break with American tradition vis-à-vis LOTEs, even though our country has been blessed, throughout its history, with mighty resources along these lines. Our Founding Fathers did not oppose LOTEs or their cultivation for posterity; they merely operated in a universe of ideas and values that were sociolinguistically uninformed and alinguistic. The massive presence of Spanish in current American life represents a last opportunity to rectify a gap that has needlessly impoverished our internal and our external modus vivendi. It represents a last chance for cultural democracy to also become a part (a long-overlooked part) of the American dream and for publicly supported linguistic repair, conservation, and growth to be added to our efforts to save from erosion and firmly establish a proactive policy on behalf of the community languages that still dot our landscapes.

References

Bauer, O. (2000/1907) *The Question of Nationalities and Social Democracy.* Minneapolis: University of Minnesota Press.

Bos Sole, A., and Hicks, D. (2004) French government cuts teaching posts for minoritized languages. *Eurolang* (Brussels, 2/26/20004).

Fischer, L. (2004) Spanish for native speakers (SNS) education: The state of the field. On WWW at http://www.cal.org./hertiage/sns/sns-fieldrpt.htm. Accessed 24.8.2004.

Fishman, J. A. (1982) Nathan Birnbaum's view of American Jews. *Judaica Book News* 18 (1), 10–12, 68–70.

Fishman, J. A. (2003) Empirical explorations of two popular assumptions: Interpolity perspectives on the relationships between linguistic heterogeneity, civil strife, and per-capita gross national product. In Tucker, G. Richard, and C. Paulston (eds) *Sociolinguistics: The Essential Readings* (pp. 383–393). Malden: Blackwell.

Garcia, O. (ed) (1991) Section ii: Who needs a rhinoceros or an Orangutan? (p. 57) and Section iii: Multilingualism for Minnows and Whales (p. 103). In *Bilingual Education: Focusschrift in Honor of Joshua A. Fishman on the Occasion of His 65th Birthday.* Amsterdam: Benjamins.

Kallen, H. (1998/1924) *Culture and Democracy in the United States.* New Brunswick: Transaction.

Kymlicka, W. (1995) *Multicultural Citizenship.* New York: Oxford University Press.

Lepore, J. (2002) *A Is for American: Letters and Other Characters in the Newly United States.* New York: Knopf.

Lough, J. (1982) *The Philosophes and Post-Revolutionary France.* Clarendon: Oxford University Press.

Meyer v. Nebraska (1923). 262. US 390.

Postrel, V. (2004) The eagle has landed. *The New York Times Book Review* December 19, 21–22.

Walzer, M. (1997) *Pluralism and Democracy.* Paris: Espirit.

Methodological Appendix

Survey of Latino Professionals

The preparation for the survey of successful Latinos in California involved four separate tasks: (1) the identification of existing lists of Latino professionals, (2) the development of a Web site with information about the project, (3) the development of the telephone survey instrument, and (4) the random selection of individuals from the identified lists.

Identification of existing lists of Latino professionals

Identification of existing lists of Latino professionals proved to be much more complex than we originally envisioned. We discovered that, while certain lists were available (e.g. doctors from the American Medical Association [AMA], Lawyers from the La Raza Lawyers Association of California), most of the professions in which we were interested either did not list professionals by ethnicity (e.g. law enforcement officers, dentists, chiropractors), could not provide addresses and telephone numbers for professionals, or did not want to either give us the information or sell us the information because they do not make available such lists to the public.

We were successful in obtaining lists for the following eight professional groups: professors in the California State University system, professors in the University of California system, judges, lawyers, doctors, teachers, elected and appointed officials, and businesspersons. However, because of the difficulty in obtaining the necessary lists, preparation for the survey extended beyond the 3 months anticipated in our original timeline. Below, we briefly describe some of the difficulties encountered in carrying out what had appeared to us to be a simple task.

In the case of doctors and lawyers, we found it necessary to purchase lists of Latino doctors from the AMA, Latino-surnamed lawyers from the La Raza Lawyers Association, and businesspersons from the *Journal of Hispanic Business*. Because the information we purchased came as address labels, we had to enter the names into a database, locate counties by zip code, and find phone numbers for these individuals on different professional Web sites (e.g. California Bar Organization Member and Searchpointe Physician). The lists that we were not able to purchase were obtained as follows: for the California State University (CSU) and University of California (UC) professors we searched the CSU and UC school's departmental Web sites looking for Latino surnamed assistant, associate and full professors. From these sites we were able to obtain email and phone numbers for these target groups. In order to get High School teachers we had to call principals and assistant principals so that they could recommend or refer individuals who fit our criteria. For the judges we came across a directory of Minority Judges that divided the judges by ethnicity. With this information we then went back to the California Bar Web page to locate current information for them, or search through the county judicial Web sites for current information. Through a contact at the National Association of Latino Elected and Appointed Officials (NALEO) we were able to get a copy of their 2000 directory, which listed Latino officials by rank and county while simultaneously offering us their contact information. All of the information that we obtained from our different efforts was then entered into a searchable database so that we could locate and find random samples of individuals by county and occupation designation.

Development of a web site describing the project

While not originally included as a project task, it became clear that developing a Web page describing the project would be essential to the success of the project. We determined that individuals asked to participate in a telephone survey were more willing to participate if they could access a complete overview of the project as well as information about the researchers involved in the study. We were fortunate in being able to secure the services of a student who was willing to develop the site in exchange for course credit, and, as a result, no project funds were expended for this purpose. The URL for the Web site is http://heritagelanguages.stanford.edu.

Development of the telephone survey instrument

Development of the telephone survey instrument was carried out as proposed and versions of the instrument were pretested. Included here as Appendix A, it covers demographic information (place of birth, country of origin, age of arrival), sociolinguistic information (patterns of English and Spanish use, education, formal study of Spanish, self-evaluation of proficiencies), views about the need for Spanish in professional life, efforts made to improve Spanish, and attitudes toward varieties of Spanish.

Random selection of individuals from the identified lists

While we originally proposed to survey a total of 100 Latino professionals, we decided to increase the number to 200 to more adequately sample the various professional groups in counties both below and above the mean with respect to Latinos in the local population.

In selecting individuals from the identified lists, we sought to select approximately equal numbers of individuals from eight occupational professional groups and two Hispanic population density strata (counties with a Hispanic population at or above the state mean and counties with a Hispanic population below the state mean). To make our selection, the 58 counties in California were divided into two groups: those counties that, according to the Rand California Demographic and Population Statistics, contain more than the mean number of Latinos in California and those that contain less than the mean number. We determined that there are 10 counties that contain more than the mean number of Latinos and 48 that have less than the mean number of Latinos/Hispanics. The selection of 200 individuals was made by drawing two samples for each professional group, so that 100 individuals were selected from the bottom counties and 100 individuals were selected from the top counties.

Telephone survey of successful Latinos

To study the use of Spanish by Latino Professionals, we developed a telephone survey instrument. Project personnel developed and pretested the interview protocol before interviews were conducted. A total of 212 individuals were surveyed because some of the original respondents declined to be tape recorded. Therefore, for the purpose of comparability we wanted to replace those individuals with people who had agreed to be tape recorded so that we could closely listen to and take note of their answers on the open-ended questions. We had very positive feedback from the respondents, and nearly 90% of them agreed to participate in a further follow-up interview, if called upon to do so, because they felt they had a lot to contribute.

Data collection

We began calling individuals from our lists of successful Latinos in April of 2001 and finished collecting our samples in August of 2001. Throughout the interviewing phase we had on average five individuals calling on a daily basis in 2–3-hour shifts. For every 25 professionals that we actually interviewed we called an average of 125 individuals.

The first few minutes of the interview involved explaining the research project to the potential participants and reading a human subjects oral consent script. The participants were then tape recorded giving oral consent to be both interviewed and tape recorded. In addition, we asked them for a fax number or mailing address so that we could formally send them our contact information after the conclusion of the interview. A total of 218 individuals were surveyed because some of the original respondents declined to be tape recorded. For the purpose of comparability we replaced those individuals who declined to be tape recorded with people who agreed to be tape recorded so that we could closely listen to and take note of their answers on the open-ended questions.

Analysis of survey data

After the interviewing process was completed a team of researcher assistants transcribed all 200 tapes. The tapes and transcriptions were checked for accuracy by individuals who had not transcribed the particular tape being reviewed. After all interviews were transcribed, they were coded for further analysis. An extensive code book was created during the coding phase. Four researchers used this code book (Appendix B) to code each interview. Each interview transcript was coded by two research assistants, and a third research assistant checked for reliability among coders. After all 200 interviews were completely coded and checked for reliability, two identical databases were created and information was entered twice, once into each database. The two databases were then compared for consistency. Any inconsistencies were then reentered and a final database was created, which was used for later analyses using forward-selection stepwise regression analyses.

Statistical Procedures

Stepwise regressions: A brief overview

The goal of stepwise regression analysis is to better understand the relationship between a set of predictors (independent variables) and a dependent variable. In stepwise regression analysis, through a series of "steps" we take a large group of predictors and select only the ones that help understand the variation or change in the dependent variable. The adjusted R^2 values tell us how well our selected group of variables helps explain variation (either increase or decrease) in the dependent variable. The higher the value, the better the selected set of variables help explain the variation. The coefficient or beta values tell us how each predictor is related to the dependent variable. A positive beta indicates a positive relationship (i.e. an increase of one unit in the predictor results in an increase of one unit in the dependent). A negative beta indicates a negative relationship (i.e. an increase of one unit in the predictor results in a decrease of one unit in the dependent, or a decrease of one unit in the predictor results in an increase of one unit in the dependent).

Building models via stepwise regression

Stepwise model-building techniques for regression designs with a single dependent variable are described in numerous sources (e.g. see Darlington, 1990; Hocking, 1966; Lindeman *et al.*, 1980; Morrison, 1967;

Neter *et al.*, 1985; Pedhazur, 1973; Stevens, 1986; Younger, 1985). The basic procedures involve (1) identifying an initial model, (2) iteratively "stepping," that is, repeatedly altering the model at the previous step by adding or removing a predictor variable in accordance with the "stepping criteria," and (3) terminating the search when stepping is no longer possible given the stepping criteria, or when a specified maximum number of steps has been reached. The following topics provide details on the use of stepwise model-building procedures.

Forward selection regression models

Forward selection starts with an empty model. The variable that has the smallest p value when it is the only predictor in the regression equation is placed in the model. Each subsequent step adds the variable that has the smallest p value in the presence of the predictors already in the equation. Variables are added one at a time as long as their p values are small enough, typically less than 0.05 or 0.10.

Survey of High Schools and Universities with Heritage Language Programs

The preparation for the survey of schools and universities with heritage language programs included four separate tasks: (1) the identification and request for existing lists of high schools and universities with established heritage language programs (this included the expansion of our university list comprising all universities in California regardless of whether they had heritage language programs); (2) the development of the survey instrument; (3) the random selection of schools and universities from the identified lists we attained, and (4) the preparation and follow-up involved in sending the questionnaire via mail and receiving adequate numbers of respondents.

Identification and request of existing lists of high schools and universities with established heritage language programs

Through contacts at the Modern Language Association and the California Foreign Language Project, we were able to attain lists of schools and universities with established heritage language programs. Once attained, however, we had to search the California Department of Education Web site to locate high-school contact information for principals and Spanish language department administrators. The same procedure was followed for the universities, often resulting in both Internet searches for department administrators and calling of the departments themselves to confirm posted information.

We had planned contacting 100 schools and 100 universities. However, we soon learned that while there are over 250 high schools with heritage language programs in California, there are barely more than 60 universities and community colleges combined that have heritage language programs. With a smaller respondent pool, we had to focus our efforts on attaining only 50 schools and universities, instead of the intended 100. Moreover, we had to broaden our university criteria to include schools that did not have established heritage language programs to fulfill the 50 we collected. All of the information we obtained from our different efforts were then entered into a searchable database so that we could locate and find random samples of schools and universities by county.

Survey instrument

The development of the mail survey instrument was carried out as proposed and versions of the instrument were pretested by university department heads at universities outside of California who served similar populations of heritage students. Included here as Appendices C and D are the mail questionnaire and its accompanying coding scheme. The instrument targeted language department heads and/or individuals in charge of heritage programs at both the high school and college/university levels. The various sections of the survey requested information about the institution, the institution's full Spanish language program, courses designed for heritage students, placement procedures, curriculum objectives, materials, teaching practices, outcomes, and instructors' language backgrounds and preparation. The questionnaire was split into parallel portions for schools that do and do not offer heritage language programs.

The random selection of schools and universities from the identified lists we attained

While we originally proposed to survey a total of 100 schools and universities, we decided to decrease the number to 50 each because of the lack of possible universities available for survey in California. We did not want to have disproportionate amounts of information, so we downsized the high-school respondent pool to match the university respondent number.

In selecting schools from the identified lists, and expanded lists, we sought to select approximately equal numbers of schools from two Hispanic population density strata (counties with a Hispanic population at or above the state mean and counties with a Hispanic population below the state mean). To make our selection, the 58 counties in California were divided into two groups: those counties that, according to the Rand California Demographic and Population Statistics, contain more than the mean number of Latinos in California and those counties that contain less than the mean number. We determined that there are 10 counties that contain more than the mean number of Latinos and 48 that have less than the mean number of Latinos/Hispanics. The selection of 100 schools was made by drawing two samples for each institutional group, so that equal numbers of institutions were selected from the bottom counties as well as from the top counties.

Secondary school participants

The Bay Area Foreign Language Project (BAFLP), an organization that has conducted a number of surveys of foreign language instruction in the state of California, provided the project with the list of secondary schools used in selecting secondary school participants. The BAFLP list contained approximately 300 high schools that had reported implementing Spanish heritage programs. In selecting the high school sample, we used the total list of 300 high schools obtained from BAFLP and randomly selected approximately equal numbers of schools from two Hispanic population density strata (counties with a Hispanic population at or above the state mean and counties with a Hispanic population below the state mean). The total sample of selected high schools included 173 schools.

Postsecondary institution participants

A list of postsecondary institutions was obtained from the Modern Language Association (MLA), an organization that regularly conducts surveys of foreign language enrollment in institutions of higher education in the United States. The MLA list identified 63 junior colleges, colleges, and universities that had responded affirmatively to questions about heritage program implementation. The schools were identified in a survey MLA conducted in 2000. We expanded the original list of 63 institutions to include 212 other colleges, universities, and junior colleges listed on the California Department of Education Web site that were not included on the MLA list. We included on our final list all postsecondary institutions that indicated either on their Web site or through further contact via email or phone correspondence that they had a Spanish language program. The final list of postsecondary institutions to which the survey was sent was composed of a total of 173 junior colleges, colleges, and universities.

The preparation and follow-up involved in sending the questionnaire via mail and receiving adequate numbers of respondents

Once the questionnaires were photocopied and collated correctly, we then had to place tracking codes on each questionnaire. We did this so that once the questionnaires were returned to us we could identify the school each questionnaire came from in case other identifying markers were not included, for example, school name and county information. Once this process was completed, we sent each questionnaire off to a corresponding school with return envelope and postage. We sent roughly 300 packets, 150 to schools and 150 to our expanded list of universities. The expanded list of universities now included junior colleges and other institutions not listed on the MLA list.

One month after sending out the initial packages, we sent out a fluorescent reminder postcard hoping to (a) renew interest in the project and (b) remind possible participants to fill out the questionnaire either by mail or phone if they desired. From this effort we received more questionnaires via mail and also completed several questionnaires via phone.

In late November, we began calling participants who had already returned questionnaires to us, but for some reason had either skipped questions or not completed questions accurately. From this effort we were able to fill in the blanks. We received our last questionnaire in early March, bringing the total of participating institutions to 52 high schools and 52 universities. The total response rate was 30%.

Analysis of mail questionnaires sent to schools and universities

A code book for the questionnaire was created shortly after we sent out the initial packets in November. As most of the questions in the questionnaire were close-ended, the coding was straightforward. However, to code the open-ended fill-in-the-blank questions, we had to wait till all of the questionnaires were returned to us before we could come up with codes to match all the answers. Therefore, coding was done in phases. First we coded for close-ended questions, then we coded for open-ended questions.

Two code sheets were created to track answers in an organized manner. Once all the questionnaires were coded by at least two individuals, they were then entered into two SPSS databases. The databases were compared after all the survey information was entered to detect any errors in data entry. When all the codes were then entered, we began cleaning the data and running basic descriptive statistics to get a better picture of our respondents.

Preparation and contact with selected schools and universities

To select the schools and universities we intended to visit in September, a list of criteria was established to identify "successful" schools. Using our SPSS database and the established criteria, we organized a list of high schools and a list of universities. From these lists, we called the department and administrative heads to schedule our visit to the schools/universities that best meet our criteria in September. We have already started this process and hope to have the schools we would like to visit secured by mid-August.

Development of the survey instrument

To study the use of Spanish by Latino Professionals, we developed a telephone survey instrument. Project personnel developed and pretested the interview protocol before interviews were conducted. Included here as Appendix 1, it covers demographic information (place of birth, country of origin, age of arrival), sociolinguistic information (patterns of English and Spanish use, education, formal study of Spanish, self-evaluation of proficiencies), views about the need for Spanish in professional life, efforts made to improve Spanish, and attitudes toward varieties of Spanish.

Data collection

We began calling individuals from our lists of successful Latinos in April of 2001 and finished collecting our samples in August of 2001. Throughout the interviewing phase we had on average 5 individuals calling on a daily basis in 2–3-hour shifts. For every 25 professionals that we actually interviewed, we called an average of 125 individuals.

The first few minutes of the interview involved explaining the research project to the potential participants and reading a human subjects oral consent script. The participants were then tape recorded giving oral consent to be both interviewed and tape recorded. In addition, we asked them for a fax number or mailing address so that we could formally send them our contact information after the conclusion of the interview. A total of 218 individuals were surveyed because some of the original respondents declined to be tape recorded. For the purpose of comparability we replaced those individuals who declined to be tape recorded with people who agreed to be tape recorded so that we could closely listen to and take note of their answers on the open-ended questions.

Analysis of survey data

After the interviewing process was completed a team of researcher assistants transcribed all 200 tapes. The tapes and transcriptions were checked for accuracy by individuals who had not transcribed the particular tape being reviewed. After all interviews were transcribed, they were coded for further analysis. An extensive code book was created during the coding phase. Four researchers used this code book (Appendix B) to code each interview. Each interview transcript was coded by two research assistants. A third research assistant checked for reliability among coders. After all 200 interviews were completely coded and checked for reliability, two identical databases were created and information was entered twice, once into each database. The two databases were then compared for consistency. Any inconsistencies were then reentered and a final database was created and used for statistical analyses presented here.

Appendix A: Telephone Survey of Latino Professionals

Instructions for interviewer

After reading the human subjects introduction and receiving both oral consent and Fax number or email address of the participant, begin the interview. The tone of the interview should be cordial. There are several places throughout the interview where we ask the participants open-ended questions. Allow them ample time to respond. It is also OK to allow the participants to ramble on in sections where we have close-ended multiple-choice questions. When the participant gives you an answer that you think is interesting do not respond back positively, for example, good answer, or very interesting. Simply state "Thanks for your response" or something of that nature, and move on. Positive feedback or rewarding participant may not allow them to contradict previous statements as we continue on through the interview. Do not hesitate to also use conversation markers like OK, yes, uh-huh to let the participant know you are paying attention to what they are saying. Also, where needed ask clarifying questions even if they are not specifically written on the questionnaire. For example, if someone says parents were born in Texas, and they don't elaborate you might want to ask exactly where in Texas.

I. DEMOGRAPHICS

I am going to now begin the interview by asking you some background questions.

1. What is your occupation?
2. Where were you born?
3. For foreign born: What was your Age on arrival to the USA?
4. Sex.
5. How old are you?

(INSTRUCTIONS TO INTERVIEWER: *If they have an extended pause or withdrawn silence, give them the option of stating what decade they were born*).

If you feel uncomfortable answering this question will you please state in which decade you were born, for example 1950–1959 equals the 50s.

6. For US-born: What Latino or Hispanic group do you most identify yourself with?
7. Where was your mother born?
8. Where was your father born?
9. What was the highest grade completed by your mother?
10. What was the highest grade completed by your father?

11. Where did your mother complete her schooling?
    School:

    Town:

    Country:

12. Where did your father complete his schooling?
    School:

    Town:

    Country:

13. What is the highest degree you have received?
14. Have you ever attended an in-service training for your current profession in Spanish?   Yes   No

> IF NO, SKIP TO QUESTION 16

(INSTRUCTIONS FOR INTERVIEWER: *Explain what this means, another term is "Continuing your education course/program"*)

15. For how many weeks did the program or training last?
16. Did you ever study Spanish in high school?   Yes   No
17. For how many years?
18. Did you ever study Spanish in college?   Yes   No
19. For how many quarters? Semesters? (1 quarter = 0.67 semester)
20. Have you ever been enrolled in classes where Spanish was the language of instruction of subjects other than Spanish?

II. SPANISH LANGUAGE

For the following questions, I am going to read you a question that asks you to either rate your language use or the frequency in which you use Spanish. After asking you the question I will read a list of possible answers for you to choose from. Please choose the answer that best describes your language ability and usage.

21. How well do you understand Spanish?
    Not at all   Very little   Fairly well   Like a native
22. How well do you speak Spanish?
    Not at all   Very little   Fairly well   Like a native
23. As a child: did you speak Spanish at home?
    Never   Rarely   Sometimes   Often   Always

IF ANSWERS TO 21 AND 22 ARE *NOT AT ALL* AND 23 IS *NEVER*, GO
TO QUESTION 46

24. To whom most typically?

(INSTRUCTIONS FOR INTERVIEWER: *Ask this question even if the person
states* rarely only, *skip this question* only if *never is given as an answer*)

25. Currently, do you speak Spanish at home?
        Never   Rarely   Sometimes   Often   Always
26. To whom most typically?

(INSTRUCTIONS FOR INTERVIEWER: *Ask this question even if the person
states* rarely only, *skip this question if never is given as an answer*)

27. Do you read in Spanish at home?
        Never   Rarely   Sometimes   Often
    Always
28. Do you write in Spanish at home?
        Never   Rarely   Sometimes   Often
    Always
29. Do you speak Spanish at work?
        Never   Rarely   Sometimes   Often
    Always

IF *NEVER*, GO TO QUESTION 46

---

30. What kinds of activities do you carry out at work in Spanish?

(INSTRUCTIONS FOR INTERVIEWER: *For questions 31 and 32 choose the
option that fits the occupation. For example, Doctor – patients, Lawyer – clients*)

31. Do you speak Spanish with monolingual Spanish-speaking clients/
    patients/students, or constituents?   Yes   No
32. If yes, ask how frequently do you speak with *X* individuals? (If no,
    skip to 33)
        Never   Rarely   Sometimes   Often   Always
33. Do you speak Spanish with bilingual Spanish-speaking clients/
    patients/students or constituents?   Yes   No
34. If yes, ask how frequently do you speak with *X* individuals? (If no,
    skip to 35)
        Never   Rarely   Sometimes   Often   Always
35. Do you speak Spanish with monolingual Spanish-speaking employ-
    ees/support staff or colleagues?   Yes   No

36. If yes, ask how frequently do you speak with *X* individuals. (If no, skip to 37)

    Never   Rarely   Sometimes   Often   Always

37. Do you speak Spanish with bilingual Spanish-speaking employees/support staff or colleagues?   Yes   No

38. If yes, then ask how frequently do you speak with *X* individuals? (If no, skip to 39)

    Never   Rarely   Sometimes   Often   Always

39. Do you ever read professional materials in Spanish such as books, documents, or electronic data sources?   Yes   No

40. If yes, ask how frequently do you read in Spanish at work? (If no, skip to 41)

    Never   Rarely   Sometimes   Often   Always

41. Do you ever write work-related letters, articles, or instructions in Spanish?   Yes   No

42. If yes, then ask how frequently do you write *X* at work? (If no, skip to 43)

    Never   Rarely   Sometimes   Often   Always

43. Is there perhaps some other activity in which you engage in Spanish at work that I have not mentioned? _____

44. How frequently do you need to use Spanish (at work)

    Everyday   Once or twice a week

    Once or twice a month   Once or twice a year

45. Does speaking Spanish at work make you more effective professionally?

    Never   Rarely   Sometimes   Often   Always

GO TO QUESTION 47

USE ONLY IF ANSWERS TO 21, 22, and 23 ARE NEGATIVE OR ANSWER TO 29 IS NEGATIVE

46. Would speaking Spanish at work make you more effective professionally?

    Never   Rarely   Sometimes   Often   Always

47. Do you feel any interest in improving your Spanish?   Yes   No

48. If you were to improve your Spanish, what would be most important for you professionally to improve? Please choose any or all that you would find valuable professionally to improve.

    (a) speaking   (b) listening   (c) reading   (d) writing

49. If you were to improve your Spanish, what would be most important for you personally to improve? Please choose any or all that you would find valuable personally to improve.

    (a) speaking   (b) listening   (c) reading   (d) writing

50. What would you need to do to accomplish this improvement? Please choose any or all that apply from the following choices.

>   Take a course
>   Carry out independent study
>   Travel
>   Use it more
>   Or *perhaps something else I haven't mentioned* .... other _____

III. OPINIONS

In this last set of questions I will ask that you state your opinion.

(INSTRUCTIONS FOR INTERVIEWER: *Do not hesitate to ask them to clarify their statements or expand on them if you do not understand immediately what they are trying to say. These are difficult questions, so the answers may be convoluted at times.*)

51. Where in the entire Spanish-speaking world is the best Spanish *spoken*?
52. Where in the entire Spanish-speaking world is the best Spanish *written*?
53. In what way(s) is it spoken better in (insert country or region from 51) than anywhere else?
54. In what way(s) is it written better in (insert country or region from 52) than anywhere else?

(INSTRUCTIONS FOR INTERVIEWER: *In the following questions, respondents tend to get confused, and often think we are asking them to respond to questions regarding bilingual education or courses taught in elementary grade levels. Put great emphasis on the fact we are asking about high school and college courses.*)

55. Many students who are raised in homes where Spanish is spoken and who have been schooled entirely in English want to take Spanish in high school or college. Do you think that special Spanish language classes designed for these students should be offered?   Yes   No

---

IF NO, GO TO QUESTION 62

---

56. What variety of Spanish should be taught in these classes?

(INSTRUCTIONS FOR INTERVIEWER: *If they ask what you mean by variety, use the following reply. Do not explain different varieties with Spanish language examples because this will possibly feed the respondent their answer.*)

There are many varieties of English spoken throughout the world and Unite States; for example, there is a variety of English spoken by those

living in England that differs from the English spoken in Australia, which in turn differs from the varieties spoken in New York and California.

(INSTRUCTIONS FOR INTERVIEWER: *If given a response that has a negative connotation, such as Spanglish, exchange for Standard Mexican Spanish spoken in California.*)

57. Should X variety of Spanish be taught? (*again referring to high school and college courses*)
      Only to Mexican Americans   or   To all Latinos
58. Do you think that literature written in the X variety of Spanish should be studied in these classes? (*again referring to high school and college courses*)   Yes   No
59. Should it be taught to?
      Only Mexican Americans   or   To all Latinos
60. What other regional varieties of Spanish should be taught in such classes?
61. To which students should these varieties be taught?
      Only to Mexican Americans   or   To all Latinos
62. Is it important for students who have been raised in homes where Spanish is spoken to use the language with their own Spanish-speaking Latino friends outside of school? (Add "in the USA" if a foreign location is mentioned)   Yes   No
63. Is it important for students who have been raised in homes where Spanish is spoken to use the language with Spanish-speaking family members older than they are? (Add "in the USA" if a foreign location is mentioned)   Yes   No
64. Is it important for students who have been raised in homes where Spanish is spoken to use the language with Spanish-speaking family members their own age? (Add "in the USA" if a foreign location is mentioned)   Yes   No
65. Is it important for students who have been raised in homes where Spanish is spoken to use the language with Spanish-speaking family members younger than they are? (Add "in the USA" if a foreign location is mentioned)   Yes   No
66. What recommendations would you have for either high schools or colleges as they design Spanish courses for Latino students?

(INSTRUCTIONS FOR INTERVIEWER: *Push a little here: Anything else? Further comments? etc.*)

Thank you so much for your help. Your views are extremely important to us for the improvement of Spanish language instruction in American high schools and colleges.

Appendix B: Survey of Spanish Heritage Language Programs in California

Section 1: Institutional Information

1. Name of institution _____
2. Location of institution _____
3. Exact name of department _____
4. Departmental title or role of respondent in the language teaching program _____
5. Institution's current total enrollment _____ and total years of study_____

Section 2: Language Program

Tell us about your Spanish language program.

6. What is the total number of faculty teaching in your Spanish language program?_____
7. Approximately how many students enroll in your Spanish language (not Spanish literature) courses per semester? _____
8. Approximately what percentage of your students taking Spanish fall into the following categories.
   ____ % traditional foreign language students (students from non–Spanish-speaking families)
   ____ % students who grew up with Spanish at home in the United States (e.g. US-born children of Spanish-speaking families)
   ____ % newly arrived immigrant students who grew up in Spanish-speaking countries
   ____ % other (Please describe) _____

   100% = Total students in Spanish language program

9. Does your department offer a general placement examination for students enrolling in Spanish language courses for the first time?
   ____yes   ____no

If No, go to Question 12.
---

10. Is your general placement examination used to help you identify heritage students? ____ yes   ____ no

---
If No, go to question 12.
---

11. Which parts of the general examination have you found most useful in identifying heritage speakers?
   ____ listening comprehension sections of the examination

____ oral interview
____ reading comprehension sections of the examination
____ writing sections of the examination
____ sections that depend on knowledge of grammar and grammatical terminology
____ sections that depend on the use of the standard language

Other (Please describe) _____

Section 3: Courses Designed for Heritage Students

12. Do you currently offer special courses for heritage students at your institution?   ____ yes   ____ no

> If no, go to question 29. If yes, complete the remaining questions in this section.

13. When did you begin to offer special or separate courses in Spanish for heritage students?
____ before 1980
____ between 1980 and 1984
____ between 1985 and 1989
____ between 1990 and 1994
____ between 1995 and 1999
____ 2000 or after

14. What levels and types of courses does your institution currently offer for heritage students? Using the appropriate column for your institution, check all the descriptions that apply even though your courses may have different titles.

High Schools	*Institutions of Higher Education*
____1st-year Spanish for heritage speakers	____1st-year Spanish for heritage speakers
____2nd-year Spanish for heritage speakers	____2nd-year Spanish for heritage speakers
____3rd-year Spanish for heritage speakers	____Composition for heritage speakers
____4th-year Spanish for heritage speakers	____Advanced grammar for heritage speakers
____Other (describe)_____	____Oral communication for heritage speakers
	____Other (describe) _____

High Schools	Institutions of Higher Education
____AP Spanish (Language)	____Spanish conversation courses
____AP Spanish (Literature)	____Spanish composition courses
	____Spanish culture and civilization courses
	____Introductory Hispanic literature courses
	____Advanced Hispanic literature courses

15. Which courses do you usually recommend that heritage students take after they have completed the sequence designed for them. Check all that apply in the appropriate column.

Section 4: Placement Procedures for Heritage Students

16. Tell us how students are placed in courses designed for heritage students. Check all that apply.
    ____(a) Students are placed in such courses by advisors/counselors.
    ____(b) Students self-select for courses using descriptions of courses provided.
    ____(c) Students take a general Spanish placement examination designed for all newly enrolling students.
    ____(d) Students complete a language survey that asks about their use of Spanish in their everyday lives.
    ____(e) Students transfer from courses designed primarily for foreign language learners at the recommendation of their teachers.
    ____(f) Other (Please describe)_____

17. Does your department offer a specially designed placement examination for heritage students? ____ yes ____ no

If No, go to question 19

18. Check all the aspects of language proficiency that this special examination measures.
    a) Listening
       ____listening to a conversation
       ____listening to extended oral presentations (e.g. radio or television announcements, formal lectures)
       ____other (please describe) _____
    b) Speaking
       ____participation in an interview
       ____ability to make presentations
       ____other (please describe) _____

c) Reading
____reading (literature)
____reading (newspapers, informative material)
____other (please describe) _____

d) Writing
____writing on a personal topic (notes, personal experience essay)
____writing on an abstract topic (e.g. response to reading)
____other (please describe) _____

e) Structure/Grammar
____familiarity with grammatical terminology
____identification/production of specific grammatical forms
____ability to correct stigmatized (nonstandard) features
____other (please describe) _____
____other (please describe) _____
____other (please describe) _____

f) Translation
____ability to translate from English to Spanish
____ability to translate from Spanish to English
____other (please describe) _____

Section 5: Curriculum

19. Rate the importance of the following learning objectives in terms of your curriculum for heritage speakers. Place an X in the appropriate box across from each objective.

Curriculum area	Important for foreign language students	Important for heritage students	Important for both groups of students
a) Students should be able to participate in everyday face-to-face interactions using appropriate levels of Spanish.	❏	❏	❏
b) Students should be able to make oral presentations in front of an audience using appropriate levels of Spanish.	❏	❏	❏
c) Students should be able to understand and interpret extended oral presentations and information available through mass media.	❏	❏	❏

Curriculum area	Important for foreign language students	Important for heritage students	Important for both groups of students
d) Students should be able to write informal notes and personal letters.	❏	❏	❏
e) Students should be able to write narrative, informative, and persuasive essays directed to a group of unknown readers.	❏	❏	❏
f) Students should comprehend and read with ease written materials such as novels, short stories, editorials, web materials.	❏	❏	❏
g) Students should comprehend written materials on specialized business or professional topics.	❏	❏	❏
h) Students should be able to use and understand grammatical terminology.	❏	❏	❏
i) Students should be able to identify and correct anglicisms, archaisms, and other dialectal or nonstandard forms in their writing.	❏	❏	❏
j) Students should be able to identify and correct anglicisms, archaisms, and other dialectal or nonstandard forms in their speaking.	❏	❏	❏
k) Students should master the rules for using the written accent.	❏	❏	❏
l) Students should master Spanish spelling rules.	❏	❏	❏

Curriculum area	Important for foreign language students	Important for heritage students	Important for both groups of students
m) Students should develop a broad vocabulary useful in business and professions.	❑	❑	❑
n) Students should be able to demonstrate familiarity with culture of Spanish-speaking countries.	❑	❑	❑
o) Students should be able to study other disciplines using Spanish (e.g. history, geography, science)	❑	❑	❑

Section 6: Materials

20. Which textbooks and other materials do you currently use in the sequences for heritage learners? Please fill in the titles or descriptions of materials

a) _____

b) _____

c) _____

d) _____

Section 7: Teaching Practices

21. The following practices are often used in the teaching of foreign language students and in the teaching of English to fluent speakers of the language. Which of these practices have you used effectively with heritage learners of Spanish? Place an X in the appropriate box across from each practice.

Practice	Effective	Not Effective	Has not been attempted
a) Direct study of vocabulary	❑	❑	❑
b) Dictation	❑	❑	❑
c) Grammar explanations	❑	❑	❑

Practice	Effective	Not Effective	Has not been attempted
d) Oral practice of particular grammatical structures	❏	❏	❏
e) Instruction that teaches grammar only by pulling out and commenting on particular forms	❏	❏	❏
f) Correction of selected common errors by teacher in front of whole class	❏	❏	❏
g) Analysis of language and style appropriate for different types of texts	❏	❏	❏
h) Drafting, writing and rewriting of compositions by students	❏	❏	❏
i) Peer editing of compositions	❏	❏	❏
j) Projects involving ethnographic research in communities by students	❏	❏	❏
k) Web research projects by students.	❏	❏	❏
l) Group research/writing projects	❏	❏	❏
m) Independent research/writing projects	❏	❏	❏
n) Extensive reading	❏	❏	❏
o) Instruction on the ways that language varies geographically and socially	❏	❏	❏
p) Use of extensive in-class listening comprehension activities	❏	❏	❏
q) Other – please describe	❏	❏	❏
r) Other – please describe	❏	❏	❏

Section 8: Outcomes

22. Are you satisfied with the outcomes of your heritage language program? ___Yes   ___No
23. List two areas with which you are particularly satisfied.
    a) _____
    b) _____

24. List two areas in which you think your program needs to improve.
    a) _____
    b) _____

Section 9: Instructors' Language Backgrounds

25. Approximately how many of your instructors who teach heritage students fall into the following categories?
    ____ % teachers who grew up in non–Spanish-speaking families
    ____ % US Latinos who grew up with Spanish at home
    ____ % US Latinos who did not grow up with Spanish at home
    ____ % Latinos who grew up and were educated in Spanish-speaking countries
    ____ % other (Please describe) _____
    100 %

26. What is the total number of instructors in your heritage program?
    _____

27. What kind of preparation for teaching heritage speakers has your *lead instructor* in the heritage sequence received? Check all that apply.
    ____ Took special course(s) as part of a teaching certificate program
    ____ Took special course(s) as part of graduate teaching assistant training
    ____ Taught a course or courses for heritage students as part of graduate teaching assistant responsibilities
    ____ Attended summer workshop(s) on the teaching of heritage speakers
    ____ Attended sessions on the teaching of heritage speakers at professional conferences
    ____ Carried out extensive individual reading on the teaching of heritage speakers
    ____ Visited heritage language classes at nearby schools or colleges
    ____ Became member of listserv focusing on the teaching of heritage speakers
    ____ Other (please describe) _____
    ____ Learned on the job by teaching heritage learners

28. What plans are you making for expanding your heritage program in the next 5 years? Check all the options that apply.
    ____ a) We plan to increase the number of courses we now teach.
    ____ b) We plan to hire more instructors who can work with heritage speakers.
    ____ c) We plan to prepare all graduate students to teach heritage language courses.
    ____ d) We plan to publicize the program more fully in order to increase enrollment.

___ e) Other (please describe) _____

___ f) Other (please describe) _____

___ g) Other (please describe) _____

Section 10: Programs without Specialized Courses for Heritage Speakers

29. At what levels and in which types of courses do heritage students enroll? Using the appropriate column for your institution, check all the courses that combine heritage speakers and traditional foreign language students.

30. Tell us how heritage students are placed in courses. Check all that apply.

___ a) Students are placed in such courses by advisors/counselors.

___ b) Students self-select for courses using descriptions of courses provided.

___ c) Students take a general Spanish placement examination designed for all newly enrolling students.

___ d) Students complete a language survey that asks about their use of Spanish in their everyday lives.

___ e) Students transfer to higher- or lower-level courses at the recommendation of their teachers.

___ f) Other (Please describe) _____

High Schools	*Institutions of Higher Education*
___1st-year Spanish	___1st-year Spanish
___2nd-year Spanish	___2nd-year Spanish
___3rd-year Spanish	___Writing and composition
___4th-year Spanish	___Advanced grammar
___ AP Spanish (Language)	___Oral communication/conversation
___AP Spanish (Literature)	___Composition courses
___Other (Describe) _____	___ Culture and civilization courses
	___Introductory literature courses
	___Advanced literature courses
	___Other
	(Describe)_____

31. Rate the importance of the following learning objectives for your two groups of students after their first 2 years of study. Place an X in the appropriate box across from each objective.

Curriculum area	*Important for foreign language students*	*Important for heritage students*	*Important for both groups of students*
a) Students should be able to participate in everyday face-to-face interactions using appropriate levels of Spanish.	❒	❒	❒
b) Students should be able to make oral presentations in front of an audience using appropriate levels of Spanish.	❒	❒	❒
c) Students should be able to understand and interpret extended oral presentations and information available through mass media.	❒	❒	❒
d) Students should be able to write informal notes and personal letters.	❒	❒	❒
e) Students should be able to write narrative, informative, and persuasive essays directed to a group of unknown readers.	❒	❒	❒
f) Students should comprehend and read with ease written materials such as novels, short stories, editorials, Web materials.	❒	❒	❒
g) Students should comprehend written materials on specialized business or professional topics.	❒	❒	❒

Curriculum area	Important for foreign language students	Important for heritage students	Important for both groups of students
h) Students should be able to use and understand grammatical terminology.	❏	❏	❏
i) Students should be able to identify and correct anglicisms, archaisms, and other dialectal or nonstandard forms in their writing.	❏	❏	❏
j) Students should be able to identify and correct anglicisms, archaisms, and other dialectal or nonstandard forms in their speaking.	❏	❏	❏
k) Students should master the rules for using the written accent.	❏	❏	❏
l) Students should master Spanish spelling rules.	❏	❏	❏
m) Students should develop a broad vocabulary useful in business and professions.	❏	❏	❏
n) Students should be able to demonstrate familiarity with the culture of Spanish-speaking countries.	❏	❏	❏
o) Students should be able to study other disciplines using Spanish (e.g. history, geography, science).	❏	❏	❏

32. Which textbooks and other materials do you currently use in Spanish 1 and Spanish 2? Please fill in the titles or descriptions of materials.

a) _____

b) _____

c) _____

d) _____

33. Do you use other supplementary materials with your heritage students? ____yes ____no
34. If yes, please describe materials below.

_____

35. The following practices are often used in the teaching of foreign language students and in the teaching of English to fluent speakers of the language. Which of these practices have you used effectively with heritage learners in your classes? Place an X in the appropriate box across from each practice.

Practice	Effective	Not effective	Has not been attempted
a) Direct study of vocabulary	❑	❑	❑
b) Dictation	❑	❑	❑
c) Grammar explanations	❑	❑	❑
d) Oral practice of particular grammatical structures	❑	❑	❑
e) Instruction that teaches grammar only by pulling out and commenting on particular forms	❑	❑	❑
f) Correction of selected common errors by teacher in front of the whole class	❑	❑	❑
g) Analysis of language and style appropriate for different types of texts	❑	❑	❑
h) Drafting, writing, and rewriting of compositions by students	❑	❑	❑
i) Peer editing of compositions	❑	❑	❑
j) Projects involving ethnographic research in communities by students	❑	❑	❑
k) Web research projects by students	❑	❑	❑

Practice	Effective	Not effective	Has not been attempted
l) Group research/writing projects	❑	❑	❑
m) Independent research/writing projects	❑	❑	❑
n) Extensive reading	❑	❑	❑
o) Instruction on the ways that language varies geographically and socially	❑	❑	❑
p) Use of extensive in-class listening comprehension activities	❑	❑	❑
q) Other – please describe	❑	❑	❑
r) Other – please describe	❑	❑	❑

36. Approximately how many of your instructors who teach heritage students fall into the following categories?
    ____ % teachers who grew up in non–Spanish-speaking families
    ____ % US Latinos who grew up with Spanish at home
    ____ % US Latinos who did not grow up with Spanish at home
    ____ % Latinos who grew up and were educated in Spanish-speaking countries
    ____ % other (Please describe) _____

37. What is the total number of instructors in your language program?
    _____

38. In terms of heritage speakers, are you satisfied with the outcomes of your program? ____yes ____ no

39. List two areas with which you are particularly satisfied.
    a) _____
    b) _____

40. List two areas in which you think your program needs to improve.
    a) _____
    b) _____

41. What are the perceptions in your department about the need to establish special classes for heritage students? Place an X in the appropriate column for each statement that describes current views in your department.

Options	Strongly disagree	Moderately disagree	Moderately agree	Strongly agree
a) We need to establish a heritage language program within the next 5 years.	❐	❐	❐	❐
b) We don't need to establish a heritage language program within the next 5 years.	❐	❐	❐	❐
c) Heritage students have requested separate classes.	❐	❐	❐	❐
d) Instructors who have had heritage speakers in their classes have requested separate classes.	❐	❐	❐	❐
e) Instructors of upper-level courses have concerns about heritage students enrolling in their classes without adequate preparation.	❐	❐	❐	❐
f) To establish a heritage language program, instructors who can teach these courses must be hired.	❐	❐	❐	❐
g) To establish a heritage language program, graduate teaching assistants must be trained to teach such courses.	❐	❐	❐	❐
h) Other	❐	❐	❐	❐
i) Other	❐	❐	❐	❐